The
Discovery
of Poetry

mas E. Sanders
Junior College

Scott, Foresman and Company

Acknowledgements

"Limberick." From *A Seizure of Limericks* by Conrad Aiken. Copyright © 1963, 1964 by Conrad Aiken. Reprinted by permission of Holt, Rinehart and Winston, Inc.   "Six Haiku." © 1962 by Mercury Press, Inc. Reprinted from *The Magazine of Fantasy and Science Fiction* by permission of the author.   "Lady Shoppers Beware," "Off-the-Cuff Remarks on Off-the-Shoulder Dresses." From *Light Armour* by Richard Armour. Copyright, 1954 by Richard Armour. McGraw-Hill Book Company. Used by permission.   "O Where Are You Going." Copyright 1934 and renewed 1961 by W.H. Auden. Reprinted from *The Collected Poetry of W.H. Auden* by permission of Random House, Inc.   "The Unknown Citizen." Copyright 1940 by W.H. Auden. Reprinted from *The Collected Poetry of W.H. Auden* by permission of Random House, Inc.   Excerpts from "In Memory of W.B. Yeats," "III." Reprinted from *The Collected Poetry of W.H. Auden* by permission of Random House, Inc.   "Courage." Permission to publish "Courage" from *Dreamers on Horseback*, by Karle Wilson Baker, was granted by Charlotte Baker Montgomery, Literary Executrix.   "Come Come! Come Out!," "Dead My Old Fine Hopes," "Good Friend Grasshopper," "I Must Turn Over," "In a Farther Field," "In the City Fields," "In the Sea-Surf Edge," "In the Twilight Rain," "Life? Butterfly," "Mirror-Pond of Stars," "Mountain-Rose Petals," "My Two Plum Trees Are," "On Her Dead Son," "Swallow in the Dusk," From *Japanese Haiku* by Peter Beilenson. The Peter Pauper Press, Mount Vernon, New York. Used by permission.   "The Fish." From *Poems North and South* by Elizabeth Bishop. Copyright © 1955 by Elizabeth Bishop. Reprinted by permission of Houghton Mifflin Company, Boston.   "Triolet." Reprinted from *Shorter Poems of Robert Bridges* (1931) by permission of the Clarendon Press, Oxford.   "Ghost." Copyright 1935 by Alfred A. Knopf, Inc. Reprinted from *Selected Poems*, by Witter Bynner, by permission.   "Crystal Moment." Reprinted with permission of The Macmillan Company from *Yolk of Thunder* by Robert P. Tristram Coffin. Copyright The Macmillan Company 1932, renewed 1960 by Margaret Halvosa.   "The Secret Heart." Reprinted with permission of The Macmillan Company from *Strange Holiness* by Robert P. Tristram Coffin. Copyright The Macmillan Company 1935, renewed 1963 by Margaret Coffin Halvosa.   "At Melville's Tomb," "Black Tambourine," "Legend," "Praise for an Urn," "Repose of Rivers," "The Broken Tower," "Voyages II." From: *The Collected Poems of Hart Crane*. By Permission of LIVERIGHT, Publishers. Copyright © Renewed 1961, by Liveright Publishing Corporation.   Correspondence between Hart Crane and Harriet Monroe and excerpts from *General Aims and Theories* and "The Bridge of Estador." From: *The Complete Poems and Prose and Selected Letters of Hart Crane*. By Permission of LIVERIGHT, Publishers, N.Y. Copyright © 1966 by Liveright Publishing Corporation.   "War Is Kind." Reprinted from *Collected Poems*, by Stephen Crane, courtesy of Alfred A. Knopf, Inc.   "Niagara (Seen on a night in November)," "Night Winds," "November Night," "On Seeing Weather-Beaten Trees," "Release," "Song," "Susanna and the Elders," "The Guarded Wound." "The Warning," "Triad." Copyright 1915 by Algernon S. Crapsey and renewed 1954 by Adelaide T. Crapsey. Reprinted from *Verse*, by Adelaide Crapsey by permission of Alfred A. Knopf, Inc.   "Chanson Innocent." Copyright, 1923, 1951, by E.E. Cummings. Reprinted from his volume, *Poems, 1923-1954*, by permission of Harcourt, Brace & World, Inc.   "Leisure." Reprinted by permission of Katharine N. Gildersleeve from *The Collected Poems of William H. Davies* published by Alfred A. Knopf. Originally published by Cape & Smith.   "All But Blind." Reprinted by permission of The Society of Authors and The Literary Trustees for the estate of Walter de la Mare.   "Rondel." From *Formal Spring: French Renaissance Poems*, tr. R.N. Currey (Oxford University Press, 1950). Permission granted by R.N. Currey.   "Since He Is Too Young," "The Falling Flower." Reprinted from *Poetry Handbook: A Dictionary of Terms* by Babette Deutsch. By permission of the publishers, Funk & Wagnalls, N.Y.   "I Never Saw a Moor." From *Poems by Emily Dickinson*, eds. Martha Dickinson Bianchi and Alfred Leete Hampson, courtesy of Little, Brown and Company, Boston.   "Because I Could Not Stop for Death," "Faith Is a Fine Invention," "I Taste a Liquor Never Brewed," "My Life Closed Twice Before Its Close," "Presentiment," "To Make a Prairie." Reprinted by permission of the publishers and the Trustees of Amherst College from Thomas H. Johnson, Editor, *The Poems of Emily Dickinson*, Cambridge, Mass.: The Belknap Press of Harvard University, Copyright, 1951, 1955, by The President and Fellows of Harvard College.   "In After Days." From *The Complete Poetical Works of Henry Austin Dobson* (London: Oxford University Press, 1923). Used by permission.   "The Cancer Cells." From *Collected Poems 1930-1960* by Richard Eberhart. © 1960 by Richard Eberhart. Reprinted by permission of Oxford University Press, Inc.   "Love Lies A-Bleeding." Reprinted by permission of Frederick Eckman. First published in *Poetry* Magazine, July, 1960.   Excerpt from "Hamlet and His Problems." From *Selected Essays* by T.S. Eliot, courtesy of Harcourt, Brace & World, Inc.   "Journey of the Magi," "Preludes," "The Love Song of J. Alfred Prufrock." From *Collected Poems 1909-1962* by T.S. Eliot, copyright, 1936, by Harcourt, Brace & World, Inc.; copyright, 1963, 1964, by T.S. Eliot. Reprinted by permission of the publishers.   "A Summer Morning." Reprinted with permission of The Macmillan Company from *The Pointed People* by Rachel Field. Copyright The Macmillan Company 1924, 1930.   "The Silent One." Permission granted by Robert Fitch.

Table of Contents

Preface

Because it is compressed communication, emotional in concept and exacting in its demands, poetry often defeats both teacher and student—they scurry past it with quiet resignation and gentle guilt. Prose occupies them, for it seems easier to read, easier to discuss, easier to understand. All of which is unfortunate—for both teacher and student.

The demands of our society are such that the "good" reader is rewarded monetarily, psychologically, and spiritually. And nothing helps the student become a "good" reader as much as poetry. Once he has learned to comprehend through the poetic line, prose becomes much easier for him to read and to write. The compression of poetry actually serves comprehension, as a complete work can be examined on one page. The processes of organization, logical thinking, established communication—all can be pointed out in their limited confines. Prose offers no such possibilities. The lengths demanded by the various forms (short stories, essays, novels) create problems in the simple logistics of page numbers if nothing else. Once the student has mastered poetic understanding, however, he can accommodate widely spaced ideas in prose, understanding the transitional elements which poetry makes logical.

This book attempts to help both the teacher and the student. The logic of poetry is observable if it is examined from small beginnings and element is added to element until poetry of some length is reached. This book is structured on such a belief. It will serve as a guide to both the reader and the writer, for it can also be used as a step-by-step approach to the writing of poetry.

To tell a teacher how to use a book has always seemed presumptuous to me. But one suggestion does seem worth offering. It might be profitable to begin this book with the last chapter, "Writing About the Poem." It summarizes the book, and it can give students an overview, an objective towards which to work. Persuading students of that objective is, of course, often the most difficult part of teaching any literary form. But they must understand their objective before they will spend the time needed to achieve it. Emile Coué, the French psychologist whose auto-suggestive "Every day in every way I'm getting better and better" failed in America, explained: "Americans are too impatient; they just want to say, 'Oh hell, I'm well.'"

But students *do* want to read well. And learning to read poetry with comprehension and delight will make good prose readers of them. That's an understandable objective, and it seems purpose enough for this book.

Why then a preface? To thank some people who have helped me with the manuscript. If it hadn't been for their help, there probably wouldn't be a book.

Bettye Lou Nicolaides has haggled, proofread, typed, made invaluable suggestions, and forced me to revise any number of passages because, as a student, she could see communicative possibilities a teacher would miss. She should be listed as co-author.

And there's her husband, Manny, who has been deprived of a lot of her company while the whole tortured process was going on.

Phyllis Eisman has listened to the manuscript, via the telephone, so often that her ears deserve mention and her friends deserve my apologies.

Naomi Pratt has relieved me of some of the more onerous chores of living so I could have Saturdays for writing.

For allowing me to include uncopyrighted materials, I am grateful to Mabel Meadows Staats, Marlene Quaroni, Donald Baim, Darylyn Neinken, Beth Biderman, Bernice Miller, Mary Kelly Lynch, June Seligman, and Jay Casselhoff.

Walter Peek has offered so much encouragement in so many ways that I won't even bother to list them.

Then there are my students, the Miami Public Library, dozens of authors of other books, all of my past teachers, thousands of poets. . . . Good grief, I'm not sure *I* wrote this book at all! It somehow seems to belong to an unorganized committee whose members would make strange bedfellows indeed. My thanks to all of them!

Thomas E. Sanders
Miami, Florida
1966

For Grace and
Lou and Walter
P.—those three

CHAPTER I

Communication: Two Sides of the Coin

Whether your ambition is fame, making money, or learning to understand yourself, you will succeed or fail in direct relation to your ability to comprehend what you read. Experience in life is inescapable, but it becomes valuable only when we understand its meaning. Fortunately, in this regard, none of us is unique; we share the larger part of our attitudes, emotions, experiences, and responses with all other men. Thus we can make some progress toward understanding the meaning of our experiences by seeing how similar experiences have affected the lives of other people. And to guide us in this attempt, the writers of the world have left us their record. It is a record which, perhaps more than any other, offers us a comprehensive view of man, his needs, his aspirations, and the meaning of his experiences. E. B. White, in *The Elements of Style,* has observed: "All writing is communication; creative writing is communication through revelation—it is the Self escaping into the open." Thus the writer, a man like other men, reveals himself as he records his observations. We, as readers applying these revelations to ourselves, can reveal ourselves to ourselves, possibly for the first time.

But it is not enough merely to read; it is necessary to learn how to read intelligently. You must learn how to read with your intellect rather than with your emotions. You will have to learn to read what the writer says, rather than what you would prefer to have him say. In short, you must first learn to *read,* before you can begin to *interpret,* knowing that the intelligent man first understands the directions before he applies his experience to create shortcuts. Once you have learned to read poems, short stories, dramas, and novels with care and intelligence, you will be ready to apply your experience to them, interpreting them in relation to your own personal needs.

To take an example, think of the instructions in a "do-it-yourself" kit. If you read the instructions carefully and understand them thoroughly before you even examine the components, you will have no difficulty in assembling the object in the kit. If, on the other hand, you decide the instructions are unnecessary and either read them casually or disregard them completely, you will probably end up wasting your time in a futile effort to assemble the item. You will be compelled at last to begin again with a careful analysis of the instructions. Eventually, of course, you will get the pieces together. But how much time and emotional effort you might have saved had you heeded the instructions of someone, not necessarily wiser than you, but more knowledgeable!

The writer offers instructions to us in at least two forms: in the form of assimilated experience, which we have already discussed, and in the form of the techniques which he uses.

But let us pause briefly here to consider more closely the question: What *is* a writer? He is, first, a person who wants, perhaps more than anything else, to see his name in print beneath the title of his work. He feels that he is aware, sensitive, valuable. He usually wants people to rise above what he considers their inadequacies. Bluntly, he is usually something of a reformer. But the writer, too, is one who realistically knows that he is never really an author until he has an audience. Walt Whitman once said: "To have great poets, there must be great audiences too." The writer's audience may be sophisticated or it may be stupid; still, it is his audience, and he knows he must respect it enough to learn to write for it. In other words, the writer knows that there are two equally important sides to the coin of communication: he is one side, his audience is the other. Consequently, every writer learns certain rules and techniques, and he employs them for the reader's benefit—to make his half of the process of communication easier.

To the extent that a reader understands something of these techniques, he is reading intelligently; he becomes a partner with the writer in the exchange of communication, and both will succeed.

There are, of course, writers—and there are writers. Some writers are self-centered to the point of failing their audiences. Their writing is so complex, so filled with ambiguity and obscurity, so turgid with hidden and private meanings, that most readers may reject the communication process altogether. Both reader and writer lose something in such instances. Some writers are really nothing more than diarists. The diarist is like a petulant child who feels that people owe him attention simply because he asks for it. *He* thinks that what he says is profound or amusing, and it may well be; but he takes no care about how he says it.

The mature writer, on the other hand, does not lament the ignorance of his audience or remain aloof from its needs. He masters the forms and techniques of whatever genre he is working in, so that his words will do what he intends them to do. The mature writer soon enters into the knowledge that communication is never easy, but that the *first* responsibility rests with the one who opens the conversation. Until the writer's statement is understood, communication cannot begin.

The mature writer doesn't want to communicate—"almost." He starts by finding the exact words to state his ideas. Then he chooses the form which will *best* accommodate and transmit those ideas to his audience. Finally, he polishes that form until it is the most effective vehicle of communication which he is capable of creating.

Until the writer has shaped his communication into such a workable form, the reader owes him nothing. But once that form has been found and polished, then the burden falls upon us, the readers. We are expected to offer the writer the attention which he deserves; we should be prepared to put almost as much effort into our reading as the author has put into his writing.

The reader who wishes to get the most out of his reading will first be sure of his knowledge of words and grammar. These are the "building blocks" of all forms of writing. Simple ideas are often communicated with simple words and in simple sentences. But complex ideas often demand bigger words and more complex grammatical constructions.

Second, a careful reader will concern himself with form and with structure, and he will try to master, almost as if he wished to become a writer himself, the techniques of the genre and writer he is studying. Archibald T. MacAllister once summarized the need for such awareness: "In our utilitarian scorn we are in danger of forgetting that a certain preoccupation with form (and even today's straight line betrays such a preoccupation) is essential to beauty."[1] Any writing that communicates is beautiful; but all beauty is structured, even in nature. The tree needs a frame of earth and sky; a trunk ties it to the earth and lifts it to heaven; limbs and twigs arrange and support the leaves which give the tree symmetry.

But since the greater part of this book will be concerned with the forms, structure, and techniques of poetry, this is a good place to give some attention to the "building blocks" just mentioned: words and grammar. First, words. You have, of course, used them from infancy, used them naturally and without much thought of their shadings, meanings, and implications. But now, as a reader of poetry, you must learn to be aware

---

1. "Introduction" to John Ciardi's translation of *The Inferno* by Dante Alighieri (New York, 1954).

of words. Try listening carefully to some conversations. Notice how often communication fails because the speaker does not use the right word, or, if he does, because his hearer does not understand the meaning of the word. The same is true of reading. Learn, too, to distinguish word shadings. A study of *Webster's New World Dictionary* is excellent for this purpose. Notice the careful shadings of meanings in synonyms in the following definition of *error:*

> SYN.—*error* implies deviation from truth, accuracy, correctness, right, etc. and is the broadest term in this comparison (an *error* in judgment, in computation, etc.); *mistake* suggests an error resulting from carelessness, inattention, misunderstanding, etc. and does not in itself carry a strong implication of criticism (a *mistake* in reading a blueprint); *blunder* implies stupidity, clumsiness, inefficiency, etc. and carries a suggestion of more severe criticism (the tactical *blunder* cost them the war); a *slip* is a mistake, usually slight, made inadvertently in speaking or writing; a *faux pas* is a social blunder or error in etiquette that causes embarrassment; *boner*, a slang term, is applied to a silly or ridiculous blunder.[1]

A good thesaurus (such as Roget's) will also prove invaluable to you, as it lists synonyms. One word of warning, however: many experts in the language insist that, with the one possible exception of *gorse* and *furze,* there are no *exact* synonyms in the English language. Before you accept a "near" synonym from a thesaurus, be sure to check the meaning of the word in a good dictionary.

While you are increasing your awareness of words, you should also try to sharpen your perceptions through conscious effort. Start by eliminating trite phrases and clichés from your own speech and writing. If you have a headache, does "splitting headache" really describe what you are feeling? Try to see familiar things and people as if you had never seen them before. Examine your family and friends: What do they really look like? Does your sister have warts? If she does, are they really warts, or are they wens, pimples, discolorations, or precisely what? What color are your father's eyes? Perhaps upon close examination you will find that words like *blue, hazel,* or *brown* are simply not exact enough. Try describing the emotions you are feeling at a given moment. If you are happy, how do you *know* you are happy? What does it feel like? How does it differ from feeling glad, thankful, elated, nervous, giddy, or exhilarated? How would you describe what you term "happiness" to someone who had never experienced it? Such a conscious striving for increased aware-

---

1. From *Webster's New World Dictionary* of the American Language, College Edition. Copyright 1966 by The World Publishing Company, Cleveland, Ohio.

ness will also make you increasingly aware of the value of words. You will be doing just what any writer must do before he sits down to write; as William Wordsworth, in the *Preface* to the *Lyrical Ballads,* said:

> For all good poetry is the spontaneous overflow of powerful feelings; and though this be true, poems to which any value can be attached were never produced on any variety of subjects but by a man who, being possessed of more than usual organic sensibility, had also thought long and deeply.

All writing shares this truth. And you, as a reader, can become a person of "more than usual organic sensibility" by consciously striving to do so. The reader who has become perceptive of himself and of those about him, and who gives thought to the words he himself might use to describe his perceptions, will necessarily become more perceptive of any writer's ideas, thus making the act of reading more rewarding.

Furthermore, in your effort to become a good reader, you must be sure that you know the fundamentals of grammar and English syntax. Unfortunately, you probably don't. Do you understand expletives? Gerunds, participles, infinitives? The terms active and passive voice? Understanding of these six grammatical terms should be basic and essential. If you are grammatically weak, ask your teacher or librarian to recommend a good grammar handbook. Devote fifteen minutes a day to it. And start learning how to diagram! You will find that diagramming can teach you the function of phrases, clauses, verbals and other sentence elements as nothing else will.

Having consciously set about mastering words and grammar, as well as having attempted to increase your awareness of the world around you, you will soon find that you have made giant strides toward becoming a good reader not only of poetry but of prose as well. You will have begun to be in a position to understand a writer's intent, rather than merely to guess at it. Remember, "interpreting," at least before you have mastered the fundamentals of reading, is often merely a synonym for "guessing."

Suggested Activities. 1. Get acquainted with your library and your librarian.

2. All writing in the Western world rests on a knowledge of the Bible, Greek and Roman mythology, and history. Be sure to include these three areas of knowledge in your reading program. And notice how often in your reading you encounter biblical, mythological, and historical allusions.

Suggested Assignments. 1. Read the following passage from *Through the Looking-Glass* by Lewis Carroll, paying close attention to what is said and how it is said:

"When *I* use a word," Humpty Dumpty said, in rather a scornful tone, "it means just what I choose it to mean—neither more nor less."

"The question is," said Alice, "whether you *can* make words mean so many different things."

"The question is," said Humpty Dumpty, "which is to be master—that's all."

Alice was too much puzzled to say anything; so after a minute Humpty Dumpty began again. "They've a temper, some of them—particularly verbs: they're the proudest—adjectives you can do anything with, but not verbs—however, *I* can manage the whole lot of them! Impenetrability! That's what *I* say!"

"Would you tell me, please," said Alice, "what that means?"

"Now you talk like a reasonable child," said Humpty Dumpty, looking very much pleased. "I meant by 'impenetrability' that we've had enough of that subject, and it would be just as well if you'd mention what you mean to do next, as I suppose you don't mean to stop here all the rest of your life."

"That's a great deal to make one word mean," Alice said in a thoughtful tone.

"When I make a word do a lot of work like that," said Humpty Dumpty, "I always pay it extra."

"Oh!" said Alice. She was too much puzzled to make any other remark.

"Ah, you should see 'em come round me of a Saturday night," Humpty Dumpty went on, wagging his head gravely from side to side, "for to get their wages, you know."

(Alice didn't venture to ask what he paid them with; and so you see I can't tell *you*.)

"You seem very clever at explaining words, Sir," said Alice. "Would you kindly tell me the meaning of the poem called 'Jabberwocky'?"

"Let's hear it," said Humpty Dumpty. "I can explain all the poems that ever were invented—and a good many that haven't been invented just yet."

This sounded very hopeful, so Alice repeated the first verse:—

" 'Twas brillig, and the slithy toves
Did gyre and gimble in the wabe:
All mimsy were the borogoves,
And the mome raths outgrabe."

"That's enough to begin with," Humpty Dumpty interrupted: "there are plenty of hard words there. 'Brillig' means four o'clock in the afternoon—the time when you begin *broiling* things for dinner."

"That'll do very well," said Alice: "and *'slithy'?*"

"Well, *'slithy'* means 'lithe and slimy.' 'Lithe' is the same as 'active.' You see it's like a portmanteau—there are two meanings packed up into one word."

"I see it now," Alice remarked thoughtfully: "and what are *'toves'?*"

"Well, *'toves'* are something like badgers—they're something like lizards—and they're something like corkscrews."

"They must be very curious-looking creatures."

"They are that," said Humpty Dumpty: "also they make their nests under sun-dials—also they live on cheese."

"And what's to *'gyre'* and to *'gimble'?*"

"To *'gyre'* is to go round and round like a gyroscope. To *'gimble'* is to make holes like a gimblet."

"And *'the wabe'* is the grass-plot round a sun-dial, I suppose?" said Alice, surprised at her own ingenuity.

"Of course it is. It's called *'wabe,'* you know, because it goes a long way before it, and a long way behind it——"

"And a long way beyond it on each side," Alice added.

"Exactly so. Well then, *'mimsy'* is 'flimsy and miserable' (there's another portmanteau for you). And a *'borogove'* is a thin shabby-looking bird with its feathers sticking out all round—something like a live mop."

"And then *'mome raths'?*" said Alice. "I'm afraid I'm giving you a great deal of trouble."

"Well, a *'rath'* is a sort of green pig: but *'mome'* I'm not certain about. I think it's short for 'from home'—meaning that they'd lost their way, you know."

"And what does *'outgrabe'* mean?"

"Well, *'outgribing'* is something between bellowing and whistling, with a kind of sneeze in the middle: however, you'll hear it done, maybe—down in the wood yonder—and, when you've once heard it, you'll be *quite* content. Who's been repeating all that hard stuff to you?"

"I read it in a book," said Alice. . . .

2. While you may disagree with Humpty Dumpty's explanation of the first verse of *Jabberwocky*, you can see how he arrived at the meanings of the words. Explain the rest of the poem, using his reasoning process as your model. Here is the poem:

Jabberwocky

'Twas brillig, and the slithy toves
    Did gyre and gimble in the wabe:
All mimsy were the borogoves,
    And the mome raths outgrabe.

"Beware the Jabberwock, my son!   *5*
    The jaws that bite, the claws that catch!
Beware the Jubjub bird, and shun
    The frumious Bandersnatch!"

He took his vorpal sword in hand:
    Long time the manxome foe he sought—   *10*
So rested he by the Tumtum tree,
    And stood awhile in thought.

And, as in uffish thought he stood,
    The Jabberwock, with eyes of flame,
Came whiffling through the tulgey wood,   *15*
    And burbled as it came!

One, two! One, two! And through and through
    The vorpal blade went snicker-snack!
He left it dead, and with its head
    He went galumphing back.   *20*

"And hast thou slain the Jabberwock?
    Come to my arms, my beamish boy!
O frabjous day! Callooh! Callay!"
    He chortled in his joy.

'Twas brillig, and the slithy toves   *25*
    Did gyre and gimble in the wabe:
All mimsy were the borogoves,
    And the mome raths outgrabe.

Lewis Carroll

Suggested Reading. *The Creative Process* by Brewster Ghiselin (Mentor pocket edition or library hardbound): several authors tell how they begin and complete creative work in literature. While the essays are not easy reading, you must begin now to stretch your mind by reading material of some difficulty. You are no longer reading merely to be amused. You are reading now to learn—though, be assured, amusement will always accompany that act.

CHAPTER II

The Language of Poetry

In the preceding chapter, it was emphasized that if you are to understand poetry and become sensitive to the subtleties of life through poetry, you must find a new awareness of words. The point is so important that this entire chapter is devoted to the subject.

In order for you to be a "good" reader—of prose as well as poetry—words must become unique and usable to you as they have never been before. You must develop an intensified, greedy hunger to hear words for the quality of their vowels, the uniqueness of their consonants, the impact of their total sound when these features are combined with the multiple meanings and sounds of every other word surrounding them. You must be willing to explore the literal or denotative meanings of words as well as their suggestive or connotative depths. And, if you can only think of one synonym for most of the words you now know, you are missing a great deal in your reading!

Words are the most basic of the writer's tools. As a mechanic works with cotter pins and gears, writers work with the words they feel will most exactly communicate their awareness or vision of reality to their readers. No good mechanic would use an oval-head bolt to do the job of a fillister-head; no adequate writer would willingly choose an inadequate word to express his meaning. The mechanic compares the hole and the bolt, and he chooses the right bolt from his inventory or experience. The writer chooses his words in much the same way—checking his catalogue of parts (a dictionary or thesaurus) if his memory is not adequate to the task. The word *chair* is not the same as the word *stool; tumult* is not *confusion; murmur* is not *whisper*. Each word does a specific and unique job: that of creating a particular image in the reader's mind.

In *The Rubáiyát of Omar Khayyám,* for example, Edward FitzGerald might easily have spoken of that *overturned* or *upside down* bowl, but his inventory included a better choice, and his line achieved communicable imagery: "And that *inverted* Bowl they call the Sky. . . ." The casual reader will, of course, fail to see the difference. All three words mean, denotatively, "not right-side-up." But *overturned* implies careless accident; and *upside down* suggests no intelligent involvement—the state exists free of any agent but is, nonetheless, "incorrect." *Inverted,* however, suggests that an intelligent agent has deliberately shaped the sky into its metaphorical form. The one word, *inverted,* sensitively read, can change the reader's initial concept of the stanza:

> And that inverted Bowl they call the Sky,
> Whereunder crawling cooped we live and die,
> Lift not your hands to *It* for help—for It
> As impotently moves as you or I.

Without an awareness of the connotative possibilities of *inverted,* the reader could mistake the implication to be that the *Sky* is synonymous with "God" and that, by extension, there is no "God" or He is powerless. An awareness of the connotation of *inverted* creates the awareness of a "God" who shaped the sky which is, in and of itself, impotent because *Sky* is *not* "God." *Sky* is a natural phenomenon; "God" is a supernatural being. He who offers prayers for help must be aware of the difference if his prayers are to be directed to a hearer. Thus, the understanding of a subtle theological concept lies in an awareness of one word.

The easiest, best, and most enjoyable way to increase your awareness of words is to read—widely, discriminately, and sensitively. If you do not already do so, you should immediately begin to read shorter works such as Shakespeare's sonnets, Hart Crane's *Voyages,* or Emily Dickinson's poems. You need not necessarily read for perfect understanding of content, but for word awareness, for sound, and for a responding of your five senses to the evocations of the words. Such reading will cause you to wonder that you were less sensitive to language before. And, as you read, you will become aware of elements other than words—phrasings, word interplay, figures of speech. The more deliberately you read, the more your awareness of all these elements will grow.

To respond initially to poetry, you need not know technical terms or structural devices; you can react to words and images, unconcerned with the techniques that make them effective. A *first* reading of any poem should be accomplished in just such a fashion. Let the words work their magic; let the images create their pictures in your mind. Allow yourself the luxury of sensuality. Try reading the following poem in this fashion, abandoning the need to understand. Allow the poet to reach whatever corner of your senses his words can—then reread the poem to see what triggered your responses:

Repose of Rivers

The willows carried a slow sound,
A sarabande the wind mowed on the mead.
I could never remember
That seething, steady leveling of the marshes
Till age had brought me to the sea.   5

Flags, weeds. And remembrance of steep alcoves
Where cypresses shared the noon's
Tyranny; they drew me into hades almost.
And mammoth turtles climbing sulphur dreams
Yielded, while sun-silt rippled them   10
Asunder . . .

How much I would have bartered! the black gorge
And all the singular nestings in the hills
Where beavers learn stitch and tooth.
The pond I entered once and quickly fled—   15
I remember now its singing willow rim.

And finally, in that memory all things nurse;
After the city that I finally passed
With scalding unguents spread and smoking darts
The monsoon cut across the delta   20
At gulf gates . . . There, beyond the dykes

I heard wind flaking sapphire, like this summer,
And willows could not hold more steady sound.

Hart Crane

Perhaps many of the words in this poem are not in your present vocabulary. After your first reading, use a dictionary. *Sarabande,* for example, is defined as a slow Spanish dance in triple time, graceful and stately, though it developed from an earlier, more lively dance. *Sarabande* refers also to the music for this dance, the emphasis coming on the second beat of the measure.

Now observe the poetic language of the first two lines. "The willows carried a slow sound" creates experience by appealing to at least two of your senses, sight and sound. Willows are graceful trees but bulky in appearance, often drooping toward the earth as if their leaves were too heavy for their slender branches. They seem to stoop under the weight of some burden, except when the wind catches their branches, lifting them slowly and languidly toward the horizon. The word *carried* implies continuous action (a subtlety desired by the poet) in a way that near synonyms (such as *brought, transmitted, conveyed,* or *transported*) could not. The phrase *slow sound* also functions poetically. The repeated *s* sounds combine with the open vowels to create an impression of slowness—not ponderousness or heaviness, but a graceful stateliness. This aural reaction is intensified by the poet's choice of *sarabande* in the next line. Willows carry their slow sound as a result of the wind's blowing through them, and the poet enlarges the image by introducing the word *wind* to perform a second action—that of mowing (cutting grass with a sickle or scythe). Since a sarabande is emphasized on the second beat of each measure, *mowed* is aptly chosen as it suggests the unemphasized upward swing of the sickle before the second action, the emphasized downward stroke of forceful cutting. Thus, the lines fuse and a total picture is presented: the reader sees a meadow bowed (as if mowed) before a wind that creates the music and motion of the sarabande in the action on the grass and in the willows. The ear hears the attendant sounds, and the sensitive reader, aided by memory-stored experience, will smell fresh cuttings and recall other memories to superimpose on the picture already conjured up by the poet.

Now examine the remainder of "Repose of Rivers" in a similar fashion, observing poetic language at work. Do not, as lazy students frequently prefer to do, mistake the author's success for sheer accident or "inspiration"—such lines are deliberate, built slowly, revised carefully by the poet until they *seem* accidental in their excellence, inspired in concept, and liquid in movement.

Can you achieve the same awareness of language from reading prose? Yes, you can. Prose—and especially the best prose—does achieve exactness, economy, intensity; but never to the same degree that poetry does. Poetry is so much more exact, so much more economical, so much more intense in its usage that it serves a more immediate end. Because of the demands of the poetic line, poetry offers better examples, more compressed rewards per page. Sample all you care to in prose (the more you read, the more your awareness develops), but demand time of your reading schedule to examine a poem or two each day—intelligently and deliberately, attempting to see what the poet achieves with words, and how.

Many people object to "poetic language." But they are objecting to a concept of diction that is both narrow and old-fashioned. This so-called "poetic language" had its genesis in standard works of poets fond of using *o'er* for *over*, *e'er* for *ever*, and *e'en* for *even*, at a time when such contractions were poetically acceptable. (They are not acceptable in modern poetry.) Many teachers too often overemphasize such poetry, not realizing that discrimination is a natural growth in the human animal; it will not be forced. Rebelling against the falseness of language so employed, and against archaic terms such as *swain* (for "shepherd") and *finny deep* (for "ocean"), readers often rebel against the whole body of poetry.

The result is lamentable, for such words are not necessarily poetic language at all. At best, they are substitutes for the longer word, a word the poet could not use because of syllable complications and aural reactions. Their inexactness alone usually weakens them, and today's poets ordinarily avoid them.

What, then, is poetic language? It is the same language that is used in speech and in prose, but it receives more careful attention from the poet. It is a more exact language because the poet seeks out the word *most* suited to his need rather than settling for one which *almost* means what he wants to convey. Selecting that one *best* word for the desired effect, he combines vocabulary with imagery, rhythm, and sensory evocation. In other words, a poet's words are everyday words used in a very special way—a sensitive, perceptive way allowing them to function completely at more than one level.

The words a poet uses are both denotative and connotative. That is, they denote the surface or literal meaning, while, connotatively, they evoke allied sensory images and unlock the mind and memory of the reader. Such use of words enables the reader to remember or evaluate experience he has stored away, experience that may have lacked meaning until the poet's language releases and unlocks the mental door to an understanding of that unused knowledge. By effectively evoking the five senses (taste, touch, sight, smell, sound), the poet creates meaning which can be perceived through them. He then urges a *sixth* sense, the *apperceptive* (which is the ability to assimilate new ideas as well as to harmonize them with already known concepts), into action. The result is that the reader experiences not only the poem, but an awareness of Self that combines with the poet's words to create a poetic understanding. For most readers, the result is as mystical an experience as they will ever achieve.

To understand poetic language, you will need to know some terms. As they are discussed below, learn their names, memorize their definitions, and begin now to use them in your own reading and writing. Most of these terms are basic not only to poetry but to prose as well. (For a discussion of rhyme, rhyme scheme, and meter, see respectively pp. 119-130, 130-131, 84-101.)

First, a *stanza* is a group of lines comprising a poetic division, corresponding to a paragraph in prose. It may be as brief as a *couplet* (two lines) or it may extend to any length the poet chooses. Among the most common stanzas are the *quatrain* (four lines), the *quintain* (five lines), the *sextain* (six lines), and the *octave* (eight lines).

Personification is the attribution of human qualities to inanimate objects or abstractions. "Love is blind" suggests that the abstraction, "love," has eyes, however sightless. "And flowers lift their faces to the sun" grants human features to stamens, pistils, and petals. Personification may be extended, as it is in the following poem:

Drinking

The thirsty earth soaks up the rain,
And drinks, and gapes for drink again.
The plants suck in the earth, and are
With constant drinking fresh and fair.
The sea itself, which one would think   5
Should have but little need of drink,
Drinks twice ten thousand rivers up,
So filled that they o'erflow the cup.
The busy sun (and one would guess
By's drunken fiery face no less)   10
Drinks up the sea, and when h'as done,
The moon and stars drink up the sun.
They drink and dance by their own light;
They drink and revel all the night.
Nothing in nature's sober found,   15
But an eternal health goes round.
Fill up the bowl, then, fill it high,
Fill all the glasses there, for why
Should every creature drink but I?
Why, man of morals, tell me why?   20

Abraham Cowley

The perceptive reader will notice many overstatements in the poem. Technically called *hyperbole,* such overstatement is exaggeration (sometimes gross exaggeration, as in "I just died laughing") designed to emphasize or create a special effect. The reader is not deceived, for hyperbole is apparent. But notice its effectiveness in

Dread

Beside a chapel I'd a room looked down,
Where all the women from the farms and town,
On Holy-days and Sundays used to pass
To marriages, and christenings, and to Mass.

Then I sat lonely watching score and score,   5
Till I turned jealous of the Lord next door. . . .
Now by this window, where there's none can see,
The Lord God's jealous of yourself and me.

John Millington Synge

The opposite of overstatement is, of course, *understatement.* The value of understatement lies in what it leaves unsaid, what it forces or allows the reader to supply. Notice the effect of understatement in the last line of

She Dwelt Among the Untrodden Ways

She dwelt among the untrodden ways
    Beside the springs of Dove,
A Maid whom there were none to praise
    And very few to love:

A violet by a mossy stone   5
    Half hidden from the eye!
—Fair as a star, when only one
    Is shining in the sky.

She lived unknown, and few could know
    When Lucy ceased to be;   10
But she is in her grave, and, oh,
    The difference to me!

William Wordsworth

The specific effect achieved by the use of the word *difference* can be seen clearly if you substitute *agony, misery,* or the phrase *pain and hurt,* all containing the same number of syllables. Note also the slight overstatement in the first line. *Untrodden* states that no one walked in that remote country. Obviously Lucy did; obviously Wordsworth did. The use of hyperbole in line 1 to balance the understatement in line 12 intensifies the effect of the understatement.

A *simile* is a comparison likening two things that are, in most respects, completely dissimilar. One shared characteristic or quality creates the comparison which is expressed with the words *like, as,* or *than.* Everyday speech frequently employs the simile: "Her lips are sweeter than honey"; "She looked like death warmed over"; "He's as ugly as a mud fence." Percy Bysshe Shelley opened his "Hymn to Intellectual Beauty" with a stanza containing six similes:

> The awful shadow of some unseen Power
>> Floats though unseen among us,—visiting
>> This various world with as inconstant wing
> As summer winds that creep from flower to flower,—
> Like moonbeams that behind some piny mountain shower,   *5*
>>> It visits with inconstant glance
>>> Each human heart and countenance;
> Like hues and harmonies of evening,—
>> Like clouds in starlight widely spread,—
>> Like memory of music fled,—   *10*
>> Like aught that for its grace may be
> Dear, and yet dearer for its mystery.

The most useful figure of speech in poetry is the *metaphor,* a comparison of two seemingly unlike things which do share comparable characteristics or qualities. The metaphor states that one thing *is* another: "His hand was a hammer of steel." The poet can thus capture the essential quality of the experience by appealing immediately to the senses, either singly or in combination. The metaphor's concreteness is derived from its ability to establish a comparison, fuse it with a reader's stored sensory memories, and create new, allied images. Sometimes considered mere poetic decoration, metaphor should serve a two-fold function of definite purpose in the poem. Mere decoration is not justifiable usage. In Sonnet 73, William Shakespeare employs three metaphors, building in intensity and subtlety to the final two lines. Notice the metaphor within a metaphor in line 4:

Sonnet 73

> That time of year thou mayst in me behold
> When yellow leaves, or none, or few, do hang
> Upon those boughs which shake against the cold,
> Bare ruin'd choirs where late the sweet birds sang.
> In me thou see'st the twilight of such day   *5*
> As after sunset fadeth in the west,

Which by and by black night doth take away,
Death's second self, that seals up all in rest.
In me thou see'st the glowing of such fire
That on the ashes of his youth doth lie,   *10*
As the death-bed whereon it must expire,
Consum'd with that which it was nourish'd by.
    This thou perceiv'st, which makes thy love more strong,
    To love that well which thou must leave ere long.

William Shakespeare

When a metaphor is employed at some length, it assumes strength in the extension. In the Twenty-Third Psalm, God is, metaphorically, a shepherd who leads me (metaphorically, the human is a sheep) to clear, calm water and grassy pasture land (those places serving my best interests) as a competent shepherd should. Danger in metaphorical usage arises when enthusiasm joins unrelated metaphors to create ludicrous situations: "Sleep is a kind of dying; this alarm clock, Gabriel's horn." Even poets of the stature of Longfellow have encountered difficulties with the metaphor. His "A Psalm of Life" contains a metaphor that works to achieve the opposite of his intention:

    Lives of great men all remind us
      We can make our lives sublime,
    And, departing, leave behind us
      Footprints on the sands of time.

The metaphor was employed to suggest permanent memory. Unfortunately, Longfellow did not consider the impermanence of a footprint in sand: it is obliterated by the next wave.

An identification by the use of an associated word for a literal meaning is called *metonymy:* "He took the *wheel* and drove us safely home"— *wheel* = control of the automobile. In Genesis, God assures Adam: "In the sweat of thy face shalt thou eat bread"—*sweat* = hard labor.

Synecdoche is an identification through substitution of a part for the whole, or a whole for a part. When the part represents the whole, it must be the most closely associated part: "There were many willing *hands*" = workers (who work with their hands); "Please accept this *rhyme*" = a poem (which includes rhymes). William Wordsworth opens his sonnet "The World Is Too Much With Us" with a synecdoche substituting the whole for a part:

    The world is too much with us; late and soon,
    Getting and spending, we lay waste our powers.

World = material possessions, as Wordsworth indicates in the second line. *Onomatopoeia* is, literally, "name-making." Words which, in their very sounds, imitate the sounds they symbolize are onomatopoetic. "Snap, crackle, pop" is a familiar cereal advertisement suggesting the sound of the crisp cereal inundated. Such words as *murmur* and *coo* are more aesthetic examples. Words arranged in sound patterns may achieve onomatopoeia, as in the following famous examples, the first from "The Princess" by Alfred, Lord Tennyson, the second from "The Raven" by Edgar Allan Poe:

> The moan of doves in immemorial elms,
> And murmuring of innumerable bees.

> And the silken, sad, uncertain rustling of each purple curtain . . .

Deliberate *repetition* of words, phrases or clauses is often used to intensify mood or emphasize an idea. Nowhere is repetition more effective than in Shakespeare's *Hamlet* soliloquy: "To be or not to be. . . ." Also notice the effect in

Cried the Fox

I run, cried the fox, in circles
narrower, narrower still,
across the desperate hollow,
skirting the frantic hill,

and shall till my brush hangs burning   *5*
flame at the hunter's door
continue this fatal returning
to places that failed me before!

Then, with his heart breaking nearly,
the lonely, passionate bark   *10*
of the fugitive fox rang out clearly
as bells in the frosty dark,

across the desperate hollow,
skirting the frantic hill,
calling the pack to follow   *15*
a prey that escaped them still.

Tennessee Williams

A reference to an historical person or event, a place connotatively rich in association, and so on, is called an *allusion*. Observe the italicized allusions in the first nine lines of " On His Deceased Wife," a sonnet by John Milton:

> Methought I saw my late espousèd saint
> Brought to me like *Alcestis* from the grave,
> Whom *Jove's great son* to her glad husband gave,
> Rescued from death by force though pale and faint.
> Mine as whom washed from spot of *child-bed taint*, 5
> Purification in the *old law* did save,
> And such, as yet once more I trust to have
> Full sight of her in Heaven without restraint,
> Came vested all in white, pure as her mind.

Clusters of associated images usually attach themselves to allusions, making lengthy explanations unnecessary—the name *Helen* automatically suggests great female beauty; *Waterloo* suggests defeat.

Irony refers to a deliberate statement which indicates a reverse attitude. A mother, hopefully offering "healthy" but unappetizing food to her child, says, "You'll like this." When he responds, "*Sure* I will," emphasizing the *sure,* he employs irony. At its most unsubtle level, irony becomes *sarcasm* (cutting language, intended to wound), which in Greek means, "I strip the flesh from the bones." Recent political use of sarcasm is apparent in the term "little old ladies in tennis shoes." In Shakespeare's *Julius Caesar,* Antony's insistence that Brutus and the other conspirators are "honorable men" is subtle irony when first employed. As he repeats it, enlarging on his intent, it becomes obvious sarcasm which even the plebeians will understand. Job's statement to the people in the Old Testament is more subtle, more mockingly and sharply ironic: "No doubt but ye are the people, and wisdom shall die with you." When irony extends to sarcasm and the two are sustained throughout a literary work, *satire* results. The most skillfully sustained irony in our literature is Jonathan Swift's *A Modest Proposal,* in which the starving Irish are encouraged to breed excessively and sell their offspring as food to their English landlords. Understatement too is usually a kind of irony: read, for example, the last line of Wordsworth's "She Dwelt Among the Untrodden Ways" (p. 15), keeping the possibility of irony in mind. Also observe the many devices of irony in

The Latest Decalogue

Thou shalt have one God only; who
Would be at the expense of two?
No graven images may be
Worshiped, except the currency.
Swear not at all; for, for thy curse   5
Thine enemy is none the worse.
At church on Sunday to attend
Will serve to keep the world thy friend.
Honor thy parents; that is, all
From whom advancement may befall.   10
Thou shalt not kill; but need'st not strive
Officiously to keep alive.
Do not adultery commit;
Advantage rarely comes of it.
Thou shalt not steal; an empty feat,   15
When it's so lucrative to cheat.
Bear not false witness; let the lie
Have time on its own wings to fly.
Thou shalt not covet; but tradition
Approves all forms of competition.   20

The sum of all is, thou shalt love,
If anybody, God above:
At any rate shall never labor
More than thyself to love thy neighbor.

Arthur Hugh Clough

An assertion that seems to contradict itself but which is, nevertheless, true, is called a *paradox*. Irony is usually a major ingredient. Religion often employs paradox: Jesus said, "For whosoever will save his life shall lose it; but whosoever shall lose his life for my sake and the gospel's, the same shall save it." Politics too employs paradox:

Of Treason

Treason doth never prosper. What's the reason?
For if it prosper, none dare call it treason.

Sir John Harington

Paradox also abounds in

Holy Sonnet XIV

Batter my heart, three-personed God; for you
As yet but knock, breathe, shine, and seek to mend;
That I may rise and stand, o'erthrow me, and bend
Your force to break, blow, burn, and make me new.
I, like an usurped town, to another due,   5
Labor to admit you, but oh, to no end;
Reason, your viceroy in me, me should defend,
But is captived, and proves weak or untrue.
Yet dearly I love you, and would be loved fain,
But am betrothed unto your enemy: 10
Divorce me, untie or break that knot again,
Take me to you, imprison me, for I
Except you enthrall me, never shall be free,
Nor ever chaste, except you ravish me.

John Donne

The term *apostrophe* means direct address to an absent person ("Oh, Shakespeare, I would write as you!"), to an abstract quality ("Love, let me feel your quiet strength"), or to a person who doesn't exist ("Sweet dream child, make of yourself flesh"). Authors of epic poetry invoked the muse Calliope to inspire them and their work. In the opening lines of *Paradise Lost,* Milton invokes the power that inspired Moses:

Sing, Heavenly Muse, that on the secret top
Of Oreb, or of Sinai, didst inspire
That shepherd who first taught the chosen seed
In the beginning how the heavens and earth
Rose out of Chaos. . . .

In "Voyages II," Hart Crane asks: "Bind us in time, O Seasons clear, and awe."

Image and *imagery* mean, quite literally, "pictures." Similes and metaphors create images by establishing relationships: "Jane's hair is like spun gold" creates an immediate picture of fine, shimmering color, receptive to light. Sunshine is implicit in the image, even though it is not explicitly mentioned. The image creates the picture, but the picture is not static; it quickly broadens to suggest other possibilities. Value is associated with gold; therefore, Jane is a valued person. *Spun* suggests the delicate but strong, for only pure elements may be spun—impurities create weak spots which break. Further, as the sun is captured in the image, it creates a halo of light around the head, strengthening the "pure" suggestion through religious association. The image sets in motion many responses in the reader. When these responses further empower the image, it becomes *imagery,* a series of interrelated impressions growing out of one picture, eventually to create a richer impression than either the poet or reader could achieve alone.

Such poetic imagery may be said to have originated with the Italian sonneteer Petrarch, who described his lady-love in highly complimentary comparisons. Elizabethan poets, enamored of his devices, borrowed them, creating new situations in which to use the similes and metaphors (called *conceits* as they became mere conventions). Teeth were like pearls, hair was like gold wires, lips were like rubies. Shakespeare, too, employed the Petrarchan conceit, but, growing a little bored with it or anxious to celebrate his dark-haired, olive-skinned lady, he wrote

Sonnet 130

My mistress' eyes are nothing like the sun;
Coral is far more red than her lips' red;
If snow be white, why then her breasts are dun;
If hairs be wires, black wires grow on her head.
I have seen roses damask'd, red and white,   5
But no such roses see I in her cheeks;
And in some perfumes is there more delight
Than in the breath that from my mistress reeks.
I love to hear her speak, yet well I know
That music hath a far more pleasing sound;   10
I grant I never saw a goddess go;
My mistress, when she walks, treads on the ground:
And yet, by heaven, I think my love as rare
As any she beli'd with false compare.

William Shakespeare

Poets such as John Donne and George Herbert extended the comparison growing from a single simile or metaphor, developing it ingeniously on many levels. Turn back to p. 21 and re-examine Donne's "Holy Sonnet XIV" to see the *metaphysical conceit* elaborately used to equate the human heart and the walled town, the poet and the conquered, Satan and the conqueror, God and the liberator. Samuel Johnson once defined metaphysical poetry as that poetry wherein "the most heterogeneous ideas are yoked by violence together." This is a harsh definition, but it is true that metaphysical poetry may at first seem difficult to read until it is seen as juxtapositions of thought, suddenly conceived and skillfully blended; the materials *are* heterogeneous, but the poet employs all his intellect in unifying the seemingly unrelated into a logical whole. T. S. Eliot described the metaphysical conceit as "the elaboration of a figure of speech to the farthest stage to which ingenuity can carry it."

Paradox may be employed in poetic imagery if the contradictions are very subtle but completely logical. Called *oxymoron,* such paradox is apparent in Milton's description in *Paradise Lost* of Satan's first view of Hell when he recovers from his nine days' fall from Heaven. Awaking, he sees

> A dungeon horrible, on all sides round,
> As one great furnace flamed; yet from those flames
> No light; but rather darkness visible
> Served only to discover sights of woe.
>
> *(I, 61-64)*

The omission of a verb at the end of line 3 establishes the paradox. Flames *should* cause light, so *darkness visible* is flatly contradictory—therefore, oxymoron. That such darkness serves to reveal *sights of woe* extends oxymoron, but a grim logic makes the image work as the reader's conditioned responses to sin and Hell are woven into the picture. Irony is frequently employed in combination with oxymoron in everyday speech. A friend's intelligence might be assessed: "He's about as sharp as a wet noodle." A second device here employed is *syllepsis,* linking one word with two unrelated words to create comparisons not otherwise possible. In "He's as sharp as a tack," *sharp* means "alert or clever" in relation to the human, "pointed, penetrating" in relation to the tack. Imagery results from the hearer's associative powers. Alexander Pope employs the same device in "The Rape of the Lock":

> Here thou, great Anna! whom three realms obey,
> Dost sometimes counsel take—and sometimes tea.
>
> *(III, 7-8)*

When opposing ideas are placed in grammatical parallel, *antithesis* results. Sarcasm may be an element, as you can see in the following summary by a mother: "My daughter *daily* falls in love *eternally.*" In the next excerpt from "The Rape of the Lock," there are more examples of antithesis than there are lines:

> But since, alas! frail beauty must decay,
> Curled or uncurled, since locks will turn to grey;
> Since painted, or not painted, all shall fade,
> And she who scorns a man, must die a maid;
> What then remains but well our power to use,   5
> And keep good humor still whate'er we lose.
>
> *(V, 25-30)*

Imagery, then, results from skillfully employed literary devices, used singly or in combination.

A *symbol* is a word or image signifying not only the actual object or idea, but all the ideas, attitudes, and responses associated with it. The compounding of many meanings in one word creates a larger idea. As the image establishes a primary-secondary relationship, the symbol obliterates the relationship, giving the image freedom to work at many levels at once. In "Voyages II," Hart Crane used the sea image as a major symbol to represent several different things—the literal body of water, the original source of life, the receiver of all dead things, the present source of life, personified woman, demigoddess, musician, music manuscript, delight and terror of lovers . . . all in ten lines!

> And yet this great wink of eternity,
> Of rimless floods, unfettered leewardings,
> Samite sheeted and processioned where
> Her undinal vast belly moonward bends,
> Laughing the wrapt inflections of our love;   5
>
> Take this Sea, whose diapason knells
> On scrolls of silver snowy sentences,
> The sceptred terror of whose sessions rends
> As her demeanors motion well or ill,
> All but the pieties of lovers' hands.   10

Or notice Crane's use of the bell as a symbol in his final poem, "The Broken Tower":

> The bell-rope that gathers God at dawn
> Dispatches me as though I dropped down the knell
> Of a spent day—to wander the cathedral lawn
> From pit to crucifix, feet chill on steps from hell.

The bell-rope is no less a physical bell-rope because it serves as a physical signal, a spiritual collector, and a psychological dispatcher. It is a concrete object even as it is a conveyance for meaning. That meaning is personal to the poet and personal to the reader, but it becomes shared meaning through the symbol.

At the most obvious level, *allegory* is a depiction of political, religious, social, or moral attitudes through personifications. Aesop's *Fables* are peopled by animals behaving as humans. In the medieval morality play *Everyman,* characters are abstractions with names such as Fellowship, Death, Knowledge, and Beauty. Bunyan's *The Pilgrim's Progress* is also a religious allegory; George Orwell's *Animal Farm* is a political allegory wherein animals represent people. Allegory, at a less obvious level, is symbolism extended until it becomes an interpretive part of the reader's experience. When Chaucer in the *Canterbury Tales* observes:

> This world nis but a thurghfare full of wo,
> And we ben pilgrimes, passing to and fro,

he begins with metaphor. The world is a road; we are travelers. The metaphor extends to symbol, however, as the comparison assumes personal meaning from our religious backgrounds. Memory causes literature (the *Canterbury Tales*) to combine with history (the pilgrims were traveling to a holy place) and, finally, to become personal in application (What is *my* purpose on earth?). At this point, allegory emerges: the "world" becomes "my life," "pilgrim" becomes "me." I am, hopefully, a traveler going to a holy place which is somewhere at the end of the road of life —eternity. Symbol has now become personal allegory.

The word *tone* refers to the dominant quality of sound in a poem or portion of a poem. As the poet wishes to achieve an emotional attitude in the poem, he chooses words which denotatively, connotatively, and in vowel-consonant quality establish the attitude or tone. A bell *rings*— that's neutral; but it *peals* joyfully, it *tolls* mournfully. Degrees of joy and age are revealed in the choice of words such as *laugh, cackle, chuckle, chortle, smile, snicker,* and *grin.* The sound of words blends with their sense, and sentences emerge correspondingly. The sedate, solemn, ponderous are encompassed in complex, compound, or compound-complex constructions. The happy, excited, tense are conveyed in simple sentences or fragments. Furthermore, color overlays sound and sense: *blue* creates serene skies or dreary moods, *green* suggests envy or fecundity, or *red* rages passionately through any number of emotions. All of these elements of tone then determine the prevailing mood of the work.

The poet's experienced and communicated feeling which emerges as emotional atmosphere in which the reader exists as he reads is called *mood.* As a person's happy mood, ugly mood, or pensive mood results from a combination of things, a poem may, in its overall effect, evoke one dominant feeling. All elements of the poem combine to create mood. Sometimes *atmosphere* (description employed to create mood) is confused with mood. The atmosphere of Poe's "The Raven," for example, is dark, dusty, and decaying as a result of such descriptive phrases as "midnight dreary," "volume of forgotten lore," and "pallid bust of Pallas." Rich trappings suggest the Gothic setting: silk, purple curtains; the velvet, violet lining of the cushioned seat. Knowledge of the lost Lenore, awareness of grief that is near-madness, sympathy for the lonely scholar—all of the reader's emotional responses to another human being now combine with responses to the atmosphere. A suffocating discomfort settles on the reader. The discomfort grows as old gods (Pallas Athene and Pluto) and pagan sites (Hades and Lethe) are juxtaposed against Judeo-Christian allusions (seraphim, Gilead, Aiden) to create a sense of spiritual conflict in the reader. Black bird of ill-omen perches on the pale bust of wisdom and casts a gaunt shadow on the floor. That shadow holds the poet's soul (is the soul merely a shadow too?) in thrall. A mournful, frightening tone results from such phrases as "weak and weary," "surcease of sorrow," and "fantastic terrors." The reader succumbs to atmosphere, symbol, tone, and narrative impact as the word *Nevermore* hypnotizes him with its monotonous repetition. A weary, defeated, helpless mood results. Solitude and decay combine with darkness and metronomic sound to hold the reader, as well as the poet, inert and helpless in the shadow on the floor. A mood of emotional and spiritual exhaustion has been created from many elements. As mood is the dominant impression established through devices of tone, it causes the reflective questioning to which a reader submits himself: "What does this mean to me? How do these revelations enrich or explain life as I understand it?"

Alliteration is repetition of consonant sound, usually at the beginning of two or more consecutive words or syllables: "*S*am *s*at *s*tiffly in *s*tubborn *s*ilence"; "*P*eter *P*iper *p*icked a *p*eck of *p*ickled *p*eppers." Alliteration may also result from repetition of initial consonants in words separated in the line:

> Hast thou forgot me then, and do I seem
> Now in thine eye so foul, once deemed so fair.
> *John Milton (Paradise Lost, II)*

This repetition seems to bind the words together, creating unity through emphasis. When it can be achieved naturally, without forcing, it is effective; when it is mechanical or artificial, it becomes obvious and weakens the line.

Repetition of vowel sounds—especially in stressed (accented) syllables —is termed *assonance.* The consonants need have no relation; vowels are paramount: "Al*o*ne, the *o*cean r*oa*ms the world's l*o*ne sands." Notice in the following lines by William Collins how assonance, like alliteration, seems to bind the lines together, creating unity through emphasis. The lines create a memory of sound, as rhyme does (see p. 120), but that binding device is not employed; a *sense* of rhyme is created by assonance, alliteration, and consonance:

> If ought of oaten stop, or pastoral song,
> May hope, chaste Eve, to soothe thy modest ear,
> Like thy own solemn springs,
> Thy springs, and dying gales . . .
>
> *Ode to Evening*

Consonance is resemblance of consonants. The term is applied to imperfect rhymes dependent on consonant rather than vowel sounds: *flesh, flash, flood, fled* or *cripple, apple, maple, supple.* Sometimes consonance is substituted for end rhyme, as in this fragment from "III" by W. H. Auden:

> You are the one whose part it is to lean,
> For whom it is not good to be alone,
> Laugh warmly turning shyly in the hall
> Or climb with bare knees the volcanic hill.

Poems for Study

The poems that follow should be examined in terms of language, figures of speech, tone, mood, alliteration, and all the other aspects of poetic language discussed so far. Read each poem carefully. Use a dictionary for unfamiliar words; do not hesitate to check a word if you feel your definition is inexact or questionable. Note the language use as it produces the poetic sound. You should begin now to see how the sense of any poem is bound up with the sound of its words. Imagery, too, builds into communicable form as much from sound as from word meanings. One suggestion: write a *précis* of each poem. A *précis* is a shortcut or a brief. It is abstracted thought, reduced to the pithiest essence possible. Comprehension in reading is indicated by the excellence of your précis —and all of your writing about poems should begin in a précis which you can later expand. You should learn to follow five general steps in abstracting a précis from a poem:

Step 1: Read the material. Check the major words in a dictionary. Do not assume you need only check unfamiliar words. Common words too may have any number of meanings with which you are unfamiliar. Understand all words as completely as possible—both denotatively and connotatively.

Step 2: Reread the poem, eliminating details, retaining only major or essential points.

Step 3: Decide which is the *one* central idea in the poem to which all other ideas contribute.

Step 4: Paraphrase (rewrite in your own words) that central idea. If one sentence will suffice, fine. If more than one sentence is required, be sure the ideas are in logical order.

Step 5: Condense your paraphrase until it is as brief as possible, yet adequate. You now have a précis.

After you have written the précis, reread the poem carefully to glean whatever richness you have thus far missed. And, above all, be sure to read the poems for their offered delight.

With Rue My Heart Is Laden

With rue my heart is laden
   For golden friends I had,
For many a rose-lipt maiden
   And many a lightfoot lad.

By brooks too broad for leaping   *5*
   The lightfoot boys are laid;
The rose-lipt girls are sleeping
   In fields where roses fade.

             A. E. Housman

To Autumn

Season of mists and mellow fruitfulness,
   Close bosom-friend of the maturing sun;
Conspiring with him how to load and bless
   With fruit the vines that round the thatch-eaves run;
To bend with apples the moss'd cottage-trees,   *5*
   And fill all fruit with ripeness to the core;
     To swell the gourd, and plump the hazel shells
   With a sweet kernel; to set budding more,
And still more, later flowers for the bees,
Until they think warm days will never cease,   *10*
     For Summer has o'er-brimmed their clammy cells.

Who hath not seen thee oft amid thy store?
   Sometimes whoever seeks abroad may find
Thee sitting careless on a granary floor,
   Thy hair soft-lifted by the winnowing wind;   *15*
Or on a half-reap'd furrow sound asleep,
   Drows'd with the fume of poppies, while thy hook
      Spares the next swath and all its twinéd flowers:
And sometimes like a gleaner thou dost keep
   Steady thy laden head across a brook;   *20*
   Or by a cider-press, with patient look,
      Thou watchest the last oozings hours by hours.

Where are the songs of Spring? Ay, where are they?
   Think not of them, thou hast thy music too,—
While barréd clouds bloom the soft-dying day,   *25*
   And touch the stubble-plains with rosy hue;
Then in a wailful choir the small gnats mourn
   Among the river sallows, borne aloft
      Or sinking as the light wind lives or dies;
And full-grown lambs loud bleat from hilly bourn;   *30*
   Hedge-crickets sing; and now with treble soft
   The red breast whistles from a garden-croft;
      And gathering swallows twitter in the skies.

John Keats

Beauty

The usually hateful crow:
he, too—this morning,
on the snow!

Matsuo Basho
(tr. *Harold G. Henderson*)

Dust of Snow

The way a crow
Shook down on me
The dust of snow
From a hemlock tree

Has given my heart   *5*
A change of mood
And saved some part
Of a day I had rued.

Robert Frost

In the Pauper's Turnip Field

Crow, in pulpit lone and tall
Of yon charred hemlock, grimly dead,
Why on me in preachment call—
Me, by nearer preachment led
Here in homily of my hoe.   *5*
The hoe, the hoe,
My heavy hoe
That earthward bows me to foreshow
A mattock heavier than the hoe.

Herman Melville

O Where Are You Going

"O where are you going?" said reader to rider,
"That valley is fatal when furnaces burn,
Yonder's the midden whose odours will madden,
That gap is the grave where the tall return."

"O do you imagine," said fearer to farer,   *5*
"That dusk will delay on your path to the pass,
Your diligent looking discover the lacking
Your footsteps feel from granite to grass?"

"O what was that bird," said horror to hearer,
"Did you see that shape in the twisted trees?   *10*
Behind you swiftly the figure comes softly,
The spot on your skin is a shocking disease?"

"Out of this house"—said rider to reader,
"Yours never will"—said farer to fearer,
"They're looking for you"—said hearer to horror,   *15*
As he left them there, as he left them there.

W. H. Auden

Epitaph on Himself

Good friend, for Jesus' sake forbear
To dig the dust enclosed here;
Blest be the man that spares these stones,
And curst be he that moves my bones.

William Shakespeare

The Barley Field

Up the barley rows,
   stitching, stitching them together,
      a butterfly goes.

Sora (tr. Harold G. Henderson)

The Sudden Chillness

The piercing chill I feel:
   my dead wife's comb, in our bedroom,
      under my heel . . .

Buson (tr. Harold G. Henderson)

Dirge of Love

Come away, come away, death,
   And in sad cypress let me be laid.
Fly away, fly away, breath;
   I am slain by a fair cruel maid.
My shroud of white, stuck all with yew,   5
            O, prepare it!
My part of death, no one so true
            Did share it.

Not a flower, not a flower sweet,
   On my black coffin let there be strown.   10
Not a friend, not a friend greet
   My poor corpse, where my bones shall be thrown.
A thousand thousand sighs to save,
            Lay me, O, where
Sad true lover never find my grave,   15
            To weep there!

William Shakespeare (Twelfth Night, Act II, sc. iv)

Flower in the Crannied Wall

Flower in the crannied wall,
I pluck you out of the crannies,
I hold you here, root and all, in my hand,
Little flower—but *if* I could understand
What you are, root and all, and all in all,   5
I should know what God and man is.

Alfred, Lord Tennyson

On Limited Warfare

Don'tcha worry, honey chile,
   Don'tcha cry no more,
It's jest a li'l ole atom bomb
   In a li'l ole lim'ted war.

It's jest a bitsy warhead, chile,   *5*
   On a li'l ole tactical shell,
And all it'll do is blow us-all
   To a li'l ole lim'ted hell.

                Anonymous

Love Not Me

Love not me for comely grace,
For my pleasing eye or face,
Nor for any outward part:
No, nor for a constant heart!
For these may fail or turn to ill: *5*
   So thou and I shall sever.
Keep therefore a true woman's eye,
And love me still, but you know not why!
So hast thou the same reason still
   To doat upon me ever.   *10*

                Anonymous

The Cancer Cells

Today I saw a picture of the cancer cells,
Sinister shapes with menacing attitudes.
They had outgrown their test-tube and advanced,
Sinister shapes with menacing attitudes,
Into a world beyond, a virulent laughing gang.   *5*
They looked like art itself, like the artist's mind,
Powerful shaker, and the taker of new forms.
Some are revulsed to see these spiky shapes;
It is the world of the future too come to.
Nothing could be more vivid than their language,   *10*
Lethal, sparkling and irregular stars,
The murderous design of the universe,
The hectic dance of the passionate cancer cells.
O just phenomena to the calculating eye,
Originals of imagination. I flew   *15*
With them in a piled exuberance of time,

My own malignance in their racy, beautiful gestures
Quick and lean: and in their riot too
I saw the stance of the artist's make,
The fixed form in the massive fluxion.   *20*

I think Leonardo would have in his disinterest
Enjoyed them precisely with a sharp pencil.

Richard Eberhart

Subway

Everyday I step into a coffin
with strangers.

Nailing hurriedly
my own coffin,

I go toward the city   *5*
to be buried alive.

Etsurô Sakamoto
(tr. Ichiro Kono and John Theobald)

In a Station of the Metro

The apparition of these faces in the crowd;
Petals on a wet, black bough.

Ezra Pound

Rain on a Cottage Roof

From within
Slight rain seems to purr,
A heavier shower murmur,
As bees hum.

Huge hands pummel and knead   *5*
The roof under
Thunder's indigo stampede.

Rain hoofs thrum.
Now hear the house become
A drum.   *10*

Freda Laughton

The poems in the next section share a common theme. Two are by students, two by accomplished poets. Read them, observing the language and achievements of each poet. Decide why one student's poem is much better than the other's; decide which of the four poems seems most effective as a result of the author's understanding and use of language.

The Wanderer

He travels over many a mile,
Rambling down life's highway,
Searching all the while,
Never ceasing to stray.
He is enroute to somewhere,   5
Running all alone,
He is enroute to nowhere,
Like a rolling stone.
He leaves the past behind,
Reaching ahead at the highest peaks,   10
But yet he cannot find
What it is that he seeks.
So he must search,
So he must longingly search.

A Student

All Roads Lead Somewhere

In this world, or any other,
There must be a road that leads *not* somewhere;
Adventurous souls, now dead, let chance
Choose destinies without a glance,
But modern man sees no old need   5
For paths not straight, for paths not true
To somewhere—anywhere.
Today, a road's a miracle,
Straight as a ruler, hard as a rock,
Well-lit, smooth, and hopelessly boring: 10
Signs *tell* us; we know where we're going . . .
And when we'll arrive.
I'd jump at a chance to walk—not ride—
A meandering path whose destiny
Is all but known—   15
Whose course is crooked, wild, and dark,
To travel into endless time.

But even this road leads—well—*somewhere*.
I am afraid, alas, alack,
That *all* roads lead somewhere.   *20*

Donald Baim (student)

The Road Not Taken

Two roads diverged in a yellow wood,
And sorry I could not travel both
And be one traveler, long I stood
And looked down one as far as I could
To where it bent in the undergrowth;   *5*

Then took the other, as just as fair,
And having perhaps the better claim,
Because it was grassy and wanted wear;
Though as for that the passing there
Had worn them really about the same,   *10*

And both that morning equally lay
In leaves no step had trodden black.
Oh, I kept the first for another day!
Yet knowing how way leads on to way,
I doubted if I should ever come back.   *15*

I shall be telling this with a sigh
Somewhere ages and ages hence:
Two roads diverged in a wood, and I—
I took the one less traveled by,
And that has made all the difference.   *20*

Robert Frost

Shooting the Sun

Four horizons cozen me
To distances I dimly see.
Four paths beckon me to stray,
Each a bold and separate way.
Monday morning shows the East   *5*
Satisfying as a feast.
Tuesday I will none of it,
West alone holds benefit.
Later in the week 'tis due
North that I would hurry to.   *10*

> While on other days I find
> To the South content of mind.
> So I start, but never rest
> North or South or East or West.
> Each horizon has its claim   15
> Solace to a different aim.
> Four-soul'd like the wind am I,
> Voyaging an endless sky,
> Undergoing destiny.
>
> *Amy Lowell*

Suggested Activity. Record any poem you find particularly pleasing. Extract the part that pleases you and copy it into your journal. Be sure you make a complete bibliographical note of the poem so that you do not, at some future date, forget the source or, worse still, forget the author and the title. Unidentifiable fragments can be distressing as they may demand identification at some future time.

Suggested Assignment. Write a carefully considered, well-organized, three-paragraph analysis of one of the *Poems for Study*. Your paper need not be long, but it should reveal your understanding of this chapter. Do not attempt to evaluate every element in the poem; choose, rather, to discuss those elements that can be encompassed within three unified paragraphs.

The following sample analyses of "Ruth" will illustrate three different approaches you might take in your paper. You should now be able to write an analysis comparable to the first example. Later you should become capable of the second, which was written by a student. Eventually you should be able to write a more sophisticated study such as the third example. As your ability to understand poetry increases, your ability to write about it will also improve.

Ruth

> She stood breast-high amid the corn,
> Clasp'd by the golden light of morn,
> Like the sweetheart of the sun,
> Who many a glowing kiss had won.
>
> On her cheek an autumn flush,   5
> Deeply ripen'd;—such a blush
> In the midst of brown was born,
> Like red poppies grown with corn.

Round her eyes her tresses fell,
Which were blackest none could tell,   *10*
But long lashes veil'd a light,
That had else been all too bright.

And her hat, with shady brim,
Made her tressy forehead dim;—
Thus she stood amid the stooks,   *15*
Praising God with sweetest looks:—

Sure, I said, Heav'n did not mean,
Where I reap thou shouldst but glean,
Lay thy sheaf adown and come,
Share my harvest and my home.   *20*

Thomas Hood

Analysis 1: Gleanings

The Old Testament story of Ruth and Naomi is familiar to almost everyone because "whither thou goest" is quoted so often. Few people can recall the name of Boaz though. In the poem "Ruth," Thomas Hood concentrates on the love of Boaz for the widow from Moab. The reader gains a new insight into the old tale as its religious significance becomes secondary to a love story. This love is as modern as today: Boaz is any man, Ruth is any woman. Allusion to the Bible makes the poem more meaningful, however, because Ruth is a symbol of devotion and loyalty. Remembering how unhappy her life has been, the reader is pleased as Boaz recognizes Ruth's beauty and purity as she stands in the ripe wheat (English "corn").

In all lands, harvest days are a time of thanksgiving, colorful and warm. The reader remembers his own autumns as he sees Ruth clasping the yellow wheat in her arms in the same way personification allows her to be "clasp'd by the golden light of morn." Warmth of the sun becomes emotional warmth as simile extends through the rest of the stanza. In stanza two, Hood uses seasons and color associations to paint a picture of a healthy, mature woman. She becomes exotic in stanza three as Boaz describes her black hair and eyes in hyperbole. In stanza four, he realizes she is good and pure. His character is revealed also. He has to be interested in more than the physical to recognize the fact that she is "praising God with sweetest looks."

The marriage proposal would seem too impetuous if the biblical allusion were not so completely a part of this poem. The language of the last stanza could come from the King James version of the Bible, and it makes Boaz seem very modest. He doesn't brag of wealth in hyperbole. Instead, he reveals his love in understatement as he raises Ruth to importance. The reader can almost see her blush and lower her long lashes. The alliteration of *b*'s from *blush-brown-born* in stanza two and *l*'s in *long lashes-light* in stanza three comes to mind again, and the poem ends on a happy note.

Analysis 2: *New Crops from Old Fields*

The title of Thomas Hood's "Ruth" is an allusion, rich in association, to the Bible. However, the poem is detailed description focused on one magic moment from the unadorned narrative line of the complete biblical work. Here Ruth stands surrounded by the brilliance of God's sun and the warmth of Boaz's love. As he watches her, Boaz concludes that Heaven sent Ruth not only to glean in his fields but also to share his home.

The romantic mood and restrained tone of the poem are established by such words as *clasp'd, sweetheart, kiss, cheek, blush* and *born,* in quatrains one and two. Restraint in the character of Boaz is indicated by the consonance of gentle *n*'s combined with the soft *o* and *u* assonance in such words as *corn, morn, sun, won, brown, born* and *grown.* His happiness builds from the contemplative in the first two quatrains to the joyous in the third where consonance in light *l* sounds recurs in the words *fell, tell, blacked, long lashes, veil'd, light, else, all.* Boaz ends his brief narrative with the original restraint as the last two quatrains return to *o* assonance in *adown, come, home.*

Among Hood's poetic devices, personification, metaphor and simile are notable. Ruth is "clasp'd by the golden light of morn" which makes her "the sweetheart of the sun." Flowers bloom in her cheeks as "a blush" is "like red poppies." Hyperbole is introduced in the description of her eyes and hair: "which were blackest none could tell." Understatement of great subtlety follows: Boaz sees Ruth praising God, merely by existing—"with sweetest looks." The sensuality of Moab and the restraint of Judah combine as *harvest* and *home* indicate the physical and emotional ties binding Boaz to his heritage. And that heritage was to be enriched by a later harvest of this love. Hood plants its seeds in this poem.

June Seligman (student)

Analysis 3: *From Allusion to Allegory*

In his poem "Ruth," Thomas Hood employs allusion to recall the Old Testament story of Ruth and Boaz, to remove the characters from the realm of religion, and to reduce them to the point of reader identification. Pastoral imagery creates a vivid picture of Ruth, a ripely mature woman, surrounded by nature's harvest. The divine qualities of beauty, fruition, and love are intimately explored in language designed to create sensual responses and spiritual awarenesses at the same time. The paradoxical possibility becomes apparent as Ruth is compared to the corn (English wheat) amid which she stands in the first stanza. As the wheat grows as high as her breast, she is diminutive. Alliteration and personification bind *clasp'd* to *corn,* and sense allows the comparison to include Ruth; so both she and the corn are surrounded by sunlight (with its implications of growth properties in physical nature and spiritual properties in God and love). Similes expand the growing tone of spiritual sensuality as "sweetheart" of the sun applies to corn and Ruth, and sun becomes both star and God. As literal sun and light of God's love ripen the plant and the woman, the opiate beauty of poppies among the corn introduces intoxicating perfumes and passionate color to the metaphorically ripe plant, ready for the harvest, that Ruth has become.

Oxymoron brings light from darkness in stanza three, empowering it with the paradoxical suggestion that the dark recesses of beauty, the unexplored, create light for the lover. Surrounded by the harvested sheaves ("stooks") of stanza four, Ruth is set apart, contrasted with that which has been gathered. Understatement suggests she is, thereby, made vulnerable to the harvester's blade, a blade honed on awareness of her spiritual as well as physical ripeness. Even in the space of four stanzas, time has passed, action has flowed around Ruth and Boaz in their arrested moment. In stanza one, she stood "amid" the corn; in stanza two, the image becomes imagery as a blush appears in the "midst" of her cheek as poppies grow "amid" the corn. In stanza four, she stands "amid" the harvested corn—repetition has enchanted time as a series of mental possibilities occur to Boaz. Assonance, consonance and alliteration carry the moments forward to this point. Boaz's changing wonder is traced in the consonance of his changing o's and "uh's" to the final stanza's strength in long e's. His sensuous associations of bread (wheat) as physical food, and beauty as spiritual food, move softly on the implication that man does not live by bread alone.

Understatement reveals the character of Boaz in the last stanza as his descriptive delight in Ruth becomes a proposal. The hyperbole of "God made you for me" would be impossible for a man of Boaz's stature—stature now completely revealed. In the first line of the poem, his physical height was established as he described the diminutive Ruth "breast-high"—to himself—a deliberately ambiguous phrase. His humility is now revealed in *litotes* (understatement made for emphasis wherein an affirmative statement is made by denying its contrary). Minimizing himself, he emphasizes Ruth's importance with, "Heav'n did not mean/Where I reap thou shouldst but glean." Agrarian symbolism now creates a rich mosaic of possible meanings within the framework of allusion. The fertility symbols of emotional needs, the hushed passion of alliteration in *s, h,* and *sh* combinations—all combine to create imperative needs in Boaz that the reader can understand and share. Sound and sense almost create a picture of the powerful landowner placing his great hand on the lips of a diminutive Ruth, gently "shushing" any objections she might utter. At this moment, the scene, the characters become the reader's experience, and he knows the complete identification created by allegory. Synecdoche elevates this man and this woman to become Man and Woman, immediately reducing the whole to its parts again as Man and Woman become You and Me in a timeless application. The poet's language has become shared experience, and the reader has known the birth of love—at least vicariously.

Suggested Reading

Louis Untermeyer, *Modern American Poetry; Modern British Poetry*
Oscar Williams, *Immortal Poems of the English Language*
Dr. William Doster and Martha McDonough, *Poetry Is For People*
Josephine J. Curto, *Writing With Understanding*
William Strunk, Jr., and E. B. White, *The Elements of Style*

CHAPTER III

The Meaning of Poetry

Year after year, students regret the necessity of studying poetry. Yet they all quote and misquote poetry unknowingly, using lines and phrases from the Bible and Shakespeare which have long since become commonplaces of the language. Furthermore, they all compose it in their daily speech, for it so happens that our language is constructed on a poetic principle: an accent pattern of stressed and unstressed vowels. As these vowels assume an observably repeated pattern, rhythm emerges to become poetry. For example, an indignant young man whose girlfriend has just jilted him might observe:

> "And *man*, she *lied*! I *knew* she *lied*!
> What's *more*, she knew *I* knew *she lied*!"

Certainly, this young man is unaware his indignation is poetic; but, because he intuitively realizes poetry is more powerful than prose, he weakens stress on some words, strengthens it on others, and artfully constructs a poetic statement unconsciously.

Note that in the young man's statement the italicized words are accented and the others are unaccented. In his first two sentences, he states his belief; in the third, he intensifies it. With a limited vocabulary, he achieves power by switching rhythmical stress. In line 1, the act is important; in line 2, the people are. At the end of line 2, both the girlfriend and the act of lying are vilified in a poetic foot called a *spondee* (two equally stressed syllables). The young man has placed ideas in tension, one against the other; he has placed accents in tension; and he has, thereby, placed emotions in tension—all of which are techniques of poetry. With the aid of centuries of language-builders who established a poetically patterned language for him, he has effectively damned the young lady.

"But textbooks, newspapers, stock market reports—they're all written in *prose!*" that same young man might still argue. "Why should I bother with poetry? How much money will it help me earn? What will it add to my life?"

Answers to his questions are standard truisms: "Man needs beauty," or "The soul needs food too." These are truisms, but they still seem unsatisfactory—too vague, too abstract. The immediacies of life seem more important than vague possibilities. For example, neither the young man nor his (ex-) girlfriend would refuse to ride in an automobile merely because statistics reveal that thousands of people are killed annually in highway accidents. They want to go somewhere, and, as they step into an automobile, they hope and trust they will be safe. At any rate, they'll worry about such things as accidents when they happen; they refuse to anticipate. Life, not death, is important.

Still, when we have conquered the immediacies of daily living, a void remains. Grades, jobs, houses, cars—all fail to supply answers to certain questions we cannot escape: "Who am I?" "Is God dead?" "What is my purpose in life?" The complexities of such questions defy prose, possibly because there are no satisfactory prosaic answers. The questions arise out of our emotional, spiritual, unconscious depths, and our need of answers is imperative. Technology can supply us with motors, and science does search for the secrets of *physical* life. But we eventually realize that "man doth not live by bread only." Eventually we begin to grapple with the old truisms simply because contemporary absolutes are inadequate and our lives are incomplete. Then it is that we must turn to art rather than to science, to poetry rather than to prose, for, as Lionel Goitein, a scientist, observed in a book entitled *Art and the Unconscious*:

> It is the eternal verities that give life its coherence, Birth, death and eternity, joy, pain, and the psychic continuum of Memory. The importance of art symbolisms resides in the fact that they follow a favorite device of the Unconscious when the going becomes tough. Art, because it is an aspect of the Unconscious, resorts to allegories, conventional symbols and stylized representations for concrete realization of abstract concepts. Serpent, Crown and Anchor used for Faith, Hope and Charity, are obvious examples. It is only when overwhelming ideas, such as passion, struggle for expression, defying all commentaries, that the artist is reduced to the most primitive symbolism, taxing his resources to the point of obscurity.[1]

Demanding his right to equality, human dignity, freedom of expression —every man shares moments of doubt about life, its meaning, and the meaning of his own life in the greater framework of human existence.

1. New York, 1948.

Knowing that because he was born, he must die—living in the shadow of that awful knowledge, man searches always for his *raison d'être*.

In *An Essay on Man*, Alexander Pope considered at length the dilemma of man, a dilemma we have faced since the beginning of the race:

> Know then thyself, presume not God to scan,
> The proper study of mankind is man.
> Placed on this isthmus of a middle state,
> A being darkly wise, and rudely great:
> With too much knowledge for the skeptic side,   5
> With too much weakness for the stoic's pride,
> He hangs between; in doubt to act, or rest;
> In doubt to deem himself a god, or beast;
> In doubt his mind or body to prefer;
> Born but to die, and reasoning but to err;   10
> Alike in ignorance, his reason such,
> Whether he thinks too little or too much:
> Chaos of thought and passion, all confused;
> Still by himself abused or disabused;
> Created half to rise and half to fall;   15
> Great lord of all things, yet a prey to all;
> Sole judge of truth, in endless error hurled:
> The glory, jest, and riddle of the world!
>
> *(Epistle II, i)*

But, in search of answers to this "riddle," man is limited by his five senses. He can see physical objects; he can touch, taste, and smell them. He can hear sounds. Still, can "love" be perceived through those five senses? Can "God"? Is "man" himself perceivable, or does he merely fancy himself more than a machine made of flesh that can be so perceived? What is his personality? His "soul"?

Science and technology cannot answer such questions for us. In fact, they continually reduce us to numbers, to reports, to the realm of the impersonal. The poet objects to such reduction, he rebels, and a little of our dignity is restored as we are, at least momentarily, caught up in that rebellion:

The Unknown Citizen
(*To JS/07/M/378 This Marble Monument Is Erected by the State*)

He was found by the Bureau of Statistics to be
One against whom there was no official complaint,
And all the reports on his conduct agree
That, in the modern sense of an old-fashioned word, he was a saint,

For in everything he did he served the Greater Community.   5
Except for the War till the day he retired
He worked in a factory and never got fired,
But satisfied his employers, Fudge Motors Inc.
Yet he wasn't a scab or odd in his views,
For his Union reports that he paid his dues,   10
(Our report on his Union shows it was sound)
And our Social Psychology workers found
That he was popular with his mates and liked a drink.
The Press are convinced that he bought a paper every day
And that his reactions to advertisements were normal in every way.   15
Policies taken out in his name prove that he was fully insured,
And his Health-card shows he was once in hospital but left it cured.
Both Producers Research and High-Grade Living declare
He was fully sensible to the advantages of the Instalment Plan
And had everything necessary to Modern Man,   20
A phonograph, a radio, a car and a frigidaire.
Our researchers into Public Opinion are content
That he held the proper opinions for the time of year;
When there was peace, he was for peace; when there was war, he went.
He was married and added five children to the population,   25
Which our Eugenist says was the right number for a parent of his generation,
And our teachers report that he never interfered with their education.
Was he free? Was he happy? The question is absurd:
Had anything been wrong, we should certainly have heard.

                                                            W. H. Auden

Fortunately, man has "a sixth sense," a sense called *apperception,* which enables him to understand concepts such as "soul," "God," "love." Apperception is a sense that systematizes and classifies everything we have experienced (either actually or vicariously) and allows us knowledge of abstractions that cannot be scientifically explained or investigated. In other words, it is the ability to assimilate and interpret new ideas or impressions with the help of past experience. To understand the process of apperception, examine your hand. It is, scientifically speaking, a digital appendage designed to lift, push, squeeze, and manipulate physical things. How, then, can it communicate so much as you gently touch the cheek of someone you love? Science can explain the physical act, the psychological motivation, the stimulus and the response of the action, but it cannot explain Romeo's

> See, how she leans her cheek upon her hand!
> O, that I were a glove upon that hand,
> That I might touch that cheek!
>
> *Romeo and Juliet (Act II, sc. ii)*

Yet you can apperceive Romeo's longing because you have known or hope to know such longing yourself. Such apperception is the poetic quality in man that allows him to *know* "love" or "dignity" or "God." And, if *knowing* such concepts is important to you, poetry is *very* important!

Before we can know "love" or "dignity" or "God" when they enter our experience for the first time, we must have developed an awareness of their possibility—an awareness that comes not from experience, but from the vicarious experience someone else shares with us. It is like wanting to learn about electronics—it would be foolish to try and learn from a limited amateur; you need to find an expert or something written by experts. Now, the basic, vital human emotions and ideas are, certainly, more abstract than electronics; so it is pretty foolish to assume they can be learned from inarticulate amateurs or superficial dilettantes. Published, respected poets are the experts in such matters. It is they who examine and formulate the textbooks we need in the spiritual science of "love," "dignity," or "God." When Socrates observed, "The unexamined life is not worth living," he doubtless realized the difficulties involved in such examination. But the poet devotes his life to examining, and it is he who can best help us who are more limited in time, who cannot pursue that examination twenty-four hours a day and still have time to work and to play.

All men share behavioral patterns: we aspire, we hate, we love. The poet can prepare us for those moments when we first encounter them. If you have never known the anguish of saying goodbye to one who has fallen out of love with you, a poem can prepare you for that inevitable moment:

Idea 61

> Since there's no help, come let us kiss and part,—
> Nay I have done, you get no more of me;
> And I am glad, yea, glad with all my heart,
> That thus so cleanly I myself can free.
> Shake hands for ever, cancel all our vows,   5
> And when we meet at any time again,
> Be it not seen in either of our brows
> That we one jot of former love retain!

Now at the last gasp of Love's latest breath,
When, his pulse failing, Passion speechless lies,   *10*
When Faith is kneeling by his bed of death,
And Innocence is closing up his eyes,
    Now if thou would'st, when all have given him over,
    From death to life thou might'st him yet recover!

Michael Drayton

When anything as important as love is lost, it will, naturally, be accompanied by present and future regret. Preparation for such regret is offered in

When We Two Parted

When we two parted
    In silence and tears,
Half broken-hearted
    To sever for years,
Pale grew thy cheek and cold,   *5*
    Colder thy kiss;
Truly that hour foretold
    Sorrow to this.

The dew of the morning
    Sunk chill on my brow—   *10*
It felt like the warning
    Of what I feel now.
Thy vows are all broken,
    And light is thy fame;
I hear thy name spoken,   *15*
    And share in its shame.

They name thee before me,
    A knell to mine ear;
A shudder comes o'er me—
    Why wert thou so dear?   *20*
They knew not I knew thee,
    Who knew thee too well—
Long, long shall I rue thee,
    Too deeply to tell.

In secret we met—   *25*
  In silence I grieve,
That thy heart could forget,
  Thy spirit deceive.
If I should meet thee
  After long years,   *30*
How should I greet thee?—
  With silence and tears.

          George Gordon, Lord Byron

Perhaps being prepared will not make such experience less painful for you, but it will certainly make it less bitter. You will know, in that agonizing moment, that you are not unique. Others have shared the sorrow, and they have left a record of it. You are not reduced to *hoping* others will understand.

Poetry works *after* such experience also. If, quite unaware of such records as the two poems which follow, you should suffer the loss of love and then discover the poems, reading them might assuage some of the grief, perhaps even allow you to understand the nature of it for the first time. Your personal experience thus intensifies the power of such poems, making the communication more vital. Since, as we have said, apperception is defined as the interpretation of new ideas or impressions with the help of past experience, it is really the mind's being conscious of its consciousness. The poet, then, helps us understand what we know—or know what we understand.

With the help of such a poem as Walt Whitman's *"Good-Bye, My Fancy,"* for example, you may, at a rash moment, be able to change your mind and the direction of your words, to discover new wonder in an old love:

Good-bye, my Fancy!
Farewell, dear mate, dear love!
I am going away, I know not where,
Or to what fortune, or whether I may ever see you again,
So Good-bye, my Fancy.   *5*
Now for my last—let me look back a moment;
The slower fainter ticking of the clock is in me,
Exit, nightfall, and soon the heart-thud stopping.
Long have we lived, joy'd, caress'd together;
Delightful!—now separation—Good-bye, my Fancy.   *10*

Yet let me not be too hasty:
Long indeed have we lived, slept, filter'd, become really blended into one;
Then if we die we die together (yes, we'll remain one),
If we go anywhere we'll go together to meet what happens,
May-be we'll be better off and blither, and learn something,   *15*
May-be it is yourself now really ushering me to the true songs (who knows?),
May-be it is you the mortal knob really undoing, turning—so now finally,
Good-bye—and hail! my Fancy.

The poet cannot oversimplify complex ideas, but, as he attempts to communicate with the reader, he does not employ deliberate complexities. A poet succeeds only when the reader suddenly feels, "Why, I know just what he means! That's what I feel but can't express!" To achieve that moment, the poet attempts to make the poem a part of the reader's actual experience. Hart Crane explains just such an intention in his essay "General Aims and Theories":

> I would like to establish [the poem] as free from my own personality as from any chance evaluation on the reader's part. (This is, of course, an impossibility, but it is a characteristic worth mentioning.) Such a poem is at least a stab at a truth, and to such an extent may be differentiated from other kinds of poetry and be called 'absolute.' Its evocation will not be toward decoration or amusement, but rather toward a state of consciousness, an 'innocence' (Blake) or absolute beauty. In this condition there may be discoverable under new forms certain spiritual illuminations, shining with a morality essentialized from experience directly, and not from previous precepts or preconceptions. It is as though a poem gave the reader as he left it a single, new *word*, never before spoken and impossible actually to enunciate, but self-evident as an active principle in the reader's consciousness henceforward.

If the poem is to give the reader that "new *word*," to become an active principle in his consciousness henceforward, the poem itself does not "mean" anything in and of itself. If the poet can free the poem from his own personality so it becomes the *reader's* experience, he simultaneously frees it from the possibility of *chance* evaluation. If it then becomes an absolute experience (one as intense as if gained actually rather than vicariously), the reader will evaluate it in its context as well as within the body of his own experience, rather than merely interpret it as a literary exercise. As such an absolute, it attains "being" as an experience, not "meaning" as a poem. Until the reader makes the poem a part of his intellectual self, it remains merely words. But once the statement becomes a part of the reader's experience and changes him into something new and better, the poem "means" something within the experience of the reader—the only place it should "mean" anything.

Archibald MacLeish suggests the way a poem becomes that "new *word*" in

Ars Poetica

A poem should be palpable and mute
As a globed fruit,

Dumb
As old medallions to the thumb,

Silent as the sleeve-worn stone   5
Of casement ledges where the moss has grown—

A poem should be wordless
As the flight of birds.

                    *

A poem should be motionless in time
As the moon climbs,   10

Leaving, as the moon releases
Twig by twig the night-entangled trees,

Leaving, as the moon behind the winter leaves,
Memory by memory the mind—

A poem should be motionless in time   15
As the moon climbs.

                    *

A poem should be equal to:
Not true.

For all the history of grief
An empty doorway and a maple leaf.   20

For love
The leaning grasses and two lights above the sea—

A poem should not mean
But be.

If MacLeish's poem meant little to you, consider its language. First, the poem is a series of seven similes (one of which is reinforced through repetition) and two metaphors, culminating in a statement. The similes are structured on concrete images which have no meaning until the five senses are utilized, experience recalled, and apperception invited. Basic to an understanding of the structure, however, is an understanding of the individual words: *palpable* = "tangible, capable of being perceived by the five senses to become clear to the mind"; *mute* = "voluntarily silent or incapable of speech"; *dumb* = "lacking the power of speech"; *medallions* = "large medals" (a coin is a medallion); *silent* = "speechless, making no sound"; *casement* = "an outward opening, hinged window frame"; *ars* (art) = "creativeness, the application of a skill." The vocabulary choice establishes the tone of the poem—quietly contemplative, resting in memory. Paradox imbues the imagery with depth and a gentle irony implying that the reader who can't utilize memory or make application to symbols will not understand a poem anyway.

With vocabulary and structural awareness, reread the poem. Do you see, in the first two lines, the paradox in a poem's being "mute/As a globed fruit"? It is "voluntarily silent," but it speaks through *all* of the senses in the same way a globed fruit (an apple or an orange, for example) does: by being perceived with the fingers, with the eyes, the mouth, the nose. A globed fruit cannot be perceived through sound alone. A *deaf* person can know the experience of an apple as completely as one who hears. The poem is a failure, then, if it is composed of words lacking connotative power.

The next two lines extend the simile structure. Close your eyes and examine a John F. Kennedy half dollar with your fingers to understand lines 3-4 completely. You will react to the feel of silver (different from the feel of iron or tin), the figures and words in bas-relief. You should be aware of the commemorative nature of the coin as you become aware of the bust of John F. Kennedy and recall his assassination. No words pass, but you have reacted to the coin as more than an economic medium of exchange. It is dumb in that it lacks the physical power of speech, but it speaks eloquently through your sense of touch so that you see the face in memory, recall the grief of a nation, and endow the coin with meaning beyond its basic, literal use.

The third simile extends the paradox into a more abstract realm, introducing unstated allusion and a romantic concept. The casement ledge that will accommodate moss is made of stone. Such windows exist in castles or great stone mansions suggestive of titles and wealth—that the ledge is stone establishes the allusion. That it is sleeve-worn suggests many inhabitants of that dwelling have leaned on the ledge, out the open window, watching and waiting for someone. Ladies awaiting the return of their lords, their lovers? Stone wears slowly under the gentle abrasion of women's garments—a further indication of the age of the building. The fact that moss has possessed the ledge suggests it has been many years since such sleeves brushed this stone. Do you need words to understand the romance inherent in the scene? Do you not re-create for yourself a vivid tapestry, chivalric and exotic, embellishing it with many added touches, from vicarious experience and memory?

Thus far, a series of adjectives has been established (observe the commas after lines 2 and 4). The dash after line 6 serves a "gathering" function for the sentence, as it would in a sentence such as "Boys, girls, men, women—all people live briefly." *Wordless* is that adjective gathering up *palpable, mute, dumb,* and *silent*. The poem, naturally constructed of words, should evoke images *through* the words rather than present a series of intellectually acceptable, unemotional symbolic tags. It should evoke memory; and memory—like the flight of birds—is not describable in concrete terms. It crosses the mind fleetingly and is gone, leaving new memories of itself.

The first function of a poem ends with line 8. The second begins with line 9 and extends through line 16.

Time implies the motion of change in day to night, week to month, month to season, season to year. Yet MacLeish suggests a poem should be motionless in the same way the moon is—as it climbs. Can its passing be marked or is the progression too subtle for the eye to follow? Even though it climbs the arch of the sky, is this moon not in this place always as time nullifies its journey from east to west? The reality of that moon is as constant as the truth of a poem. Love, for example, remains love throughout the centuries. Man's concepts may change, but the emotion remains constant—as does the moon.

The participle *leaving* modifies *poem* in line 9 and gains its object in *mind* in line 14. The poem should, then, enter the mind as the moon enters a tree—not physically, but with illuminative power. Just as the moon touches each twig, illuminates it briefly, and passes on, the poem should touch each memory in the mind and pass on after illuminating that memory briefly. The moon, touching the twigs, does not change them; therefore, it is *motionless*. The reinforcement of repetition in lines 15 and 16 *insists* the reader understand the image.

Section 1, then, suggested a poem should evoke memory. Section 2 suggests it should, further, illuminate memory, enabling the reader to see stored images. Section 3 extends the poetic function. Though a poem is equal to truth, it is not truth itself. Memory of an experience is not the experience itself, but it is equal to the experience in intensity. Mac-

Leish offers two examples. An empty doorway and a maple leaf both suggest a cleaving. A person no longer fills the doorway; the leaf has been separated from the tree. Leaves cannot return. The implication: neither can a person return who has once left (either emotionally or through death). In man's long history, his great grief has always concerned loss of someone. Yet that loss exists in nature (leaf) as it does in man's constructed world (doorway). The symbols are not grief; therefore, not true; but they equal it if their image evokes memory of loss.

Love is not leaning grasses and two lights above the sea, but the image is equal to the abstraction. Leaning grasses are, together, capable of touching each other, taking strength from leaning on each other, but they are forever chained to their own root systems. Still, those root systems supply the strengths and weaknesses they share in leaning. They grow on land at water's edge, another meeting in constant separation. Water gives life to land; all life returns to the sea. Two lights (of ships or fireflies) above that great birth-image may meet and pass, but they may not inseparably merge; they must pursue their individual courses over the vastness of the sea. These possibilities become vital if the reader recalls comparable scenes he has observed. And the poignant memory is equal to the poignancy of love; it is not love.

Gathering the examples and directing lines 23 and 24 back to lines 17 and 18, MacLeish concludes that a poem, then, evokes memory, illuminates memory, enables the reader to apply that memory, creating apperception out of the perceived. The poem itself means nothing. It merely exists. The apperception of the reader *means,* but it is not the poem. The poem allowed apperception to occur. That was its function. And this is *ars poetica,* the art (meaning both the poet's craft and the reader's application) of poetry.

Once again, why should you concern yourself with such "art"? Because you have so little time to live—and, at times, so little apparent reason. Ezra Pound's argument in his essay "How to Read" is: "The function of literature as a generated prize-worthy force is precisely that it does incite humanity to continue living; that it eases the mind of strain, and feeds it, I mean definitely as *nutrition of impulse.*"

But why such attention to detail? Why not read widely, merely for "big" ideas rather than slowly for "one" idea? Pound answered that question too:

It is an error to think that vast reading will automatically produce any such knowledge or understanding. Neither Chaucer with his forty books, nor Shakespeare with perhaps half a dozen, in folio, can be considered illiterate. A man can learn more music by working on a Bach fugue until he can take it apart and put it together, than by playing through ten dozen heterogeneous albums.

And again, the questions: "Why bother? What will poetry add to my life?" As a human, you must live in the world of man. His concerns are your concerns. Nor have they changed throughout man's history—regardless of his technological and scientific advances. Man remains a troubled animal attempting to learn how to live. And, as each of us utilizes poetry at an elementary level in our own speech, we live it in our own life, as Wallace Stevens has said in

Men Made Out of Words

What should we be without the sexual myth,
The human reverie or poem of death?

Castratos of moon-mash—Life consists
Of propositions about life. The human

Reverie is a solitude in which   5
We compose these propositions, torn by dreams,

By the terrible incantations of defeats
And by the fear that defeats and dreams are one.

The whole race is a poet that writes down
The eccentric propositions of its fate.   10

Suggested Activity. Begin now to seek a poet you would like to understand at some length. Do not make a hasty decision; merely begin your search. Once you have found him, plan to devote some considerable time to exploring each of his poems until you understand it with some thoroughness. Do not be influenced by the quantity of a poet's work. Some of the most rewarding poets left a small body of poems; others left such a large body it seems almost impossible to study all the poems intelligently. This should be a project of several years; therefore, do not let such considerations influence your choice.

Suggested Assignment. Choosing one of the poems of parting in this chapter, analyze your reasons for preferring it to the others. Give specific reasons, supporting your ideas by direct reference to lines and phrases from the poem.

Suggested Reading
Milton Crane, ed., *Fifty Great Poets*
Oscar Williams, ed., *A Pocket Book of Modern Verse*

CHAPTER IV

From Syllables—Poems

Ralph Waldo Emerson once observed, "Poetry teaches the enormous force of a few words." You can easily see the truth of this statement in some of the brief poetic forms; the longer ones are more demanding as a result of length. For that reason, we will begin with shorter forms, working constantly toward longer, more complex ones. However, as you learn new techniques of understanding and add them to old ones, the longer forms will eventually seem to be no more complex than the shorter ones. They will merely be longer. Let's begin with some brief poetic forms from the Orient, as their brevity allows sudden insight, thus bypassing the difficulty of extended *explication* (exposition, examination, and interpretation).

Haiku

The Japanese, somewhere in the mists of antiquity, recognized the fragility of memory, of associated emotions. Always delighted with understatement, preferring it in their use of words as well as in their floral arrangements, they created *hokku*. Literally, the word meant "starting verse," for such was the form's original function. At the royal court, one of the pastimes was the composition of *tanka* (see pp. 62–63), a five line verse with a set number of syllables in each line: 5, 7, 5, 7, 7, to total 31—no more, no fewer. This intellectual game was played by two people. The first created the hokku (the first three lines of 17 syllables); the second supplied the last two lines of 14 syllables. Adding the two lines was called "verse capping."

At some unknown date, the first three lines of the tanka became independent, self-contained units, though they retained the name *hokku* (or, as it is more commonly seen in English, *haiku*). You have already read three examples of haiku in Chapter II: one each by the Japanese poets Sora and Basho and one by the American Ezra Pound. Though anthologists usually classify Pound's "In a Station of the Metro" as free verse, it does meet the requirements of haiku. Its 18 syllables are closer to the required length than many English translations of haiku from the Japanese. This is because the content of some haiku (the word is both singular and plural) requires the translator to use more or fewer syllables in order to retain the mood, meaning, and tone of the original.

Since the number of syllables in haiku has been emphasized, it may be well to review the syllable as a unit of language. A *syllable* is, by definition, a word or portion of a word pronounced as one uninterrupted sound. It is usually composed of a vowel or a diphthong and the consonants clustered around it. Such words as *one, friend, love* contain one syllable. *Agree* (a•gree), *endure* (en•dure), *proceed* (pro•ceed) are two-syllable words. *Activate* (ac•ti•vate), *constantly* (con•stant•ly), *diatribe* (di•a•tribe) contain three syllables.

A haiku contains 17 such syllables in three lines, each with a set number of syllables: 5, 7, 5. Other essential elements in each haiku are: a reference to a season of the year, an emotion associated with that season, and an indicated spiritual insight. Brevity demands conciseness, but that conciseness is not necessarily syntactical: a haiku need not contain a clause; it may be composed entirely of related phrases or interrelated words creating images.

The older definition of haiku as "starting verse" is also indicative of another of its functions—it is supposed to create a response in the reader. That response triggers other responses, and the eventual, final statement is achieved in the reader's mind. The haiku has thus opened memory, begun a series of thoughts. Aesthetically, these thoughts may carry the reader far from the original one, giving him greater insight into himself and his world as they expand—like the ripples from a stone cast into a pond.

Babette Deutsch's version of a haiku by Moritake will illustrate the simplicity of language, the combination of responses:

> The falling flower
> I saw drift back to the branch
> Was a butterfly.

The word *butterfly* establishes the season—spring. An emotional response begins in the suggested beauty of a flower falling gracefully from a tree or shrub. The response is intensified by the awareness that the mind has been too hasty: the "flower" is falling upwards, "back to the branch." (The Japanese call this *saṁvegha,* "poetic shock.") No flower has died; rather, a butterfly, colorful and graceful, has created an illusion. A spiritual insight results: beauty does not die; it takes new, allied forms in the compensatory pattern of nature. The reader can see the flower falling because he has seen actual flowers fall and his mind has stored the image until, as he reads the haiku, that memory is unlocked and the scene re-created. Superimposed on this is the other memory of butterflies floating to rest on branches or flowers. And childhood too is restored briefly, for such memory-images are usually from that leisurely and wondrous time. Thus, the spiritual insight broadens to include not only the truth of nature's compensations but the compensations of youth recaptured—the ability to be delighted, for example. When this happens, allied memories of childhood flow one after another, unbidden and nostalgic. The haiku has worked its magic.

In the following haiku by Issa, observe poetic shock at work. Notice, however, it is not an effort to outwit the reader:

> Snow melts
> and the village is overflowing—
> with children.
>> (tr. *Harold G. Henderson*)

The reader is prepared by the end of the second line for spring flood imagery. He is delightfully surprised with the rebirth of spring life in the exuberance of children released from winter's cold jail.

Examine the next haiku, remembering moons you have seen reflected in water:

> ### The Short Night (I)
> Night that ends so soon:
> in the ford there still remains
> one sliver of the moon.
>> *Buson* (tr. *Harold G. Henderson*)

Summer is suggested in the title, "The Short Night." Once seen, a sliver of moon reflected in water at dawn is never forgotten. The image is merely stored away. Memory unlocked, the response is nostalgia, delight, sadness, or whatever allied memory the reader holds. Inherent is that great truth that the end of night is the beginning of day, or that beauty repeats itself in nature (two moons exist—the reflected one possibly more perfect in its blurred image than the original).

Not all haiku "work" for all readers. You will find you respond to some and not to others. In Japan, reading the haiku is considered as much an art as writing it. As you read, then, remember: you are reading at three levels: 1) you want to know what the poet says; 2) you want to know what it means *to you;* and 3) you want to find that element that makes you and the poet, at least briefly, one fused identity, for, through that fusing, you share something with all men.

Another haiku by Buson works a different spell. If the word "caterpillar" is offensive to you, try to read this haiku as a Japanese would. Caterpillar means silkworm, of such vital economic importance to many households that he is even respectfully addressed as "sama" or "sir."

The Short Night (III)
The short night is through:
on the hairy caterpillar,
little beads of dew.
(tr. *Harold G. Henderson*)

Caterpillar and *short night* indicate summer. The caterpillar as a natural work of art is aesthetically complex. His movement is fluid, his body a living length of fairy filaments, fragile as gossamer. Morning dew, evanescent and ephemeral, forms crystal worlds of prismed color. The caterpillar will soon spin a cocoon from which will be unwound the silken threads as fine as his hair. And he will emerge a butterfly—thus extending his almost infinite capacity for beauty. Feeding on mulberry leaves, he is surrounded by dark green foliage, brown wood, and berries shaded from pale green to deep purple, depending on ripeness. Man's short night gives way to morning sun or death; the caterpillar's short night of sleep gives way to beauty or death if his cocoon is unwound for its silken threads. Distillate dew softens and refines the emotional response as memory of mornings recaptured are triggered in the reader's mind. Night giving way to day, caterpillar becoming butterfly which will lay eggs from which will come caterpillars—these realities suggest nature's recurring pattern, and spiritual awareness is born.

Fragility and sensitivity lie in the heart of haiku—and composing and reading them are intellectually rewarding, emotionally satisfying, spiritually pleasing adventures. If the haiku "work" and the reader shares the poet's simple mystical act of recalling and associating images and memories, then both the poet and the reader can know the profound joy of creation.

Examine the following haiku, paying attention to their structure and their ability to evoke response, to join it to associated memories, and to create spiritual awareness. If one does not cause a reaction in you, pass it by. The Japanese suggest reading a number of haiku until one generates awareness, then taking that one to bed.

> Dead my old fine hopes
> and dry my dreaming but still . . .
> Iris, blue each spring.
> *Shushiki (tr. Peter Beilenson)*

This haiku employs understatement in the third line. *Hopes* are immensely more important than the *Iris.* Yet, in the understatement, man's values are placed in new perspective—and so is a flower.

Observe the ends of lines in the next haiku:

> My two plum trees are
> so gracious . . . see, they flower
> one now, one later.
> *Buson (tr. Peter Beilenson)*

Are ends the first line, and a period could make of this a complete, meaningful clause: the trees *do* exist. However, the thought is carried over to the predicate adjective, *gracious,* of the second line, thereby creating a second image to add to that of the first line. *Flower* ends the second line and a period could be inserted here also, creating proof of the assertion. But the line extends into the third to complete the images of lines 1 and 2. In this fashion, the language and syntax work as a single unit to urge memory onto memory, creating a kind of mosaic. This is the element of *economy*—using no more words than are needed to complete the poetic task. Many other words could have been employed to create the overlaid images, but, as these few can do the work, the poet arranges them accordingly, and economy results.

In the next haiku by Basho, note how the repeated *s* sounds work alliteratively to create the onomatopoetic sound of the sea whispering along the sands:

> In the sea-surf edge
> mingled with bright small shells . . .
> bush-clover petals.
> *(tr. Peter Beilenson)*

Consonance in *shells* and *bush, mingled* and *small,* combine with the softness of assonance throughout to intensify the onomatopoeia. To describe your emotional response—if any—to this haiku will probably be almost impossible. Yet you should try. You will probably find yourself describing a sea-surf edge where water meets the sand, mingling the small petals of bush-clover plants with the agitated sand. Physical description accomplished, however, chances are you will still be at a loss to explain the evocative power of the scene. Yet you may recognize the disquieting response in your memory of similar scenes. Memory is, sometimes, so fragile that it defies examination.

Note especially the punctuation in this next haiku by Issa:

> In the city fields
> contemplating cherry-trees . . .
> strangers are like friends.
> *(tr. Peter Beilenson)*

Punctuation is effectively omitted at the end of line 1 to create a subtle image of the earth also looking upward at the beauty above it. Punctuation is frequently a powerful element in poetry, as its omission or inclusion changes the possible readings of a line—sometimes limiting, at other times enlarging, the possibilities of meaning. As line 1 of this haiku is an adverbial prepositional phrase, a comma at the end of the line would indicate its grammatical function. However, were there a comma, then the subtlety of nature contemplating nature, of earth admiring its own offspring—this delightful subtlety would be utterly lost. The deliberate omission of a comma intensifies the possibilities for the sensitive reader, while, at the same time, it does not obscure the literal meaning.

A poet might omit more than punctuation for equally valid reasons. In the following Basho haiku, you will notice the omission of a verb:

> Mountain-rose petals
> falling, falling, falling now . . .
> waterfall music.
> *(tr. Peter Beilenson)*

As there is no clause (the verb *are* is omitted), the work is composed exclusively of phrases and interrelated words (*falling* is a participle which functions as an adjective). The movement of petals leads logically and musically into the music of the waterfall. The waterfall image is a reflection of the mountain image which begins the poem, as each is a flowing curvature of line against the sky. The eye is urged upward, involved in the gentle, downward wafting of rose petals, bathed in the cold power of falling water, and suddenly submitted to the blurred images of mist and petals intermingled. The ear, too, has been caught in the imagery, and the reader fancies he can hear the petals fall, though, obviously, they make no sound. Such oxymoron allows saṁvegha to create a confusion in the senses—a confusion that allows apperception to exist.

The versatility of haiku is perhaps nowhere better illustrated than in Karen Anderson's "Six Haiku." The demands of science fiction seem far removed from the subtle fragility of haiku, but observe the natural wedding of the two:

1
The white vapor trail
Scrawls slowly on the sky
Without any squeak.

2
Gilt and painted clouds
Float back through the shining air,
What, are there stars, too?

3
In the heavy world's
Shadow, I watch the sputnik
Coasting in sunlight.

4
Those crisp cucumbers
Not yet planted in Syrtis—
How I desire one!

5
In the fantastic
Seas of Venus, who would dare
To imagine gulls?

6
When Proxima sets
What constellation do they
Dream around our sun?

Tanka

Tanka, as we mentioned earlier, allows the poet an additional 14 syllables, a total of 31, for his verse. This permits the poet to communicate an image or series of images and ideas too complex for reduction to the 17 syllables of haiku. There are five lines in tanka, and the 31 syllables are allotted 5, 7, 5, 7, 7. However, the last two lines of 7 syllables each serve *only* to "cap" the haiku, to extend the image, to illuminate it—*not* to introduce other ideas.

Ten centuries ago, the Japanese poet Okura wrote the following tanka on the death of his son:

> Since he is too young
> To know the way, I would plead:
> Pray accept this gift,
> O Underworld messenger,
> And bear the child pick-a-back.
>
> (tr. *Babette Deutsch*)

Notice that the starting verse (the first three lines) is complete. The child is a precious gift given into immediate custody since his youth makes him incapable of a solitary journey. The haiku is then capped with 14 syllables extending the image and imbuing the whole series of sorrowful images with consoling charm in an earthly act.

This intensification of emotion from the first three lines as a result of the capping verse is particularly noticeable in

> Come and gone is the year,
> No tidings yet of my love.
> My silk sleeve is damp with tears.
> Like silkworm curled in cocoon
> My heart is hidden in darkness.
>
> *Author unknown*
> (tr. *Glenn Hughes* and *Yozan Iwasaki*)

Serious poetry of both the East and the West contains many puns. Irresistible to English poets such as John Donne and Shakespeare, the pun is equally dear to the Japanese. You will observe it in the words *Fusi* and *Few see* in the next tanka, where translation, however, makes it less amusing than it is in the original Japanese:

Mount Fusi has fires,
    But they are hidden from sight.
Mount Fusi I said,
    But I meant myself—Few see
    The fires of my secret heart.

Author unknown
(tr. *Glenn Hughes* and *Yozan Iwasaki*)

Sometimes the intensification of emotion in the final fourteen syllables of tanka seems to add new ideas. However, closer examination will usually reveal the presence of the ideas, however subtle, in the first three lines:

An avenue of blossoms—
    The same soft colors as in other springs—
And perfumes still the same—
But he who planted them no longer here—
Then never say this whiff of spring's the same.

Tsurayuki (tr. *Glenn Hughes* and *Yozan Iwasaki*)

Gentle sadness pervades the haiku as author and reader recall other years from a more recent vantage point. Are things recalled "the same" or are they colored with nostalgia? What of the loss, the absence of some thing or someone which makes us need to persuade ourselves of the immutability of nature? Once an awareness of our self-delusion arises, it is logical to admit to the sorrowful truth of loss and self-pity. Even if "he who planted them" is not a second person (and may it not be the speaker himself?), is there not a loss? Are you the same person this year that you were a year ago? Have months left you unchanged, or, in the process of change, have you lost something that was precious? Your earlier ability to see experience as wonderful, for example? Can you still delight in that which was exciting a year ago? Or has new sophistication been paid for with loss of naivete?

This sense of loss has occupied man since Adam and Eve first looked out of Eden to find that

The world was all before them, where to choose
Their place of rest, and Providence their guide:
They hand in hand, with wandering steps and slow,
Through Eden took their solitary way.

Paradise Lost (XII, 646-649)

Henry David Thoreau spoke of it when he wrote:

> Time is but the stream I go a-fishing in. I drink at it; but while I drink I see the sandy bottom and detect how shallow it is. Its thin current slides away, but eternity remains. I would drink deeper; fish in the sky, whose bottom is pebbly with stars. I cannot count one. I know not the first letter of the alphabet. I have always been regretting that I was not as wise as the day I was born.
>
> *"Where I Lived, and What I Lived For," Walden*

Such loss, like "love," "grief," or "joy," cannot be re-created in exposition, descriptive prose, or explanatory words. At best, you must try to find distinct metaphors when attempting to explain to someone what, say, "love" is to you: "Love is like skyrockets and being lost when you were little." But to really attempt to state the unstatable, memory must be utilized, emotion must be evoked, as it is in haiku and tanka. This process is the major element in most poetry. T. S. Eliot termed it the finding of an *objective correlative:*

> The only way of expressing emotion in the form of art [in this case poetry] is by finding an 'objective correlative'; in other words, a set of objects, a situation, a chain of events which shall be the formula of that *particular* emotion; such that when the external facts, which must terminate in sensory experience, are given, the emotion is immediately evoked.
>
> *"Hamlet and His Problems," Selected Essays*

One last aspect of the poems you have been reading deserves mention here—the fact that the poems are all translations. Because of the often unheralded work of translators, little of the world's poetry is denied you. Translators devote their lives to trying to find the best way to render Greek, Latin, German, Japanese, and all the other languages of the world, into English. Still, much of the original effect is invariably lost, of course, simply because languages differ in sound and in effect. Worse, nuances of meaning are lost as ideas are tugged out of one language and made to fit into another.

To understand some of the difficulties of translation, you may find the following discussion helpful. It is from Harold Stewart's *A Net of Fireflies:*

> The most famous of all haiku may be quoted again here to illustrate this need for stylistic and structural modification, inevitable if something of the same *rênso,* or constellation of ideas, is to be given in English. To present the reader with a baldly literal version such as

Furu ike ya	The old pond!
Kawazu tobi-komu	A frog jumps in:
Mizu no oto.	The sound of the water!

is to fail completely to evoke in his mind's ear and eye the associations and atmosphere which this verse has for every Japanese, who can recite it by heart; and which have been dissected and discussed at deadly length by both their critics and ours. The poet must supplement this bare statement with much that the Japanese memory and imagination offer spontaneously, but which ours do not. He must give a poetic realization, if he is to capture the atmosphere.

In a Temple Garden
The old green pond is silent; here the hop
Of a frog plumbs the evening stillness: plop!

Much of the effect of the original depends on the onomatopoeia, in which the assonance of short "o" sounds, repeated no less than five times, suggests to the ear the water-sound when the frog jumps in. By a happy coincidence, it has been found possible to reproduce these in the poetic paraphrase.

Despite a few such liberties taken, a large proportion of these versions in verse are quite literal, sometimes more so than those previous renderings on whose foundations they have in part been built. As an illustration of the method adopted, a well-known haiku by Sôkan may be shown in the various stages of its passage into English poetry:

Romanized Transliteration:
  Koe nakuba
  Sagi koso yuki no
  Hitotsurane.

Literal Pidgin-English Version:
  Voice if-were-not
  White-herons only snow's
  One-line-see?

Translation into Haiku-Form:

If they gave no cry,	*5 syllables*
See, those white herons would be	*7 syllables*
But one line of snow!	*5 syllables*

Poetic Paraphrase into Couplet:

The Voice of Snow

That flight of egrets, if they gave no cry,
Would be a streak of snow across the sky.

Additional Haiku for Study

The following are poetic paraphrases into couplets by Harold Stewart:

On the Road to Nara

Because of early spring, this nameless hill
Is knee-deep in the gauze of morning still.

Basho

One Sense of Beauty

On white plum-petals that were pure and sweet,
The nightingale now wipes its muddy feet.

Issa

Spring Dawn

Up comes the bucket from the well of gloom,
And in it floats—a pink camellia bloom.

Kakei

Unseen Till Now

How visibly the gentle morning airs
Stir in the caterpillar's silky hairs!

Buson

The Art of Archery

After the sudden shower, along the strand
Green pine-needles are sticking in the sand.

Shiki

The Broken Resolution

Another year departs: the bell is tolled.
—And I intended never to grow old!

Jokun

Split by the Wind
The butterfly, with airy stitches, sews
Together again the barley's parted rows.

Sora

Gone Out
The paper lanterns on the graves are torn
By heavy dew in the chill autumn dawn.

Rankô

Considerate
I must turn over, crickets, so beware
Of local earthquakes in the bed we share!

Issa

Since It Must Be So . . .
You must remain. I must depart.
Two autumns falling in the heart.

Buson

The Three Loveliest Things
I have seen moon and blossoms; now I go
To view the last and loveliest: the snow.

Rippo (his death-poem)

The following haiku are translated by Peter Beilenson:

Life? Butterfly
on a swaying grass that's all . . .
But exquisite!

Soin

On Her Dead Son
In what windy land
wanders now my little dear
dragonfly hunter?

Chiyo-Ni

In a farther field
a scarecrow kept me company . . .
walking as I walked.

Sanin

Swallow in the dusk . . .
   spare my little buzzing friends
among the flowers.

Basho

Come come! Come out!
   From bogs old frogs command the dark
and look . . . the stars!

Kikaku

Good friend grasshopper
   will you play the caretaker
      for my little grave?

Issa

Mirror-pond of stars . . .
   suddenly a summer shower
      dimples the water.

Sora

In the twilight rain
   these brilliant-hued hibiscus . . .
      a lovely sunset.

Basho

I must turn over . . .
   Beware of local earthquakes
      bedfellow cricket!

Issa

The following haiku are translated by Harold G. Henderson:

On a withered branch
   a crow has settled—
      autumn nightfall.

Basho

The beginning of all art:
   a song when planting a rice field
      in the country's inmost part.

Basho

Persistence
Did it yell
    till it became *all* voice?
    Cicada-shell!

Basho

Leaving the House of a Friend
Out comes the bee
    from deep among peony pistils—
    oh, so reluctantly!

Basho

Near the Great Shrine, Ise
From what tree's bloom
    it comes, I do not know,
    but—this perfume!

Basho

An Invitation to Etsujim
Snow that we two
    looked at together—this year
    has it fallen anew?

Basho

The World Upside Down
A trout leaps high—
    below him, in the river bottom,
    clouds flow by.

Onitsura

The Unseen Road
Warehouses in a row—
    behind them is a road, where swallows
    come and go.

Buson

Suggested Activities. 1. Attempt to write a haiku. You will find it quite possible. The technical demands of the haiku are relatively simple; and, certainly, as Thomas Carlyle observed, "A vein of poetry exists in the hearts of all men." In Japan, even the lowliest laborer enjoys such composition as a relaxing pastime. If you are satisfied enough with one to share it with the class, submit it.

2. To understand a haiku is often reason enough for you to want to "cap" it. If one appeals to you, attempt to intensify it with the additional 14 syllables to form a tanka.

Suggested Assignments. 1. In a well-organized paragraph, explicate one of the haiku from the *Additional Haiku for Study.*

2. Compare two translations of the same haiku, stating your reasons for preferring one to the other.

3. Discuss the objective correlative as it is employed in one of the haiku.

4. Compare the prose statement of Thoreau and "The World Upside Down" by Onitsura to reveal similar techniques in prose and poetry.

Fan Pieces or Fireflies

The *epigram* has been a favored unpleasantness in the western world for many centuries. As early as the second century before Christ, the Roman, Lucillius, wrote

Mucilla Dyes Her Locks
Mucilla dyes her locks, 'tis said,
   But 'tis a foul aspersion;
She buys them black, they therefore need
   No subsequent immersion.

(tr. William Cowper)

The epigram is a brief, witty, and penetrating statement, in either poetry or prose, which emphasizes a human weakness or reduces a hallowed idea to ruin with a neatly-turned phrase. Oscar Wilde saw much to dislike in his Victorian England, as you can see from two of his prose epigrams:

Children begin by loving their parents; as they grow older they judge them; sometimes they forgive them.

The Picture of Dorian Gray

What is a cynic? A man who knows the price of everything, and the value of nothing.

Lady Windermere's Fan

The Japanese too developed a kind of epigram, called *senryu*. Written in haiku form, it depicted the stupidities and folly of humans in amusing or unacceptable social situations. Considered vulgar by the more sensitive Japanese, it will not concern us here except to introduce the *fan piece,* a happy combination of the best of haiku and the least offensive epigrammatic element of senryu.

Instead of making a direct statement, the fan piece employs personification or metaphor and places the resulting symbol in a situation familiar to humanity. Just as it is in the epigram, paradox is usually at the heart of the fan piece. (Notice the paradoxical use of language in Wilde's definition of a cynic.) Fan pieces usually consist of two parts: the introduction establishes the comparison or sets the tone; the conclusion makes the main point, often with the use of saṁvegha. The resulting epigram is "written" (actually, painted with a brush) on a fan and, when the fan is opened, an "illumination" of a human problem is briefly revealed. Because the illumination is brief, fan pieces are also known as *fireflies*.

You can see how a fan piece is constructed by examining a haiku that contains the best elements of senryu:

> Disliked by all, refusing still to die
> Even when weak with age: a winter fly.
> *Kikaku (tr. Harold Stewart)*

Nature is observed and a parallel is drawn: flies that have lived beyond their season are like old people who have outlived theirs. Paradox is employed: nature ordinarily allows no will to be imposed on its design; yet the will to live is often strong enough to force imposition. The paradox is extended: other living things are inconvenienced by the tenacious creature and resent the lengthening of life, but they too contain that will and may, one day, employ it. As nature rejects the useless, their inability to function should destroy the will, but that will exists throughout nature and is, therefore, "natural."

To understand the metaphorical imagery in this verse is to illuminate understanding in two ways. First: although the reality of the statement is unpleasant, it is unavoidable. Second: man can temper his vision with mercy by observing a harsh reality in symbols, thus forgiving himself for his necessary cruelty.

Admittedly very subtle, the paradox of the fan piece is rewarding in the insight transmitted from author to reader. If it were less subtle, it would be vulgar indeed, for harsh truth cruelly stated contains little to excuse its shock to the sensitive ear. No reader wishes to be assaulted, and the writer is addressing himself to the reader. He must, as a result, find his way to make the unacceptable acceptable. The fan piece offers one way.

Rabindranath Tagore, the Nobel prize winner (1913), found the subtlety and beauty of haiku and fan pieces adaptable to his Hindu philosophy. In 1928, he published his *Fireflies,* stating: *"Fireflies* had their origin in China and Japan where thoughts were very often claimed from me in my handwriting on fans and pieces of silk." Tagore was Indian by birth, but a British subject since India was, during his lifetime, a part of the Empire. Having studied in England, he frequently wrote in English. The following fan pieces are not translations. Tagore's verses are untitled and unrhymed, observing no set number of syllables in English, though their effect is achieved in brevity.

Note how the epigrammatic quality in Tagore's works is refined away from the harsh, and elevated to gentler subjects:

> The butterfly counts not months but moments,
>   and has time enough.

The paradox in this verse rests in the unstated complaint of people who excuse inactivity with a plea of not having enough time. A butterfly, which lives such a short time, serves nature by cross-pollinating flowers; some species serve man by laying eggs from which caterpillars hatch to spin cocoons, the threads of which make silk. The butterfly is its own excuse for being, simply because it is beautiful, and sometimes that beauty is enjoyed by man too. To accomplish so much, the butterfly has only one short season to live before winter kills it. Yet it "has time enough." The paradox: All things existing in time have time enough if they use it well, concerning themselves with action rather than with selfishness or regret.

This firefly is complete in 14 syllables. In addition to paradox, it achieves its power through perceptive analysis of the thought to be communicated and contrast in implied metaphor: people should not count time, thereby wasting time; they should be like butterflies, working, not clock-watching. Alliteration is employed (*months-moments*), consonance (*counts-months-enough-moments* and *moments-time*), and assonance (*counts not months but moments*).

In the next firefly, notice the structure of paradox. The first line establishes the comparison and sets the tone through language, simile, and consonance; the last one makes the main point. The use of an objective correlative is apparent in the simile, without which the first line would not convey an image. Remove it and no association is evoked:

> My thoughts, like sparks, ride on winged surprises, carrying a single laughter.
> The tree gazes in love at its own beautiful shadow which yet it never can grasp.

The sunlight simile in this next one pervades the lines:

> Let my love, like sunlight, surround you
> and yet give you illumined freedom.

Established as an image in the first line, *sunlight* has the connotation of brilliance and warmth, which extends to the participle *illumined*. The paradox lies in the words *surround* (which implies imprisoning) and *freedom*. Alliteration is employed in *let-love-like* and *sunlight-surround*. Assonance is apparent in *sunlight-surround* and *you-illumined*. The tone of the words *sunlight-surround-illumined* establishes a mood of easy surrender into luxurious safety.

Now try to analyze the following fireflies in terms of language, paradox, simile, metaphor, tone, mood, the use of an objective correlative, and all the techniques discussed so far:

> Days are coloured bubbles
> that float upon the surface
> of fathomless night.

> My offerings are too timid to claim your remembrance,
> and therefore you may remember them.

> The soil in return for her service keeps the tree tied to her,
> The sky asks nothing and leaves it free.

> Gods, tired of their paradise, envy man.

> While God waits for His temple to be built of love,
> men bring stones.

> The flower which is single
> need not envy the thorns
> that are numerous.

> Love punishes when it forgives
> and injured beauty by its awful silence.

> The glow-worm while exploring the dust
> never knows that stars are in the sky.

> Though the thorn in thy flower pricked me, O Beauty,
> I am grateful.

In the last firefly, note how a complex metaphor becomes a symbol which, in turn, becomes allegory. The rose is beautiful; it therefore *becomes* the abstract concept, *Beauty*; the abstract concept is personified by the act of consciously pricking the poet. The poet becomes all men who encounter beauty and are both grateful for and hurt by it. Personification is completed in the apostrophe "O Beauty," which carries all these implications. This is thus a clear instance of how effectively personification and apostrophe can work in combination with the objective correlative.

Suggested Activity. The construction of fan pieces is not beyond your ability. They do demand, however, that you examine reality through your own eyes—not through the trite phraseology of everyday commonplaces. Attempt one or two. Once you have arrived at your basic thought, consciously and deliberately employ the devices of poetry you have learned about so far. Observe the improvements that will follow from attention to sound (alliteration, assonance, and so on) and how sense will expand as a result.

Suggested Assignments. 1. Examine the following Tagore fireflies:

Beauty is truth's smile
    when she beholds her own face
        in a perfect mirror.

The dew-drop knows the sun
    only within its own tiny orb.

I am able to love my God
    because He gives me freedom
        to deny Him.

2. In a brief composition, explain the effectiveness of one of the above fireflies. Remember that, based on haiku, fireflies can be very similar to haiku, but differ in that they are *didactic,* or morally instructive; they depend on sudden illumination of that which you already know but are unaware of knowing until the epigrammatic treatment forces you into awareness.

3. Read further in this form to gain greater familiarity with it. Many of the best elements of the fan piece are employed by American and English poets. If you can understand those elements here, they should present fewer problems later. The epigrams of such authors as Martial, Ben Jonson, John Donne, and Oscar Wilde may provide you with ideas. By way of exercise, you might try restating such epigrams in fire-

fly form. As an example, Oscar Wilde's definition of a cynic (p. 70) might, in such treatment, become:

> Offering orchids,
> cynics complain
> when women prefer
> common daisies.

The Cinquain

You have now examined three simple poetic forms and learned a great deal, at least indirectly, about all poetry. The fourth unmetered form you will study contains elements of the three you have already mastered. It is a relatively new form, the *cinquain*. Its originator was Adelaide Crapsey, the sensitive young daughter of a minister. She admired haiku, and, from it, she evolved the cinquain. The cinquain rests, like the tanka, on a five line pattern, but its syllable count is 2-4-6-8-2, for a total of 22 syllables.

The emotional response basic to haiku is one ingredient of the cinquain. The extension of imagery in the capping verse of tanka is also a component, and the didactic quality of the epigrammatic fan piece frequently finds its way into the line. *Poignancy* (the sharply painful to the emotions) usually colors this form, for it is somehow suited in its structure to an examination of the deeply personal attitudes we all hold. Through this form, such attitudes can be explored and communicated, as it is a fragile container of thought.

Note how the title may set the mood of the cinquain:

Niagara
(Seen on a night in November)

How frail	2 syllables
Above the bulk	4 syllables
Of crashing water hangs	6 syllables
Autumnal, evanescent, wan,	8 syllables
The moon.	2 syllables

Adelaide Crapsey

The consonance of repeated *n*'s in the title and subtitle are unhappy in sound. *Niagara* is, of course, associated with honeymooners—especially June ones. *November* is, however, an autumn month, cold and lonely. It evokes a response in the reader that is associated with "aloneness" rather than "togetherness." This poem seems, even in the title, suggestive of a person alone in a place usually reserved for two people in close harmony. And that one person is not here in a happy season.

Frail in the first line intensifies the mood, almost by paradox, for strength in union and happiness is associated with Niagara Falls. Line 2 is strong in its heavy *b* consonance which dismisses misty, rainbow images; this is a big, unsentimental phenomenon. Line 3 extends the harshness of line 2 with the aural violence of *crashing water,* only to end the line with *hangs,* a word evoking mist images. Line 4 develops the mist image and restates the title imagery by repeating the *n* consonants in *autumnal* (maturing in autumn, beginning to die), *evanescent* (tending to fade or vanish, as love might do), and *wan* (sickly, pale). But the mist is not enchanted by summer and love; it is cold and old and sick as an unloved person might be or seem to see it, especially when alone. It is even possible that a progression (such as birth-life-death) is suggested in the beginning letters of the adjectives in line 4, A-E-W, letters which begin the alphabet and almost end it. This subtlety may even be extended in the strength of the word sounds: *autumnal* is strong with a heavy accent at mid-word; *evanescent* shifts the accent into the last half of the word, a weak sound, not strong as is the "tum" syllable of *autumnal; wan* is a very weak-sounding, one-syllable word, ending the line as if overtaken with exhaustion. Gentle saṁvegha exists in the moon image; the reader has been led to expect *mist.* And the poetic shock beclouds that pale moon with the mists we have envisioned, making it more remote, colder, lonelier. The moon and the moon-viewer become even lonelier now; there is only one moon and one viewer—and they are widely separated by space and time. Between them is the fertile, crashing water of Niagara, but they are held sterile and apart by it—making the single viewer and the dead satellite even more barren. Sadness and hopelessness combine to create the atmosphere of these 22 syllables, for the reader has been moved to supply his memories too.

In the next cinquain, "Susanna and the Elders," allusion and understatement combine to indict not only the elders but the enemies of beauty everywhere:

Susanna and the Elders

"Why do
You thus devise
Evil against her?" "For that
She is beautiful, delicate.
Therefore."

Adelaide Crapsey

For those who do not know the Old Testament Apocrypha story, it is, briefly: Two Jewish elders attempted the chastity of Susanna, a girl of great beauty and purity. When they were unsuccessful, they brought charges of adultery against her, charges which, if proved, meant death. They were unsuccessful. Daniel proved her innocence, and the elders were put to death. One of the most provocative stories for artists and writers, it is frequently employed in music, painting, and literature.

(Allusion such as this is, of course, successful only if the reader knows the event or person referred to; but a dictionary will usually provide enough information to give you basic understanding. And remember this: poets do not choose obscure allusions simply to challenge their readers, thereby revealing their own cleverness or extensive knowledge. If elaborate allusion or obscure reference accomplishes the communicative purpose as no simpler symbol can, poets do not hesitate to use such allusion. The truly interested reader will always undertake whatever research becomes necessary if he thinks the poem is important enough.)

The 23 syllables of "Susanna and the Elders" comprise a dialog fragment. Question and answer are unequally important; therefore, the question is stated in 11 syllables, the answer in twelve, the cinquain being divided in the middle of the third line. Both question and answer are biblical in tone, deliberately archaic in syntax to intensify the content the reader expects from the title. The question lacks anger: it is a statement of almost innocent wonder wanting explanation. Thus the answer, in its terseness, provokes contrast. The contrast is strengthened through the choice of words. *She is beautiful* implies "We are not"; *delicate* implies "We lack delicacy." Such implication extends the image of a *young* girl in contrast to *old* men. Also implicit is the physical and emotional gulf between youth and age. Understatement in the word *therefore* indicates two possibilities: 1) the elders cannot verbalize and answer and are reduced to the cliché, "You know what I mean"; or 2) they know the answer very well, and stating it in the heavy, hard *therefore* reveals the depth of their cynicism, a cynicism determined to destroy that which it cannot possess. Their use of *therefore* is, then, designed to circumvent rebuttal. The ugly, legalistic word characterizes the elders as insensitive cynics who plot evil against beauty and delicacy as a psychological compensation for their own aesthetic inadequacies.

The element of "sudden revelation" in the firefly is beautifully illustrated in this cinquain by Mabel Meadows Staats:

Spring Thaw

If birds
Return to build
Each spring when winter goes
Must you recall cold words and stay
Away?

The title suggests the end of winter (the bare, the cold, the hard—as ice) and the beginning of spring (new life, warmth, and softness—as ice melts). The first three lines extend the title's suggestions, adding a nest image—a receptacle for eggs, small, new beginnings. The second element of the growing paradox is a contrast in unnatural human behavior, or pride's overcoming the instinctively natural (as the return of birds is "natural"). Implicit is the idea that the heart is a nest willing to receive precious, fragile words which are also small, new beginnings, like eggs. The objective correlative is employed with considerable skill in the comparisons. The winter of misunderstanding should end in reawakened friendship so that the emotional cycle can continue just as birds continue the cycle of nature.

The cinquain employs line endings as haiku does: to bring one thought to a suggested conclusion, yet, at the same time, to reinforce, extend or change it subtly into the next, thus utilizing words completely. In line 2 of "Spring Thaw," *build* suggests that a direct object, *nests,* will be the next word. However, *spring* is an adverbial noun, telling "when," and implying direct object function. Birds do not literally "build spring," but, as spring is as much an attitude as it is a season, birds build it symbolically as they build their nests. Any denial of promise is unnatural in nature; so, as *return* leads into *stay,* expectation suggests that the word *angry* will come after *stay.* The suggestion includes, at least, the physical presence of the person. However, *away* reduces even that possibility and *away* contrasts with *return* so harshly that the realization of loss is spiritually defeating. The physical structure of the cinquain further emphasizes the contrast by balancing the first eight syllables against the last eight. The middle four (*when winter goes*) modify each half of the metaphor. Light vowels in the first eight syllables are balanced against woeful alliteration and consonance of *w*'s introduced by the middle four syllables and extended through the remaining eight. Long *a*'s seem to overlay the question with their own answer—aye (yes) —and sense becomes so intricately bound up with sound that they cannot be separated.

Intensity mounts in "Spring Thaw" as each observation is extended into the next. If such transitions seem overly subtle to you, remember that you are accustomed to using such progressions in your own prose. Starting with the least important idea, you build to the most important one: "I enjoy television program X; I usually watch program Y; I *never miss* program Z." A similar progression is obvious in

Triad

These be
Three silent things:
The falling snow . . . the hour
Before the dawn . . . the mouth of one
Just dead.

Adelaide Crapsey

Each line ends powerfully. *Be* means *exist;* these things do exist—nor can their existence be stopped. *Things* are matters of concern, ordinarily not of a living nature. Falling snow is a thing—completely removed from you except for your ability to experience it with your five senses. You can never share the emotion of a snowflake, nor can it become a part of your spiritual self. You can only respond to the silence of it, understanding something of your own attitude toward silence. The hour before the dawn is also a "thing," but it is more immediately capable of being experienced. You can exist *in* it as you cannot exist *in* a snowflake. The hour before the dawn not only influences your reaction to the dawn; it creates the setting for it. Thus, the second image is more personal than the first. As the earth is not yet stirring, as the implication of silent aloneness exists in the image, it is a sharpened extension of the snowflake silence. The third image is immediately personal. Even if you have never known the awesomeness of death in your own family, you share, with all men, the knowledge of your own impending death. As death will probably come to your parents or friends first, you can imagine your reaction to their lips sealed in stillness by death. That unpleasant awareness easily extends to a contemplation of your own lips frozen in eternal silence. Since *hour-one-dead* complete the lines, you should be aware of the denotative impact of the words: *hour* = limited time; *one* = singleness; *dead* = completion. All of your connotative awarenesses should overlay these denotative possibilities and be intensified through the process of accretion, as *dawn* combines with *hour,* and *one* combines with *dead.* Sound, too, adds emotional impact in the progression of vowels: *snow, hour, dawn, mouth, one . . . dead.* Finality becomes crushing in the final word.

In "November Night," aural memory is imperatively demanded in line 1, and imagery builds through the next four lines to create emotional response in the final syllables:

November Night

Listen . . .
With faint dry sound,
Like steps of passing ghosts,
The leaves, frost-crisped break from the trees
And fall.

Adelaide Crapsey

The simile, "like steps of passing ghosts," may be an aural impossibility to the scientist, but the emotions are not scientific in their selection, and oxymoron becomes logical. *Frost crisped* is onomatopoetic as the ear remembers the sharp snapping sounds of leaves in autumn. The limitless sound of double *l* seems to linger, growing fainter and fainter in the distance of memory as one recalls seeing the falling of the leaves; but one's ear is allowed no stored memory of their sound at the moment of impact. Perhaps the reader realizes that leaves return to earth to become humus—which is the ghost of themselves. At that moment, the reader knows he is scarcely more than a leaf in nature, destined for humus himself—and immediately he blots out that conscious awareness, happy to accept the imagery of *leaf,* which symbolizes him to the point of allegory. Unconscious allegory is often more acceptable than stark truth.

Suggested Activity. Attempt a cinquain. An understanding of poetry becomes simpler if you encounter some of the same problems the poet has. This form is still undemanding enough to allow you success.

Suggested Assignments. 1. Choose one of the following cinquains. Explicate it, explaining the ways sense and sound combine. Do not attempt to exhaust all possibilities. Ezra Pound's belief that a man can learn music through the process of taking a fugue apart and putting it together again will make more and more sense to you as you learn more about the sound and sense of poetry. Remember that your paper must be an organized unit, exhibiting coherence and unity. If some of your ideas and realizations must be abandoned in the interests of creating a composition that is organically complete, do not hesitate to omit them.

The Warning

Just now,
Out of the strange
Still dusk . . . as strange, as still . . .
A white moth flew. Why am I grown
So cold?

Adelaide Crapsey

Rain

Listen!
Silver needles
Of rain catch up the threads
Of thought and knit them round our hearts
Tightly.

Mary Linda Gross (student)

The Guarded Wound

If it
Were lighter touch
Than petals of flowers resting
On grass, oh still too heavy it were,
Too heavy.

Adelaide Crapsey

Night Winds

The old
Old winds that blew
When chaos was, what do
They tell the clattered tree that I
Should weep?

Adelaide Crapsey

Release

With swift
Great sweep of her
Magnificent arm my pain
Clanged back the doors that shut my soul
From life.

Adelaide Crapsey

2. If you composed a cinquain, explicate it, revealing your intentions as you think you achieved them.

3. In the following poem, you will find portions which could easily stand alone as haiku (note particularly section III). Mr. Fletcher writes tanka, in intent if not in strict form, in section IV; and fireflies, like their counterparts in nature, illumine line after line.

Read the entire poem, first for the magic of the words. Then reread it for meaning. Finally, read it once again, observing the combinations of forms you have just learned about, and seeing *how* the poet unlocks memory for you:

from *Irradiations*
III

Over the roof-tops race the shadows of clouds;
Like horses the shadows of clouds charge down the street.

Whirlpools of purple and gold,
Winds from the mountains of cinnabar,
Lacquered mandarin moments, palanquins swaying and balancing   *5*
Amid the vermilion pavilions, against the jade balustrades.
Glint of the glittering wings of dragon-flies in the light:
Silver filaments, golden flakes settling downwards,
Rippling, quivering flutters, repulse and surrender,
The sun broidered upon the rain,   *10*
The rain rustling with the sun.

Over the roof-tops race the shadows of clouds;
Like horses the shadows of clouds charge down the street.
IV

Flickering of incessant rain
On flashing pavements:
Sudden scurry of umbrellas:
Bending, recurved blossoms of the storm.

The winds come clanging and clattering   *5*
From long white highroads whipping in ribbons up summits:
They strew upon the city gusty wafts of apple-blossom,
And the rustling of innumerable translucent leaves.

Uneven, tinkling, the lazy rain
Dripping from the eaves.   *10*
VI

O seeded grass, you army of little men
Crawling up the long slope with quivering, quick blades of steel:
You who storm millions of graves, tiny green tentacles of earth,
Interlace yourselves tightly over my heart,
And do not let me go: *5*
For I would lie here forever and watch with one eye
The pilgrimaging ants in your dull, savage jungles,
The while with the other I see the stiff lines of the slope
Break in mid-air, a wave surprisingly arrested;
And above it, wavering, dancing, bodiless, colorless, unreal,   *10*
The long thin lazy fingers of the heat.

John Gould Fletcher

CHAPTER V

Prosody: Syllables Into Feet

You have now examined four poetic forms which rely on syllable count to establish line length and stanza form. You have considered language, figures of speech, and the various poetic devices used to achieve compression, economy of words, mood, tone, and imagery, as well as to evoke association and response in the reader. And you probably "listened" to the lines of the quoted poems, reading them aloud until the imagery and sound combined to create the pictures your participation made possible.

"Listening" for that sound came unbidden and naturally to you, for poetry is natural to man, and, like music, it is intended to be heard. Much of its effectiveness lies in its rhythm. In fact, a poem can be defined as a literary composition in rhythmical and metrical language, expressing a strongly felt emotion or a thought with strongly felt emotional overtones. Poetry is, essentially, music created with words rather than with notes. It may be light and gay to express joy, stately and proud to create patriotism, sonorous or sad to convey sympathy—like music, it is adaptable. And, like music, poetry depends on tempo and beat. So you "listened," and, when the line communicated the poet's intent to you in a way that was pleasing to your ears, it became poetry. Until that time, it was merely words strung together.

Siegfried Sassoon, a successful poet himself, once said, "A man may be a born poet, but he has to make himself an artist as well. He must master the instrument." The reader too must become an artist in listening to and understanding the use of the poet's instrument. You are ready now to learn more technical information about the instrument you have learned to enjoy a little. A study of the basic principles of verse structure is called *prosody*. It includes *meter, rhyme,* and *stanza form.* You will study these terms in that order.

Meter

As *meter* refers to the rhythm pattern of the poetic line, you have already dealt with it unknowingly in the preceding chapters. It results when the poet chooses syllables to create a pattern that is measurable by accent and repetition. In Chapter IV, you saw that *agree, endure,* and *proceed* are two-syllable words. Each contains one unaccented and one accented syllable. The unaccented syllable is called *feminine* because it is weak in stress; the accented syllable is called *masculine* because it is strong. The usual way to mark unaccented or feminine syllables is with a rocker (˘); accented syllables are marked with a dash (—). Accent is determined by the pitch or stress (or both) which you give a word when you pronounce it. If you say *agree* aloud, you hear *agrēe*. The masculine *-gree* is more heavily stressed than the feminine *a-* because you use more wind to make the sound. Similarly, *endure = endŭre*, and *proceed = procēed*. That expenditure of wind is caused by the length of time you hold the vowels. The longer you hold them, the heavier the accent.

In three-syllable words, the stress pattern is: *āctĭvāte, cōnstantlў, dĭātrĭbe.* The first syllable of all three of these words is masculine; but the feminine syllables fall in various patterns. In *activate* and *diatribe,* the accent is slightly heavier on the first syllable than it is on the third. The heavier accent is called a *primary accent;* the lighter is called a *secondary accent.* Both primary and secondary accents are masculine. But, in a given line of poetry, sounds on either side of a word may weaken a secondary accent to make it almost feminine, or they may intensify it into a primary accent. Observe this action on *woodwind.* It has a primary-secondary accent pattern, or two masculine syllables: *wōodwīnd.* Notice the shift of the secondary accent in two different sentences:

Sōftlў blew the woodwinds then. (*-winds* weakens to feminine)

Blōw, blow, grēat woodwinds! Blōw! (*-winds* intensifies to primary)

Mark the masculine and feminine syllables in the following words. Say each aloud to hear the accent before marking it. Then check your ear by comparing your accent patterns with those in the dictionary:

abduct	accessory	anapest
abduction	amiable	antipodes
able	amphibrach	antique
abrupt	amphimacer	barbarous

boohoo	heptameter	spondee
cacaphonous	hexameter	tetrameter
caesura	iambic	trimeter
dactylic	monometer	trochaic
dimeter	octameter	trochee
gravule	pentameter	truncate

(Incidentally, did you read the definitions of any unfamiliar words? Any time you see an unfamiliar word in your reading or in the thesaurus, check it in the dictionary—for two things: the *exact* meanings and the *correct* pronunciation. Do not guess at either. Readers as well as writers must be sure of these things if communication is to take place.)

You are now ready to learn the first step in scanning. To *scan* is to mark (or measure) the masculine and feminine syllables in a line of poetry in order to indicate the regularly repeated accent pattern. It is that repetition which creates poetry and separates it from prose, which does not have a *repeated* pattern. In fact, the main difference between poetry and prose is that poetry is *measurably* rhythmical, while prose is not.

Using your dictionary for any word you are not *positive* about, scan the following sentence. *Do not read beyond the sentence until you have followed this direction.*

> And we heard, brushing in flowers ankle-deep, the milk that bubbled in the pail and buzzings of the honeyed hours behind the woodbine veil.

While scanning, were you aware enough of what you have already learned to notice onomatopoeia, alliteration, assonance and consonance? They are effective in prose also. If you are progressing as you should be, you noticed! If you didn't, you need to be sharpening your observation powers more than you are. Your scansion marks should be:

˘ ˘ — — ˘ ˘ — ˘ — ˘ — ˘ — ˘ — ˘ ˘ —
And we heard, brushing in flowers ankle-deep, the milk that bubbled in the pail

˘ — ˘ ˘ ˘ — ˘ — ˘ — ˘ — — —
and buzzings of the honeyed hours behind the woodbine veil.

While some repetition of accents is apparent in this line, it is not a regularly recurring pattern; therefore, the line is prose.

In the next sentence, the phrases and clauses have been kept intact, but they have been rearranged into a more rhythmical pattern. Scan it:

> And, brushing ankle-deep in flowers, we heard, behind the woodbine veil, the milk that bubbled in the pail and buzzings of the honeyed hours.

Your ear should hear the difference in the rhythm because the pattern is now much more regular. It should be:

˘ — ˘ —˘ — ˘ — ˘ ˘ — ˘— ˘ — — — ˘
And, brushing ankle-deep in flowers, we heard, behind the woodbine veil, the

— ˘ — ˘ ˘ ˘ — ˘ — ˘ ˘ ˘ — ˘ —
milk that bubbled in the pail and buzzings of the honeyed hours.

As you read this version, you should have heard it as *almost* regular in repeated pattern. It is a stanza from "In Memoriam" by Tennyson, removed from stanza form and written as a prose sentence.

Now scan the actual poetic stanza. You will find some of the accents changing. Do not *now* rely on your dictionary. Let your ear supply accent:

> And brushing ankle-deep in flowers,
> We heard behind the woodbine veil
> The milk that bubbled in the pail,
> And buzzings of the honeyed hours.

Your scansion pattern should now be:

˘ — ˘ —˘ — ˘ —
And brushing ankle-deep in flowers,

˘ — ˘ — ˘ — ˘ —
We heard behind the woodbine veil

˘ — ˘ — ˘ — ˘ —
The milk that bubbled in the pail,

˘ — ˘ — ˘ — ˘ —
And buzzings of the honeyed hours.

The accents have now become very regular in their repetition, almost a lulling drone that, in combination with the onomatopoeia, re-creates a
— ˘   —
drowsy country afternoon. In line 1, *flowers* was shortened to "flours," a pronunciation allowed by dictionaries and created naturally by the rhythm of the line. In line 2, *-bine* lost its accent because the rhythmical pattern reduced your stress on the word. In line 3, *in* became accented because the pattern caused you to pronounce it with stress. The same thing happened to *of* in line 4.

The pattern that has emerged is a feminine (unaccented) syllable followed by a masculine (accented) syllable. And this, as it happens, is the most common metrical foot in English. It is called an *iambic foot*. A *foot* is a group of *two* or *three* syllables working together as a metrical unit. The *iambic* foot (called an *iamb*) is marked ˘ —.

However, to complete the scansion of this stanza, you need to learn two more terms and the marks to indicate their use. The *virgule* is used to *separate* feet, to show where each begins and ends. The virgule mark is | . If there are four feet to a line, you will use 3 virgules:

˘ — ˘ — ˘ — ˘ —

And brush|ing ank|le-deep|in flowers

The virgule may come at the end of any syllable; therefore, it frequently divides words, especially in lines containing polysyllabic words. The *caesura* is a very short pause (as if for breath or emphasis) within a line. It may be dictated by the thought alone or by indicated punctuation, and it may come anywhere in a line, depending on the poet's need and use of it. It is especially useful to the poet if he wishes to add variety to a line without changing the meter, for it has no count. As a result, it may come in the middle of a foot without changing the accent pattern. The caesura is most easily recognized in the lyrics to songs. If you have ever noticed a vocalist's almost gasping for breath between phrasings, you have heard the "soundless" caesura. It is marked || .

Alexander Pope delighted in shifting the caesura in his lines to give them versatility of rhythm. Read the following lines from his "The Rape of the Lock" to feel yourself pausing in the reading as the caesura is employed:

> Whether the nymph||shall break Diana's law,
> Or some frail china jar||receive a flaw;
> Or stain her honour,||or her new brocade;
> Forget her pray'rs,||or miss a masquerade;
> Or lose her heart,||or necklace,||at a ball;   5
> Or whether heav'n has doomed||that Shock must fall.
>
> *(II, 105-110)*

These lines are all *end stopped;* that is, a pause occurs at the end of each, retaining the general meaning in the line. If, on the other hand, a thought is not contained in one line but runs on into the next, the line is said to be *enjambed*. Pope enjambs lines later in this same poem:

> Gums and pomatums shall his flight restrain,
> While clogged he beats his silken wings in vain;
> Or alum styptics with contracting power
> Shrink his thin essence like a riveled flower;

> Or, as Ixion fixed, the wretch shall feel   5
> The giddy motion of the whirling mill,
> In fumes of burning chocolate shall glow,
> And tremble at the sea that froths below!
>
> *(II, 129-136)*

Lines 3 and 4 are enjambed as are lines 5, 6, 7, and 8. You will remember the effectiveness of haiku carry-over lines (pp. 56-61). They too are a form of enjambment, but the use of such enjambment in haiku produces different results than it does in English poetry. English-speaking poets of the Imagist School do often use oriental enjambment, however.

You are now ready to scan the Tennyson lines completely. This you do by marking the syllables, inserting the virgules, and adding any caesuras. Your scansion should be:

$$\breve{} \quad \bar{} \quad \breve{} \quad \bar{} \breve{} \quad \bar{} \breve{} \quad \bar{}$$
And brush|ing ank|le deep|in flowers,

$$\breve{} \quad \bar{} \quad \breve{} \quad \bar{} \breve{} \quad \bar{} \quad \breve{} \quad \bar{}$$
We heard‖behind|the wood|bine veil

$$\breve{} \quad \bar{} \quad \breve{} \quad \bar{} \breve{} \quad \bar{} \breve{} \quad \bar{}$$
The milk|that bubb|led in|the pail,

$$\breve{} \quad \bar{} \quad \breve{} \quad \bar{} \breve{} \quad \bar{} \breve{} \quad \bar{}$$
And buzz|ings of|the hon|eyed hours.

You now have a certain mastery of the iambic foot. But good poets do not usually employ only one foot in a poem, as it tends to become sing-songy. A different foot (called a *relief* or *variant foot*) is often employed to break up the rhythm and keep it from becoming too monotonously regular. Still, the *dominant foot* establishes the meter of the poem; so, if a poem has more iambs than any other foot, it is iambic.

Scan the following stanzas, noting that each has one foot that is *not* an iamb:

> The Moving Finger writes, and, having writ,
> Moves on; nor all your Piety nor Wit
>   Shall lure it back to cancel half a Line
> Nor all your Tears wash out a Word of it.
>
> And that inverted Bowl they call the Sky,   5
> Whereunder crawling cooped we live and die,
>   Lift not your hands to *It* for help—for It
> As impotently moves as you or I.
>
> *The Rubáiyát of Omar Khayyám*
> (tr. *Edward FitzGerald*)

Your scansion should be:

ˇ ⎯ ˇ ⎯ ˇ ⎯ | ˇ ⎯ ˇ ⎯
The Mov|ing Fin|ger writes,‖and, hav|ing writ,

⎯ ˇ ˇ ⎯ ˇ ⎯ ˇˇ ˇ ⎯
Moves on;‖nor all|your Pi|ety|nor Wit

ˇ ⎯ ˇ ⎯ ˇ ⎯ ˇ ⎯ ˇ ⎯
Shall lure|it back|to can|cel half|a Line

ˇ ⎯ ˇ ⎯ ˇ ⎯ ˇ ⎯ ˇˇ
Nor all|your Tears|wash out|a Word|of it.

ˇ ⎯ ˇ ⎯ ˇ ⎯ ˇ ⎯ ˇ ⎯
And that|invert|ed Bowl|they call|the Sky,

ˇ ⎯ ˇ ⎯ ˇ ⎯ ˇ ⎯ ˇ ⎯
Whereun|der crawl|ing cooped‖we live|and die,

⎯ ˇ ˇ ⎯ ˇˇ ⎯ ˇ ⎯ ˇ ⎯
Lift not|your hands|to *It*|for help—‖for It

ˇ ⎯ ˇ ⎯ ˇ ⎯ ˇ ⎯ ˇˇ
As im|potent|ly moves‖as you|or I.

The meter of these stanzas is regular except for the first foot of lines 2 and 7. Was Edward FitzGerald unable to work iambs into his line? Hardly! You will notice the stanzas employ caesuras to vary the rhythm and save it from monotony. However, they did not supply enough for his satisfaction; so he varied the meter. Through shifting the accent onto the opening syllables of the lines, FitzGerald also emphasized the words by jarring the reader's attention into an awareness of them. *Moves* becomes an inexorable word. *Lift* begins an imperative sentence, doubly imperative as a result of the accent shift.

Iambics create *rising meter,* because stress raises the voice at the end of each foot. This creates a joyful, happy rhythm. If a poet wishes to establish this happiness at the very beginning of a line of iambs, he may drop the feminine syllable (the *head* of the iamb) and start with the masculine syllable (the *trunk*). This device is called *truncation.* Observe it in these lines from Ben Jonson's *Volpone:*

⎯ ˇ ⎯ˇ ⎯ ˇ ⎯
∧Come,|my Cel|ia,‖let|us prove,

⎯ ˇ ⎯ ˇ ⎯ ˇ ⎯
∧While|we can,‖the sports|of love.

Impetuosity of tone results from the truncation, almost as if the feminine head were lost in the poet's gasping for breath to hurry into the line and the suggested physical activity. As *rests* (intervals of silence) compensate for the feminine syllables, the *carat* (∧) at the beginning of the lines is used to indicate the omission. (A second feature of this device will be discussed with the next foot.)

The variant feet of the lines just quoted from the *Rubáiyát* are exactly opposite in construction from the iamb; each contains two syllables, as does the iamb, but the accent is reversed. The masculine syllable comes before the feminine syllable. This foot is called a *trochee,* and is marked — ◡. Words like *lyric* and *falling* indicate its pattern. As it is accented on the first syllable, it creates *falling meter* and is useful in conveying solemn or emphatic ideas. Though the iambic pattern is more natural in English sentences, most two-syllable words in the language are trochaic in accent pattern.

Scan the following excerpt from W. H. Auden's "In Memory of W. B. Yeats":

> Earth, receive an honoured guest;
> William Yeats is laid to rest:
> Let the Irish vessel lie
> Emptied of its poetry.

The mournful quality of this stanza owes its effectiveness to the excellent metaphor and the artful use of trochaic feet. A constantly falling rhythm intensifies sadness from the first masculine syllable of line 1. Your scansion should be:

$$\text{Earth,} \overset{\shortparallel}{|} \text{re} | \text{ceive an} | \text{honoured} | \text{guest;} \wedge$$

$$\text{William} | \text{Yeats is} | \text{laid to} | \text{rest:} \wedge$$

$$\text{Let the} | \text{Irish} | \text{vessel} | \text{lie} \wedge$$

$$\text{Emptied} || \text{of its} | \text{poetry.}$$

The first three lines end in trochees from which the unstressed syllables have been dropped. This truncation deepens the sadness. This form of truncation (dropping feminine syllables from the end of the line) is called *catalexis*; lines employing the device are said to be *catalectic* (shortened). As the device was not employed in line 4, the line has its full complement of syllables and is, therefore, *acatalectic* (not shortened).

Another example of catalexis of the trochee appears in the following lines from Shelley's "Music When Soft Voices Die":

$$— \smile \;|| \; — \quad — \smile \; — \smile \; —$$

Music,|| when soft|voices|die, ∧

$$— \quad \smile \quad \smile \smile \quad — \; \smile\smile$$

Vibrates|| in the | memory.

The trochees in both examples are enforced by other poetic devices. In Shelley's lines, *music,* the subject of the clause, occurs in line 1; *vibrates,* its verb, appears in line 2. Enjambment creates a caesura after the verb, and *in the memory* becomes saṁvegha as the reader realizes the vibration is mental rather than physical. *Memory* adds one feminine foot to become a dactyl (see below for definition). In Auden's stanza, line 3 is enjambed into line 4 in the same haiku manner. *Emptied* is followed by a caesura, intensifying melancholia as it creates saṁvegha in the following feet. And the final foot adds one more feminine syllable to its end to become a dactyl.

The *dactyl* is a three-syllable foot accented on the first syllable, as in

$$— \smile\smile \qquad — \smile \smile \qquad — \smile\smile$$

mannikin, carnival, and *popular.* It is marked — ⌣ ⌣. Dactyls are effective in creating gloom and despair, for they are, as you can see, simply a trochee plus another unstressed syllable. Together, the feminine syllables create a more falling meter than the trochee.

Longfellow's opening line of "Evangeline" is the classic model of the dactylic foot, for it immediately establishes a forbidding, sunless tone. In this line, dactyls and language become a singularly effective unit. As you scan it, expect a variant foot at the end of the line:

This is the forest primeval. The murmuring pines and the hemlocks

As the sixth foot is truncated into a trochee through the omission of the second feminine syllable, your scansion should be:

$$— \smile\smile \; — \smile \; \smile \; — \smile \;. \; — \; — \smile\smile \; — \quad \smile \smile \; — \smile$$

This is the|forest pri|meval.''The|murmuring|pines and the|hemlocks

As the dactyl truncated into a trochee naturally, the carat is not needed to indicate an incomplete dactyl. The poet desired the effect achieved by substituting a trochee: it varied the meter slightly and strengthened the images in *pine* and *hemlock.* The dactylic foot, *pines and the,* creates the image of an elongated tree. In contrast, as the meter does not have as far to fall in *hemlocks,* the trochee adds bulk to the tree image, tying it to the earth. Notice the caesura which falls within the third dactyl. It does not break the metrical pattern, but it varies the line.

In "The Bridge of Sighs," Thomas Hood truncated dactyls to create a mood of gentle concern. The effect will be obvious as you scan the lines:

> Take her up tenderly,
> Lift her with care;
> Fashion'd so slenderly,
> Young and so fair!

Your scansion should be:

— ˘ ˘ — ˘˘
Take her up | tenderly

— ˘ ˘ —
Lift her with | care ∧∧

— ˘ ˘ — ˘˘
Fashion'd so | slenderly

— ˘ ˘ —
Young and so | fair ∧∧

If one poet could be called the master of any metrical foot, Longfellow would probably garner the dactyl laurel. Although most of his poetry is eminently forgettable, his dactylic effects are memorable. Scan the opening lines of "Curfew" to observe his metrical achievements:

> Solemnly, mournfully,
> Dealing its dole,
> The Curfew Bell
> Is beginning to toll.

Longfellow truncated the second dactyl of line 2 to achieve a specific effect. The alliterative *d*'s create the mournful bell's sonorous voice which is abruptly silenced at the end of the line as life deserts the streets. A reverberation remains after the sound is gone, that reverberation existing in the truncated syllables. To reinforce the reverberative effect, compensation is employed in lines 3 and 4. (*Compensation* is the addition of extra syllables to feet elsewhere in the stanza to repair an earlier loss.) Your scansion should be:

— ˘ ˘ — ˘˘
Solemnly, ‖ mournfully,

— ˘ ˘ —
Dealing its | dole, ∧∧

˘ — — —
The Cur | few Bell

˘ ˘— ˘ ˘ —
Is beginning | to toll.

One of the lost syllables is repaired in the equally stressed foot of line 3 which should be an iamb but lengthens to two stressed syllables because there is no caesura after the adjectival *Curfew.* Two unaccented syllables equal an accented one in quantity, so half the repair job is accomplished. In addition, the equally stressed syllables create the slow, steady sound of clapper against iron, adding a new dimension to the lines.

The second unstressed syllable is picked up in the last line where it is appended to the first foot. In its present progressive form, the verb is ponderous and slow, the alliterative *b*'s of *Bell-beginning* combining with the consonantal *n-g* combinations to repeat the reverberative sound. *Is begin-* creates an anapest; the compensatory *-ing* is added to it, lessening the joy of the rising meter by dropping it to destroy delight and recall the embargo on life. The iambic *to toll* extends the melancholy result by placing sound in tension against sense.

The *anapest,* like the dactyl, is a three-syllable foot. Its scansion pattern is the opposite of the dactyl's. An anapest is composed of two unaccented and one accented syllables, marked ⌣ ⌣ — . As a feminine syllable added to the end of a trochee created the dactyl, a feminine syllable added to the head of an iamb creates the anapest. As the iamb is rising meter, the anapest is extended rising meter. It is particularly useful in expressing joy and sprightly action. Such words as *violin, luncheonette,* and *cavalier,* are anapestic.

Scan the following lines from Shelley's "The Cloud" to see anapests used without variant feet:

> Like a child from the womb, like a ghost from the tomb,
> I arise and unbuild it again.

Your scansion should be:

$$\text{Like a child} | \text{from the womb,} \| \text{like a ghost} | \text{from the tomb,}$$

$$\text{I arise} \| \text{and unbuild} | \text{it again.}$$

You should have noticed the first line seems to divide in the middle. Anapests, used in an unrelieved pattern, usually suffer this division, as they create a galloping meter. This "hop and a trot and a gallop" rhythm is often employed by satirists and humorists. James Russell Lowell uses it in "A Fable for Critics." Scan his lines to see the effectiveness:

> There are one or two things I should just like to hint,
> For you don't often get the truth told you in print.

Your pattern should be:

```
 ˘  ˘  —  ˘  ˘  — ˘  ˘  — ˘  ˘  —
There are one|or two things|||I should just|like to hint,
```

```
 ˘  ˘  — ˘ ˘  — ˘  ˘  — ˘  ˘  —
For you don't|often get|||the truth told|you in print.
```

In humor, as you can see, the anapestic line falls apart advantageously.

In combination with the iamb, the anapest becomes a lilting foot. Eliminating one feminine foot reduces the trotting rhythm to a sprightly, dancing measure. Edgar Allan Poe used the combination with great effectiveness in "Ulalume." Scan the first five lines:

> The skies they were ashen and sober;
> The leaves they were crispéd and sere,
> The leaves they were withering and sere;
> It was night in the lonesome October
> Of my most immemorial year.

Your scansion should be:

```
 ˘  —  ˘  ˘  — ˘  ˘  — ˘
The skies|||they were ash|en and so|ber;
```

```
 ˘  —  ˘  ˘  — ˘  ˘  —
The leaves|||they were crisp|ed and sere,
```

```
 ˘  —  ˘  ˘  — ˘ ˘  ˘  —
The leaves|||they were with|ering and sere;
```

```
 ˘  ˘  — ˘  ˘  — ˘  ˘ ˘ ˘
It was night|in the lone|some Octo|ber
```

```
 ˘  ˘  — ˘  ˘  — ˘ ˘ —
Of my most|immemor|ial year.
```

The lines are successful for a variety of reasons. Tone, mood and atmosphere become immediately obvious through autumnal images in the words *ashen, sober, crispéd, sere, withering,* and *October.* Consonance, assonance and alliteration are combined to create onomatopoeia throughout the first three lines as the poet reproduces the dry, whispering sound of dead leaves. *N*'s, *m*'s, *o*'s in the last two lines are melancholy and lonely. Vivid imagery results from the combination of these elements, but it is presented in the lilting rhythm of the iamb-anapest combination to produce a mixed response in the reader. He becomes two people reacting simultaneously. This effect is deliberate as the poem reveals the poet walking through a mystical, mythical land of imagination, and he is accompanied by Psyche, his soul. A symbolic splitting of the personality is achieved through the dual emotions established in the reader as language strains against rhythm. A careful scansion and examination of the total poem will teach you a great deal about prosody.

Lines 1, 3, and 4 of "Ulalume" probably presented problems for you. An extra unaccented syllable stands alone at the ends of lines 1 and 4, while one is added at the head of the last foot in line 3. The explanation is this: since lines are said to be catalectic when feminine syllables are dropped, and acatelectic when a full complement of syllables is employed, they are called *hypercatalectic* when extra feminine syllables are added. The *-ering* syllables in line 3 blend almost to the value of one syllable. In Poe's third line, the extra syllable combines with repetition from line 2, creating a ghostly, extended echo, as if apparitional loneliness followed at a distance, whispering melancholy through the autumnal forest of the soul.

In the following lines from "A Fable for Critics," Lowell criticizes the dull writing of James Fenimore Cooper. Scan the lines for: 1) a headless foot, 2) a foot you haven't scanned before, and 3) two hypercatalectic lines, the first of which borrows a syllable from the second as it enjambs the line in thought as well as in meter:

> Choose any twelve men, and let C. read aloud
> That one of his novels of which he's most proud,
> And I'd lay any bet that, without ever quitting
> Their box, they'd be all, to a man, for acquitting.

Your scansion should be:

$$\smallsmile \;\; \_\smallsmile \smallsmile \;\; \_ \; \smallsmile \smallsmile \_ \smallsmile \; \smallsmile\_$$
∧ Choose an|y twelve men,‖and let C.|read aloud

$$\_ \;\; \_\smallsmile \smallsmile \; \_\smallsmile \smallsmile \;\; \_ \; \smallsmile \;\; \smallsmile \; \_$$
That one|of his nov|els‖of which|he's most proud,

$$\smallsmile \; \smallsmile \_\smallsmile \smallsmile \_ \; \smallsmile \; \_\smallsmile \smallsmile \; \_ \smallsmile$$
And I'd lay|any bet|that‖without|ever quit|ting

$$\smallsmile \; \_ \;\; \smallsmile \; \smallsmile \_\smallsmile \smallsmile \_ \; \smallsmile \smallsmile \_ \smallsmile$$
Their box,‖they'd be all|to a man‖for acquit|ting.

The first foot is a headless anapest. To "hear" the dropped syllable, read "so" or "you" as the first word of the line. Line 2 starts with the unfamiliar foot. Line 3 becomes hypercatalectic by "borrowing" the first feminine syllable from the anapest of line 4, doubly enjambing the line.

Line 4 compensates by adding the hypercatalectic syllable at the end. The first syllable of line 2 is called a *spondee*.

While the spondee is not one of the major feet in English metrics, it is the one most often used as a variant foot. Composed of two equally accented syllables, it can substitute for any of the four major feet. As it contains two stresses, it is a heavy, ponderous foot that is used to express power, to slow a line, or to halt the forward flow of rhythm completely, as in *football, childhood, bookcase.* As spondaic words are exceedingly rare in English, the spondee is usually composed of two monosyllabic words such as *deep sleep.*

A second variant foot is the *pyrrhic.* As it is the opposite of the spondee, it is composed of two unstressed syllables. No single word in the English language represents the pyrrhic, for any word of two syllables or more will be accented on one of the syllables. *Of the* represents the pyrrhic pattern, for example. Now, expecting both pyrrhics and spondees, scan these lines:

> Here flaking the bright sun to endure cold,
> Gods plead with men and shake the embalmed earth.

The first line contains two spondees, two pyrrhics, and one iamb. The second contains two spondees, one pyrrhic, and two iambs. Your scansion should be:

> Here flak|ing the|bright sun|to en|dure cold,

> Gods plead|with men|and shake|the em|balmed earth.

Neither spondees nor pyrrhics will predominate in a poem. They are relief feet, substituted to achieve effect. The pyrrhic speeds the line along; the spondee slows or halts it. So strong is the spondee that one masculine syllable may create a spondaic foot, the remainder of the measure being a rest—another aspect of compensation. The voiceless pause commands the same amount of time a voiced syllable would.

In Tennyson's "Break, Break, Break," the spondee creates awesome power and dismal loneliness. Scan these two lines:

> Break, break, break,
> On thy cold gray stones, O Sea!

The *b* and *k* sounds are made in different parts of your mouth. Your lips are closed for the *b* but opened for the *k*. Time is required for you to rearrange your mouth in speaking the words. That time creates the rest portion of the spondee. Read the first line with exaggerated slowness, noticing the formation of the words as your mouth creates the sounds. Your scansion of the two lines should be:

$$\overline{\text{Break,}}\wedge \mid \overline{\text{break,}}\wedge \mid \overline{\text{break,}}\wedge$$

$$\underbrace{\text{On thy}}_{\smile\ \smile} \overline{\text{cold}} \mid \overline{\text{gray}}\ \overline{\text{stones,}} \parallel \overline{\text{O}}\ \overline{\text{Sea!}}$$

In the opening lines of "Lines Composed a Few Miles Above Tintern Abbey," Wordsworth varies the rhythm with spondees and pyrrhics. Scan the lines:

> Five years have passed; five summers, with the length
> Of five long winters! and again I hear
> These waters, rolling from their mountain-springs.

Did you hear the agonizing slowness of *five years,* the speeding along of *summers, with the* in preparation for the interminable time span created by meter and pronunciation of the *f-f-l-g-w* combination in *of five long winters?* Did you then notice how the pyrrhic led into the tripping, joyful iambs? Did you observe the contribution of the caesuras to the mood and tone? Your scansion should be:

$$\overline{\text{Five}}\ \overline{\text{years}} \mid \underset{\smile}{\text{have}}\ \overline{\text{passed;}} \parallel \overline{\text{five}}\ \overline{\text{summ}} \mid \underset{\smile}{\text{ers,}}\ \underset{\smile}{\text{with}} \mid \underset{\smile}{\text{the}}\ \overline{\text{length}}$$

$$\underset{\smile}{\text{Of}}\ \overline{\text{five}} \mid \overline{\text{long}}\ \overline{\text{win}} \mid \underset{\smile}{\text{ters!}} \parallel \underset{\smile}{\text{and}}\ \underset{\smile}{\text{a}} \mid \underset{\smile}{\text{gain}} \mid \underset{\smile}{\text{I}}\ \overline{\text{hear}}$$

$$\underset{\smile}{\text{These}}\ \overline{\text{wa}} \mid \underset{\smile}{\text{ters,}}\ \overline{\text{roll}} \mid \underset{\smile}{\text{ing}}\ \underset{\smile}{\text{from}} \mid \underset{\smile}{\text{their}}\ \overline{\text{moun}} \mid \overline{\text{tain-springs.}}$$

The emotions are readily affected by rhythm, as you know from your own choices of music. If you are happy, you prefer not to hear solemn or mournful music, for it will alter, if not completely destroy, your happy mood. If, on the other hand, you are sad, you will prefer solemn or mournful music, for it serves as adequate background against which to enjoy your melancholia. Poets, naturally, realize these values of rhythm and utilize them for their multiplicity of effects. Sound becomes a definite part of the sense of a poem through such metrical attention—and the poet needs every device at his disposal to communicate with you. At times, he may deliberately employ light, lilting meters with distressing ideas, the better to create ambivalences in the reader. Ambivalences, uncertainties, doubts—all are components of sadness, fear, mental turmoil.

Therefore, the ambivalence created by placing sound in tension with sense communicates itself to the reader, and he remembers his own unrest at other moments of ambivalence. When a poet enlists your unconscious memory patterns in such a fashion, using them to supply new possibilities to the poem, *identification* can occur. You read about the reactions of the poet or the person in the poem, but, simultaneously, you begin to read about yourself. As your response becomes more intense, you stop (at least to a limited degree) being yourself, and the person in the poem stops being himself. Both blend to create a new person: the emotional product of the reading experience.

By the way, if you are experiencing difficulty in scanning, your problem may lie in an inattention to word sounds. No poet could afford such inattention, no matter how slight it might be; nor can you. In your scansion of the Wordsworth lines, did you, for example, place the virgule between the *m*'s of *summer*? If you did, you are pronouncing the word "sum-mer." With that pronunciation, the word becomes a spondee because of the second *m*. Your dictionary will reveal the pronunciation "sum'ĕr," a trochee. Did you scan *rolling* as *rol-ling*? Learn to check words, even if you are reasonably sure you know their pronunciations and meanings. Poets cannot afford to be almost right; they must try to be exact. If you are to share their communication, you must also strive for exactness.

The six metrical feet you have now learned are only about one-fifth of the total number in English poetry. However, the remaining twenty-five or twenty-six are so infrequently used that you need have no great knowledge of them. If you learn to work with the six, the others will be obvious as variant feet, and your ear should establish their acceptability in whatever line of poetry you are reading. By way of review and for quick reference, the following chart may prove helpful. Two relief feet in addition to the pyrrhic and spondee are included for your convenience.

SCANSION	NAME	EXAMPLE	ORDER OF SYLLABLES		
⌣ ⌣	pyrrhic	*of the*	F	F	
‒ ‒	spondee	*football*	M	M	
⌣ ‒	iamb	*inflict*	F	M	
‒ ⌣	trochee	*science*	M	F	
⌣ ⌣ ‒	anapest	*luncheonette*	F	F	M
‒ ⌣ ⌣	dactyl	*history*	M	F	F
⌣ ‒ ⌣	amphibrach	*forgotten*	F	M	F
‒ ⌣ ‒	amphimacer	*radio*	M	F	M

You are now ready to scan any poetry you wish to attempt. While you have been introduced to only four basic metrical feet and four relief feet, any variants should cause you little trouble. Being able to name a foot is not, in and of itself, important. It is important that you *hear* a metrical foot so you can read poetry in such fashion that its definite metrical pattern becomes apparent. Being aware of that rhythm will make you aware of mood and tone as you combine sound patterns of metrics with sound and meanings of words. Then, when a line seems to be unduly obscure, you can analyze the metrics to discover how they work with or against the words to create impressions.

Wide reading will help as nothing else. Many excellent anthologies of American and English poetry are available in inexpensive paperback editions. Buy one or two and read carefully. Listen for feet, trying to find examples of the twenty-odd relief feet not pointed out to you. Watch for effective figures of speech, and, when a line sounds so "right" you wish you had written it, take it apart scientifically. Scan it; examine the language; dissect it to see every device employed by the poet. In this way you will learn to read well.

Perhaps a brief lesson by a major poet will help you. Samuel Taylor Coleridge once wrote a metrical letter to his young friend, Derwent, to help the boy with prosody. Read the poem carefully, noting particularly the advice in lines 11-14. While that advice may seem a bit syrupy by your standards, the reasoning is sound. Poetry allows more emotional excess than prose does. Scan the poem to see the feet creating themselves:

Metrical Feet
lesson for a boy

Trochee trips from long to short;
From long to long in solemn sort
Slow Spondee stalks; strong foot! yet ill able
Ever to come up with Dactyl trisyllable.
Iambics march from short to long;—   *5*
With a leap and a bound the swift Anapests throng;
One syllable long, with one short at each side,
Amphibrachys hastes with a stately stride;—
First and last being long, middle short, Amphimacer
Strikes his thundering hoofs like a proud highbred racer.   *10*
If Derwent be innocent, steady, and wise,
And delight in the things of earth, water, and skies;
Tender warmth at his heart, with these meters to show it,
With sound sense in his brains, may make Derwent a poet,—

> May crown him with fame, and must win him the love
> Of his father on earth and his Father above.
>   My dear, dear child!
> Could you stand upon Skiddaw, you would not from its whole ridge   *15*
> See a man who loves you as your fond S. T. Coleridge.

Anapests and iambs dominate in the poem since it is a happy task for the poet. You doubtless noticed certain syllables that would not rhythmically be forced into the feet you have learned. Those are variants occasioned by the imposed vocabulary of the poem. As this is, obviously, a tour de force, ragged metrics are to be expected, but every foot in the poem is defensible.

Your scansion should resemble the following:

Trochee | trips from | long to | short; ∧

From long | to long | in sol | emn sort

Slow Spon | dee stalks; ‖ strong foot! ‖ yet ill able

Ever to | come up with | Dactyl tri | syllable.

Iam | bics march | from short | to long; —

With a leap | and a bound | the swift An | apests throng;

One syll | able long, ‖ with one short | at each side,

Amphibrach | ys hastes with | a state | ly stride; —

First and last | being long, ‖ middle short, ‖ Amphimacer

Strikes his thun | dering hoofs | like a proud | highbred racer.

If Derwent | be innocent, ‖ steady, | and wise,

And delight | in the things | of earth, wa | ter, and skies;

Tender warmth | at his heart, ‖ with these me | ters to show it,

With sound sense | in his brains, | may make Der | went a poet, —

⌣ — ⌣ ⌣ — ⌣ ⌣ — ⌣ ⌣ —
May crown|him with fame,‖and must win|him the love

⌣ ⌣ — ⌣ ⌣ — ⌣ ⌣ — ⌣ ⌣ —
Of his fa|ther on earth|and his Fa|ther above.

⌣ — — —
My dear,|dear child!

⌣ ⌣ — ⌣— — ⌣ ⌣ — ⌣ ⌣ ⌣ — —
Could you stand|upon Skiddaw,‖you would not‖from its whole ridge

⌣⌣ — ⌣ ⌣ —⌣ ⌣ — ⌣⌣ — —
See a man|who loves you|as your fond|S. T. Coleridge.

Line 1 employs truncation. Line 3 ends in a *ditrochee* (two trochees considered a compound foot). Line 9 ends with a *second paeon* (its class being determined from the placement of the one accented syllable among the three unaccented ones). Line 10 ends with a *fourth epitrite* (its class being determined from the placement of the one unaccented syllable among the three accented ones). The second foot of line 11 is a *first paeon* (notice the placement of the accented syllable), while lines 13 and 14 both end in *third paeons*. The third foot of line 12 is a *bacchius*. Line 18 contains two variant feet: the second foot is an *antispastic,* and the final one is a *minor ionic.* The end foot of line 19 is a matching minor ionic which makes for clever metrics but one of the worst examples of rhyme in the English language.

Because Derwent had requested the lesson in metrics, we can safely assume he had been exposed to the basic feet. Coleridge exhibits a trait common to good teachers in offering a little more than the student really asked for.

Suggested Assignment. Scan "A Child's Grace" and one other of the following poems. In a brief paper, discuss the effective use of metrics to achieve the poet's intention. Discuss poetic devices as they combine with metrics and vocabulary and syntax of the lines to create a combination of sound and sense. Several questions follow each of the poems to aid you in your analyses.

A Child's Grace

Here a little child I stand,
Heaving up my either hand;
Cold as Paddocks though they be,
Here I lift them up to Thee,
For a Benison to fall   5
On our meat, and on us all. *Amen.*
                    Robert Herrick

a. Why is truncation employed in lines 1-4, but not in lines 5-6?

b. What emotional change do the metrics of lines 5-6 indicate? How effective is the metrical shift?

At Tea

The kettle descants in a cozy drone,
And the young wife looks in her husband's face,
And then at her guest's, and shows in her own
Her sense that she fills an envied place;
And the visiting lady is all abloom,   5
And says there was never so sweet a room.

And the happy young housewife does not know
That the woman beside her was first his choice,
Till the fates ordained it could not be so . . .
Betraying nothing in look or voice   10
The guest sits smiling and sips her tea,
And he throws her a stray glance yearningly.

Thomas Hardy

a. Metrics are almost as important in "At Tea" as the words themselves. How are they varied to weld sound to sense, actually creating a kind of sense by themselves?

b. The final foot of the second stanza is a pyrrhic—a curious foot to end a line, not to mention a poem. Explain why the foot is so effective.

Eldorado

Gayly bedight,
A gallant knight,
In sunshine and in shadow,
Had journeyed long,
Singing a song,   5
In search of Eldorado.

But he grew old,
This knight so bold,
And o'er his heart a shadow
Fell as he found   10
No spot of ground
That looked like Eldorado.

And, as his strength
Failed him at length,
He met a pilgrim shadow—   *15*
"Shadow," said he,
"Where can it be,
This land of Eldorado?"

"Over the Mountains
Of the Moon,   *20*
Down the Valley of the Shadow,
Ride, boldly ride,"
The shade replied,
"If you seek for Eldorado!"

                    Edgar Allan Poe

a. How do the metrics establish a sense of "two-ness" throughout the poem? How many of the groupings or pairs of attitudes, objects, and so on, are introduced by metrical shifts?

b. Explain compensation in the poem.

Spring and Fall: To a Young Child

Márgarét, are you gríeving
Over Goldengrove unleaving?
Leaves, líke the things of man, you
With your fresh thoughts care for, can you?
Ah! ás the heart grows older   *5*
It will come to such sights colder
By and by, nor spare a sigh
Though worlds of wanwood leafmeal lie;
And yet you wíll weep and know why.
Now no matter, child, the name: *10*
Sórrow's spríngs áre the same.
Nor mouth had, no nor mind, expressed
What heart heard of, ghost guessed:
It ís the blight man was born for,
It is Margaret you mourn for.   *15*

                    Gerard Manley Hopkins

a. How do metrics and enjambment create a mood in this poem?

b. How does the syntax work with the metrics to create sense as sound strengthens the tone of the poem?

Line Length

Syllables compound into disyllabic (two-syllable) or trisyllabic (three-syllable) feet. Feet follow one another to create the line (which usually begins with a capital letter even though it is not necessarily a complete sentence) and the line is named according to the dominant foot as well as the total number of feet.

With the exception of free verse (see pp. 237-280), poems will usually have either a regular number of feet in each line throughout the poem or a repeated pattern, such as five in the first line, three in the second, five in the third, three in the fourth, and so on. The following limerick will illustrate:

> There was a young lady from Niger,
> Who smiled as she rode on a tiger.
> They came back from the ride
> With the lady inside,
> And the smile on the face of the tiger.

Lines 1, 2, and 5 contain three feet; lines 3 and 4 contain two. The limerick is anapestic with an iamb opening lines 1 and 2. (Did you notice the hypercatalectic feet?)

As meter is the measure of the syllable, a poem is iambic, trochaic, anapestic or dactyllic according to the prevailing foot throughout the poem. The dominant line length (number of feet to the line) is also named. Thus, the limerick is anapestic trimeter (three anapests to the line).

Lines of from one to six feet are common in English; lines of from seven to eight, uncommon; lines of nine or more, rare. The names of the lengths are:

one foot:	monometer	five feet:	pentameter
two feet:	dimeter	six feet:	hexameter
three feet:	trimeter	seven feet:	heptameter
four feet:	tetrameter	eight feet:	octameter

Scan the following examples to see the different effects of varying line length. As you study the various line lengths, identify the scansions as anapestic dimeter, trochaic hexameter, dactyllic tetrameter, iambic pentameter, and so forth.

First, *monometer*. Few poems are written exclusively in monometer. Those few usually exhibit metrical cleverness rather than serious intent. Such a verbal exercise is

Lines on the Antiquity of the Microbe
Adam

Had 'em.

Strickland Gillilan

This poem is complete in two lines of one foot each, a total of four syllables. No example could more effectively suggest the importance of the title to a poem. Not just a tag, the title should contribute to the poem's total effect. In this case, of course, the poem would be meaningless without the title. As humor frequently relies on surprise, the solemnity of the falling trochees works against the lightness of the observation, and the two monometer lines contain only one-third the number of syllables of the title. An unarguable statement, the poem delights the reader who knows he has been pleasantly outwitted.

A rare, serious example of monometer is

Upon His Departure Hence
Thus I

Pass by,

And die:

As one

Unknown   *5*

And gone.

I'm made

A shade

And laid

I'th' grave: *10*

There have

My cave

Where tell

I dwell.

Farewell.   *15*

·*Robert Herrick*

The strict monometer of this poem is accomplished at the expense of *in the,* the two words being unnaturally contracted in line 10. Such contraction, called *elision,* is the slurring together of two syllables or the outright omission of one to force the meter or syllable count of a line to conform to the poem's metrical pattern. Seldom very successful, it can be useful in minimizing accent. Turn back to p. 99 and examine the second foot, line 11, of "Metrical Feet." *Innocent* would ordinarily be accented on the first syllable. However, *be* absorbs the stress of the first syllable, making a diphthong of the *e-i* combination and creating a three-syllable English word without an accent—a theoretical impossibility. Monometer lends itself, because of its brevity, to refrain lines in poems of longer line length.

Dimeter, the two-foot line, is scarcely common in English-language poetry, but it is not rare. Its lines are frequently varied with lines of greater length or with monometer for certain effects. While dimeter dominates the following poem, many interesting variations are included. Examine them for their contributions to

Absent Yet Present

As the flight of a river
   That flows to the sea
My soul rushes ever
   In tumult to thee. .

A twofold existence   5
   I am where thou art;
My heart in the distance
   Beats close to thy heart.

Look up, I am near thee,
   I gaze on thy face;   10
I see thee, I hear thee,
   I feel thine embrace.

As the magnet's control on
   The steel it draws to it,
Is the charm of thy soul on   15
   The thoughts that pursue it.

And absence but brightens
   The eyes that I miss,
And custom but heightens
   The spell of thy kiss.   20

It is not from duty,
   Though that may be owed,—
It is not from beauty,
   Though that be bestowed;

But all that I care for,   25
   And all that I know,
Is that, without wherefore,
   I worship thee so.

Through granite it breaketh
　　A tree to the ray;　　　　　*30*
As a dreamer forsaketh
　　The grief of the day,

My soul in its fever
　　Escapes unto thee;
O dream to the griever!　　　*35*
　　O light to the tree!

A twofold existence
　　I am where thou art;
Hark, hear in the distance
　　The beat of my heart!　　　*40*

Edward Bulwer-Lytton, Lord Lytton

A series of images flows from the opening line as a series of comparisons is drawn. The parallelism is compounded as iambs and anapests rush after each other, like the river of line 1, through hypercatalectic line after hypercatalectic line. The skillful use of pyrrhics and spondees speeds or slows the tumultuous, headlong flight of emotion as the extra feminine syllable enjambs hypercatalectic line into acatalectic line, and caesuras shift happily through the stanzas. The dimeter line lends itself to the impassioned outpouring.

Various feet are skillfully blended in "Résumé," but the prevailing foot is established in lines 1, 3, 5, and 7. The irony of the dimeter observations is intensified as trochees are balanced against the two-foot line: falling meter versus happy length. The resultant contrast creates a bitter, but charming, resignation in the last two lines as trochees give way to the final iamb and anapest:

Résumé

Razors pain you;
Rivers are damp;
Acids stain you;
And drugs cause cramp.
Guns aren't lawful;　　　*5*
Nooses give;
Gas smells awful;
You might as well live.

Dorothy Parker

One of the reading problems frequently necessitated by short lines in contemporary poetry is *inversion,* a placing of words out of normal sentence order. Generally discouraged in contemporary poetry, it is quite a standard practice in older works. As the poet constantly attempts brevity, the device is an aid to him but a hindrance at times to the reader trying to thread his way through the syntax of the line. It can be used effectively, however, as you will notice in

All But Blind

All but blind
   In his chambered hole
Gropes for worms
   The four-clawed Mole.

All but blind   *5*
   In the evening sky,
The hooded Bat
   Twirls softly by.

All but blind
   In the burning day   *10*
The Barn-Owl blunders
   On her way.

And blind as are
   These three to me,
So, blind to Someone   *15*
   I must be.
         Walter de la Mare

Catalexis in the lines beginning with *All* establishes an uncertainty of mood that is developed in the choices of "all but blind" creatures. The dimeter lines are varied rhythmically as anapests relieve iambs, and compensation creates singular imagery in the last two lines of stanzas 3 and 4. Moral observations such as "blind to Someone/I must be" would be unpalatable without the seeming ingenuousness of the dimeter lines.

Trimeter, the three-foot line, lends itself to melancholia because its length seems sobbed. Scan the following poems carefully, noticing the cumulative effect of the repeated words:

The Day

The day was a year at first
When children ran in the garden;
The day shrank down to a month
When the boys played ball.

The day was a week thereafter   5
When young men walked in the garden:
The day was itself a day
When love grew tall.

The day shrank down to an hour
When old men limped in the garden;   10
The day will last forever
When it is nothing at all.

Theodore Spencer

Defend your scansion of this poem, pointing out two alternate scansions for the second line of each stanza and giving your reasons for rejecting them. How does "The Day" utilize language to enlarge and to diminish time? How do action and state of being verbs contribute to the processes?

The contribution of line length to the sound and sense of a poem becomes very clear in the rearrangement of stanza 1 of "The Day" which follows. You will notice nothing has been changed except the line length. Trimeter has been reduced to dimeter with one monometer line; yet the overall change seems much greater:

The day was a year
At first when children
Ran in the garden;
The day shrank down
To a month   5
When the boys played ball.

Vocabulary, grammar, syntax, poetic device, metrics—all remain constant; only line length differs. Yet a subtle change pervades the stanza. The mood has been violated.

Poets must be sure that *all* elements work together to create unity of impression in a poem. When coherence combines with technical subtleties, the poetic experience becomes very rewarding to the reader. Observe the way meaning shifts the emphasis on *If* to vary the foot containing it in the following poem:

Rondel

If I'm at church these days
It's just to see her there,
Fresh as new roses are.

Why gossip, then, and raise
Interest in the affair,   *5*
If I'm at church these days?

Whatever paths or ways
I follow lead to her;
Fool, to say fool, and stare
If I'm at church these days.   *10*

Christine de Pisan
(tr. R. N. Currey)

Although "If I'm at church these days" is a repeated line, it does not function in "Rondel" as a refrain, for its scansion pattern changes with the sense of the lines. In line 1, *If I'm* is an iamb; in line 6, it is a trochee; in line 10, it is a spondee. Reading the lines within the framework of such stress patterns, observe the additional implications. The initial trochees in lines 3 and 5 are also interesting in their implications. Explain them. One pyrrhic foot is used in the poem—where? Discuss the reason. Lines 9 and 10 are technically rich—a richness that creates the final, unified tone. Can you see the scansion possibilities of the lines? How do caesuras work to contribute to the effect?

Understatement in the *refrain* of a poem (a line regularly repeated with exactly the same meaning each time) is particularly effective for two reasons: 1) the repeated sound emphasizes the sense, calling the importance of the ideas to the reader's attention; and 2) understatement becomes richly apparent as a constant redirection of attention to it enforces the metrics, making any tension between sound and sense apparent. "They are all gone away" in the next poem can be read as iambic trimeter, but tone demands anapestic dimeter. "There is nothing more to say" picks up the anapest in the opening foot, unifying the refrain lines and creating empty sadness as the lilting meter is juxtaposed against the hopelessness of the statements:

The House on the Hill

They are all gone away,
   The House is shut and still,
There is nothing more to say.

Through broken walls and gray
   The winds blow bleak and shrill: *5*
They are all gone away.

Nor is there one today
   To speak them good or ill:
There is nothing more to say.

Why is it then we stray,   *10*
   Around that sunken sill?
They are all gone away,

And our poor fancy-play
   For them is wasted skill:
There is nothing more to say.   *15*

There is ruin and decay
   In the House on the Hill:
They are all gone away,
There is nothing more to say.
             Edwin Arlington Robinson

In arriving at a conclusion about the poet's intention in "The House on the Hill," you might speculate on the capital *H*'s in lines 2 and 17.

Tetrameter, the four-foot line, is a popular length for accomplished poets, and an easy one for beginners. Light, graceful forms such as villanelles (pp. 222-223), ballades (pp. 218-219), rondeaus (p. 219), and triolets (pp. 221-222) are particularly suited to iambic tetrameter. In fact, if someone with a melodious voice should read the following villanelle aloud, you could probably dance any fox trot step to it without difficulty:

Villanelle

A dainty thing's the Villanelle;
   Sly, musical, a jewel in rhyme,
It serves its purpose passing well.

A double-clappered silver bell
   That must be made to clink in chime,   *5*
A dainty thing's the Villanelle;

And if you wish to flute a spell,
   Or ask a meeting 'neath the lime,
It serves its purpose passing well.

You must not ask of it the swell   *10*
   Of organs grandiose and sublime—
A dainty thing's the Villanelle;

And, filled with sweetness, as a shell
   Is filled with sound, and launched in time,
It serves its purpose passing well.   *15*

Still fair to see and good to smell
   As in the quaintness of its prime,
A dainty thing's the Villanelle,
It serves its purpose passing well.

              William Ernest Henley

The deceptive simplicity of tetrameter may also be employed for subtle persuasion, as the delicacy of the line belies the seriousness of sense:

Brahma

If the red slayer think he slays,
   Or if the slain think he is slain,
They know not well the subtle ways
   I keep, and pass, and turn again.

Far or forgot to me is near;   *5*
   Shadow and sunlight are the same;
The vanished gods to me appear;
   And one to me are shame and fame.

They reckon ill who leave me out;
   When me they fly, I am the wings;   *10*
I am the doubter and the doubt,
   And I the hymn the Brahmin sings.

The strong gods pine for my abode,
   And pine in vain the sacred Seven;
But thou, meek lover of the good!   *15*
   Find me, and turn thy back on heaven.

              Ralph Waldo Emerson

Details chosen carefully, observed freshly, and offered in descriptive progression create harmony of the senses within the short tetrameter line. The brief quality of the line allows rapid building of image on image. Notice the effective use of simile to create the overall color tone of

Symphony in Yellow

An omnibus across the bridge
   Crawls like a yellow butterfly,
   And, here and there, a passer-by
Shows like a little restless midge.

Big barges full of yellow hay   *5*
   Are moved against the shadowy wharf,
   And, like a yellow silken scarf,
The thick fog hangs along the quay.

The yellow leaves begin to fade
   And flutter from the Temple elms,   *10*
   And at my feet the pale green Thames
Lies like a rod of rippled jade.

                     Oscar Wilde

Your daily speech is imperfect iambic *pentameter,* or five-foot lines. While some of your friends may assume poetry is too esoteric for them, were you to record their conversations and scan them, you could demonstrate a ragged iambic pattern emerging. And there would be five iambs to the line that would regularly re-create itself. Such is the natural rhythmical pattern of the English language, and, as a result, more English and American poetry is written in this meter than in any other. Certain forms, such as the sonnet, demand it.

The first three stanzas of Thomas Gray's "Elegy Written in a Country Church-Yard" will help reveal to you your own familiarity with the rhythm. Notice how easy it is to scan; also notice how simple it is to read aloud—even for people who have difficulty reading poetry:

The curfew tolls the knell of parting day,
   The lowing herd wind slowly o'er the lea,
The plowman homeward plods his weary way,
   And leaves the world to darkness, and to me.

Now fades the glimmering landscape on the sight,   *5*
   And all the air a solemn stillness holds,
Save where the beetle wheels his droning flight,
   And drowsy tinklings lull the distant folds;

Save that from yonder ivy-mantled tower
   The moping owl does to the moon complain   *10*
Of such as, wandering near her secret bower,
   Molest her ancient solitary reign.

   The following sonnet is written in iambic pentameter, but you should
notice the relief feet as you scan it. They work with the caesuras to create a musing, introspective statement, intensely personal, yet unblush-
ingly shared:

What Lips My Lips Have Kissed

What lips my lips have kissed, and where, and why,
I have forgotten, and what arms have lain
Under my head till morning; but the rain
Is full of ghosts tonight, that tap and sigh
Upon the glass and listen for reply,   5
And in my heart there stirs a quiet pain
For unremembered lads that not again
Will turn to me at midnight with a cry.
Thus in the winter stands the lonely tree,
Nor knows what birds have vanished one by one,   10
Yet knows its boughs more silent than before:
I cannot say what loves have come and gone,
I only know that summer sang in me
A little while, that in me sings no more.

                              Edna St. Vincent Millay

Justify the lost lovers-ghosts-tree-bird images as they build to the final
two lines. Have metaphors been mixed, or are they logical in their
progression?
   Hexameter, the six-foot line, is seldom used extensively in English.
More often, it is employed as a relief line in truncated form. Sidney Lanier's "The Marshes of Glynn" contains the following excerpt. (Caution:
as you scan it, expect truncations!)

Ye marshes, how candid and simple and nothing-withholding and free
Ye publish yourselves to the sky and offer yourselves to the sea!
Tolerant plains, that suffer the sea and the rains and the sun,
Ye spread and span like the catholic man who hath mightily won
God out of knowledge and good out of infinite pain   5
And sight out of blindness and purity out of a stain.

As the marsh-hen secretly builds on the watery sod,
Behold I will build me a nest on the greatness of God:
I will fly in the greatness of God as the marsh-hen flies
In the freedom that fills all the space 'twixt the marsh and the skies.   10

In France, the six-foot line was used extensively in heroic verse (poetry recounting the exploits of Alexander the Great), and, since the English borrowed this length from their French contemporaries, the line came to be called an *alexandrine*. Its most successful use in English poetry is found in Edmund Spenser's *The Faerie Queene,* a *metrical romance* (highly imaginative narrative poetry chronicling the adventures of knights and their ladies). For his own purposes, Spenser evolved the *Spenserian stanza,* eight lines of iambic pentameter and a ninth of iambic hexameter (the alexandrine). Notice the effect of the ninth line in the first stanza of this elaborate allegory:

> A Gentle Knight was pricking on the plaine,
>> Ycladd in mightie armes and silver shielde,
>> Wherein old dints of deepe wounds did remaine,
>> The cruell markes of many a bloudy fielde;
>> Yet armes till that time did he never wield.   *5*
>> His angry steede did chide his foming bitt,
>> As much disdayning to the curbe to yield.
>> Full jolly knight he seemd, and faire did sitt,
>> As one for knightly giusts and fierce encounters fitt.

If you know the American folk ballad "Frankie and Johnny," you have already encountered a highly irregular hexameter line, rich in variant feet. The tetrameter refrain lines reduce syllable count and employ shifting emphasis and changing feet to create remarkable suggestion. Be aware of it as you read:

Frankie and Johnny

Frankie and Johnny were lovers, O, how that couple could love.
Swore to be true to each other, true as the stars above.
He was her man, but he done her wrong.

Frankie she was his woman, everybody knows.
She spent one hundred dollars for a suit of Johnny's clothes.   *5*
He was her man, but he done her wrong.

Frankie and Johnny went walking, Johnny in his bran' new suit,
"O good Lawd," says Frankie, "but don't my Johnnie look cute?"
He was her man, but he done her wrong.

Frankie went down to Memphis; she went on the evening train.   *10*
She paid one hundred dollars for Johnny a watch and chain.
He was her man, but he done her wrong.

Frankie went down to the corner, to buy a glass of beer;
She says to the fat bartender, "Has my loving man been here?
He was my man, but he done me wrong."   *15*

"Ain't going to tell you no story, ain't going to tell you no lie,
I seen your man 'bout an hour ago with a girl named Alice Fry.
If he's your man, he's doing you wrong."

Frankie went back to the hotel, she didn't go there for fun,
Under her long red kimono she toted a forty-four gun.   *20*
He was her man, he was doing her wrong.

Frankie went down to the hotel, looked in the window so high,
There was her lovin' Johnny a-lovin' up Alice Fry;
He was her man, but he done her wrong.

Frankie threw back her kimono; took out the old forty-four;   *25*
Roota-toot-toot, three times she shot, right through that hotel door.
She shot her man, 'cause he done her wrong.

Johnny grabbed off his Stetson. "O good Lawd, Frankie, don't shoot."
But Frankie put her finger on the trigger, and the gun went roota-toot-toot.
He was her man, but she shot him down.   *30*

"Roll me over easy, roll me over slow,
Roll me over easy, boys, 'cause my wounds is hurting me so,
I was her man, but I done her wrong."

With the first shot Johnny staggered; with the second shot he fell;
When the third bullet hit him, there was a new man's face in hell.   *35*
He was her man, but he done her wrong.

Frankie heard a rumbling away down under the ground.
Maybe it was Johnny where she had shot him down.
He was her man, and she done him wrong.

"Oh, bring on your rubber-tired hearses, bring on your rubber-tired hacks,   *40*
They're takin' my Johnny to the buryin' groun' but they'll never bring him back.
He was my man, but he done me wrong."

The judge he said to the jury, "It's plain as plain can be.
This woman shot her man, so it's murder in the second degree.
He was her man, though he done her wrong."   45

Now it wasn't murder in the second degree, it wasn't murder in the third.
Frankie simply dropped her man, like a hunter drops a bird.
He was her man, but he done her wrong.

"Oh, put me in that dungeon. Oh, put me in that cell.
Put me where the northeast wind blows from the southeast corner of hell.   50
I shot my man 'cause he done me wrong."

Frankie walked up to the scaffold, as calm as a girl could be,
She turned her eyes to heaven and said, "Good Lord, I'm coming to thee.
He was my man, and I done him wrong."

Repetition of words with minor changes creates a sense of narrative progression in the refrain line of each stanza. As the emphasis shifts in the line, the meter changes slightly from refrain line to refrain line. Can you see how sound and sense are combined in this shift? As folk ballads are changed by each singer, the subtlety of such metrics becomes the best possible argument for rhythm's being natural to every human. When such variations occur within a poem, incremental rather than normal refrain results. Each change adds new depth and dimension to the overall effect, but the value of refrain is not lost. The folk always manage to have their cake and eat it too.

Heptameter, the seven-foot line, is difficult to keep intact, since its length becomes labored. James Whitcomb Riley's "When the Frost Is on the Punkin" utilizes it. Impossible to defend as "good" poetry, it has still enjoyed enormous popularity, possibly because of its nostalgic appeal in recalling a bucolic past. The first stanza will reveal the line. Notice the way it seems to divide somewhere around mid-line even though no caesura falls naturally at that point:

> When the frost is on the punkin and the fodder's in the shock,
> You can hear the kyouck and gobble of the struttin' turkey-cock,
> And the clackin' of the guineys, and the cluckin' of the hens,
> And the rooster's hallylooyer as he tiptoes on the fence.
> O, it's then's the times a feller is a-feelin' at his best,   5
> With the risin' sun to greet him from a night of peaceful rest,
> As he leaves the house, bareheaded, and goes out to feed the stock,
> When the frost is on the punkin and the fodder's in the shock.

The heptameter line becomes cumbersome indeed in trisyllabic feet. You will probably find the first five lines of Algernon Charles Swinburne's "In the Water" easy to scan but difficult to enjoy. The sound obscures the sense of the line, and the reader abandons thought for aural enjoyment:

The sea is awake, and the sound of the song of the joy of her waking is rolled
From afar to the star that recedes, from anear to the wastes of the wild wide shore.
Her call is a trumpet compelling us homeward: if dawn in her east be acold,
From the sea shall we crave not her grace to rekindle the life that it kindled before,
Her breath to requicken, her bosom to rock us, her kisses to bless as of yore?

Octameter, the eight-foot line, is familiar to almost everyone because of one poem, Poe's "The Raven," which employs acatalectic octameter in lines 1 and 3 of each stanza. Observe the truncated feet in the other lines. Regardless of the poem's weaknesses and flaws, an analysis of the metrics and effects achieved through simile, metaphor, symbol, mood, tone, and so forth, will repay any reader. Stanza 1 is reproduced below:

Once upon a midnight dreary, while I pondered, weak and weary,
Over many a quaint and curious volume of forgotten lore—
While I nodded, nearly napping, suddenly there came a tapping,
As of some one gently rapping, rapping at my chamber door.
" 'Tis some visitor," I muttered, "tapping at my chamber door—   5
Only this, and nothing more."

Suggested Activity. As this is the most difficult chapter of this book, attention should be given to it until you have mastered scansion. Work with any portion of this chapter until you are thoroughly comfortable in your knowledge. Attention to metrics is of importance in prose as well as in poetry, for much of the best prose owes its major effect to a blending of apt language and interesting cadences. In fact, many passages from such writers as Thomas Wolfe, Henry David Thoreau, Frederic Prokosch, and Truman Capote can be rearranged into metrically defensible lines of poetry. Prose that depends on the elements of poetry for its aural impact and emotional evocations is called *poetic prose.* You might wish to find a selection from your favorite author and attempt to arrange it into poetic lines.

Suggested Assignment. Search for one poem written in each of the metrical line lengths and major feet. Some will not be easy to find. Share your findings with the class. If one strikes you as being particularly interesting, prepare a brief discussion to present orally, pointing out your observations, illustrating them with lines from the poem. You might be amazed as your classmates point out areas you have overlooked.

CHAPTER VI

Rhyme and Stanza Pattern

Just as meter and rhythm are difficult to understand, rhyme and stanza pattern are simple. Children learn easily and early to rhyme for the pleasure of repeated sound. Nor is it necessary to teach them; they discover rhyme quite naturally for themselves. Long before they can master such complicated consonants as *r* and *l*, they intuitively employ subtle rhyme in such pleasantries as "Siwy Biwy" or "cwazy-wazy" or "Moe-Joe" as toy names.

Popular tunesmiths are often less inventive. Any-one who has heard popular songs is unfortunately familiar with rhymes such as *spoon-June-Moon, kiss-bliss,* or *trees-breeze.* This agonized rhyming is not a recent invention. Alexander Pope (1688-1744) was irritated by it when he wrote *An Essay on Criticism,* from which the following lines are excerpted. You will find in these lines, also, advice against judging poetry by any *one* element. All of the techniques you are considering are employed simultaneously by the good poet:

> But most by numbers judge a poet's song,
> And smooth or rough with them is right or wrong:
> In the bright Muse though thousand charms conspire,
> Her voice is all these tuneful fools admire;
> Who haunt Parnassus but to please their ear,   *5*
> Not mend their minds; as some to church repair,
> Not for the doctrine, but the music there.
> These equal syllables alone require,
> Though oft the ear the open vowels tire;
> While expletives their feeble aid do join,   *10*
> And ten low words oft creep in one dull line:
> While they ring round the same unvaried chimes,
> With sure returns of still-expected rhymes:
> Where'er you find "the cooling western breeze,"
> In the next line it "whispers through the trees";   *15*

If crystal streams "with pleasing murmurs creep,"
The reader's threatened (not in vain) with "sleep";
Then, at the last and only couplet fraught
With some unmeaning thing they call a thought,
A needless Alexandrine ends the song,   20
That, like a wounded snake, drags its slow length along.

(ll. 337-357)

Did you notice how Pope illustrated many of his observations by making his metrics, word choice, or poetic device re-create the fault? There are ten words in line 11, for example; line 21 is an alexandrine. Did you look up any new words, such as "numbers"? In lines 362-365 of this same poem, Pope suggests a writer must know his craft, just as you, the reader, must understand it if you are to understand what you read:

True ease in writing comes from art, not chance,
As those move easiest who have learned to dance.
'Tis not enough no harshness gives offense;
The sound must seem an echo to the sense.

By definition, *rhyme* is the repetition of vowel or consonantal sounds in one or more masculine or feminine syllables. *Perfect rhyme* repeats the vowel sound, which must be preceded by a different consonant (*tall-small-wall-call*). Such words as *right-write* or *sum-some* are not rhymes however, because they are exactly the same sounds, not an *echo* of sound. (Compare *identical rhyme,* p. 126.) This echoing quality of rhyme endears it to memory. Few people can remember the number of days in our months without the mnemonic device of

Thirty days hath September,
April, June, and November;
All the rest have thirty-one
Excepting February alone,
Which hath but twenty-eight, in fine,   5
Till leap year gives it twenty-nine.

This little memory aid utilizes many aspects of rhyme. *Fine-nine* are *masculine rhymes*—rhymes in which a final stressed syllable contains the correspondence of sound. Such rhymes are strong and forceful. *Feminine rhymes* are represented by *September-November.* Such rhymes contain corresponding sounds in two consecutive syllables, the second of which is unaccented. Notice the rhyme is carried in the *-tem-* and *-vem-* syllables of *September-November.* Other examples are *blighted-sighted, sewing-going,* and *brighten-tighten.* Feminine rhyme adds lightness and delicacy to a line.

A third type of rhyme, not represented in "Thirty days," is *triple rhyme,* in which the correspondence of sound is carried through three consecutive syllables, as in *laborious-glorious-victorious.* Triple rhyme is particularly effective in humorous or satirical verse.

The rhyming of *one-alone* represents *slant rhyme*—rhymed words of similar though not exact correspondence. Also called *near, imperfect,* or *half rhyme,* this form lends itself to subtlety of thought. It is useful to the poet who wishes to retain rigid meter in a poem, as it compensates for extended regularity, breaking the singsong quality.

Lines concluding in rhyme are said to be *end rhymed,* and, as the repetition of metrical accent is comparable to the "beat" in music, end rhyme is comparable to the return to the keynote in music. This "keynoting" arouses expectation in the reader. He knows it will be repeated, expects it, and is satisfied when it occurs. It acts, in a sense, as an echo. If you expect an echo which fails to come, you are disappointed. The recurring echo established by rhyme also sets the line apart as a complete rhythmical unit comparable to a musical phrase. It further supplies the organizational pattern of stanzas, as you will discover later. The end rhyme in stanza 1 of Alexander Pope's "Solitude" is masculine:

> Happy the man, whose wish and care
> A few paternal acres bound,
> Content to breathe his native air
> In his own ground.

Did you observe the effect Pope achieved by decapitating two full feet from line 4? How can you tell the shortening occurs at the head rather than from the trunk of the line?

Robert Louis Stevenson's "Good and Bad Children" is characterized by delicacy and lightness as a result of the feminine rhymes: ,

> Children, you are very little,
> And your bones are very brittle;
> If you would grow great and stately,
> You must try to walk sedately.
>
> You must still be bright and quiet   5
> And content with simple diet;
> And remain, through all bewild'ring,
> Innocent and honest children.

Happy hearts and happy faces,
Happy play in grassy places—   *10*
That was how, in ancient ages,
Children grew to kings and sages.

But the unkind and the unruly,
And the sort who eat unduly,
They must never hope for glory—   *15*
Theirs is quite a different story!

Cruel children, crying babies,
All grow up as geese and gabies,
Hated, as their age increases,
By their nephews and their nieces.   *20*

Feminine slant rhyme is employed in lines 7 and 8. Did you check the dictionary for *gabies?* If you didn't, you are still far away from being a good reader. *Gaby* is a legitimate word, still in use.

Stevenson's use of alternating feminine and masculine end rhyme in "Marching Song" is effective. Can you see why?

Bring the comb and play upon it!
  Marching, here we come!
Willie cocks his highland bonnet,
  Johnnie beats the drum.

Mary Jane commands the party,   *5*
  Peter leads the rear;
Feet in time, alert and hearty,
  Each a Grenadier!

All in the most martial manner
  Marching double-quick;   *10*
While the napkin like a banner
  Waves upon the stick!

Here's enough of fame and Pillage
  Great commander Jane!
Now that we've been round the village,   *15*
  Let's go home again.

Jane's leadership is stated in stanza 2, but her tomboyishness and power are established more clearly in the rhyme and implications throughout the poem. Scan "Marching Song" to see the careful use of metrics in combination with end rhyme. Do not expect the foot to remain constant! Be alert to headless and truncated feet!

Robert Herrick utilizes alternated masculine and feminine end rhyme in this well-known poem:

To the Virgins, To Make Much of Time

Gather ye rosebuds while ye may,
　Old Time is still a-flying;
And this same flower that smiles today,
　Tomorrow will be dying.

The glorious lamp of heaven, the sun,　　*5*
　The higher he's a-getting,
The sooner will his race be run,
　And nearer he's to setting.

That age is best which is the first,
　When youth and blood are warmer;　　*10*
But being spent, the worse and worst
　Times still succeed the former.

Then be not coy, but use your time,
　And while ye may, go marry;
For, having lost but once your prime,　　*15*
　You may forever tarry.

How does the scansion of the lines with masculine end rhyme differ from those with feminine end rhyme? Why? Account for the use of *ye* in stanzas 1 and 3, of *you* in stanza 4. Why is the change made? This poem belongs to the *carpe diem* (seize the day) school of poetry which suggests, "Eat, drink, and be merry, for tomorrow we die." Poets have often used the argument as an encouragement to their intended mistresses. Sixteenth and seventeenth century English poets excelled in such argument.

Sometimes, to make sure the reader will be aware of rhyme, poets indent lines to set off matched pairs. Notice, in "To the Virgins," that the indented lines rhyme, and the flush lines rhyme. Notice, also, the indented rhymes are feminine, the flush lines masculine.

In Chapter v, you scanned the following lines from Hood's "Bridge of Sighs":

> Take her up tenderly,
> Lift her with care;
> Fashioned so slenderly,
> Young and so fair!

The triple rhymes in the dactyls are especially effective in contrast with the masculine rhymes in the truncated second and fourth lines. Again you see rhyme and meter working together. *Remember:* A poem results from the poet's use of many devices, *consciously* and *simultaneously.* Concentration on only one element assures bad verse, not good poetry. Your concentration on only one element of poetry insures imperfect reading, not complete communication.

Triple rhyme is particularly agreeable to the satirist or humorist as it leads to *outrageous rhyme*—the distortion of words to make them rhyme humorously, as in

The Platitude

Does the duckbilled Platitude
Give you Social Latitude?
If so, knock that Attitude
Into a cocked Hattitude!

Enid Williams

Sir W. S. Gilbert used triple end rhyme and double internal rhyme to humorous advantage in his light opera lyrics. *Internal rhyme* occurs when a word within a line, usually just before a caesura, rhymes with a word further along in the line:

from *Nightmare*

When you're lying awake with a dismal headache, and repose is taboo'd by anxiety,
I conceive you may use any language you choose to indulge in, without impropriety;
For your brain is on fire—the bedclothes conspire of usual slumber to plunder you:
First your counterpane goes, and uncovers your toes, and your sheet slips demurely
   from under you;
Then the blanketing tickles—you feel like mixed pickles—so terribly sharp is the
   pricking,   5
And you're hot, and you're cross, and you tumble and toss till there's nothing 'twixt
   you and the ticking.
Then the bedclothes all creep to the ground in a heap, and you pick 'em all up in a
   tangle;
Next your pillow resigns and politely declines to remain at its usual angle!

The internal rhyme word may rhyme with the last word of the line, as it does in Poe's

> Once upon a midnight dreary, while I pondered, weak and weary,
> Over many a quaint and curious volume of forgotten lore—
> While I nodded, nearly napping, suddenly there came a tapping,
> As of some one gently rapping, rapping at my chamber door.
> " 'Tis some visitor," I muttered, "tapping at my chamber door—   5
>   Only this and nothing more."
>
> *"The Raven"*

Slant rhyme, if carefully and imaginatively used, can be an asset and an aid to the poet. It does not contain the same correspondence of vowels and consonants as perfect rhyme and, therefore, slants the sound. Emily Dickinson used it with ease and grace. *Heaven-given* in the second stanza of "I Never Saw a Moor" illustrates feminine slant rhyme:

> I never saw a moor,
> I never saw the sea;
> Yet know I how the heather looks,
> And what a wave must be.
>
> I never spoke with God,   5
> Nor visited in heaven;
> Yet certain am I of the spot
> As if the chart were given.

The inversion in line 3 is interesting. The meter would remain the same had the poet written "Yet I know how the heather looks," but the meaning would shift. *I know how* is a simple statement of fact; *know I how* emphasizes *know* and makes it assert, "I understand emotionally, physically, spiritually and intellectually." Such inversions are acceptable at any time, but they should always be as deliberate and as effective as this one.

Examine Emily Dickinson's use of slant and perfect rhyme in "Presentiment" to distinguish time indications:

> Presentiment—is that long Shadow—on the lawn—
> Indicative that Suns go down—
>
> The Notice to the startled Grass
> That Darkness—is about to pass—

Rhyme has, in addition to the major elements, many less obvious and subtle uses. As it does carry an echo, it combines sound impressions with stated time intervals, thereby pleasing the ear. Because this time interval is expected by the reader, a poet repeats the rhyme regularly. It occurs every other line or every third line. To allow four or five lines to lapse before the rhyme is offered causes the reader to lose sight of the rhyme and, consequently, of the meaning of the poem. To allow the sixth line to establish a rhyme is to expect more of the reader than he can give. By that time, he has decided there is no rhyme; the echo has faded so completely he will probably overlook the rhyme when it occurs or be disturbed as if he had been asked to remember something he couldn't quite recall.

Identical rhyme repeats a word, usually adding new connotations from intervening lines. It is used with caution, however, for poets must first decide it is justifiable rather than convenient. Humorous poets have found it effective, certainly. A famous bit of nonsense is

The Purple Cow

I never saw a Purple Cow,
I never hope to see one;
But I can tell you, anyhow,
I'd rather see than be one.

Gelett Burgess

Even here the fourth line is reinforced by rhymes within the line in the words *see-be* which create *double rhyme*—notice, neither *see* nor *be* would be followed by a caesura except for the rhyme, but the rhyme does not extend to *one.*

Burgess was astonished at the popularity of his whimsy, so astonished he wrote a second "Purple Cow" some years later, abandoning the double rhyme:

Ah, yes, I wrote the "Purple Cow"—
I'm sorry, now, I wrote it!
But I can tell you, anyhow,
I'll kill you if you quote it.

Observe the slant rhyme in *tell-kill,* however.

Identical rhyme can be serious and effective too. Notice the intensification in line 4 as, connotatively, the element of justification or rationalization is added in Coleridge's stanza from "The Rime of the Ancient Mariner":

Then all averred, I had killed the bird
That brought the fog and mist.
'Twas right, said they, such things to slay,
That bring the fog and mist.

Line 3 contains a defensible inversion in *said they,* as we frequently use *said John* or *said the President* to indicate an important statement or speaker. Had the inversion been employed merely to gain the rhyme of *they-slay,* however, it would be much harder—if not impossible—to defend. The inversion in *such things to slay* adds power to the line. To end it with *things* would weaken it measurably, making the progression from the specific to the general rather pointless. Lines such as 1 and 3 contain internal rhyme that clearly reveals the caesura. It breaks the line into two units of equal metrical length. Examination will reveal its advantages, but poets are cautious in its use. It can become merely a testament to their ingenuity.

Sidney Lanier used internal rhyme elaborately in "The Symphony," placing it in positions removed from mid-line. You will notice slant rhyme is used internally also:

"Each day, all day" (these poor folk say),
"In the same old year-long, drear-long way,
We weave in the mills and heave in the kilns,
We sieve mine-meshes under the hills,
And thieve much gold from the Devil's bank tills,   5
To relieve, O God, what manner of ills?—"

Lanier's prosody in the complete poem, "The Symphony," is worth the time you might spend examining it. The total structure is particularly interesting in its use of alliteration and assonance. These two devices are also elements of rhyme as the repetition of consonants and vowels creates the lingering echo. Examine the examples in Chapter II, considering their contribution to the effect of rhyme. Much poetry, notably Anglo-Saxon, *blank verse* (unrhymed iambic pentameter; see pp. 223-236), and contemporary free verse (see pp. 237-280), utilize alliteration, assonance, and consonance instead of end rhyme. The effectiveness of these techniques will be apparent in the first ten lines of *The Vision of William concerning Piers the Plowman,* translated by W. A. Neilson and K. G. P. Webster:

> In a summer season, when soft was the sun,
> I clad me in rough clothing, a shepherd as I were;
> In habit of a hermit, unholy of works,
> Went I wide in this world, wonders to hear.
> But on a May morning on Malvern Hills   5
> To me befell a marvel, a fairy thing methought.
> I was weary of wandering and went me to rest
> Under a broad bank by a burn side;
> And as I lay and leaned and looked on the waters,
> I slumbered in a sleep, it sounded so pleasant.   10

Light verse has always enjoyed broad appeal, utilizing curiosities of rhyme. *Light rhyme,* a feature of many ballads, employs an end rhyme of final feminine syllables. The Mother Goose "Goosey Goosey Gander" is familiar to almost everyone:

> Goosey Goosey Gander, where shall we wander
> Up stairs and down stairs and in my Lady's chamber.
> Old father long legs will not say his prayers,
> Take him by the left leg and throw him down the stairs.

Old Mother Goose understood the effectiveness of internal and slant rhyme, if we may judge from *Gander-wander-chamber.* She was also aware of assonance, consonance, and alliteration—all of which may explain her appeal to children who need not know the meaning of her verse. The music of the lines is quite enough to make the young remember them without conscious effort.

A contemporary light versifier, Richard Armour, uses light rhyme in

Lady Shoppers, Beware
> Show-window manikins
> Have slenderer fannykins.

Clever use of slang, interestingly combined words, or coinages are more acceptable in humor than in traditional poetry. The euphemistic *fannykins,* you notice, constitutes an anapest. The iamb lends itself in another of Armour's light rhyme observations, titled

Off-the-Cuff Remark on Off-the-Shoulder Dresses
> Here's one conviction that I hold
> I've never been in error:
> If low-cut dresses leave you cold,
> You're probably the wearer.

Ogden Nash utilizes light rhyme in combination with lines of elaborate meter and length to create his widely admired humor. Examine this poem for its diversity of rhyme usage:

The Terrible People

People who have what they want are very fond of telling people who haven't what
    they want that they really don't want it,
And I wish I could afford to gather all such people into a gloomy castle on the
    Danube and hire half a dozen capable Draculas to haunt it.
I don't mind their having a lot of money, and I don't care how they employ it,
But I do think that they damn well ought to admit they enjoy it.
But no, they insist on being stealthy   5
About the pleasure of being wealthy,
And the possession of a handsome annuity
Makes them think that to say how hard it is to make both ends meet is their
    bounden duity.
You cannot conceive of an occasion
Which will find them without some suitable evasion.   10
Yes, indeed, with arguments they are very fecund;
Their first point is that money isn't everything; and that they have no money anyhow
    is their second.
Some people's money is merited,
And other people's is inherited,
But wherever it comes from,   15
They talk about it as if it were something you got pink gums from,
This may well be,
But if so, why do they not relieve themselves of the burden by transferring it to the
    deserving poor or to me?
Perhaps indeed the possession of wealth is constantly distressing,
But I should be quite willing to assume every curse of wealth if I could at the same
    time assume every blessing.   20
The only incurable troubles of the rich are the troubles that money can't cure,
Which is a kind of trouble that is even more troublesome if you are poor.
Certainly there are lots of things in life that money won't buy, but it's very funny—
Have you ever tried to buy them without money?

Ogden Nash

Suggested Assignments. 1. Examine the end rhyme in Shelley's "Hymn to Intellectual Beauty" (p. 16). Why is it effective? Where are echoing qualities achieved through alliteration, assonance, and consonance? Why are words repeated?

2. Examine John Keats' "To Autumn" (p. 28) in the same way. How is the metaphor strengthened by rhyming devices?

3. W. H. Auden's "O Where Are You Going" (p. 30) employs almost every rhyming device. Explain why each is effective as it is used in the poem. Explain the use of caesuras as they relate to rhyme.

4. Explain the correspondence of lines 2 and 4 in "The Cancer Cells" (p. 32).

5. How does the rhyme contribute to the total effect of "Rain on a Cottage Roof" (p. 33)?

Stanza Patterns

You will remember the definition of a stanza from Chapter II: "A group of lines comprising a poetic division corresponding to a paragraph in prose." This division may be fixed by poetic convention or it may be arbitrarily chosen by the poet, depending on his intention. Meter and rhyme scheme dictate structure in the *fixed forms* (sonnets, for example; see pp. 197-214); meter and thought-grouping suggest it in *blank verse;* poetic sense and sensitivity indicate it in *free verse.*

The fixed forms in traditional western poetry are "fixed" by the pattern of meter and the pattern of end rhyme (both of which, however, may be varied if the poet has reason to do so). The pattern of end rhyme in the fixed forms is called *rhyme scheme,* and rhyme scheme establishes the immediately apparent pattern in poetry. To indicate the rhyme scheme, we label rhymes with letters of the alphabet to show repetition and change. Two successively rhymed lines would be lettered *aa*. Three would be *aaa*. The letters indicate the rhyme has remained constant. If the rhyme scheme of a poem is *aa,* two lines stand alone as a poem. A three-line stanza with all lines rhyming would be *aaa*. The letters *aba* indicate a three-line stanza wherein lines 1 and 3 rhyme; line 2 has no correspondingly rhymed mate. If the next three line stanza has a rhyme scheme of *cbc,* the *b* rhyme from stanza 1 has been picked up. A third stanza in the poem would be rhymed *ded.* The sequence *abab* indicates four lines with lines 1 and 3 corresponding in rhyme, as do 2 and 4.

In scanning a poem, you will place the letter indicating rhyme at the end of each line, in parentheses. As you will have established the metrical pattern for the line, you will note the number of feet at the upper right of the rhyme scheme letter. For example a^5 would indicate an initial pentameter line; c^3 would indicate the third end rhyme in a stanza, the line being trimeter. The Tennyson lines you scanned earlier now become:

And brush|ing ank|le deep|in flowers, a^4

We heard||behind|the wood|bine veil b^4

The milk|that bubb|led in|the pail, b^4

And buzz|ings of|the hon|eyed hours. a^4

It is an iambic tetrameter quatrain (four-line stanza) with an *abba* rhyme scheme.

The most common stanzas are:

couplet: 2 lines, rhymed *aa* when standing alone; *aa, bb, cc,* etc., in poems of more than one couplet.

tercet or *triplet:* 3 lines, rhymed *aaa, bbb,* alone. If *interlocking rhyme* (repetition of rhyme in a new stanza from a line in the previous one) is employed, *terza rima* (*aba, bcb, cdc,* etc.) results.

quatrain: 4 lines, rhymed *abab, abba, abcb,* etc. The rhyme scheme usually remains constant in the quatrains throughout the poem. A pair of couplets may be fused into a quatrain: *aabb.*

quintain: 5 lines, rhymed *aabbb, ababb,* etc. The quintain is a combination of the couplet and the tercet.

sestet: 6 lines, rhymed *ababab, abbabb,* etc. Two tercets may be fused into the sestet as may a couplet and a quatrain. The rhyme scheme possibilities become numerous.

septet: 7 lines (also called *heptet*). As this stanza is a combination of couplets, tercets, quatrains, and quintains, the rhyming possibilities are almost endless. The most notable form is in iambic pentameter rhymed *ababbcc,* called *rime royal.* It was used by Chaucer, Spenser, and other English poets.

octave: 8 lines, rhymed as two quatrains fused; a couplet, a quatrain, and a couplet; two tercets and a couplet, etc. An Italian octave, *ottava rima,* is rhymed *abababcc.* While Italian poets employed eleven syllables to the line, English poets preferred iambic pentameter (the heroic lines in each language). The *Spenserian stanza* is an octave rhymed *ababbcbc* plus the ninth line *c.*

These are merely the most commonly used stanzas. Any number of lines may be used to create the stanza most suitable to the poet's purpose.

The Total Poem: An Analysis of "God's World"

You now have the information you need to dissect a poem with some thoroughness. A study of a successful lyric poem will reveal some of the things Sassoon meant by "A man may be a born poet, but he has to make himself an artist as well. He must master the instrument." You might remember Pope's statement also if you begin to question whether the poet "has all these things in mind":

> True ease in writing comes from art, not chance,
> As those move easiest who have learned to dance.
> 'Tis not enough no harshness gives offense;
> The sound must seem an echo to the sense.

In her poem "God's World," Edna St. Vincent Millay lifts words into the realm of music. As the words to songs are called "lyrics," you can easily understand why such poetry must "sing." The physical structure of the poem increases this musical quality through rhythm in the metrics and echo in the rhyming devices. First, read the poem as if it were written in prose paragraph form:

O world, I cannot hold thee close enough! Thy winds, thy wide gray skies! Thy mists, that roll and rise! Thy woods, this autumn day, that ache and sag and all but cry with colour! That gaunt crag to crush! To lift the lean of that black bluff! World, World, I cannot get thee close enough! Long have I known a glory in it all, but never knew I this: here such a passion is as stretcheth me apart,—Lord, I do fear Thou'st made the world too beautiful this year; my soul is all but out of me,—let fall no burning leaf; prithee, let no bird call.

The rhythm has not been damaged by the prose arrangement; the work is still a poem, but it has lost some of its effectiveness. The enforced pause in thought at the end of lines in the poetic stanza gives depth and dimension to many of the lines. The rhyme is subtle enough to lose much of its power in the prose paragraph. To see the difference, read the poem in Millay's stanza form:

God's World

O world, I cannot hold thee close enough!
    Thy winds, thy wide gray skies!
    Thy mists, that roll and rise!
Thy woods, this autumn day, that ache and sag
And all but cry with colour! That gaunt crag   5
To crush! To lift the lean of that black bluff!
World, World, I cannot get thee close enough!

Long have I known a glory in it all,
    But never knew I this:
    Here such a passion is   *10*
As stretcheth me apart,—Lord, I do fear
Thou'st made the world too beautiful this year;
My soul is all but out of me,—let fall
No burning leaf; prithee, let no bird call.

Now scan the poem carefully. Mark the feet, the rhyme scheme, caesuras, and so forth. Examine the language and syntax to understand what has been accomplished—and how.

After you have scanned the poem, examine your scansion to be sure you are satisfied with it. Can you defend your decisions? Compare your scansion with another student's. How do the two differ? Why? Discuss your reasons. Are there justifiable arguments for more than one scansion?

Now, let's go carefully through the poem.

First, the title reveals something of the tone of the lyric. It is *God's* world, not the poet's. Possession is the deity's.

The first stanza opens with apostrophe, but it is personification at an intensely personal level: notice the lower case *w* in *world*. The poet addresses it intimately, extending the personal through the line in imagery suggesting an embrace. *Thee* injects a spiritual quality which would have been lost with the more familiar "you." The exclamation point intensifies the passion of the line. Replace it with a period and the line suffers.

Line 2 repeats the biblical form, giving strength to a line built powerfully. The vastness of sky is achieved through the assonance of the *i*'s in *winds-wide-skies* and the alliteration of *winds-wide*. Notice the subtlety of spelled color. Either *grey* or *gray* is correct, but a poet must choose deliberately. The enormity of "sky" is evoked; therefore the choice of the neutral color gray rather than of a more intense blue. But neutrality without coldness is desired; so *gray* is preferred to *grey,* since the *a* spelling associates the word with *gay*. *Grey*, though it is, denotatively, the same word, suggests, connotatively, a lowering, cold cheerlessness. And as poets must sharpen their perceptions to accommodate such niceties, so must good readers! Emotion spills from the poet now—this line is exclaimed phrases, not clauses. An exclamation point intensifies this sudden burst also.

Line 3 repeats the techniques. The alliterative *roll and rise* creates a visual image in employed vowels. The *o* of *roll* creates a (⌣) image. The long *i* seems to ascend. The *s* consonance of *mists* and *rise* adds to the rising image. The exclamation mark again suggests no statement is possible. Wonder announces the phenomena, but they are too evocative to be reduced to assertion.

Line 4 continues the formal, second person usage and extends itself midway into line 5 where an exclamation point stops the impetuous flow of reaction, almost in amazement before the crag image. The lines employ language carefully. *Autumn-day-ache* and *sag* are richly emotional as the assonance creates a weary sound, embodies it in the season, and suggests that the exclaimed intensities of lines 1, 2, and 3 have brought the viewer to emotional fatigue. The line flows on *a* assonance into line 5, extending the evoked response into near-exhaustion as understatement combines with the word *cry*—the logical end of the progression. But, before the reader can be caught completely, saṁvegha (see p. 57) is employed in *with colour*. (Notice the similarity of this line to the Issa haiku use of *village overflowing with children,* p. 57. Poetic shock acts once again to lift the spirit to new intensity.) Saṁvegha is employed immediately once more as the elevated emotion is brought sharply against *That gaunt crag* erected in hard *g* consonance.

Line 6 redirects the crag image, however, as haiku lines do, into the understood wish of "Oh to be strong enough to crush something that strong!" The wish establishes the smallness of the human figure. The line softens in the alliteration of *lift-lean*, only to create massive imagery through contrast with the alliteration in *black bluff*, intensified by the *f* consonance in *lift-bluff* by directing the sound back on itself. *That* as an adjective before *crag* and *bluff* creates distance and diminishes the mortal even more.

Line 7 subtly deifies *world* by changing lower case *w* to capital *W*. The personal element of line 1 is replaced by wondrous adoration. A second subtle shift occurs in the near-repetition of line 1. The intimacy of *hold* is replaced by *get*. Hyperbole is suggested throughout in the exclamation points, but it never occurs completely since the poet's restraint has avoided completed clauses except in lines 1 and 7.

Stanza 2 empowers the images with applied meaning that is *almost* didactic, but the lyric quality of language and image reduces the deified world to a physical sphere in God's hand; the poem ends in understatement, once again establishing the frailty of the mortal.

The "glory" image built in the prevailing tone of stanza 1 is established in line 1 of stanza 2 by the *l-g* consonance in *long-glory-all*. A very subtle pun is employed in line 2 in the word *knew*. The pun rests in the statement growing from line 1: I have been aware of "a" (indefinite article) glory in the world, but never knew I "this" (definite adjective) glory; so the knowledge is "new." The two lines employ language at its most meaningful level.

Lines 3 and 4 utilize *p-s* consonance effectively and *stretcheth* serves two functions: it intensifies the biblical quality of the language (especially effective as God is being directly addressed) and lengthens the word almost onomatopoetically. Notice how much longer *stretcheth* seems than *stretches*, yet the syllable count is the same. *Do* is used in the line to intensify *fear*, making the statement stronger through emphasis. The hyperbole in line 5 is effective, for only hyperbole is adequate in complimenting God.

Immediately following the hyperbole, understatement reduces the mortal to ecstatic exhaustion in *My soul is all but out of me*. The understatement extends itself in the remainder of line 6 and through line 7 to compound the ecstasy of spiritual exhaustion. The mortal in the presence of the world exercised no great self-control. This breathlessness of restrained hyperbole in exclamation points is absent in stanza 2. It refines the rush of words. Image does not outrush image here. In God's presence, the poet's language is not fragmented. Stately clause follows stately clause. But even God's presence cannot dwarf the poet utterly when she is enraptured by beauty. The final understatement, though humbled by *prithee* (I pray You), is stated in the imperative mood!

You will notice the first stanza is joyful in its rhythm. The metrics are, of course, responsible for that. And Millay was responsible, indeed, for her metrics! Did you count the syllables for *any* reason? You should have. Both stanzas have exactly the same number, line by line, though the numbers and kinds of feet vary between the stanzas.

If you feel you may have been hasty, re-scan the lines.

The scansion which follows this paragraph is one *possible* scansion. Observe: one possible. To know what the poet intended, we would need her scansion. Even then we might disagree with her! Your scansion may not match the one presented here. Language, by its very nature, causes even isolated sounds to seem different to any two people—even two people who have reliable ears. When sounds are combined, when denotation and connotation set in, when your speech background is superimposed on the poet's, when the emotion of a line grips you, possibly in a different way from which it did the poet—when these things happen simultaneously, any number of scansions become possible. One will not, of necessity, be "right" and all others "wrong." Just as the poet relies on that inner voice of music for many of his effects, so must the perceptive reader. Just as the poet masters his instrument that he may improvise and create new rhythms from old rules, so must the reader. But a good poet can defend his reasons, reveal how they are solidly based in rules. So must you be able to give reasons for scanning as you do. Merely to say, "Well, it just sounds that way," is not an adequate defense. What happens in one line to make you think another one should be scanned in a curious fashion? What technique of assonance, alliteration, and so on, may work to prove your scansion? You must be able to defend your reasoning, not so you can argue with anyone, but so you can reason with yourself. If a technique works, how and why does it work? From such understanding, you too, in time, may learn to improvise brilliantly on the reading instrument—or even on the writing instrument.

Syllables

10	O world, ‖ I can‖not hold‖thee close‖e nough!	a^5
6	Thy winds, ‖ thy wide‖gray skies!	b^3
6	Thy mists,‖that roll‖and rise!	b^3
10	Thy woods, ‖ this au‖tumn day,‖that ache‖and sag	c^5
10	And all‖but cry‖with co lour!‖That gaunt crag	c^4
10	To crush!‖To lift‖the lean‖of that‖black bluff!	a^5
10	World, World, ‖ I can‖not get‖thee close‖enough!	a^5
10	∧Long‖have I known‖a glor‖y in‖it all,	a^5
6	But nev‖er knew‖I this:	b^3
6	∧Here‖such a pa‖ssion is	b^3
10	As stretch‖eth me‖a part,—‖Lord,∧‖I do fear	c^5
10	Thou'st made‖the world‖too beau‖ti ful‖this year;	c^5
10	My soul‖is all‖but out‖of me,—‖let fall	a^5
10	No burn‖ing leaf;‖prith ee,‖let no‖bird call.	a^5

By distorting word stress in this poem, you might have marked the lines unrelieved iambics. Such scansion would do indefensible violence to some of the feet where meaning shifts the iamb into another foot through emphasis on a word.

Line 1 contains five iambs with a caesura after the first, demanded by direct address. The first iamb employs *hovering accent,* a fine attention to related vowel sounds merging as a result of placement within the line. The feminine *O* is a long sound, held for measurable extended time without receiving stress. The formation of the vowel sound ends in a *w* placement of the lips which must hold the end of the *O* sound and blend it into the new *w* formation. This seems to make the stress placement uncertain. Should it come on *O* or *wo-?* The uncertainty makes the sound hover between the two. This device is also called *distributed stress,* because the stress is literally distributed between the two words. This hovering or distribution creates a lingering effect as if the poet is unwilling to relinquish the image. Millay sets the tone of the poem in this first iamb. The whole poem is a plea to hold the world at this mystical moment of perfection—a plea stated in the final lines of stanza 2 when she asks God to allow no further change.

The emotional response created by the iamb extends through the statement in the first line and the next six, to be restated in the last line, a reinforcing through repetition. Lines 2 and 3 are shortened to three iambs each, establishing the impetuous wonder. Line 4 employs two caesuras to re-establish the idea of this one perfect period. Line 5 varies the meter for two reasons: 1) the rhythm could become too regular; 2) the first two iambs lead effectively into the amphimacer (see p. 98), a variant foot for iambs and anapests. Had Millay used the anapest here, the meter would be lilting, an undesirable effect. The amphibrach (see p. 98) creates the exhausted tone, as it almost creates a deep sigh. To hear the effect of the ‿ — ‿ rhythm, sigh deeply, attempting to measure stress in your breathing. Note how the sigh begins in low stress, builds to strong, slackens away softly. Such is the rhythm of the amphibrach. A second possibility suggests itself—and it creates the same effect. If Millay so chose, she may have used *anacrusis,* an upward or back beat of one or more unaccented syllables at the beginning of a line before the regular rhythm is established. In such case, *And* is an extra unaccented syllable so used and *all but* becomes a trochee, as do *cry with* and *colour.* Such trochees create the same exhausted tone mentioned above.

A change of emotional tone is needed immediately to indicate a new image has intruded itself to capture the poet, literally forcing her into new awareness. The *bacchius* (‿ — —) does this, just as you use it to express appreciation in such a fragment as "That sweet man!" This foot might be scanned as a *molossus* (— — —) if stress is placed on *that*—a reading that is defensible but less interesting. If you scanned this line as five iambs, defend your scansion. Remember: "It sounded right" is not enough defense.

Line 6 returns to the iambic rhythm in order to build to the powerful *black bluff* image, which is spondaic. Color and bulk blend into an image of equal attention to the two parts. The alliteration reinforces the effect of both tone and metrics. Line 7 emphasizes the importance of the World in an initial, strong spondee, intensified from the opening line's hovering accent of *O world*. Four iambs bring the stanza to a close in the resignation of the repeated line.

Stanza 2 opens with a headless iamb, a truncation chosen to re-create the length of time denoted in the word. The caesura works in combination to achieve the effect. The second foot compensates, picking up the extra syllable and using it to create an anapest followed by an iamb to establish a lilting happiness in the knowledge of glory. The pyrrhic followed by an iamb speeds the line into *all,* tying it to *glory* metrically, as the *l*'s do alliteratively. If you scanned the first three feet as iambs, defend your reasoning.

Lines 9 and 10 repeat the pattern of shortened lines from stanza 1, but they are structured to make the wonder a spiritual, rather than an excited, reaction. Line 10 employs the headless iamb and caesura to emphasize the word *here,* meaning "this world at this moment." Line 11 contains a rest spondee, strengthened by the emphatic bacchius. Could two iambs be justified as scansion here? The spondee at mid-line in line 12 indicates an emotionally overpowering experience. The spondees in lines 13 and 14 intensify the imperative while the trochaic middle foot in line 14 shifts the emphasis slightly to the poet as *prithee* means "I pray you." The stress on the first syllable subtly emphasizes the "I" element.

Throughout the poem, rhyme serves as a lingering echo (here intensifying the great size of the world) and a binder to give form to the seven-line stanzas. Lines 2 and 3 in each stanza are indented, not as a whim, but to emphasize their shortened length and to call attention to their end rhyme which, you will notice, is particularly interesting in stanza 2. The repeated use of saṁvegha owes much of its effectiveness to the end rhyme, as the emotional stopping leaves us unprepared for the poetic shock of the next line.

After making such a study of the language, punctuation, special effects, rhyme, and prosody of the poem, you can see how intimately they work together to create a total unit—a unit that must evolve from "art not chance."

Suggested Activity. Choose a poem *not in this book* that you particularly like. Do not choose a long one, but do allow yourself the pleasure of choosing one of greater length than a single couplet, tercet or quatrain. Scan it and dissect it for effectiveness in meaning, imagery, language, metrical technique, rhyme, and so on. Try to exhaust the poem in such a way that, after you have written it on the board and explained it to the class, no one can find anything to add. If there is a variant scansion possibility, defend your choice before it is challenged. Remember: words are both denotative and connotative. Is paradox an element? Is saṁvegha? You may find that a poem you like will reveal no depth of structure or content under such close examination. If this happens, choose another poem. By such processes, your critical discrimination grows.

Suggested Assignment. Choose one of the poems from the following group. Examine it in a brief paper, much as "God's World" is examined. Make every effort to reveal your understanding of the way in which sound and sense work together in the poems.

Constancy

Out upon it, I have loved
   Three whole days together!
And am like to love three more,
   If it prove fair weather.

Time shall moult away his wings   5
   Ere he shall discover
In the whole wide world again
   Such a constant lover.

But the spite on't is, no praise
   Is due at all to me: 10
Love with me had made no stays,
   Had it any been but she.

Had it any been but she,
   And that very face,
There had been at least ere this   15
   A dozen dozen in her place.
                  Sir John Suckling

Simplex Munditiis

Still to be neat, still to be drest,
As you were going to a feast;
Still to be powd'red, still perfumed:

Lady, it is to be presumed,
Though art's hid causes are not found,   *5*
All is not sweet, all is not sound.

Give me a look, give me a face,
That makes simplicity a grace;
Robes loosely flowing, hair as free:
Such sweet neglect more taketh me   *10*
Than all th' adulteries of art.
They strike mine eyes, but not my heart.

                              Ben Jonson

Art Above Nature, to Julia

When I behold a forest spread
With silken trees upon thy head;
And when I see that other dress
Of flowers set in comeliness;
When I behold another grace   *5*
In the ascent of curious lace,
Which like a pinnacle doth show
The top, and the top-gallant too.
Then, when I see thy tresses bound
Into an oval, square, or round;   *10*
And knit in knots far more than I
Can tell by tongue; or true-love tie;
Next, when these lawny films I see
Play with a wild civility:
And all those airy silks to flow,   *15*
Alluring me, and tempting so;
I must confess, mine eye and heart
Dotes less on Nature, than on Art.

                              Robert Herrick

The Garden of Love

I went to the Garden of Love,
And saw what I never had seen:
A Chapel was built in the midst,
Where I used to play on the green.

And the gates of this Chapel were shut,   *5*
And "Thou shalt not" writ over the door;
So I turned to the Garden of Love
That so many sweet flowers bore;

And I saw it was filled with graves,
And tombstones where flowers should be;   10
And Priests in black gowns were walking their rounds,
And binding with briars my joys and desires.

William Blake

Mother, I Cannot Mind My Wheel

Mother, I cannot mind my wheel;
   My fingers ache, my lips are dry:
Oh! if you felt the pain I feel!
   But oh, who ever felt as I?
No longer could I doubt him true—   5
   All other men may use deceit;
He always said my eyes were blue,
   And often swore my lips were sweet.

Walter Savage Landor

Suggested Reading

John Bartlett, *Familiar Quotations*
Francis Turner Palgrave, *The Golden Treasury*
Oscar Williams, *The Silver Treasury of Light Verse*

CHAPTER VII

Understanding Fixed Forms—Preliminaries

Many of your efforts in understanding poetry will, predictably, be discouraging. You will miss the mark widely as you concentrate on one area (such as metrics) and overlook another (such as tone). You should not expect to master the reading of poetry with too much haste. You are involved in *many* processes: extracting the poem's essence, understanding its structure, seeing it in relation to the poet as another human being, and applying the communicated ideas to your own experience to create a new awareness of Self through revelation.

On the other hand, in at least one area you should be experiencing considerable success. Your powers of discrimination should be markedly improved. Learning what to observe from a body of rules should help create new sensitivity in you. Obvious rhyme, the trite phrase, unimaginative treatments (and you will find all of these in published poetry) should by now be irritating to you. If, as you examine a work—even an excellent one—you feel annoyance at the poet's overlooking a technique you feel would have improved his line, you are distinguishing a great deal. Such is discrimination, a necessity for the reader as well as for the writer. If you are making no such distinctions, consider Wordsworth's statement: "Minds that have nothing to confer find little to perceive." The grim realities of this should make you work harder.

With the aid of sensitivity, discrimination, and learned rules, you are now ready to read the fixed forms. Your poetic awareness began with a confined but free verse form, the haiku. The freedom of that form was limited by syllable count and seasonal reference. Greater freedom was granted in the tanka's and cinquain's additional syllables and lines. However, since each form bound the line with a definite syllable count, you have already begun to work at understanding fixed forms. Fanpieces removed the fixed restrictions, and you learned to understand limited free verse confined only by brevity. You are now ready to begin the cycle again with meter, rhyme, and stanza.

At this point, you must learn a term that is vital to all good poetry and prose.

The success of any word structure rests on an understanding of *scene*. This word is used here in a different sense from the one you probably know. It is not the location of action; nor is it a division of an act in a play; nor is it a panorama viewed from a geographical point. "Scene," as used here, is an abstraction loosely synonymous with "now-ness." It suggests involvement of the reader within the framework of the written form.

Have you known people who mutilated a joke so it was never funny? Have you known others who told the same joke in such a way that the audience was amused even if the joke was well-known? The person who tells a joke well has a sense of scene. It is the effect achieved not by "telling" something, but by observing it, isolating the ingredients to see the function of each, recombining the ingredients to omit the non-essential and sharpen what is retained, and, in general, reporting the incident in such a way that the hearer feels caught up in the immediacy of the experience. He experiences the events or emotions in his imagination almost as concretely as if he were undergoing them in actuality. This immediacy, this involvement, when applied to literature, is a result of scene in the work.

Millay achieved this sense of scene in "God's World" (p. 132) through language, metrics, rhyme, and an overall sincerity. For example, she did not merely state, "Black bluffs loom skyward." She did not say, "The crag was gaunt." She did not complain that Nature's beauty exhausted her. By objectively reporting concrete details through carefully selected sensory images, she created experience that includes the reader, forces him to participate utterly. If one more leaf should fall, one more bird call, he, like the poet, would be emotionally responsive. Scene has enmeshed him.

There is no rule of scene, no one way for the writer to achieve it except through a sensitive awareness of his reader's needs. Try to remember your anguish if you have ever read something so poorly written you resented the author. You felt as if he were telling you *what* you should see, *how* you should feel, and you experienced only irritation because the obvious and unimaginative lines did not capture your emotions. At such times, you objected to a lack of scene. Another author may establish scene so sharply that you "live" the work. Incidentally, good detective writers and authors of the supernatural are frequently so effective in handling scene that the reader becomes afraid of ordinary noises. When such happens, scene is at work.

Samuel Taylor Coleridge achieves scene in "Kubla Khan," a work sometimes termed *pure poetry*—poetry designed for the joy of sound alone. The sense in such poetry is either unimportant or utterly lacking. "Pure" poetry does not attempt to instruct the reader or convert him to any belief. It exists merely for the pleasure it can give a reader in sound and imagery. Even though the location is remote in "Kubla Khan," the characters exotic and unnamed, the descriptions rare and strange, the reader "participates" in the poem. He knows the darkness, the joy of sensuousness, the ice and greenery. In short, scene pervades the poem as a result of the poet's wedding his own sensitivity to poetic devices to capture the sensitivity of the reader. The poem becomes the reader's, not the poet's:

Kubla Khan

In Xanadu did Kubla Khan
A stately pleasure-dome decree:
Where Alph, the sacred river, ran
Through caverns measureless to man
    Down to a sunless sea.   *5*
So twice five miles of fertile ground
With walls and towers were girdled round:
And there were gardens bright with sinuous rills,
Where blossomed many an incense-bearing tree;
And here were forests ancient as the hills,   *10*
Enfolding sunny spots of greenery.

But oh! that deep romantic chasm which slanted
Down the green hill athwart a cedarn cover!
A savage place! as holy and enchanted
As e'er beneath a waning moon was haunted   *15*
By woman wailing for her demon-lover!
And from this chasm, with ceaseless turmoil seething,
As if this earth in fast thick pants were breathing,
A mighty fountain momently was forced:
Amid whose swift half-intermitted burst   *20*
Huge fragments vaulted like rebounding hail,
Or chaffy grain beneath the thresher's flail:
And 'mid these dancing rocks at once and ever
It flung up momently the sacred river.

Five miles meandering with a mazy motion   *25*
Through wood and dale the sacred river ran,
Then reached the caverns measureless to man,
And sank in tumult to a lifeless ocean:
And 'mid this tumult Kubla heard
Ancestral voices prophesying war!   *30*
    The shadow of the dome of pleasure
    Floated midway on the waves;
    Where was heard the mingled measure
    From the fountain and the caves.
It was a miracle of rare device,   *35*
A sunny pleasure-dome with caves of ice!

    A damsel with a dulcimer
    In a vision once I saw:
    It was an Abyssinian maid,
    And on her dulcimer she played,   *40*
    Singing of Mount Abora.
    Could I revive within me
    Her symphony and song,
    To such deep delight 'twould win me,
That with music loud and long,   *45*
I would build that dome in air,
That sunny dome! those caves of ice!
And all who heard should see them there,
And all should cry, Beware! Beware!
His flashing eyes, his floating hair!   *50*
Weave a circle round him thrice,
And close your eyes with holy dread,
For he on honey-dew hath fed,
And drunk the milk of Paradise.

Samuel Taylor Coleridge

Examine the poetic devices. What does specific vocabulary contribute? How effectively do metrics and rhyme work together? What is the mood and how is it achieved? Consider the tone and atmosphere. What figures of speech are used effectively? How does the total effect become successful scene? You probably became completely aware of scene if you realized that the line "Could I revive within me" is a personal line—you too could build that dome in air. Scene causes you to experience the effect of the words.

Small Beginnings—The Couplet

As man learns from small beginnings, then progresses to the increasingly complex, and finally masters the difficult, we will begin with the briefer forms, progress to the longer, and finally you will be able to cope with the most demanding lengths.

The smallest poetic unit in western poetry is the *couplet,* a name which indicates the basic structure of the stanza pattern. A "couple" in love is two people bound to each other by emotional ties. "To couple" a trailer to a car is to join the two into one working unit. A couplet, then, is two lines bound by end rhyme, each working together to form a unit. As a well-matched couple must be intellectually, emotionally, physically, and spiritually in harmony if they are to establish "oneness," the lines of a couplet are closely knit and harmonious in thought, language, and syntax to create an illusion of complete unity. Couplets may exist as complete poems in two lines; they may be used in sequence to create a poem of several couplets; or they may be utilized within long poems of other stanza patterns.

In the unmetered forms, you saw how the poet accommodates an idea in a limited number of syllables to communicate his idea to you. In the couplet, the poet increases or decreases syllables as his subject demands. The antiquity of microbes, for example, was observed in only four syllables (p. 105). The general rule a poet follows is this: use not one syllable more than is necessary for the statement. Padding is nowhere more obvious than in the couplet. Its brevity demands greater attention to individual syllables than do lengthier forms, and, for this reason, your awareness of the individual words as they are juxtaposed against each other must be sharpened. Such sharpening will also allow you to observe *motion* (the movement in time the poet uses to establish and develop his idea) and *countermotion* (a change of mood or tone within the time construction of the poem to intensify or clarify the idea). *Pace* is the speed of motion or countermotion. As the poet begins with his basic idea (his précis), he chooses his words to involve the reader and begin the process of perception as rapidly as possible. He concerns himself with words which will, denotatively, establish the concrete details he wishes and those which will, connotatively, evoke layers of meaning from the reader's stored images and memories. This selection requires that he decide which ideas will most effectively be communicated through his use of diction and which through his use of idiom. *Diction* is that body of standard, accepted language constructions (free of trite phrases and slang) chosen by anyone who uses the language effectively; *idiom* is such language structured to create an impression sometimes contrary to the literal meaning of the words. "The house burned up" and "The house burned down" are both idioms for "Fire destroyed the house," the statement couched in diction. A poet's idiom may grow out of his unique associations, becoming richly symbolic in the process. In "The Love Song of J. Alfred Prufrock," T. S. Eliot states:

> In the room the women come and go
> Talking of Michelangelo.

The first line utilizes leisurely-paced diction to create the scene of women strolling back and forth within the confines of a room which allows no extensive movement possibilities. The second line, if the language were intended to function *only* at the level of diction, would mean, quite denotatively, "Discussing the artist Michelangelo." Such is not the case, however. Eliot uses Michelangelo to symbolize an acceptable topic of conversation at the gathering. Implicit is the non-personal quality of the conversation, the freedom from fear of personal revelation in the conversational exchange, and a judgment that the conversational depth of the participants is shallow at best. Symbol and irony combine to create personal idiom that the reader can readily understand. Saṁvegha (see p. 57) is employed brilliantly in line 2.

Metrics, line length, poetic device, rhyme or the absence of it—all contribute to the pace of motion and countermotion of the lines. Notice how many elements contribute to the communication in these lines:

$$\breve{}\breve{} - \breve{} - \breve{} \mid - \breve{} -$$
In the room | the women | come and go

$$- \breve{} \breve{} - \breve{} - \breve{}\breve{} -$$
Talking | of Mi | chelan | gelo.

The trisyllabic feet of line 1 establish a pleasant air of proud gentility. The initial anapest speeds the reader into the line where its lilting rhythm is slowed by the amphibrach (which, as Coleridge once said, "hastes with stately stride"). The final amphimacer (which "strikes its hoofs like a proud, high-bred racer") reveals the women's self-knowledge of background and breeding. Stately assonance of repeated *o*'s and the onomatopoetic effect of consonance in *m*'s create a murmuring undertone. The motion of the line is sprightly in metrics, gentle in poetic device, direct in the denotative language of statement, but tempered by *come and go* with its connotative suggestion of gentle motion. An image almost Victorian grows from the line as the reader realizes men are present, but they are nowhere in evidence. A sweet painting of graceful, strolling women emerges.

That gentle tone is shattered as saṁvegha combines with the harsh consonants of the trochaic *talking*. Connotative possibilities in the word choice become obvious if you substitute *speaking* for *talking* or *discussing* for *talking of*. All mean, denotatively, much the same, and the syllable count remains constant, but the meaning is altered. The sadness of the trochee is ironic in its destruction of the sweet picture, and the feminine syllables of the first two feet hurry the reader to the harsh *Mi* (My) which connotation directs back to *talk-,* creating the notion of a series of unshared monologues (My talk). The three iambs (*of Michelangelo*) place light, lyrical metrics in tension against the conversational subject (the great genius of art). The reader becomes aware of the shallowness of their discussion and the pretentiousness of their conversational choice as "iambics trip from short to long." When the rhymed syllable *-lo* occurs, it becomes connotatively "low," contrasting to the spirited gait of the iambs. Countermotion is achieved as the painting of lovely women is flawed by their shallow, gushing non-communication; and the word *Michelangelo* seems to trail away on the connotation of "low" as the women go and distance diminishes sound. The unassertive but sensitive personality of J. Alfred Prufrock is revealed in these two lines as implication through countermotion reveals his complex and introverted nature.

The notion that tone can be established in a couplet through the author's choices in idiom and diction, metrics and rhyme will become apparent if you turn back to the lines on the antiquity of microbes on p. 105. How would the word *them* have affected the second line of that couplet? Why were trochees more effective than iambs would have been?

The structural development of poetry is exceedingly obvious in the couplet because of its brevity, so this is a good place to broach that subject. In writing a poem, a poet may choose any one of several structural forms. Notice the different effects achieved in the following couplets as a result of using various types of structure.

First, a couplet using *expository structure:*

Goodbye

As a leaf in spring flourishes, then dies,
So must each human being relinquish earthly ties.

Samuel Jacob Casselhoff (student)

The expository method asserts a generality and supports it with a specific illustration or example; or, it may reverse the process: a generally profound observation may be supported by intensified statement. You are familiar with exposition from writing themes and essays. In "Good-bye," a specific example leads into a generality. Notice the time patterns incorporated in the metrics. Compare *flourishes-dies*—notice pace in the duration of the first, the finality of the second. The pattern is repeated in *relinquish-ties*. Example is also employed in

English Lesson

Nouns and verbs are quite complex
When the noun is "boy" and the verb is "necks."

Darylyn Neinken (student)

In "Net Worth," an observation is extended:

Net Worth

A human body's a delicate hulk,
Worth more in essence than in bulk.

Donald Baim (student)

The next poem, "The Secret Heart," employs eleven couplets, asserting the statement in couplet 1, expanding it to a bright conclusion in couplet 11. Scene is effectively established in this poem so the reader can share the experience. The pace of metrics and language combines with the poet's sharp awareness of verb usage to create a sense of reader presence. Verbs of being and passive voice verbs are absent. The poem leaps from image to image on strong, active voice verbs and metrics skillfully blended with childish idiom. The resultant emotional tone recalls childhood's fright on awakening suddenly, only to be soothed by the love of a parent. The image of the cupped hands becomes the symbol of memory. Observe the scansion of each line; it will reveal how pace of sense and sound work together:

The Secret Heart

˘ — ˘ — ˘ — ˘ —
Across | the years | he could | recall

˘ — ˘ — ˘ — ˘ —
His fa | ther one | way best | of all.

— ˘ — ˘ — ˘ —
In the still | est hour | of night

˘ — ˘ — ˘ ˘ ˘ —
The boy | awakened | to a light.

— ˘ — ˘ — ˘ —
Half in dreams, | he saw | his sire

˘ ˘ — — — ˘ —
With his great | hands full | of fire.

The man had struck a match to see

∧ If his son slept peace fully.

He held his palms each side the spark

His love had kin dled in the dark.

His two hands were curved apart

In the sem blance of a heart.

He wore, it seemed to his small son.

A bare heart on his hid den one,

A heart that gave out such a glow

No son awake could bear to know.

It showed a look upon a face

Too ten der for a day to trace.

One in stant, it lit all about,

And then the se cret heart went out.

But it shone long enough for one

To know that hands held up the sun.

Robert P. Tristram Coffin

Another common mode of development in poetry is *chronological structure,* which develops a statement with attention to time. One thing happens before another; the first enables the second to occur:

Epitaph Intended for Sir Isaac Newton
Nature and Nature's Laws lay hid in Night,
God said, Let Newton be! and all was Light.
Alexander Pope

In this first example, notice the double allusion. A biblical reference lies in the first line, so time is established: literal night (symbolic ignorance) existed. Nature and science were therein concealed. Irony pervades the second line. Seemingly adding an eighth day to a busy week of creation, God commands still another miracle: the existence of Sir Isaac Newton in order to illuminate the dark night of science. The King James language, assonance, consonance, and alliteration raise clever irony to brilliant satire.

A gravestone yields this next couplet which employs the pun (*done for* means either "killed off" or "copulated with") and light rhyme. Examine your reaction to it: why do you laugh at the humor? Is it humor, or is it a grim reminder that all life is of a brief duration? Is grim irony a component of the couplet? Is there an answer to the infant's query? What do metrics contribute to the effectiveness of the *distich* (a couplet that stands alone as a complete poem)?

On an Infant Eight Months Old

Since I have been so quickly done for,
I wonder what I was begun for.

Future chronology is projected in "Time Out." Enjambment of lines, shifting caesuras, and variant feet create a moment of resignation. The shared communication owes most of its effect to metrics here, as the idiom of the poem is couched in trite phrases. Explain the power of *It* in couplet 3:

Time Out

I have given myself a little while
In which to remember how to smile.

I will not think, or speak, or act,
Or weep. I will wait. And the numbing fact

Will grow familiar and I will face   5
It—sooner or later—with smiling grace.

I will not wonder, since hearts grow tough,
Whether a lifetime is long enough.

Jane Merchant

Scene emerges in the four couplets because the *numbing fact* is not specifically identified. The poem may be applied to any situation involving hurt. While understatement is not employed, a sense of understatement lingers in the lines. Had anguished hyperbole been employed, would scene be as apparent?

In the following epitaph, chronological structure and outrageous rhyme are combined:

On Will Smith
Here lies Will Smith—and what's something rarish,
He was born, bred, and hanged, all in the same parish.

Editorial structure is a third method of development available to the poet. In newspapers, the editorial usually observes a situation, then comments on it. In editorially structured poetry, an epigram may be employed or an ironical contrast included. Motion and countermotion are very evident in the epigram. Pope understood the value of lines sharply juxtaposed against each other:

Engraved on the Collar of a Dog, Which I Gave to His Royal Highness
I am his Highness' dog at Kew;
Pray tell me, Sir, whose dog are you?
Alexander Pope

A silence seems to separate lines 1 and 2 as transition is avoided. The implication growing from omission is shocking—and inescapable.

To understand the observation of the ·next couplet, remember the overt actions and reactions of students around you as they first examine a dreaded test:

You Beat Your Pate
You beat your pate, and fancy wit will come:
Knock as you please, there's no body at home.
Alexander Pope

In the following couplet, the allusion is to a widely held, though untrue, belief that swans never sing until they are ready to die. Then they sing one beautiful song. From this belief came the phrase "swan song," meaning a final great or beautiful accomplishment. The epigram refers to inept poets. Observe the starting point of countermotion in the couplet:

On a Volunteer Singer
Swans sing before they die—'twere no bad thing
Should certain persons die before they sing.
Samuel Taylor Coleridge

The historical allusion in the next couplet is to history's failure to record the birthplace of Homer, the Greek poet to whom are attributed *The Iliad* and *The Odyssey*. The ironic observation recalls the realization that prophets are without honor in their own lands:

On Homer

Seven wealthy towns contend for Homer dead
Through which the living Homer begged for bread.

Anonymous

Another common form of development is *argument structure,* in which a single argument or series of arguments is employed for or against an existing situation. In "Leisure," the couplets are closed. Notice the effective use of repetition in lines 1 and 13 as countermotion balances motion. Personification is worthy of notice also. Scene results from the accretion of the loved and familiar actions:

Leisure

What is this life if, full of care,
We have no time to stand and stare?

No time to stand beneath the boughs
And stare as long as sheep or cows.

No time to see when woods we pass,   *5*
Where squirrels hide their nuts in grass.

No time to see, in broad daylight,
Streams full of stars, like skies at night.

No time to turn at Beauty's glance,
And watch her feet, how they can dance.   *10*

No time to wait till her mouth can
Enrich that smile her eyes began.

>

A poor life this if, full of care,
We have no time to stand and stare.

W. H. Davies

The *pivot* of this poem (that point at which countermotion becomes obvious) occurs at the beginning of the seventh couplet. You will notice it is as if a silence had fallen after couplet 6. Countermotion ends that silence. You will recall the device from Pope's dog-collar couplet. Mark the pivot with >. Argument structure frequently employs repetition.

End rhyme, onomatopoeia, caesuras, contemporary allusions—all combine to make argument in the next poem a delight. Scene is supplied by reader memory—for everyone has at some time been irritated by cereal packaging and advertising. Recollection is a great aid to scene when sentiment or irritation is involved:

I'm Apt To Be Surly Getting Up Early

Although it seems a trifling thing, a matter immaterial
I bear my malice toward the men who manufacture cereal.

I'm looking for a muffled meal, no wham, no pop, no swish,
That settles down inert and shy, relaxing in the dish.

The early hours are bleak and gray; the early news is drastic,   *5*
So why are all the breakfast foods so darned enthusiastic?

I feel in troubled times like these, somebody ought to quiet
The built-in boom and crackle of the current morning diet.

I'm not impressed by prizes, rings, or matching silver service.
I simply want some nourishment that doesn't make me nervous.   *10*

I'm weary of the cowboy and the package he endorses;
No doubt he'd rather eat the stuff than have it scare the horses.

> I plan to burn each noisy box of vitamins and bulks
The happy day I run across a cereal that sulks.

C. S. Jennison

Another common mode of development in poetry is *descriptive structure.* In descriptive structure, details are employed. (You will remember Oscar Wilde's use of this method in "Symphony in Yellow," p. 113.) In the following poems composed of couplets, notice the progression from simple description to a final statement reaching beyond the immediate confines of the poems:

A Summer Morning

I saw dawn creep across the sky,
And all the gulls go flying by.
I saw the sea put on its dress
Of blue midsummer loveliness,

And heard the trees begin to stir   5
Green arms of pine and juniper.
I heard the wind call out and say:
"Get up, my dear, it is today!"
>   *Rachel Field*

The countermotion of "A Summer Morning" begins with that silence marked by the pivot. The technique of haiku is apparent in such poems. As countermotion is change within the time construction of the poem, it may occur after the physical poem has ended. The process of memory extends the poem into unwritten possibilities supplied by the reader. Your memory of such days allows you to continue the poem at your own reflective leisure.

In "Crystal Moment," the structure is descriptive, but any number of other developmental methods are also employed. Isolate them, being able to present your reasons for choosing as you do. Notice the metrics of the poem as imagery becomes symbol and symbol becomes allegory:

Crystal Moment

Once or twice this side of death
Things can make one hold his breath.

From my boyhood I remember
A crystal moment of September.

A wooded island rang with sounds   5
Of church bells in the throats of hounds.

A buck leaped out and took the tide
With jewels flowing past each side.

With his high head like a tree
He swam within a yard of me.   10

I saw the golden drop of light
In his eyes turned dark with fright.

I saw the forest's holiness
On him like a fierce caress.

Fear made him lovely past belief,   15
My heart was trembling like a leaf.

He leaned towards the land and life
With need about him like a knife.

In his wake the hot hounds churned,
They stretched their muzzles out and yearned.   20

They bayed no more, but swam and throbbed,
Hunger drove them till they sobbed.

Pursued, pursuers reached the shore
And vanished. I saw nothing more.

So they passed, a pageant such   25
As only gods could witness much,

Life and death upon one tether
And running beautiful together.

Robert P. Tristram Coffin

One More Line—The Tercet

Tercets seldom stand alone, and, when they do, the *aaa* rhyme scheme seems contrived and artificial in the third line. When two triplets comprise a poem, the problem minimizes itself with the introduction of a second set of rhymes.

Mother Goose combined many poetic devices in

Come, let's to bed,
Says Sleepy-head;
Tarry a while, says Slow.

Put on the pot,
Says Greedy-gut,   5
We'll sup before we go.

The *aabccb* rhyme scheme ties the poem together nicely. Language is apt, and the slant rhymed *pot-gut* is interesting. Slight and didactic though it may be, it is effective. What is the structural device?

Tennyson uses *aaabbb* in "The Eagle." As you read it, listen to the caesuras in lines 3 and 6:

The Eagle

He clasps the crag with crooked hands;
Close to the sun in lonely lands,
Ringed with the azure world, he stands.

The wrinkled sea beneath him crawls;
He watches from his mountain walls,   5
And like a thunderbolt he falls.

Alfred, Lord Tennyson

While descriptive structure is obvious, the major structural approach in "The Eagle" is *contrast* (differences or dissimilar characteristics of two ideas, people, or things). Scene emerges as imagery establishes "nowness"—the bird is created in stanza 1, and a food image is suggested in the larger element of stanza 2. As the wrinkled sea crawls, a worm emerges connotatively. Worm becomes snake for the reader; snake equals sin and the Garden of Eden. The eagle is a noble bird associated with gods. Even its abode in stanza 1 is "of the heavens." Judeo-Christian symbolism attaches itself to such imagery, creating an unconscious awareness in the reader. Extending such imagery to its ultimate possibility, the reader may find parable emerging as Good (Eagle) hurls itself (like the avenging thunderbolt of Zeus) toward Evil (snake and sea as sex images). Redemption of man after the fall becomes implicit in such extensions. Contrasts occur in air, sea, and land (for what does the sea crawl over?) as well as in good and evil. Notice contrasts in language: eagle *clasps,* sea *crawls;* bird *stands,* then *falls.*

The interlocking rhyme scheme of tercets in terza rima (*ababcbcdc,* etc.; see p. 131) is relieved by couplets in each section of Shelley's

Ode to the West Wind

I

O wild West Wind, thou breath of Autumn's being,
Thou, from whose unseen presence the leaves dead
Are driven, like ghosts from an enchanter fleeing,

Yellow, and black, and pale, and hectic red,
Pestilence-stricken multitudes: O thou,   5
Who chariotest to their dark wintry bed

The wingéd seeds, where they lie cold and low,
Each like a corpse within its grave, until
Thine azure sister of the Spring shall blow

Her clarion o'er the dreaming earth, and fill   *10*
(Driving sweet buds like flocks to feed in air)
With living hues and odors plain and hill:

Wild spirit, which art moving everywhere;
Destroyer and preserver; hear, oh, hear!

II

Thou on whose stream, 'mid the steep sky's commotion,   *15*
Loose clouds like earth's decaying leaves are shed,
Shook from the tangled boughs of Heaven and Ocean,

Angels of rain and lightning: there are spread
On the blue surface of thine aëry surge,
Like the bright hair uplifted from the head   *20*

Of some fierce Maenad, even from the dim verge
Of the horizon to the zenith's height,
The locks of the approaching storm. Thou dirge

Of the dying year, to which this closing night
Will be the dome of a vast sepulcher,   *25*
Vaulted with all thy congregated might

Of vapours, from whose solid atmosphere
Black rain, and fire, and hail will burst: oh, hear!

III

Thou who didst waken from his summer dreams
The blue Mediterranean, where he lay,   *30*
Lulled by the coil of his crystalline streams,

Beside a pumice isle in Baiae's bay,
And saw in sleep old palaces and towers
Quivering within the wave's intenser day,

All overgrown with azure moss and flowers   *35*
So sweet, the sense faints picturing them! Thou
For whose path the Atlantic's level powers

Cleave themselves into chasms, while far below
The sea-blooms and the oozy woods which wear
The sapless foliage of the ocean, know   *40*

Thy voice, and suddenly grow gray with fear,
And tremble and despoil themselves: oh, hear!

IV

If I were a dead leaf thou mightest bear;
If I were a swift cloud to fly with thee;
A wave to pant beneath thy power, and share   45

The impulse of thy strength, only less free
Than thou, O uncontrollable! If even
I were as in my boyhood, and could be

The comrade of thy wanderings over Heaven,
As then, when to outstrip thy skyey speed   50
Scarce seemed a vision; I would ne'er have striven

As thus with thee in prayer in my sore need.
Oh, lift me as a wave, a leaf, a cloud!
I fall upon the thorns of life! I bleed!

A heavy weight of hours has chained and bowed   55
One too like thee: tameless, and swift, and proud.

V

Make me thy lyre, even as the forest is:
What if my leaves are falling like its own!
The tumult of thy mighty harmonies

Will take from both a deep, autumnal tone,   60
Sweet though in sadness. Be thou, Spirit fierce,
My spirit! Be thou me, impetuous one!

Drive my dead thoughts over the universe
Like withered leaves to quicken a new birth!
And, by the incantation of this verse,   65

Scatter, as from an unextinguished hearth
Ashes and sparks, my words among mankind!
Be through my lips to unawakened Earth

The trumpet of a prophecy! O Wind,
If Winter comes, can Spring be far behind?   70

Percy Bysshe Shelley

Contrasting structure and *aabccb* end rhyme are used in the following Pindar translation. The two tercets have been successfully fused into a simple sentence, each tercet containing half of the clause:

Lord of Nature

God can wake light
  Out of black night
    To untarnished ray,

And in dark cloud
  Deeply can shroud   *5*
    The pure light of day.
Pindar (tr. Lionel W. Lyde)

The triplet lends itself to complex grammatical structures, as phrases and dependent clauses can be isolated, making great sense as a unit, yet being closely knit to the overall sense through syntax and the unification of stanzas. Marianne Moore's "A Talisman" is, structurally, a simple sentence stating, "A shepherd found a sea-gull." Besides the clause, tercets 1 and 2 contain an adverbial prepositional phrase (line 1) and three participial phrases (lines 2, 3, and 5). Tercets 3 and 4 modify *sea-gull* through an appositive (*scarab*), as well as through prepositional, participial, and infinitive phrases. As the triplets enjamb into one another gracefully and evocatively, the reader reconstructs any number of scenes from the descriptive elements he is offered:

A Talisman

Under a splintered mast   of lapis lazuli,
torn from the ship and cast   a scarab of the sea,
  near her hull,   with wings spread—

a stumbling shepherd found,   curling its coral feet,   *10*
embedded in the ground,   *5*   parting its beak to greet
  a sea-gull   men long dead.
Marianne Moore

In the next poem, "Anthesis," contrasting structure results from a rhymeless tercet preceding a rhymed tercet. Assonance, consonance, and alliteration are all effectively used in the first stanza to create the monotonous mood. Rhyme absence slows the lines to create further dullness. The joyous anapests and slant rhyme of stanza 2 re-create the released joy of children:

Anthesis

The metronome drones against pendulous columns,
Imprisoning bodies whose dreams are unlocking
A fistful of daisies, a kiss of the sun.

With a whoop and a bound and a roll in the clover,
The children, as one, fling their books and discover *5*
The first of July to the last of forever.

Bernice Miller (student)

If *anthesis* is an unfamiliar word to you, did you look it up?

Other poems in triplets worth re-examination are "The House on the Hill" (p. 110) and "Villanelle" (p. 111). The couplet and tercet are combined in "Shooting the Sun" (p. 35).

Compounding—The Quatrain

Since poetry is intended for a reader, a poet must periodically remind himself of that reader. No reader *has* to admire the poet's cleverness or *has* to be impressed with what the poet says. If the poet offers glib generalities, the reader has no reason to read the work. *He* is as capable as the poet at generalizing, at assuming erroneously, at thinking in abstractions unrelated to the concrete. He wants something perceptive and original to be said in the poem or he would not be reading it.

A good poet constantly attempts to *share* experience with his reader, to illuminate his own imperfect perceptions to make them meaningful to himself and others. Poetic device, metrics, tone, atmosphere, scene—in short, the combined techniques you have examined—all must be utilized by the poet as he perceives freshly whatever he wishes to communicate to you, the reader.

In a quatrain of two couplets, in expository structure, utilizing symbols, William Blake accomplishes such communication:

A Cradle Song

Sleep, Sleep, beauty bright,
Dreaming o'er the joys of night.
Sleep, Sleep: in thy sleep
Little sorrows sit and weep.

The *immediate* intention of the poet is the creation of a lullaby which, through musical sound, will soothe a child and induce sleep. Repetition of the suggestion is woven into the poem five times in the word *sleep,* a sixth in the rhyme *weep,* and in the overall euphony of language—a euphony created, in part, by assonance. Scene is created in the lulling music, the gentle psychology of the quatrain, and the anticipated use of the poem. A rhyme scheme of *abab* would be less euphoric, as it would lack the echo which hovers over the poem. A scheme of *abba* would stretch the expectation span of the child, serving to arouse rather than to soothe him. Night fears are minimized by *joys.*

A *second* intention lies in a philosophical statement which is suggested. Night, as a time of rest, minimizes the problems of day—problems which were magnified by growing weariness. Such *sorrows* exhaust themselves as the sleeper rests; so, he will be stronger in the morning. Another possibility: the soothing lullaby ends at the colon in line 3; then comes the poet's *frightening* wisdom, which the child, of course, could never appreciate: that even in sleep there are the sorrows of our dreams. But *little* sorrows, since it is just a child—how beautiful to make them *little!* But the point is that even a child dreams, and even in the almost pristine beauty of this child's sleep are the seeds of the essentially tragic human condition. The little sorrows are personified, and they sit and weep just as the child might do. Finally, if the reader wishes to envision death as a kind of sleep, he is free to do so for whatever comfort the lullaby offers. The idea was a common conceit during Blake's lifetime, and is familiar from Hamlet's "To be or not to be" soliloquy.

Perhaps you can see the subtle differences between "shared ideas" and "stated" attitudes by comparing two quatrains with the same general meaning. In "Maud," Tennyson asserts an emotional attitude. The following quatrain from that poem lacks scene and starts no reaction in the reader, who might state the same thought equally well:

> O that 'twere possible
> After long grief and pain
> To find the arms of my true love
> Round me once again!

An anonymous sixteenth century poet treated the same emotion with more subtlety, allowing a structured comparison and suggested description to frame themselves in expository structure: there is a progression from general to specific, with a symbol leading into a stated desire. Understatement makes acceptable what would, in hyperbole, be merely vulgar. Note: the appeal to the deity is apostrophe. Do not allow contemporary carelessness in such matters to cause you to misread *Christ* as an interjection!

Western Wind

Western wind, when will thou blow,
    The small rain down can rain?
Christ, if my love were in my arms,
    And I in my bed again!

A comparison is drawn between Nature and the nature of man. The first needs the life element of rain (gentle rain rather than torrential, spring rain brought by the western wind, hence *small*), as man needs the vitality of love. Winter (or drought) is the time when rain and love are absent. An exhaustion attends each, but the exhaustion can be relieved by the return of the familiar. It is within expectation that the western wind will end Nature's winter; but there is no forseeable end to the drought of love. Rain will return fecundity to the earth, but the arms and bed of the poet seem destined to remain empty. Psychological associations exist in the fertile imagery of rain received by earth, and in the appeal throughout the poem to all five senses. While a casual reading may not reveal the poet's achievements to the reader, he *experiences* them. His experience results from the poet's employing and combining associative images. The images work together to create a controlled series of associations which become symbolic.

To achieve such symbolism, the poet must first know what he wishes to communicate, and then he must find the techniques which will work to convey that communication to the reader who is interested in the meaning, which comes to him only if the poet's intellect affords the idea a pathway to that goal. The poet may *know* something, but he can make the reader perceive it only if he phrases the idea in language the reader can associatively incorporate into his own existence. The poet's images must accrue into a symbol, and that symbol must communicate itself to the reader.

Sometimes the poet wishes to suggest associated themes without explicit application. When you read a poem constructed to trigger reader associations, you may make an application far removed from the poet's imagery. In other words, it merely sets your responses in motion, in much the same fashion that haiku does. Examine the next poem, noticing that while it is ostensibly concerned with horses, those animals are devices used to trigger memory, rather than concrete symbols:

Horses of the Sea

The horses of the sea
    Rear a foaming crest,
But the horses of the land
    Serve us best.

The horses of the land   *5*
Munch corn and clover,
While the foaming seahorses
Toss and turn over.
Christina Rossetti

That same horse image may be used as a definite symbol, however. In the next poem, metaphor begins in simple statement, assumes proportion through visual imagery, is superimposed against a commonplace image (*sky*) and becomes a complete symbol in the last four lines. Effective ambiguity results from the poet's seemingly careless punctuation and attention to stanza form. The first line of the second quatrain is attached to quatrain 1. The resulting form is almost free verse—which you will study later. Notice the two possible readings of the last five lines and you will understand the poet's deliberate ambiguity—an ambiguity you are free to resolve as you see best by supplying punctuation or simply accepting two ideas interwoven to create a third:

Ride a Wild Horse

Ride a wild horse
with purple wings
striped yellow and black
except his head
which must be red.   *5*

Ride a wild horse
against the sky—
hold tight to his wings

before you die
whatever else you leave undone   *10*
once ride a wild horse
into the sun.
Hannah Kahn

The words *wild horse* are richly evocative as a phrase standing alone. In response, you may recall a picture you have seen of that proud animal, mane flying in the wind, nostrils distended as powerful hoofs carry him across unfenced grasslands. Or you may remember movies or television plays wherein possession of a wild horse became the single aim of a romantically conceived cowboy on western plains against a backdrop of rugged mountains. Or you may relive the storybook nostalgia of a young boy's friendship with a sleek animal too powerful to be tamed by the physical strength of less sensitive adults.

Line 1 of "Ride a Wild Horse" introduces the concrete image, which line 2 immediately abstracts. Wings are added to the animal and the mythological Pegasus emerges, or even just the red trademark of Mobil Oil service stations, or a combination of both. But the image of line 1 has become metaphor in line 2. The mighty wings that can lift the graceful bulk of a horse have freed your imagination from the solid earth of reality. Once realized, *poetic license* (liberties a poet may take as he deviates from standard practices of word usage, grammar, syntax, image construction—any liberty he may employ to achieve a desired effect) frees the poet as it frees the reader, and the metaphor becomes symbol as image is added to image.

Stanza 2 employs ambiguity in the word *against*. Does it mean "into" or "silhouetted against the sky"? The dash after *sky* indicates an explanation will follow. However, *hold tight to his wings* might be read "pinion his wings" or "cling to his wings." As the sentence continues without final punctuation, it enjambs into the third stanza. Does line 1 of stanza 3 complete line 3 of stanza 2? Or does it introduce line 2 of stanza 3, making that line parenthetical? If so, is there a need of the parenthetical repetition of idea? Can you decide *positively* where motion becomes countermotion?

Exercising poetic license, the poet deliberately employs ambiguity to juxtapose and fuse several ideas into a mosaic of possibility, enlarging the symbol into elaborate abstraction. The last two lines extend the ambiguity as *into the sun* may mean "up into the sky toward the sun," or "across the land in the direction of the sun," or, literally, "into the purifying fire of the sun." The reader who cannot abstract himself from land, even in imagination, is caught in the magic of image as thoroughly as the reader who can free himself from sullen earth to soar skyward. Ambiguity allows the poem to work for both. And for the fortunate reader, it can work at the two levels simultaneously.

What, then, does the horse symbolize? Only you can answer that question. And no two readers will answer it the same way. Whatever the horse symbolizes for you, the abstraction can be only vaguely stated in prose, but it can be completely experienced in poetry. For that reason, Pegasus has long been the symbol of poetry—but this does not suggest this poem *means* "Experience at least one poem before you die." It doesn't preclude that as *one* of the many possibilities; but it doesn't insist upon it, either. The wild horse, a concrete image, becomes *equal* to the abstraction; it does not *become* the abstraction, for abstractions cannot become concrete. In Archibald MacLeish's terms, the poem is "equal to:

not true." But that degree, that value, is more important to the reader than the true could ever be if it were reducible to the concrete.

Four lines achieve great statement through illustration in "Outwitted." Contrast in countermotion strengthens the structure as couplet strains against couplet. Lines 1 and 4 employ an effective repetition that binds the poem into a close-knit unit:

Outwitted

He drew a circle that shut me out—
Heretic, rebel, a thing to flout.
But Love and I had wit to win:
We drew a circle that took him in!

Edwin Markham

The expository statement in the next poem is acceptable to the reader because it achieves universality without preachiness:

Death Stands Above Me

Death stands above me, whispering low
I know not what into my ear:
Of his strange language all I know
Is, there is not a word of fear.

Walter Savage Landor

The unpleasant becomes bearable as metaphor pervades the birthday observation of James Russell Lowell:

Sixty-Eighth Birthday

As life runs on, the road grows strange
With faces new, and near the end
The milestones into headstones change,
'Neath every one a friend.

In the following poem by Emily Dickinson (who used no titles) two quatrains are structured to make a personal observation which furnishes the basis for the last two lines:

[My Life Closed Twice]

My life closed twice before its close—
It yet remains to see
If Immortality unveil
A third event to me

> So huge, so hopeless to conceive   5
> As these that twice befell.
> Parting is all we know of heaven,
> And all we need of hell.

Did you read the first quatrain with a period at the end of the fourth line? If so, read it again. Line 4 is enjambed into the first line of the second quatrain. Did hyperbole bother you in the opening line of the poem? Can you explain your reaction?

You should be *very* aware of the final lines in most poems, since the poet usually places the idea of greatest importance there. The *climax* (point of highest interest) should come at the end. If the poet's best lines are at the beginning of the poem, *anticlimax* may occur—once the greatest moment is over, anything else is disappointing. Anticlimax may be used effectively, however, when the poet wishes to reveal unresolved attitudes or a humorous withdrawal.

One of Edna St. Vincent Millay's most quoted poems is a quatrain employing anticlimax with maximum effect. The first two lines para-phrase a cliché which suggests the candle of life (either physical or intel-lectual) grows short as a result of dissipations. But how effectively the cliché is used here! Such a realization of life's fragility is climactic in any life. Countermotion in the quatrain makes light of the realization, how-ever, as the poet deliberately makes light (the pun is very much in-tended) of the two statements in lines 1 and 2:

First Fig

My candle burns at both ends;
  It will not last the night;
But ah, my foes, and oh, my friends—
  It gives a lovely light!

Climax may be *foreshadowed* (suggested in advance in such a way that it is not totally unexpected when it occurs) in opening lines, but it is most effective in final lines. Notice foreshadowing and climax in

I Meant To Do My Work Today

I meant to do my work today,
But a brown bird sang in the apple tree,
And a butterfly flitted across the field,
And all the leaves were calling me.

And the wind went sighing over the land,⠀⠀⠀*5*
Tossing the grasses to and fro,
And a rainbow held out its shining hand—
So what could I do but laugh and go?
⠀⠀⠀⠀⠀⠀⠀⠀⠀⠀⠀⠀*Richard Le Gallienne*

Characterization (the indication of personality and behavioral pattern) may furnish the essential pivot in a poem. In this one, notice the comparisons which are juxtaposed to create the final statement:

The Silent One

You say you cannot live without
My kiss, my love, my touch;
I do not speak and yet, my dear,
I worship you as much.

You count your feelings by the stars,⠀⠀*5*
I count mine by the sun;
So go and die your thousand deaths
While I die but my one.
⠀⠀⠀⠀⠀⠀⠀⠀⠀⠀⠀⠀*Robert Fitch*

A parallel structure creates and contrasts two characters in "The Silent One." The *you* and the *I* of the poem are balanced by the "words" of the first quatrain, the "actions" of the second. While character does, indeed, supply the essential pivot of the poem, explain the pivot of *So* in line 7. Is the tone of the poem the same in the last two lines as it was in the preceding six?

A certain danger lurks in parallel structure if the poet is not very careful. An often quoted poem, the following overworks imagery, and thereby creates a ludicrous parallel:

The Night Has a Thousand Eyes

The night has a thousand eyes,
⠀⠀And the day but one;
Yet the light of the bright world dies
⠀⠀With the dying sun.

The wind has a thousand eyes,⠀⠀⠀⠀⠀*5*
⠀⠀And the heart but one;
Yet the light of a whole life dies
⠀⠀When love is done.
⠀⠀⠀⠀⠀⠀⠀⠀⠀⠀⠀⠀*Francis William Bourdillon*

In "Legacy," see how many techniques you can isolate. Do not read beyond the poem until you are sure you've exhausted it:

Legacy

Late afternoon held all the world
Upon its sunny palm
And offered it, in soft hours wrapped
And tied with bits of lawn.

The seagrapes stretching to the sun   *5*
Cleaved water in the pool;
A sudden shower fermented time
In crystal alcohol.

As neighbors called the children in,
Their laughter died away,   *10*
And I—abruptly orphaned—
Inherited the day.

Thomas E. Sanders

The metrical structure of "Legacy" is: quatrains $a^4b^3c^4b^3$ in iambs. Line 11 is truncated by one syllable to intensify the image. The structural development is descriptive-chronological. The pivot occurs at the beginning of line 11. The rhyme is slant in stanzas 1 and 2, perfect in stanza 3. Personification occurs in *afternoon* as a giver of gifts, *shower* as a brewer, and *seagrapes* as bathers. The scene relies on the reader's memory, all five senses being appealed to directly or indirectly. Movement is achieved through action verbs and participles. Character is developed in what the *I*-narrator chooses to observe. Ordinary elements assume symbolic meaning. Psychological change pivots on *a sudden shower*. Eternal optimism is revealed in the shift from loneliness (*abruptly orphaned*) to self-containment (*inherited the day*). The ambivalence in the last two lines grows from uncertainty; is it self-containment or rationalization? This ambivalence is intensified from lines 5 and 6 where the reflection of seagrapes creates two plants—the actual and the mirrored. The title suggests that which is a gift but receivable only after loss—a compensation. The poet is an adult; childhood is lost, but the ability to evaluate experience is the compensation. Is it enough to balance loss? Can an adult be orphaned by the loss of children? The climax is foreshadowed by the title, and is reached in the last two lines. There are caesuras in line 3: *it-in*; line 5: *seagrapes-stretching*; and line 11: *I-abruptly*. The précis of the poem is: Loss may be compensated for—but imperfectly.

If you observed more devices at work in this poem than are mentioned here, you can now see how a poet may be unaware of his own work!

Suggested Activity. Read *The Rubáiyát of Omar Khayyám,* translated by Edward FitzGerald. It is available in any number of editions in all libraries. As FitzGerald made several translations of the work, compare a few stanzas you like in the various translations. Decide why you prefer one translation to another.

3 + 2 = 5: The Quintain

You have already worked with one form of the five line stanza, Adelaide Crapsey's cinquain. And you are probably already all too familiar with the quintain dear to many confirmed "poetry-haters," the *limerick.* When glasses are lifted and spirits soar, this ubiquitous form comes tripping into the conversation on its tipsy anapests and settles down in the mixed company with unblushing ease. The language of the most often quoted limericks forbids their inclusion here, but a few of the "early evening" variety will illustrate the form.

As it is a popular form, variant feet abound in the limerick, but a typical pattern is usually observed: five anapestic lines $a^3a^3b^2b^2a^3$. Just where the limerick originated—or when—is speculative at best. The earliest recorded examples appear in Loane's *History of Sixteen Wonderful Old Women,* published in 1821. They later became widely popular with the publication of Edward Lear's *Book of Nonsense* in 1846. At that time, lines 1 and 5 repeated the *a* rhyme word:

> There was an old Man of the Dee,
> Who was sadly annoyed by a Flea;
>> When he said, "I will scratch it!"
>> They gave him a hatchet
> Which grieved that Old Man of the Dee.
>
> *Edward Lear*

Utilizing all devices of rhyme, outrageous puns, and frequent allusion, the limerick is, too often, uncomfortably like senryu (see pp. 70-71). Even religion becomes the target at times:

> ### *Faith Healer*
> There was a faith-healer in Deal
> Who said, "Although pain isn't real,
>> If I sit on a pin
>> And it punctures my skin,
> I dislike what I fancy I feel."
>
> *Anonymous*

Nor is science spared:

Relativity

There was a young lady named Bright,
Who travelled much faster than light,
She started one day
In a relative way,
And returned on the previous night.

Anonymous

Nor poets:

An Old Looney of Rhyme

There was an old Looney of Rhyme
Whose candor was simply sublime:
When they asked, "Are you there?"
He said, "Yes, but take care,
For I'm never 'all there' at a time!"

Anonymous

Nor business:

Real Estate

There was a young lady of Wantage
Of whom the Town Clerk took advantage.
Said the County Surveyor,
"Of course you must pay her;
You've altered the line of her frontage."

Anonymous

Nor morals:

A Young Lady of Kent

There was a young lady of Kent,
Who said that she knew what it meant
When men asked her to dine,
And served cocktails and wine;
She knew, oh she knew!—but she went!

Anonymous

Nor law:

An Old Party of Lyme

There was an old party of Lyme,
Who lived with three wives at one time.
When asked, "Why the third?"
He replied, "One's absurd,
And bigamy, sir, is a crime!"

Anonymous

Nor even the limerick itself:

A Limerick on Limericks

A limerick gets laughs anatomical
Into space that is quite economical.
But the good ones I've seen
So seldom are clean,
And the clean ones so seldom are comical.

Anonymous

In short, no area of human foible is spared. Nor are all limericks anonymous. Some of the best poets have been delighted by the limerick as a "natural" for the pun—and few poets can resist a play on words:

Benjamin

There was a brave girl of Connecticut
Who flagged the express with her petticut,
Which critics defined
As presence of mind,
But deplorable absence of ecticut.

Ogden Nash

Limberick

It's time to make love. Douse the glim.
The fireflies twinkle and dim.
The stars lean together
Like birds of a feather,
And the loin lies down with the limb.

Conrad Aiken

More respectable quintains are equally numerous, both as individual poems and as stanzas in longer works. Capping a tercet with a couplet, Emily Dickinson wrote

[To Make a Prairie]

To make a prairie it takes a clover and one bee,
One clover, and a bee,
And revery.
The revery alone will do,
If bees are few.

Deceptively simple, this quintain begins with an alexandrine and reduces syllable count in succeeding lines, establishing the motion of the poem. Revery itself (the daydream) follows such a pattern. Countermotion in line 4 lengthens syllable count to recall the dreamer briefly, as day-dreams do, and allows refinement of the dream. Can you justify Dickinson's changing "*a* clover and *one* bee" (line 1) to "*one* clover, and *a* bee" (line 2)?

The brevity of quintain stanzas, especially when short line lengths are used, creates a thoughtful, graceful form. For this reason, poets generally avoid a strict observance of line length throughout quintain stanzas, preferring to shorten or lengthen alternating lines. Edmund Waller's "Go, Lovely Rose"—an example from the *carpe diem* school of poetry—is composed of such stanzas ($a^2b^4a^2b^4b^4$). The symbol and its message imprint themselves doubly on the reader's mind, and he is unsure of the reason until he reads short lines as couplets, free of the *b* rhymed lines. Then he sees a précis emerge:

Go, Lovely Rose!

Go, lovely rose!
Tell her, that wastes her time and me,
That now she knows,
When I resemble her to thee,
How sweet and fair she seems to be.   5

Tell her that's young
And shuns to have her graces spied,
That hadst thou sprung
In deserts, where no men abide,
Thou must have uncommended died.   10

Small is the worth
Of beauty from the light retired;
Bid her come forth,
Suffer herself to be desired,
And not blush so to be admired.   15

Then die! that she
The common fate of all things rare
May read in thee:
How small a part of time they share
That are so wondrous sweet and fair!   20

Edmund Waller

This same tour de force may be observed in George Herbert's "The Gifts of God," with its $a^3b^5a^5b^5a^3$ stanzas. You will notice that only the trimeter lines carry the précis:

The Gifts of God

When God at first made Man,
Having a glass of blessings standing by;
Let us (said He) pour on him all we can:
Let the world's riches, which dispersèd lie,
    Contract into a span.   *5*

    So strength first made a way;
Then beauty flowed, then wisdom, honour, pleasure:
When almost all was out, God made a stay,
Perceiving that alone, of all His treasure,
    Rest in the bottom lay.   *10*

    For if I should (said He)
Bestow this jewel also on my creature,
He would adore my gifts instead of me,
And rest in Nature, not the God of Nature:
    So both should losers be.   *15*

    Yet let him keep the rest;
But keep them with repining restlessness:
Let him be rich and weary, that at least,
If goodness lead him not, yet weariness
    May toss him to my breast.   *20*

                             George Herbert

Percy Bysshe Shelley found the quintain adaptable to the *ode*—a dignified, highly intellectual lyric designed to reveal intense emotion. The imaginative quality of the form can best be seen if you scan the lines of "To a Skylark," paying particular attention to the varied metrics and the alexandrine concluding each stanza. Probably no poem in the language appeals to all five senses as this one does:

To a Skylark

Hail to thee, blithe Spirit!
Bird thou never wert,
That from heaven, or near it,
Pourest thy full heart
In profuse strains of unpremeditated art.   *5*

Higher still and higher
   From the earth thou springest
Like a cloud of fire;
   The blue deep thou wingest,
And singing still dost soar, and soaring ever singest.   *10*

In the golden lightning
   Of the sunken sun,
O'er which clouds are bright'ning,
   Thou dost float and run;
Like an unbodied joy whose race is just begun.   *15*

The pale purple even
   Melts around thy flight;
Like a star of Heaven
   In the broad daylight
Thou art unseen, but yet I hear thy shrill delight,   *20*

Keen as are the arrows
   Of that silver sphere,
Whose intense lamp narrows
   In the white dawn clear
Until we hardly see—we feel that it is there.   *25*

All the earth and air
   With thy voice is loud,
As, when night is bare,
   From one lonely cloud
The moon rains out her beams, and Heaven is overflowed.   *30*

What thou art we know not;
   What is most like thee?
From rainbow clouds there flow not
   Drops so bright to see
As from thy presence showers a rain of melody.   *35*

Like a Poet hidden
   In the light of thought,
Singing hymns unbidden,
   Till the world is wrought
To sympathy with hopes and fears it heeded not: *40*

Like a high-born maiden
   In a palace-tower,
  Soothing her love-laden
   Soul in secret hour
With music sweet as love, which overflows her bower: 45

Like a glow-worm golden
   In a dell of dew,
  Scattering unbeholden
   Its aërial hue
Among the flowers and grass, which screen it from the view: 50

Like a rose embowered
   In its own green leaves,
  By warm winds deflowered,
   Till the scent it gives
Makes faint with too much sweet these heavy-wingéd thieves. 55

Sound of vernal showers
   On the twinkling grass,
  Rain-awaken'd flowers,
   All that ever was
Joyous, and clear, and fresh, thy music doth surpass.   60

Teach us, Sprite or Bird,
   What sweet thoughts are thine:
  I have never heard
   Praise of love or wine
That panted forth a flood of rapture so divine.   65

Chorus hymeneal,
   Or triumphal chant,
  Matched with thine would be all
   But an empty vaunt,
A thing wherein we feel there is some hidden want.   70

What objects are the fountains
   Of thy happy strain?
  What fields, or waves, or mountains?
   What shapes of sky or plain?
What love of thine own kind? what ignorance of pain?   75

With thy clear keen joyance
   Languor cannot be:
Shadow of annoyance
   Never came near thee:
Thou lovest—but ne'er knew love's sad satiety.   *80*

Waking or asleep
   Thou of death must deem
Things more true and deep
   Than we mortals dream,
Or how could thy notes flow in such a crystal stream?   *85*

We look before and after,
   And pine for what is not:
Our sincerest laughter
   With some pain is fraught;
Our sweetest songs are those that tell of saddest thought.   *90*

Yet if we could scorn
   Hate, and pride, and fear;
If we were things born
   Not to shed a tear,
I know not how thy joy we ever should come near.   *95*

Better than all measures
   Of delightful sound,
Better than all treasures
   That in books are found,
Thy skill to poet were, thou scorner of the ground!   *100*

Teach me half the gladness
   That thy brain must know,
Such harmonious madness
   From my lips would flow
The world should listen then—as I am listening now.   *105*

                                 Percy Bysshe Shelley

The English skylark is an unobtrusive, little, brown bird of no visual distinction. Leaving the ground, he flies straight upward in a spiraling fashion, singing his glorious song. The *fire* simile of stanza 2 creates a multi-level sensory impression of that upward flight. Stanza 3 almost creates a concrete image from the abstraction *joy* as the reader "sees" the emotion rather than the bird. In the seventh stanza, sound assumes physical form to galvanize the reader's sense of touch, just as gentle spring rain does. The senses are deceived, one doing the work of another, as language, imagery, and metrics conspire to create new experience out of old memories.

In Greece, where it originated, the ode was a choral interlude in a play. Divided into three parts, it was chanted to music as the chorus moved up one side of the stage during the strophe (first statement), down the other during the antistrophe (answer to the statement), and finally stood still during the epode (a summary or application). You can see a similar design in Shelley's poem. Stanzas 1-6 constitute the strophe in which the bird is identified as symbol. Stanzas 7-12 create the antistrophe in which the symbol is diffused through nature. The remainder of the poem is the epode, generally didactic in its application, becoming very personal in application in the final stanza. To see the progression from general to specific application, compare "Teach *us*" in stanza 13 with "Teach *me*" in stanza 21.

Suggested Assignment. Edgar Allan Poe employed the quintain in "To Helen," but he took many liberties with it. Examine the poem carefully and write a three-paragraph defense of his liberties:

To Helen

Helen, thy beauty is to me
    Like those Nicean barks of yore,
That gently, o'er a perfumed sea,
    The weary, wayworn wanderer bore
    To his own native shore.   5

On desperate seas long wont to roam,
    Thy hyacinth hair, thy classic face,
Thy Naiad airs, have brought me home
    To the glory that was Greece
    And the grandeur that was Rome.   10

Lo! in yon brilliant window-niche
    How statue-like I see thee stand,
    The agate lamp within thy hand!
Ah, Psyche, from the regions which
    Are Holy Land!   15

Edgar Allan Poe

Continued Growth—The Sestet

Understanding form in poetry becomes simpler as you build from what you have learned. You are now ready to consider three new terms: unity, coherence, and transition.

Unity is an essential relatedness of the parts of a poem. In the couplet, line 2 is an extension of line 1, while line 1 leads into line 2. The tercet extends the demands of unity, as does the quatrain. Beyond the quatrain, unity becomes a greater problem since the last two lines of a quintain or a sestet may be a couplet, and that couplet must be closely related to the first three or four lines to create a sense of "wholeness." Unity is destroyed when grammatical or syntactical errors occur. It is hampered by vague language. It fails to come into existence if cloudy thinking lies in the inception of the poem.

Coherence is the cement holding the parts of a poem together to create unity. Mixed metaphors, for instance, lack coherence, since the two elements involved cannot be cemented together. You saw this in "The Night Has a Thousand Eyes" (p. 169). Logic is the basic ingredient of coherence.

Effective *transition* in a poem helps create coherence, as it marks the passing from one point to another. It may be achieved by a word, a phrase, a suggested association, a repetition, and so forth. It is the poet's effective guiding of the reader's mind so he is not disturbed by omission. Prose allows such obvious transitions as "However . . . , First . . . , Second . . . , Next we will. . . ." Poetry, however, is too compressed, too subtle for the obvious. It ordinarily relies on the logic of image growing out of image to create transition. If logic is absent between parts, coherence is lost. An incoherent poem is like an incoherent person— intelligent people prefer to avoid both of them. The reader must be aware of the presence of these elements if he is to achieve full understanding.

Observe unity and coherence at work in

Courage

Courage is armour
A blind man wears;
The calloused scar
Of outlived despairs:
Courage is Fear
That has said its prayers.   5

Karle Wilson Baker

The *ababcb* rhyme scheme establishes some unity; metrics reinforce it. Coherence is achieved in the extension of connotative meanings in *armour*. *Definition structure* is employed in this couplet. Stated as a metaphor, the definition begins with an easily understood abstraction. As armour is a protective enclosure, a blind man is courageous as he ventures abroad. The next two lines extend the armour image, and the shift is made logically in the understandable transition indicated by the comparison. A scar is a protective barrier built naturally by the body to protect a spot vulnerable from prior injury. A callous is layers of protective scar tissue; so despairs leave scars that insulate themselves further with the protective armour of callous. This acceptable abstraction leads logically into the final two lines which indicate man's fear is like a blind man who ventures into the unknown. As the blind man's only armour is courage, man's fear is armoured by prayer, which shields him. A man so shielded is said to be courageous. The conclusion is both credible and ironic. The progression by which it is reached relies on the logic of stated elements to make new elements believable. Note finally how, if we reduce the sestet to a metrically sound quatrain, we destroy the transition beween the ideas:

> Courage is armour
> A blind man wears;
> Courage is Fear
> That has said its prayers.

Despair serves as a transition in the motion of the poem to create logic when countermotion occurs. The unity gained creates coherence.

Argumentative people frequently become incoherent as they fail to make effective transitions. What might otherwise be logical discussion suffers loss of unity, and they lose the argument. Similarly, the "argument" of an effective poem must contain effective transitions.

The immediately apparent transitional device in this next sestet is word repetition. The "within-without" contrast and the comparison of "house-body" further establish unity and coherence:

All Hushed and Still

> All hushed and still within the house;
>   Without, all wind and driving rain;
> But something whispers to my mind,
> Wrought up in rain and wailing wind:
> Never again? Why not again? Never again!   5
>   Memory has power as well as wind!

Emily Brontë

The transitions in Wordsworth's "Daffodils" are completely obvious and exceedingly effective. The many devices employed in the poem work to create coherence that reaches full unity in combination with the basic premise. Each sestet is coherent, and transitions unify the stanzas into a total communication:

Daffodils

I wandered lonely as a cloud
That floats on high o'er vales and hills,
When all at once I saw a crowd,
A host, of golden daffodils;
Beside the lake, beneath the trees,   5
Fluttering and dancing in the breeze.

Continuous as the stars that shine
And twinkle on the Milky Way,
They stretched in never-ending line
Along the margin of a bay: 10
Ten thousand saw I at a glance,
Tossing their heads in sprightly dance.

The waves beside them danced; but they
Out-did the sparkling waves in glee:
A poet could not but be gay,   15
In such a jocund company:
I gazed—and gazed—but little thought
What wealth the show to me had brought:

For oft, when on my couch I lie
In vacant or in pensive mood,   20
They flash upon that inward eye
Which is the bliss of solitude;
And then my heart with pleasure fills,
And dances with the daffodils.

William Wordsworth

The death of a toad mangled by a power mower may seem poor material for a poem; but, in three coherent sestets, the poet achieves tight unity to evoke memory through the toad image, as the haiku author did with the caterpillar (p. 58):

The Death of a Toad

A toad the power mower caught,
Chewed and clipped of a leg, with a hobbling hop has got
  To the garden verge, and sanctuaried him
  Under the cineraria leaves, in the shade
    Of the ashen heartshaped leaves, in a dim,   *5*
      Low, and a final glade.

  The rare original heartsblood goes,
Spends on the earthen hide, in the folds and wizenings, flows
  In the gutters of the banked and staring eyes. He lies
  As still as if he would return to stone,   *10*
    And soundlessly attending, dies
      Toward some deep monotone.

  Toward misted and ebullient seas
And cooling shores, toward lost Amphibia's emperies.
  Day dwindles, drowning, and at length is gone   *15*
  In the wide and antique eyes, which still appear
    To watch, across the castrate lawn,
      The haggard daylight steer.

Richard Wilbur

The subtlety of logic works disturbingly in "The Death of a Toad." Combining chance incident with penetrating observation, conscious memory, and that unconscious awareness which psychiatrists call "racial memory" or "the collective unconscious," Wilbur reminds the reader of his link with a dimly remembered, submerged, and primitive past. A toad may be found anywhere—unexpectedly—in nature. The power mower is an unnatural creation of man in conflict with his natural habitat. Controlling the machine, he loses a part of his identity with nature, for he violates its laws by attempting to control them. Caught between his mechanical present and his amphibious past (for did he not come from the sea at the dawn of life?), he has removed himself from both to wander in the misty mid-region of his life until past and present collide in such chance encounters as this. The inoffensive toad, mangled by the machine, escapes it to die in the sanctuary of a place protected from mechanical invasion—and the reader, observing a token of his own past die with the toad, sees something of his own spiritual suicide. Metaphorically the toad becomes man, a symbolism transcending allegory, for there is an actual, physical bond beyond mere similarity—the bond of shared origins.

Such a wealth of implication and application results from a unity that includes the poet, the poem, and the reader. Wilbur "sees" the incident and becomes concerned with it. A more casual observer (you or I) might be disturbed momentarily by the occurrence, but, deliberately refusing to explore its complexities, would probably shrug it off and forget it as soon as possible. Wilbur forces an examination by extracting meaning from the very heart of the incident and, analogously, from existence itself. With the poet's eye, he sees beyond the immediate physical moment, perceives a metaphysical relationship, and communicates that new vision to the reader.

The observed incident, casually reported, would be: The power mower caught a toad and cut off a leg; the toad hopped under some plants and died. But this is no casual report. It is an experience in life, and, simultaneously, it is a universal sacrament as death becomes shared experience. The opening couplet serves to establish the scene, but it subtly does more. The power mower "caught" the toad. Wherein is man's involvement? It is as if the machine functions independently of man, and the mechanical beast is as cruel as it is powerful, for the powerless toad is "chewed and clipped of a leg." *Catharsis* (a purging of the emotions through pity and fear) begins to work in the reader at this point. An omnipresent fear of power mowers and the realization of human responsibility in this act create sympathy for the toad in his clumsy, mangled locomotion. In other words, man, too, can become prey to the mower; so the reader's identification with the toad and the toad's fate begins in pity and extends through fear.

Language becomes almost mystical after the *cacophony* (harsh, discordant sounds combined with unpleasant words, deliberately designed to irritate, annoy, or make the reader uncomfortable) of "with a hobbling hop has got," an image awkward and painful after the metallic, mechanical alliteration of "caught, chewed and clipped." Death is foreshadowed in *verge* as the reader supplies denotative possibilities—for example, "on the verge." Using *sanctuary* as a verb, Wilbur emphasizes the innocence of the toad, also endowing it with a "natural" knowledge of protection and further enlisting reader identity and sympathy. Unstated is an analogous question: "Where, when *I* am on the verge, will *I* find sanctuary from the machine?" The cineraria leaves, heartshaped with ash-colored down, evoke a series of images to cluster around *sanctuaried*. The sacred heart, Ash Wednesday, death of the innocent—all attach themselves to the primitive toad as *sh* consonance creates a silence broken only by the keening wail of long *a*'s ending in the shadowy "Low, and a final glade." Gentle irony lingers in this line as "the valley of the shadow of death" seems to emerge from the sound combinations.

The second sestet creates new tensions by revealing the quiet death of the toad in gigantic proportions—as if seen under a microscope or on a large screen. All background elements are now removed; only the toad occupies the reader's attention. However, there is a recollection of the mystical quality of the first stanza—*heartsblood* recalls *heartshaped,* and the sacred heart image is refined beyond man's religions. Time and memory merge as "earthen hide" with its "folds and wizenings" magnifies to primitive Earth in its birth throes when compression and expansion created the hills and valleys of the wrinkled planet. Time begins and fires die with language working at many levels in "gutters of the banked and staring eyes." As literal eyes—the rounded *(banked)* orbs—are rimmed with lids, the gutters fill with blood. Mirrors of life-force within the body, the eyes are *banked* (covered with ashes to preserve the flame of life—recalling the ashen heartshaped cineraria leaves around the toad) against the long night of death. Vain hope pervades "as if he would return to stone"— the ancient belief was that toads possessed the ability to suspend animation and live through many centuries until the mud in which they had encased themselves turned to stone; the stone, broken, released them to life as water awakened them. But this toad will undergo no such suspension. "Soundlessly attending" (waiting), he dies "toward some deep monotone" (an uninterrupted repetition suggesting death, disintegration, and renewal in the eternal pattern of time). Amphibious *s, l, t,* consonance of the sestet submerges in the closing words to evoke an image of dark and silent deeps of timeless seas.

The final sestet narrows focus still further until even the body of the toad is outside the reader's vision. Only the eyes, now large and mind-filling, remain. Life force flows back in time toward ancient seas in boiling, bubbling *(ebullient)* torment, and to land that calls sea creatures to its "cooling shores," shores they once claimed as their domain ("Amphibia's emperies") until, in the scale of evolution, they passed it on to man. Now, in those large and ancient eyes, the life-force *(light)* dims and dies away on *d* alliteration. But still they seem to see time in its constant pattern, though wasted and worn in the evening shadows of this day of death, as it follows *(steers)* its chosen pattern across the mutilated *(castrate)* lawn. The machine has maimed not only the creatures of nature (toad and man), but nature itself (the grass).

Opening each stanza with a couplet, Wilbur presents the basic premise of the poem—the three couplets can be read as a coherent statement. The remaining lines of each sestet expand suggestion, bringing it to a near close, in haiku fashion, only to extend it in the next stanza. Metrics also create ambivalences for man caught between his present and his past. Each stanza opens with a tetrameter line, progresses through varying but greater lengths, and dies away in trimeter—as a heart might beat. Iambs combine with anapests to create a lilting measure, but shifting caesuras slow the forward motion and the final sestet expires in the final death image on 'four spondees, one of which ends the poem. In eighteen lines, motion has created awareness in man that he has violated his distant heritage. Countermotion, beginning after the final line, demands he judge himself for this act.

New Additions—The Octave

To add rule to rule may seem, at times, a bloodless approach to the study of poetry; yet it is necessary. Certainly, rules are not designed to confine or stifle pleasure. You probably can see already how they help you organize your thinking, fix it in intent, and allow you to share the poet's communication. Spontaneity should, of course, be involved in your reading of a poem. But spontaneity is not merely the sudden receiving of emotional response. In fact, what seems most spontaneous *in the poem* has probably been revised and refined until it mimics spontaneity. If spontaneity in *reading* poetry is to occur, it too must come as a result of awareness of techniques, without which the reader receives a labored, imperfect communication as a result of his partial understanding.

The octave is particularly well suited to the expression of overflowing emotion. It is long enough to accommodate a brief experience, short enough to compress that experience into a moment. In the time it takes the reader to read the poem, the experience happens. Spontaneity may then envelop the idea.

In "Jenny Kissed Me," Leigh Hunt utilizes masculine and feminine rhyme, mixed metrical feet, apostrophe, repetition, internal rhyme, and hyperbole. You will notice this octave is, in actuality, two quatrains written as a single stanza. While the poet was "expressing his feelings," they are feelings you have known too. The poem becomes your experience as a result of your spontaneity in making the moment your own:

Jenny Kissed Me

Jenny kissed me when we met,
    Jumping from the chair she sat in;
Time, you thief, who love to get
    Sweets into your list, put that in:
Say I'm weary, say I'm sad,   5
    Say that health and wealth have missed me,
Say I'm growing old, but add,
    Jenny kissed me.

Leigh Hunt

When the poet finds a point of mutuality with you, the expression of both selves may be delightful indeed. Have you not known the emotion of the following sestet?

A Legacy

You told me, Maro, whilst you live
You'd not a single penny give,
But that, whene'er you chanct to die,
You'd leave a handsome legacy:
You must be mad beyond redress,   5
If my next wish you cannot guess!

Martial (tr. *Samuel Johnson*)

Emily Brontë's life was scarcely happy. You have probably read her brooding novel, *Wuthering Heights.* Sharing a brief moment with the reader, she found joy in the symbols of death, and the delight therein, though grim, seems spontaneous. This next octave by Brontë is composed of four couplets, but the first and last are rhymed *aa.* Unity is strengthened in the repetition of *day.* Where does the pivot occur in this poem? Grammatically, what does the participle in line 4 modify?

Fall, Leaves, Fall

Fall, leaves, fall: die, flowers, away;
Lengthen night and shorten day!
Every leaf speaks bliss to me,
Fluttering from the autumn tree.
I shall smile when wreaths of snow   5
Blossom where the rose should grow;
I shall sing when night's decay
Ushers in a drearier day.

Emily Brontë

Octaves lend themselves to poems of more than one stanza because they retain a sense of spontaneity. Unity reinforces itself in eight lines as the stanza can be seemingly complete; the extension of the poem, however, seems natural rather than anticlimactic. Notice in this next poem that each octave might stand alone; together, however, they borrow unity from each other. Paradox in lines 5-8 becomes understandable in the word *creation* in line 15:

Aubade

O, Lady, awake! The azure moon
   Is rippling in the verdant skies,
The owl is warbling his soft tune,
   Awaiting but thy snowy eyes.
The joys of future years are past,   *5*
   Tomorrow's hopes are fled away;
Still let us love and even at last
   We shall be happy yesterday.

The early beam of rosy night
   Drives off the ebon moon afar,   *10*
Whilst through the murmur of the light
   The huntsman winds his mad guitar.
Then, Lady, wake! My brigantine
   Pants, neighs, and prances to be free;
Tell the creation I am thine,   *15*
   To some rich desert fly with me.

Anonymous (Nineteenth century)

Observe the different structure of the two octaves in the next poem. How does the second octave extend the rich imagery of the first? How do they differ in the use of poetic devices? Do the differences destroy or enforce unity? What elements serve to create coherence? Notice also that stanza 1 is in the indicative mood, stanza 2 in the imperative. Is this deliberate? How does it contribute to spontaneity?

A Birthday

My heart is like a singing bird
   Whose nest is in a watered shoot;
My heart is like an apple-tree
   Whose boughs are bent with thickset fruit;
My heart is like a rainbow shell   *5*
   That paddles in a halcyon sea;
My heart is gladder than all these
   Because my love is come to me.

Raise me a dais of silk and down;
   Hang it with vair and purple dyes;   *10*
Carve it in doves and pomegranates,
   And peacocks with a hundred eyes;

Work it in gold and silver grapes,
　　In leaves and silver fleurs-de-lys;
Because the birthday of my life　　　　　*15*
　　Is come, my love is come to me.

Christina G. Rossetti

An intensely personal tone runs through the next poem, "The Vaga-
bond," but the *me* of it might be anyone. In the spontaneous capturing of
a mood, Stevenson merely gives the reader a statement that becomes his
own. Scan the poem. How does the use of *me* as a repetitious rhyme add
unity to the poem? Why is the second stanza repeated as the fourth with
seek changed to *ask?* What is the structure?

The Vagabond

Give to me the life I love,
　　Let the lave go by me,
Give the jolly heaven above
　　And the byway nigh me.
Bed in the bush with stars to see,　　*5*
　　Bread I dip in the river—
There's the life for a man like me,
　　There's the life forever.

Let the blow fall soon or late,
　　Let what will be o'er me;　　　*10*
Give the face of earth around,
　　And the road before me.
Wealth I seek not, hope nor love,
　　Nor a friend to know me;
All I seek, the heaven above　　　*15*
　　And the road below me.

Or let autumn fall on me
　　Where afield I linger,
Silencing the bird on tree
　　Biting the blue finger.　　　　*20*
White as meal the frost field—
　　Warm the fireside haven—
Not to autumn will I yield,
　　Not to winter even!

Let the blow fall soon or late,   *25*
   Let what will be o'er me;
Give the face of earth around,
   And the road before me.
Wealth I ask not, hope nor love,
   Nor a friend to know me;   *30*
All I ask, the heaven above,
   And the road below me.

                           Robert Louis Stevenson

The cliché or trite phrase is probably one of your problems when you write an essay. Poets too see it as a very real danger in writing poetry of spontaneous self-expression. Losing sight of their readers' needs, they may hasten into the bad kind of shorthand thinking such phrases suggest. However, a clever poet can employ them deliberately. Notice their *effective* use in

Everything in Its Place

The skeleton is hiding in the closet as it should,
The needle's in the haystack and the trees are in the wood,
The fly is in the ointment and the froth is on the beer,
The bee is in the bonnet and the flea is in the ear.
The meat is in the cocoanut, the cat is in the bag,   *5*
The dog is in the manger and the goat is on the crag,
The worm is in the apple and the clam is on the shore,
The birds are in the bushes and the wolf is at the door.

                           Arthur Guiterman

Suggested Activity. Attempt to write a poem, however short, from what you have thus far learned. You will soon find yourself falling into the traps of generality and trite phraseology; but actually writing a poem will allow you to see and cope with those problems even more effectively than is the case with prose. If you cannot seem to avoid clichés, attempt an octave in light verse deliberately beginning or ending in a cliché. Such horrors as "Crime does not pay," "Love conquers all," or "Money won't buy happiness" may serve as starters. You might wish to re-examine Ogden Nash's "The Terrible People" (p. 129). Try shortened lines, feminine and triple and outrageous rhyme also.

Suggested Assignments. 1. In a three-paragraph paper, examine the following poem, revealing your knowledge of poetry to this point:

Child and Maiden

Ah, Chloris! that I now could sit
   As unconcern'd as when
Your infant beauty could beget
   No pleasure, nor no pain!
When I the dawn used to admire,   *5*
   And praised the coming day,
I little thought the growing fire
   Must take my rest away.

Your charms in harmless childhood lay
   Like metals in the mine;   *10*
Age from no face took more away
   Than youth conceal'd in thine.
But as your charms insensibly
   To their perfection prest,
Fond love as unperceived did fly,   *15*
   And in my bosom rest.

My passion with your beauty grew,
   And Cupid at my heart,
Still as his mother favour'd you,
   Threw a new flaming dart: *20*
Each gloried in their wanton part;
   To make a lover, he
Employ'd the utmost of his art—
   To make a beauty, she.

                Sir Charles Sedley

Remember paradox and the pun, unity and coherence, spontaneity and ambiguity. Do not overlook the obvious in seeking out the subtle; however, be *aware* of the subtle!

2. Any of the following poems might be treated as your instructor sees fit:

Cromek

A petty sneaking knave I knew—
O Mr. Cromek, how do ye do?
           William Blake

from *Hamlet*

My words fly up, my thoughts remain below:
Words without thoughts never to heaven go.
     William Shakespeare (Act III, sc. iii)

Upon the Body of Our Blessed Lord, Naked and Bloody

They have left thee naked, Lord; O that they had!
This garment too I would they had denied.

Thee with thyself they have too richly clad,
Opening the purple wardrobe in thy side.

O never could there be garment too good   5
For thee to wear, but this, of thine own blood.

Richard Crashaw

A Ballad of Trees and the Master

Into the woods my Master went,
Clean forspent, forspent.
Into the woods my Master came,
Forspent with love and shame.
But the olives they were not blind to Him,   5
The little gray leaves were kind to Him:
The thorn-tree had a mind to Him
When into the woods He came.

Out of the woods my Master went,
And He was well content.   10
Out of the woods my Master came,
Content with death and shame.
When Death and Shame would woo Him last,
From under the trees they drew Him last:
'Twas on a tree they slew Him—last   15
When out of the woods He came.

Sidney Lanier

Song

When I am dead, my dearest,
   Sing no sad songs for me;
Plant no roses at my head,
   Nor shady cypress tree:
Be the green grass above me   5
   With showers and dewdrops wet;
And if thou wilt, remember,
   And if thou wilt, forget.

I shall not see the shadows,
   I shall not feel the rain;   *10*
I shall not hear the nightingale
   Sing on as if in pain:
And dreaming through the twilight
   That doth not rise nor set,
Haply I may remember,   *15*
   And haply may forget.

                    Christina Rossetti

From a Churchyard in Wales

This spot is the sweetest I've seen in my life,
For it raises my flowers and covers my wife.

Upon Julia's Clothes

Whenas in silks my Julia goes,
Then, then, methinks, how sweetly flows
The liquefaction of her clothes.

Next, when I cast mine eyes, and see
That brave vibration, each way free,   *5*
O, how that glittering taketh me!

                    Robert Herrick

Confession of Faith

I lack the braver mind
That dares to find
The lover friend, and kind.

I fear him to the bone;
I lie alone   *5*
By the beloved one,

And, breathless for suspense,
Erect defense
Against love's violence

Whose silences portend   *10*
A bloody end
For lover never friend.

But, in default of faith,
In futile breath,
I dream no ill of Death.   *15*

Elinor Wylie

The King's Epitaph

Here lies our sovereign Lord, the King,
Whose word no man relies on,
Who never said a foolish thing,
Nor ever did a wise one.

John Wilmot, Earl of Rochester

Parting at Morning

Round the cape of a sudden came the sea,
And the sun looked over the mountain's rim:
And straight was a path of gold for him,
And the need of a world of men for me.

Robert Browning

["Faith" Is a Fine Invention]

"Faith" is a fine invention
When Gentlemen can *see*—
But *Microscopes* are prudent
In an Emergency.

Emily Dickinson

Preference

I think I'd much prefer to write
Of emerald leaves by sunlight kissed
Than read a complex book about
Photosynthesis.

Beth Biderman (student)

[I Taste a Liquor Never Brewed]

I taste a liquor never brewed—
From Tankards scooped in Pearl—
Not all the Vats upon the Rhine
Yield such an Alcohol!

Inebriate of air—am I—   *5*
And Debauchee of Dew—
Reeling—thro endless summer days—
From inns of Molten Blue—

When "Landlords" turn the drunken Bee
Out of the Foxglove's door—   *10*
When Butterflies—renounce their "drams"—
I shall but drink the more!

Till Seraphs swing their snowy Hats—
And Saints—to windows run—
To see the little Tippler   *15*
Leaning against the—Sun—

Emily Dickinson

My Girl, Thou Gazest Much

My girl, thou gazest much
    Upon the golden skies:
Would I were heaven! I would behold
    Thee then with all mine eyes.

George Turberville

Virtue

Sweet day, so cool, so calm, so bright,
    The bridal of the earth and sky,
The dew shall weep thy fall tonight,
    For thou must die.

Sweet rose, whose hue, angry and brave,   *5*
    Bids the rash gazer wipe his eye,
Thy root is ever in its grave,
    And thou must die.

Sweet spring, full of sweet days and roses,
    A box where sweets compacted lie,   *10*
My music shows ye have your closes,
    And all must die.

Only a sweet and virtuous soul,
    Like seasoned timber, never gives;
But though the whole world turn to coal,   *15*
    Then chiefly lives.

George Herbert

Art Thou Pale for Weariness

Art thou pale for weariness
Of climbing heaven and gazing on the earth,
Wandering companionless
Among the stars that have another birth,
And ever changing, like a joyless eye   5
That finds no object worth its constancy?

Percy Bysshe Shelley

Paradox

The joy that's felt within a heart
Can never be explained
To those who've never felt it
And those who've known no pain,
For only he who knows remorse   5
Can feel deep tenderness,
And only he who's once been sad
Can once again feel bliss.

Beth Biderman (student)

CHAPTER VIII

Reading the Fixed Forms

Many literary critics feel man's greatest literary achievements lie in the long poetic works of our cultural heritage. Others assert that no extended poem can sustain emotion to create a response in the reader as the short lyric can. Certainly, it is necessary to learn to read short forms well before attempting longer forms, for the demands of poetry grow increasingly greater with length. Thus we will begin our closer study of the fixed forms with poems of shorter length.

Quite possibly the most admired of all poetic lengths is the *sonnet*. Almost every poet, at one time or another, attempts this ubiquitous vehicle. The reasons for its popularity are numerous, and an examination of the sonnet will convince you of the charm and practicality of the form.

The sonnet has been universally admired since its beginnings in the thirteenth century. Probably originating in Italy, it was refined and perfected by Petrarch, who established many of the conventions which make it an intimate work. The air of intimacy is virtually inescapable in the sonnet, for it is a definite communication between two individuals. Through the sonnet, the poet speaks directly to the reader as a second person. This monolog is usually charged with emotion, therefore eloquent and elegant. But, like the haiku, the form is demanding and relatively standardized. Thus rigidity of form is juxtaposed against intensity of emotion—a pattern of one element pulling against another. This creates an intellectual tension which pervades the sonnet. It begins in the "message" of the poem, for the lines allow a meditative or reflective statement from the poet; and ends in whatever application the reader chooses to make of the poet's resolution.

The sonnet is a lyric not generally suitable for musical scoring. As its form is logical, introspective, and ingenious, it does not suggest spontaneity or winging melody. Actually, it frequently seems designed less to please the reader than to afford the poet a chance to make a statement wherein he establishes his own mental serenity or asserts an emotion that has become explosive. The statement or the emotion, however, is controlled. The demands of form allow no looseness of language, no illogicality. Argument is enforced; illustration is employed; comparison utilizes contrast; the *merely* descriptive is avoided.

As the first sonnets were addressed to a woman, a loved one who was theoretically chaste and almost holy in her remoteness, the early forms established traditions of elevated language, excessive and elaborate figures of speech, and a general disregard for reality. Later, revolting against both the specious and the precious, such poets as Shakespeare, Donne and Milton turned the form toward a wider variety of subject matter, more practical language, and more defensible imagery. As the original intent had been to elevate the "holy" loved one, sonnets were found to be ideal for statements of jealousy, sorrow in absence, farewells, gift-giving, and so on. Reverence of language and tone, combined with the conversational intimacy of the sonnet, early suggested its adaptation to conversation between lovers and, by extension, between man and God. The adoration shifted from human to divine with small effort. God could be exhorted, scolded, argued with in a personal, dramatic, intense fashion—just as lovers could exhort, scold, argue with each other.

Eventually, and inevitably, other uses suggested themselves. Nature was addressed, personal experience was narrated. The sonnet became the most widely used poetic form in the English language. It has been used amorously, religiously, speculatively, boldly, even satirically. It lends itself to any subject embodying reflective thought. Either Cupid's arrows or an assassin's bullets may be adequately dealt with in the form.

Now, what *is* the form? A sonnet usually contains fourteen lines, but it may have only eleven or as many as twenty-one. Though the best practitioners have written it in any number of metrical feet, it is ordinarily in iambic pentameter. It may consist of three quatrains and a couplet; of an octave and a sestet; or of fourteen lines without syntactical break. The sonnet is a flexible form of infinite variety, and many authors have declared they felt justified in calling themselves poets only after they had mastered it.

The Italian Sonnet

The Italian form of the sonnet (often called the *Petrarchan sonnet*) is divided into an octave and a sestet. The octave is rhymed *abbaabba* and may be composed of eight enjambed lines or broken into two quatrains. Whatever the division, the eight lines work as a unit to state the poet's desire, indignation, or vision; they may ask a question, plead a problem, or offer a profound, personal reflection. In short, the burden of the sonnet rests on the octave, in which the *call* or announcement of the sonnet's purpose is made.

The sestet may be rhymed in any tercet pattern such as *cdecde, cdcdcd, cdcddc, cdcede,* and so on. Two restrictions, however, are applied: the sestet may not conclude with a couplet, and no end rhyme beyond *e* is permissible. That is, the Italian form allows a maximum of five rhymes. In the sestet, the burden of the octave is eased, as the *response* is made to the call. Desire, indignation, vision are solaced, soothed, realized; the query or problem is answered or resolved; the reflection is illuminated.

Simply, then, the octave asks a question, states a belief, or offers a narrative comment. The sestet answers the question, makes specific application of the belief, or answers the narrative with an abstract comment.

Dante Gabriel Rossetti followed the Petrarchan pattern with great fidelity in *The House of Life,* a *sonnet sequence*—a group of sonnets devoted to a single problem or dedicated to a person. Note how octave and sestet work together in the following sonnet from Rossetti's sequence:

> The gloom that breathes upon me with these airs
>   Is like the drops which strike the traveller's brow
>   Who knows not, darkling, if they bring him now
> Fresh storm, or be old rain the covert bears.
> Ah! bodes this hour some harvest of new tares,   5
>   Or hath but memory of the day whose plough
>   Sowed hunger once,—the night at length when thou,
> O prayer found vain, didst fall from out my prayers?
> How prickly were the growths which yet how smooth,
>   Along the hedgerows of this journey shed,   10
> Lie by Time's grace till night and sleep may soothe!
>   Even as the thistledown from pathsides dead
> Gleaned by a girl in autumns of her youth,
>   Which one new year makes soft her marriage-bed.

The octave consists of two quatrains. The first reflects on current despair, likening it to rain after a storm lull. Is it a continuation of the old or the beginning of a worse, new storm? The second quatrain extends the reflective question through the restatement in stronger imagery. The sestet answers the octave, effectively making the transition by extending the imagery again. The first tercet suggests despair is always tempered by that which makes it bearable. The second observes that despair leads into the births of new delights and is, therefore, functional.

Structurally, the octave and the sestet in a sonnet are two interlocking parts of a single unit. They must meet and meld to create the whole, though each is distinct and grammatically complete. The octave introduces; the sestet resolves. The reflection is stated and resolved as the octave strains against the sestet, as emotional content strains against confinement and rigidity of form. A curious fact about most sonnets is that they seem to be structured like a human thought. The tensions, the ambivalences, the dichotomies of both are apparent. Perhaps this similarity accounts for the sonnet's popularity.

Frequently, the sonnet will employ such single syllable words as *oh, but, then, now,* to indicate the transition from octave to sestet. You can see such transition in line 9 of John Keats' "On First Looking Into Chapman's Homer," a sonnet about a translator of Homer. Notice the chronological structure which creates the "before-after" octave-sestet pattern. Comparison and contrast are embodied in the chronology. The first quatrain is a general statement of literary travels through western poetry. The second quatrain becomes more specific as Keats laments his inability to read Homer in Greek—only in translation. Chapman's translation, however, gave Keats access to the Achaean world with some fidelity. The word *Then* serves as transition into the sestet which ties the literary voyage of discovery to an historical one. As one who discovers a new planet or some explorer seeing a geographical wonder, Keats stands in awe of the new realm:

On First Looking Into Chapman's Homer

Much have I traveled in the realms of gold,
And many goodly states and kingdoms seen;
Round many western islands have I been
Which bards in fealty to Apollo hold.
Oft of one wide expanse had I been told   5
That deep-browed Homer ruled as his demesne;
Yet did I never breathe its pure serene
Till I heard Chapman speak out loud and bold:
Then felt I like some watcher of the skies
When a new planet swims into his ken;   10
Or like stout Cortez when with eagle eyes
He stared at the Pacific—and all his men
Looked at each other with a wild surmise—
Silent, upon a peak in Darien.

John Keats

Purists may object to the notion of Cortez, rather than Balboa, staring at the Pacific. Poets can make mistakes too—but, unlike non-poets, they can fall back on poetic license!

John Keats and Leigh Hunt were friends who once, as friends will, engaged in a friendly contest. On a chill December evening as they visited, their talk turned to the common English cricket. Hunt suggested a sonnet-writing contest on the very trite subject of the grasshopper and the cricket. Keats agreed and finished his sonnet first, and, though ordinarily given to extensive revision, he let it stand. Keats reveals, in this unrevised but greatly admired sonnet, a mastery of considerably more than the Petrarchan sonnet. Hunt's approach is markedly different. No absolute pronouncement can be made, but critics generally feel Keats' is the superior sonnet:

To the Grasshopper and the Cricket

Green little vaulter in the sunny grass,
   Catching your heart up at the feel of June,
   Sole voice that's heard amidst the lazy noon,
When ev'n the bees lag at the summoning brass;
And you, warm little housekeeper, who class   *5*
   With those who think the candles come too soon,
   Loving the fire, and with your tricksome tune
Nick the glad silent moments as they pass;
Oh, sweet and tiny cousins, that belong,
   One to the fields, the other to the hearth,   *10*
Both have your sunshine; both, though small, are strong
   At your clear hearts; and both were sent on earth
To sing in thoughtful ears this natural song—
   Indoors and out—summer and winter—Mirth.

                                   Leigh Hunt

On the Grasshopper and the Cricket

The poetry of earth is never dead:
   When all the birds are faint with the hot sun,
   And hide in cooling trees, a voice will run
From hedge to hedge about the new-mown mead;
That is the Grasshopper's—he takes the lead   *5*
   In summer luxury—he has never done
   With his delights; for when tired out with fun,
He rests at ease beneath some pleasant weed.
The poetry of earth is ceasing never:

On a lone winter evening, when the frost   *10*
  Has wrought a silence, from the stove there shrills
The Cricket's song, in warmth increasing ever,
  And seems to one in drowsiness half lost,
  The Grasshopper's among some grassy hills.

John Keats

In class, you might debate the merits of the two poems. Pertinent to such discussion would be, certainly, a comparison of the sestet rhyme schemes. Structural development is also worth noticing. Hunt discusses both of the insects in his octave, then comments on them in the sestet. Keats devotes his octave to one, his sestet to the other. The pivotal transitions are interesting too. Notice the punctuation at the end of each octave, the *Oh* of Hunt's sestet, the repetition of words in Keats'. Discuss the tone and mood of the two poems. How does *setting* (the physical geography or locale) contribute to *atmosphere* (the emotional quality resulting from the handling of setting)? How many settings are there in each poem? A setting may be specific (as a room in a house) or general (as all of nature). Observe the relief trochees in both poems. Which has the more interesting metrics? How are symbols employed?

The sonnet is uniquely suited to the romantic idea, and few stories are more romantic than that of Lilith:

Body's Beauty

Of Adam's first wife, Lilith, it is told
  (The witch he loved before the gift of Eve,)
    That, ere the snake's, her sweet tongue could deceive,
And her enchanted hair was the first gold.
And still she sits, young while the earth is old,   *5*
    And, subtly of herself contemplative,
    Draws men to watch the bright web she can weave,
Till heart and body and life are in its hold.
The rose and poppy are her flowers; for where
    Is he not found, O Lilith, whom shed scent   *10*
And soft-shed kisses and soft sleep shall snare?
    Lo! as that youth's eyes burned at thine, so went
    Thy spell through him, and left his straight neck bent
And round his heart one strangling golden hair.

Dante Gabriel Rossetti

You can see how Rossetti turned Lilith's dark charms to the conventional golden ones dear to sonneteers, while retaining her triple role in legend as Adam's first mate (supplied by Satan, only to be supplanted by God's Eve), the Semitic vampire who lived in ruins and desolate places, and the medieval witch who menaced little children. In quatrain 1, she is Satan's gift to the lonely ancestor of man; in quatrain 2, she retains her youthful bloom in the ruins of old earth, drawing life force from men enmeshed in physical lust. The sestet introduces Adam as the innocent bound to the witch, and all men are the children of Adam. As he bowed his head before her charms and she strangled his heart (the seat of the emotions) with needs of the flesh, she made all men her victims, perpetuating her evil. Allusion becomes the vehicle for whatever allegory you may wish to extend beyond the fourteenth line.

Abstractions such as love or freedom are often very effectively handled in abstract symbols, because no concrete one exists. The poet, however, must have concrete ideas that are not concretely statable. If he thinks in abstract terms, his communication will lack conviction. Notice the effective juxtaposition of octave and sestet in "Credo," as dismay gives way to hope—and resolution somehow attaches itself to you as a result of the poem:

Credo

I cannot find my way: there is no star
In all the shrouded heavens anywhere;
And there is not a whisper in the air
Of any living voice but one so far
That I can hear it only as a bar   *5*
Of lost, imperial music, played when fair
And angel fingers wove, and unaware,
Dead leaves to garlands where no roses are.
No, there is not a glimmer, nor a call,
For one that welcomes, welcomes when he fears,   *10*
The black and awful chaos of the night;
But through it all—above, beyond it all—
I know the far-sent message of the years,
I feel the coming glory of the Light.

Edwin Arlington Robinson

In Milton's "On His Blindness," the octave ends syntactically in the first line of the sestet. This is a Miltonic innovation designed to heighten the "call-and-answer" structure. As line and sentence are placed in taut opposition, structure, form and meaning become poised against each other. Motion and countermotion are more evident in sonnets than in any other kind of poetry. Notice the biblical allusion in *hidden talent*—it is actually a pun (a proof that the pun may be quite respectable). How would this sonnet suffer or be improved if *stand* in the last line were changed to *sit?*

On His Blindness

When I consider how my light is spent
Ere half my days in this dark world and wide,
And that one talent which is death to hide
Lodged with me useless, though my soul more bent
To serve therewith my Maker, and present   5
My true account, lest he returning chide,
"Doth God exact day-labor, light denied?"
I fondly ask. But Patience, to prevent
That murmur, soon replies: "God doth not need
Either man's work or his own gifts. Who best   10
Bear his mild yoke, they serve him best. His state
Is kingly: thousands at his bidding speed
And post o'er land and ocean without rest;
They also serve who only stand and wait."

John Milton

The traditional iambic pentameter of the sonnet is artfully varied to suit the sense of the following poem. Modern machinery and an age-old concept of God are combined with vibrancy and power by the founder of *Poetry,* a magazine dedicated to the contemporary and unconventional verse forms of the American 1920's:

A Power Plant

The invisible wheels go softly round and round—
Light is the tread of brazen-footed Power.
Spirits of air, caged in the iron tower,
Sing as they labor with a purring sound.
The abysmal fires, grated and chained and bound,   5
Burn white and still, in swift obedience cower;
While far and wide the myriad lamps, aflower,
Glow like star-gardens and the night confound.
This we have done for thee, almighty Lord;
Yea, even as they who built at thy command   10
The pillared temple, or in marble made
Thine image, or who sang thy deathless word.
We take the weapons of thy dread right hand,
And wield them in thy service, unafraid.

Harriet Monroe

The machine and God are explored in the Petrarchan form by a contemporary poet-aviator:

High Flight

Oh, I have slipped the surly bonds of earth,
And danced the skies on laughter-silvered wings;
Sunward I've climbed and joined the tumbling mirth
Of sun-split clouds—and done a hundred things
You have not dreamed of—wheeled and soared and swung   5
High in the sunlit silence. Hov'ring there,
I've chased the shouting wind along and flung
My eager craft through footless halls of air.
Up, up the long delirious, burning blue
I've topped the wind-swept heights with easy grace,   10
Where never lark, or even eagle, flew;
And, while with silent, lifting mind I've trod
The high untrespassed sanctity of space,
Put out my hand, and touched the face of God.

                                        John Gillespie Magee, Jr.

Suggested Assignment. In the following Italian sonnet, introspection or monolog may be at work. Discuss your reasons for deciding which is the case. Who or what is *thee?* Is the end rhyme effective within the framework of your argument? It should be.

The Image of Delight

O how came I that loved stars, moon, and flame,
And unimaginable wind and sea,
All inner shrines and temples of the free,
Legends and hopes and golden books of fame;
I that upon the mountain carved my name   5
With cliffs and clouds and eagles over me,
O how came I to stoop to loving thee—
I that had never stooped before to shame?
O 'twas not thee! Too eager of a white
Far beauty and a voice to answer mine,   10
Myself I built an image of delight,
Which all one purple day I deemed divine—
And when it vanished in the fiery night,
I lost not thee, nor any shape of thine.

                                        William Ellery Leonard

The English Sonnet

More flexible than the Italian form, the English sonnet may consist of either three quatrains and a concluding couplet, or of an octave and a sestet composed of a quatrain and a couplet. The two major English forms are the *Shakespearean* and the *Spenserian*. The difference lies in the number of rhymes allowable. The Spenserian holds to the five allowed in the Italian form; the Shakespearean adds two:

Shakespearean	*Spenserian*
a	a
b	b
a	a
b	b
c	b
d	c
c	b
d	c
e	c
f	d
e	c
f	d
g	e
g	e

These rhyme schemes suggest the greater possibilities of the English form. Quatrain 1 may offer a statement; quatrains 2 and 3, a variation or expansion; the couplet, a conclusion. Or the octave and sestet may work as they do in the Italian form, with the final couplet making the general conclusion. This combining of the two forms may add strength in the tension.

Iambic pentameter remains the acceptable foot, though Shakespeare himself used tetrameter and hexameter when it suited his purpose to do so.

Dante Gabriel Rossetti was as versatile in sonnet construction as any poet has ever been. The first three lines of "The Sonnet" are a masterful combination of metaphor, appositive, alliteration, consonance, and assonance. Time, death, and life are carved in the chiseled words of the octave as it creates a sensory impression of words as concrete as the sculptor's materials. The sestet reinforces the monument metaphor, as a coin is a commemorative device, in short, also a memorial—and line 1 is tied to line 9. The couplet turns the carefully controlled image back to line 1 again as the complete idea is captured in the eternal revolution of life and death:

The Sonnet

A Sonnet is a moment's monument,—
   Memorial from the Soul's eternity
   To one dead deathless hour. Look that it be,
Whether for lustral rite or dire portent,
Of its own arduous fulness reverent: 5
   Carve it in ivory or in ebony,
      As Day or Night may rule; and let Time see
Its flowering crest impearled and orient.
A Sonnet is a coin: its face reveals
   The Soul—its converse, to what Power 'tis due:—   10
Whether for tribute to the august appeals
   Of Life, or dower in Love's high retinue,
It serve; or, 'mid the dark wharf's cavernous breath,
In Charon's palm it pay the toll to Death.

                                Dante Gabriel Rossetti

Many sentiments, no matter how sincere, sound impossibly false in prose. The sonnet, controlling the line, restraining language in the metrical pattern, allows their statement to seem as heartfelt as it is simple. Paradoxically, since the sonnet is "a moment's monument," Shakespeare perpetuates the very possibility he seems to wish to negate in

Sonnet 71

No longer mourn for me when I am dead
Than you shall hear the surly sullen bell
Give warning to the world that I am fled
From this vile world, with vilest worms to dwell.
Nay, if you read this line, remember not   5
The hand that writ it; for I love you so
That I in your sweet thoughts would be forgot
If thinking on me then should make you woe.
O, if, I say, you look upon this verse
When I perhaps compounded am with clay,   10
Do not so much as my poor name rehearse,
But let your love even with my life decay,
   Lest the wise world should look into your moan
   And mock you with me after I am gone.

                                  William Shakespeare

The student well may understand the basic metaphor of "The Lessons of Nature," as it reduces a profound observation to the understandable level of an everyday occurrence—the act of reading (the metaphor being extended even to the casual marginal doodle of some previous owner of the book). The art of bookbinding indicated in lines 10-12 contrasts sharply with the functional craft revealed in the book you now read. Content is not enhanced by surface decoration, nor can expensive materials compensate for sacrificed content:

The Lessons of Nature

Of this fair volume which we World do name
If we the sheets and leaves could turn with care,
Of Him who it corrects, and did it frame,
We clear might read the art and wisdom rare:
Find out His power which wildest powers doth tame,   5
His providence extending everywhere,
In every page, no period of the same.
But silly we, like foolish children, rest
Well pleased with colour'd vellum, leaves of gold,
Fair dangling ribbands, leaving what is best,   10
On the great Writer's sense ne'er taking hold;
Or if by chance we stay our minds on aught,
It is some picture on the margin wrought.

                    William Drummond of Hawthornden

Compare the structure of the following sonnets on the subject of death. The first is Spenserian in structure with the sestet in tension against the octave, the couplet drawing the conclusion. The second is Shakespearean with the argument running from line 1 through line 16, the couplet lacking a conclusive or epigrammatic statement complete in the two lines:

What If This Present

What if this present were the world's last night?
Mark in my heart, O Soul, where thou dost dwell,
The picture of Christ crucified, and tell
Whether that countenance can thee affright,
Tears in his eyes quench the amazing light,   5
Blood fills his frowns, which from his pierced head fell.
And can that tongue adjudge thee unto hell,
Which prayed forgiveness for his foes' fierce spite?

No, no; but as in my idolatry
I said to all my profane mistresses,   *10*
Beauty, of pity, foulness only is
A sign of rigor: so I say to thee,
To wicked spirits are horrid shapes assigned,
This beauteous form assures a piteous mind.

John Donne

Ghost

He rises from his guests, abruptly leaves,
Because of memory that long moons ago
Others now dead had dined with him, and grieves
Because these newer persons he must know
Might not have loved his ghosts, his unknown dead.   *5*
There are new smiles, new answers to his quips;
But there are intervals when, having said
His dinner-table say, he hears dead lips . . .
The dead have ways of mingling in the uses
Of life they leave behind, the dead can rise   *10*
When dinner's done. But one of them refuses
To go away and gazes with dead eyes
Piercing him deeper than a rain can reach,
Leaving him only motion, only speech.

Witter Bynner

While it would be difficult to scorn such a versatile form as the sonnet, the following Shakespearean sonnet *on* the sonnet is worth reading and studying for the poetic devices employed. Tasso, Camoëns, Dante, and Milton were all especially adept with the sonnet form, each adding his own distinctive contribution to its evolution—therefore, Wordsworth's tribute to them:

Scorn Not the Sonnet

Scorn not the Sonnet; Critic, you have frowned,
Mindless of its just honors; with this key
Shakespeare unlocked his heart; the melody
Of this small lute gave ease to Petrarch's wound;
A thousand times this pipe did Tasso sound;   *5*
With it Camoëns soothed an exile's grief;
The Sonnet glittered a gay myrtle leaf
Amid the cypress with which Dante crowned
His visionary brow; a glowworm lamp,

It cheered mild Spenser, called from Faery-land   *10*
To struggle through dark ways; and when a damp
Fell round the path of Milton, in his hand
The Thing became a trumpet; whence he blew
Soul-animating strains—alas, too few!

William Wordsworth

Suggested Assignment. In a three-paragraph paper, discuss the techniques and ideas of one of the following sonnets. Attempt a penetrating analysis, utilizing everything you have thus far learned. The questions following each sonnet are designed to aid you in your analysis.

Lucifer in Starlight

On a starred night Prince Lucifer uprose.
Tired of his dark dominion swung the fiend
Above the rolling ball in cloud part screened,
Where sinners hugged their specter of repose.
Poor prey to his hot fit of pride were those.   *5*
And now upon his western wing he leaned,
Now his huge bulk o'er Afric's sands careened,
Now the black planet shadowed Arctic snows.
Soaring through wider zones that pricked his scars
With memory of the old revolt from Awe,   *10*
He reached the middle height, and at the stars,
Which are the brain of heaven, he looked, and sank.
Around the ancient track marched, rank on rank,
The army of unalterable law.

George Meredith

a. Motion and countermotion are clearly defined in "Lucifer in Starlight." Discuss the poet's technique in achieving them.

b. Contrasts are also apparent. Why are they used? Be specific!

Sonnet 104

To me, fair friend, you never can be old,
For as you were when first your eye I ey'd,
Such seems your beauty still. Three winters cold
Have from the forests shook three summers' pride,
Three beauteous springs to yellow autumn turn'd   *5*
In process of the seasons have I seen,
Three April perfumes in three hot Junes burn'd,
Since first I saw you fresh, which yet are green.

Ah! yet doth beauty, like a dial-hand,
Steal from his figure, and no pace perceiv'd;   *10*
So your sweet hue, which methinks still doth stand,
Hath motion, and mine eye may be deceiv'd;
   For fear of which, hear this, thou age unbred:
   Ere you were born was beauty's summer dead.

William Shakespeare

a. Time references abound in "Sonnet 104." How do they contribute to the total structure?

b. Explain the paradox of the couplet as it grows from the first twelve lines.

Sonnet 1

Loving in truth, and fain in verse my love to show,
That she, dear she, might take some pleasure of my pain,
Pleasure might cause her read, reading might make her know,
Knowledge might pity win, and pity grace obtain,
I sought fit words to paint the blackest face of woe,   *5*
Studying inventions fine, her wits to entertain.
Oft turning others' leaves to see if thence would flow
Some fresh and fruitful showers upon my sunburnt brain.
But words came halting forth, wanting Invention's stay;
Invention, Nature's child, fled step-dame Study's blows;   *10*
And others' feet still seemed but strangers in my way.
Thus great with child to speak, and helpless in my throes,
Biting my truant pen, beating myself for spite:
"Fool!" said my Muse to me, "look in thy heart, and write."

Sir Philip Sidney

a. From your own experience in writing answers to essay questions, themes, and in-class compositions, trace the logic of Sidney's inability to "get organized."

b. Explain the seeming paradox resulting from the last line—remembering it is the last line of a carefully structured, rule-bound form.

The Cross of Snow

In the long, sleepless watches of the night,
   A gentle face—the face of one long dead—
   Looks at me from the wall, where round its head
   The night-lamp casts a halo of pale light.

Here in this room she died; and soul more white   *5*
  Never through martyrdom of fire was led
  To its repose; nor can in books be read
  The legend of a life more benedight.
There is a mountain in the distant West
  That, sun-defying, in its deep ravines   *10*
  Displays a cross of snow upon its side.
Such is the cross I wear upon my breast
  These eighteen years, through all the changing scenes
  And seasons, changeless since the day she died.

Henry Wadsworth Longfellow

  a. Explain the metaphorical uses of color in "The Cross of Snow."
  b. Explain the similarity between the first quatrain and Buson's "The Sudden Chillness" (p. 31).

The Celestial Surgeon

If I have faltered more or less
In my great task of happiness;
If I have moved among my race
And shown no glorious morning face;
If beams from happy human eyes   *5*
Have moved me not; if morning skies,
Books, and my food, and summer rain
Knocked on my sullen heart in vain:
Lord, Thy most pointed pleasure take
And stab my spirit broad awake;   *10*
Or, Lord, if still too obdurate I,
Choose Thou, before that spirit die,
A piercing pain, a killing sin,
And to my dead heart run them in!

Robert Louis Stevenson

  a. How does Stevenson's iambic tetrameter line change the tone of the sonnet as a form? What does the heroic line (iambic pentameter) add?
  b. Poets are free, of course, to modify a form—even a fixed form —to suit the communication they wish to make. Explain the structural changes in this sonnet as they might suit Stevenson's communication.

Piazza Piece

—I am a gentleman in a dustcoat trying
To make you hear. Your ears are soft and small
And listen to an old man not at all,
They want the young men's whispering and sighing.
But see the roses on your trellis dying   *5*
And hear the spectral singing of the moon;
For I must have my lovely lady soon,
I am a gentleman in a dustcoat trying.

—I am a lady young in beauty waiting
Until my truelove comes, and then we kiss.   *10*
But what grey man among the vines is this
Whose words are dry and faint as in a dream?
Back from my trellis, Sir, before I scream!
I am a lady young in beauty waiting.

John Crowe Ransom

a. Ransom has modified the sonnet form greatly to achieve his communication in "Piazza Piece." Explain the effects and how the modifications help him achieve them.

b. Explain why this sonnet might illustrate the functions of octave and sestet better than any other you have read. Is this most nearly Italian or English in form? Justify your answer.

The Dead Crab

A rosy shield upon its back,
That not the hardest storm could crack,
From whose sharp edge projected out
Black pin-point eyes staring about;
Beneath, the well-knit cote-armure   *5*
That gave to its weak belly power;
The clustered legs with plated joints
That ended in stiletto points;
The claws like mouths it held outside:
I cannot think this creature died   *10*
By storm or fish or sea-fowl harmed,
Walking the sea so heavily armed;
Or does it make for death to be
Oneself a living armory?

Andrew Young

a. You might recall "The Death of a Toad" (p. 183) as you read "The Dead Crab." Compare the language of the two poems. Which would be a more acceptable statement to the "objective" biologist? Why?

b. Explain the psychology of the final couplet. Does it apply to you, your friends? Explain why you feel as you do.

Other Fixed Forms—Mostly French

Beyond the sonnet, there are many other common fixed forms. For general convenience, they are discussed below in alphabetical order with a typical example to illustrate each.

The *ballad* is a narrative poetry form, divided into two categories. The *popular* or *folk ballad* seems to originate out of an actual event which makes a profound impression on some unknown person who composes a song about it to suit himself. Others, heartily involving themselves, reconstruct the unwritten words as they create their own versions. Changed version follows changed version until many similar ones exist. "Frankie and Johnny" (p. 115) is an American example.

Observable features of folk ballads are their primary attention to common folk, minor nobility, or folk heroes (such as Billy the Kid or Jesse James); repeated themes of love, betrayal, and death; lack of description or characterization except as it is revealed in dialog; repetition in refrain lines or stanzas. The *ballad stanza* is, ordinarily, an iambic quatrain, $a^4b^3c^4b^3$, though any number of variations are possible—the "folk" are not as concerned with metrics as they are with emotional response and a "good story." The frequent inclusion of superstitions and the absence of transitional devices also stamp the ballad with a folk origin.

"Barbara Allen" is a Scottish ballad that was first published in 1765:

Barbara Allen

In Scarlet town where I was born,
There was a fair maid dwellin',
Made every youth cry, "Well-a-day!"
Her name was Barbara Allen.

All in the merry month of May,   5
The green buds they were swellin',
Sweet William on his death bed lay
For the love of Barbara Allen.

He sent his servant to her door,
To the place where she was dwellin',   *10*
"O Miss, O Miss, O come you quick,
If your name be Barbara Allen!"

O slowly, slowly got she up,
And slowly she came nigh him;
She drew the curtain to one side   *15*
And said, "Young man, you're dying."

"Yes, I am sick and very sick,
And grief is in me dwellin',
No better, no better, I'll never be,
If I don't get Barbara Allen."   *20*

"Do you remember the other night
When you were at the tavern?
You drank a health to the ladies all,
But you slighted Barbara Allen."

"Yes, I remember the other night   *25*
When I was at the tavern;
I gave a health to the ladies all,
And my heart to Barbara Allen."

He turned his pale face toward the wall,
For death was in him dwellin',   *30*
"Goodbye, goodbye, my dear friends all,
Be kind to Barbara Allen."

As she was walking toward her home,
She heard the death-bell knellin';
And every stroke it seemed to say,   *35*
"Cold-hearted Barbara Allen!"

She looked to the east, she looked to the west;
She saw the corpse a-coming,
"O hand me down that corpse of clay
That I may look upon it.   *40*

"O mother, mother, make my bed;
O make it long and narrow;
Sweet William died for me today,
I shall die for him tomorrow.

"O father, father, dig my grave, 45
O dig it long and narrow;
Sweet William died for love of me,
And I will die for sorrow."

A rose, a rose grew from William's grave,
From Barbara's grew a briar; 50
They grew and they grew to the steeple-top
Till they could grow no higher.

They grew and they grew to the steeple-top
Till they could grow no higher;
And there they tied a true-love knot, 55
The rose clung round the briar.

The *literary* or *art ballad* is a conscious construction in imitation of the folk ballad, but it is not intended to be sung. A strict observance of the ballad stanza is customary, though authors do not limit themselves to it. While the most famous of all literary ballads is Coleridge's "The Rime of the Ancient Mariner," it is probably so familiar that you will enjoy more the altered ballad stanzas of John Keats'

La Belle Dame sans Merci

O what can ail thee, knight-at-arms,
  Alone and palely loitering?
The sedge has wither'd from the lake,
  And no birds sing.

O what can ail thee, knight-at-arms 5
  So haggard and so woe-begone?
The squirrel's granary is full,
  And the harvest's done.

I see a lilly on thy brow,
  With anguish moist and fever dew, 10
And on thy cheeks a fading rose
  Fast withereth too.

I met a lady in the meads
   Full beautiful, a faery's child;
Her hair was long, her foot was light   *15*
   And her eyes were wild.

I made a garland for her head,
   And bracelets too, and fragrant zone;
She looked at me as she did love,
   And made sweet moan.   *20*

I set her on my pacing steed,
   And nothing else saw all day long,
For sidelong would she bend, and sing
   A faery's song.

She found me roots of relish sweet,   *25*
   And honey wild, and manna dew,
And sure in language strange she said—
   "I love thee true."

She took me to her elfin grot,
   And there she wept, and sigh'd full sore,   *30*
And there I shut her wild wild eyes
   With kisses four.

And there she lulléd me asleep,
   And there I dream'd—Ah! woe betide!
The latest dream I ever dream'd   *35*
   On the cold hill side.

I saw pale kings and princes too,
   Pale warriors, death-pale were they all;
They cried—"La Belle Dame sans Merci
   Thee hath in thrall!"   *40*

I saw their starved lips in the gloam,
   With horrid warning gapéd wide;
And I awoke, and found me here,
   On the cold hill's side.

And this is why I sojourn here,   45
   Alone and palely loitering,
Though the sedge is wither'd from the lake,
   And no birds sing.

John Keats

Even though the *ballade* is sometimes called a ballad, it should not be confused with that form. The ballade originated in France during the Middle Ages, was revived during the Renaissance and again in the twentieth century. A sophisticated form, it is relatively strict in its structure: three octaves and a quatrain called an *envoy*—occasionally ten-line stanzas are used by accomplished poets. The rhyme scheme remains constant throughout the octaves (*ababbcbc*), the envoy being *bcbc*. No rhyme word may be repeated in another stanza; the final line of all stanzas, however, is repeated as a refrain, even in the envoy which is addressed to a real patron or some high power:

The Ballad of Dead Ladies

Tell me now in what hidden way is
   Lady Flora the lovely Roman?
Where's Hipparchia, and where is Thaïs,
   Neither of them the fairer woman?
   Where is Echo, beheld of no man,   5
Only heard on river and mere—
   She whose beauty was more than human? . . .
But where are the snows of yester-year?

Where's Héloïse, the learned nun,
   For whose sake Abeillard, I ween,   10
Lost manhood and put priesthood on?
   (From Love he won such dule and teen!)
   And where, I pray you, is the Queen
Who willed that Buridan should steer
   Sewed in a sack's mouth down the Seine? . . .   15
But where are the snows of yester-year?

White Queen Blanche, like a queen of lilies,
   With a voice like any mermaiden—
Bertha Broadfoot, Beatrice, Alice,
   And Ermengarde the lady of Maine—   20
   And that good Joan whom Englishmen
At Rouen doomed and burned her there—
   Mother of God, where are they then? . . .
But where are the snows of yester-year?

Nay, never ask this week, fair lord,   25
   Where they are gone, nor yet this year,
Except with this for an overword—
   But where are the snows of yester-year?
         François Villon (tr. *Dante Gabriel Rossetti*)

Of approximately the same age as the ballade, the *rondeau* also originated in France and, when Chaucer began to use the form, came to be called the *roundel* (see below). Its structure is thirteen lines written throughout with two rhymes, plus two unrhymed refrains which are made from the first word or words of the poem—fifteen lines in all. The refrain follows lines 8 and 13 (counting rhymed lines only):

In After Days

In after days when grasses high
O'er-top the stone where I shall lie,
   Though ill or well the world adjust
   My slender claim to honoured dust,
I shall not question or reply.   5

I shall not see the morning sky;
I shall not hear the night-wind sigh;
   I shall be mute as all men must
      In after days!

But yet, now living, fain were I   10
That some one then should testify,
   Saying—"He held his pen in trust
   To Art, not serving shame or lust."
Will none?—Then let my memory die
      In after days!   15
         Henry Austin Dobson

The *roundel* is a variation of the Chaucerian roundel, and was created by Algernon Charles Swinburne. Its structure is nine lines containing two rhymes, plus two brief refrain lines rhyming with the second of the two rhymes. The refrain is taken from the first word or words of the poem and follows the first and third tercets:

The Roundel

A roundel is wrought as a ring or a starbright sphere,
  With craft of delight and with cunning of sound unsought,
That the heart of the hearer may smile if to pleasure his ear
    A roundel is wrought.

Its jewel of music is carven of all or of aught—   5
Love, laughter, or mourning—remembrance of rapture or fear—
That fancy may fashion to hang in the ear of thought.

As a bird's quick song runs round, and the hearts in us hear
Pause answer to pause, and again the same strain caught,
So moves the device whence, round as a pearl or tear,   10
    A roundel is wrought.

Algernon Charles Swinburne

An almost impossibly complicated French form, the *sestina* dates from about 1100 A.D. Its primary use has been to reveal the cleverness of poets, since its involvements are so great. In structure, it is usually six stanzas of six lines, each ending with the *same six words*. A final stanza of three lines caps the poem, all six words being used in it—three at mid-line, three at line's end.

In "Sestina of the Tramp-Royal," the key words are *all, world, good, long, done,* and *die.* The seven stanzas have this pattern:

Stanza 1: abcdef
2: faebdc
3: cfdabe
4: ecbfad
5: deacfb
6: bdfeca
7: b—e
   d—c
   f—a

Sestina of the Tramp-Royal

Speakin' in general, I 'ave tried 'em all—
The 'appy roads that take you o'er the world.
Speakin' in general, I 'ave found them good
For such as cannot use one bed too long,
But must get 'ence, the same as I 'ave done,   5
An' go observin' matters till they die.

What do it matter where or 'ow we die,
So long as we've our 'ealth to watch it all—
The different ways that different things are done,
An' men an' women lovin' in this world;   10
Takin' our chances as they come along,
An' when they ain't, pretendin' they are good?

In cash or credit—no, it aren't no good;
You 'ave to 'ave the 'abit or you'd die,
Unless you lived your life but one day long,   *15*
Nor didn't prophesy nor fret at all,
But drew your tucker some'ow from the world,
An' never bothered what you might ha' done.

But, Gawd, what things are they I 'aven't done!
I've turned my 'and to most, an' turned it good,   *20*
In various situations round the world—
For 'im that doth not work must surely die;
But that's no reason man should labour all
'Is life on one same shift—life's none so long.

Therefore, from job to job I've moved along.   *25*
Pay couldn't 'old me when my time was done,
For something in my 'ead upset it all,
Till I 'ad dropped whatever 't was for good,
An' out at sea, be'eld the dock-lights die,
An' met my mate—the wind that tramps the world!   *30*

It's like a book, I think, this bloomin' world,
Which you can read and care for just so long,
But presently you feel that you will die
Unless you get the page you're readin' done,
An' turn another—likely not so good;   *35*
But what you're after is to turn 'em all.

Gawd bless this world! Whatever she 'ath done—
Excep' when awful long—I've found it good.
So write, before I die, " 'E liked it all!"

Rudyard Kipling

The forerunner of the rondeau, the *triolet* is an octave with two rhymes only. The entire first line is repeated as the fourth and seventh lines, the second line as the eighth. Rhyme scheme, then, is *ABaAabAB,* capital letters indicating lines which are repeated:

Triolet

When first we met, we did not guess
That Love would prove so hard a master;
Of more than common friendliness
When first we met we did not guess.

Who could foretell this sore distress,   *5*
This irretrievable disaster
When first we met?—We did not guess
That Love would prove so hard a master.

Robert Bridges

Triolet

Worldly designs, fears, hopes, farewell!
Farewell all earthly joys and cares!
On nobler thoughts my soul shall dwell,
Worldly designs, fears, hopes, farewell!
At quiet, in my peaceful cell,   *5*
I'll think on God, free from your snares;
Worldly designs, fears, hopes, farewell!
Farewell all earthly joys and cares.

Patrick Carey

Originating around 1650, the *villanelle* contains five tercets, and ends with a quatrain; the refrain employed forms eight of the nineteen lines:

Pan

O Goat-foot God of Arcady!
   Cyllene's shrine is grey and old;
This northern isle hath need of thee!

No more the shepherd lads in glee
   Throw apples at thy wattled fold,   *5*
O Goat-foot God of Arcady!

Not through the laurels can one see
   Thy soft brown limbs, thy head of gold:
This northern isle hath need of thee!

Then leave the tomb of Helicé,   *10*
   Where nymph and faun lie dead and cold,
O Goat-foot God of Arcady;

For many an unsung elegy
   Sleeps in the reeds our rivers hold:
This northern isle hath need of thee.   *15*

And thine our English Thames shall be,
   The open lawns, the upland wold,
O Goat-foot God of Arcady,
   This northern isle hath need of thee!

                             Oscar Wilde

Villanelle of His Lady's Treasures

I took her dainty eyes, as well
   As silken tendrils of her hair:
And so I made a Villanelle!

I took her voice, a silver bell,
   As clear as song, as soft as prayer;   *5*
I took her dainty eyes as well.

It may be, said I, who can tell,
   These things shall be my less despair?
And so I made a Villanelle!

I took her whiteness virginal   *10*
   And from her cheeks two roses rare:
I took her dainty eyes as well.

I said: "It may be possible
   Her image from my heart to tear!"
And so I made a Villanelle!   *15*

I stole her laugh, most musical:
   I wrought it in with artful care;
I took her dainty eyes as well;
   And so I made a Villanelle!

                            Ernest Dowson

Blank Verse—Everything But Rhyme

Blank verse differs from other fixed forms in that it is not fixed by end rhyme—a feature completely absent from the form. Instead a dominant foot (iambic) and line length (pentameter) fix it as firmly as rhyme fixes other forms. The difficulties involved in finding a rhyme to meet the demands of meaning in a line are familiar to all poets. Classical writers such as Homer and Virgil did not employ rhyme, choosing assonance, alliteration, consonance, and various kinds of hovering accent to establish echo. By the middle of the sixteenth century, English poets were in limited rebellion against rhyme for two reasons: 1) it imposed restrictions they wished to minimize; and 2) the classical humanists argued that, as it was not found in classical writers, it was a crutch contemporary writers should avoid.

English authors (Surrey, Sackville and Norton, and Gascoigne) dropped end rhyme from their iambic pentameter lines. Christopher Marlowe accepted the precedent they established. Shakespeare and John Milton later employed the unrhymed form, lifting it from the dramatic and didactic poetry to which it had been confined and allowing it to sing in their lyrical poetry as well as it had in the sonorous grandeur of the narrative and dramatic work of earlier writers. Because it is so well suited (as a result of the lack of rhyme) to the impressive statement authoritatively delivered, it seems most fitted to narrative, dramatic, and philosophical poetry. The plays of Shakespeare, Milton's *Paradise Lost,* the plays of such twentieth-century writers as Christopher Frye and T. S. Eliot, and Robert Frost's *A Masque of Reason*—all employ it.

Because rhymed iambic pentameter was used for heroic (epic) poetry in English, it was called *heroic verse.* When the iambic pentameter lines were rhymed couplets, they were called *heroic couplets.* Milton, abandoning the rhyme but not the meter, prefaced his long narrative poem, *Paradise Lost,* with a description of its form as "English Heroic verse, without rime . . ." and emphatically defended its use. His poetry offers his most eloquent defense, however, and invites your profitable study.

In reading the following conversation between Satan and Beëlzebub, observe the richness of sound. Scan the lines and list the devices used to achieve this musical wealth:

> ". . . Here at least
> We shall be free; the Almighty hath not built
> Here for his envy, will not drive us hence:
> Here we may reign secure; and, in my choice,
> To reign is worth ambition, though in hell: 5
> Better to reign in hell than serve in heaven.
> But wherefore let we then our faithful friends,
> The associates and copartners of our loss,
> Lie thus astonished on the oblivious pool,
> And call them not to share with us their part   10
> In this unhappy mansion, or once more
> With rallied arms to try what may be yet
> Regained in heaven, or what more lost in hell?"

So Satan spake; and him Beëlzebub
Thus answered: "Leader of those armies bright   15
Which, but the Omnipotent, none could have foiled!
If once they hear that voice, their liveliest pledge
Of hope in fears and dangers—heard so oft
In worst extremes, and on the perilous edge
Of battle, when it raged, in all assaults   20
Their surest signal—they will soon resume
New courage and revive, though now they lie
Grovelling and prostrate on yon lake of fire,
As we erewhile, astounded and amazed; ·
No wonder, fallen such a pernicious highth!"   25

(ll. 258-283)

Blank verse may seem easier to read than rhymed iambic pentameter, but to the poet it offers greater difficulties than any other form. So close to naturally spoken English, it should, seemingly, be simple to write, but it suffers from that nearness. If blank verse is to be richly alive, rather than pale and insipid as is most speech, it must utilize all possible poetic devices save rhyme. To compensate for the loss of that echo, the poet relies on shifting the metrical stress through careful utilization of relief feet, shifting the caesura in the line, enjambing lines so they create verse paragraphs, varying the language and metrics to separate passages, and varying the speech patterns of speakers (in dramatic poetry) to establish their unique identities. In blank verse more than in any other form, you should be especially sure to read from the beginning of the line to the end of the thought-break. If you pause at the end of each line, you will lose all sense of meaning as rhyme absence removes the memory aid of echo. By fragmenting the line, you will lose the sense of complete sentence units.

Your scansion of the lines should resemble the following:

". . .Here|at least

We shall|be free;|| the Al|mighty|hath not built

Here for|his en|vy,"will|not drive|us hence:

Here"we|may reign|secure;|| and,"in|my choice,

To reign|is worth|ambition,|| though in hell:

Better|to reign|in hell|than serve|in heaven.

But where|fore let|we then|our faith|ful friends,

The asso|ciates and|copart|ners of|our loss,

Lie thus||aston|ished on|the obliv|ious pool,

And call|them not|to share||with us||their part

In this|unhapp|y man|sion,"or|once more

With rall|ied arms||to try|what may|be yet

Regained|in Heaven,|or what|more lost|in hell?"

So Sa|tan spake;||and him|Beël|zebub

Thus answered:||"Leader of|those arm|ies bright

Which,"but|the Omni|potent,"none∧|could have foiled!

If once|they hear|that voice,|| their live|liest pledge

. Of hope||in fears|and dangers—||heard so oft

In worst|extremes,|and on|the per|ilous edge

Of batt|le, when|it raged,|in all|assaults

Their sur|est sig|nal—"they|will soon|resume

New cour|age and|revive,||though now|they lie

Grovelling|and pros|trate on|yon lake|of fire,

As we|erewhile,||astound|ed and|amazed;

No won|der,"fall|en such|a perni|cious highth!"

Satan's speech is majestic in assonance, mighty in the diction of proud nobility. The reader does not doubt his greatness, his regal bearing.

Shifting caesuras add grandeur to his statements, and the metrics subtly reveal his character. Notice the line

$$\overline{}\;\overline{}\;\smile\;\overline{}\;\smile\;\overline{}\;\smile\;\overline{}\;\overline{}$$
Here‖we|may reign|secure‖and‖in|my choice . . .

The opening spondee might as easily have been written *We here*—an iamb. But the equation of person and place would have been destroyed: the removal of the caesura would have de-emphasized both. The final two feet of the line are a pyrrhic and a spondee, designed to intensify *my* and *choice*—choice as Satan's, not God's. *Secure* and *choice* are also equated through the simple conjunction *and*. The line might have been written *yet in my choice*—but gone, then, would be the equating element; removed, the caesura; strength would vanish, and the admirable egotism of Satan would not manifest itself.

The biblical transition acts as a stage direction, and Beëlzebub's vocabulary lacks the polysyllabic grandeur of Satan's; it seems more ordinary, rising to greatness only in *Leader* and *Omnipotent*. The compensation here is noteworthy also. As transition enjambs into dialog, an amphibrach precedes a dactyl. The caesura emphasizes *Leader* to characterize Beëlzebub as a fawning opportunist. The line is reduced to four feet, but the syllable count remains at ten. The remainder of his speech is designed to reveal his strength by minimizing the weakness of the other fallen angels and calling attention to his superior powers of recovery.

Attention to such small and subtle detail creates greatness in blank verse. An ear sensitive to such effect responds to that greatness, finding blank verse more rewarding than rhymed forms.

Polonius' advice to Laërtes in Shakespeare's *Hamlet* (which is written in dramatic blank verse) owes its effectiveness not only to the meaning of the words but to the devices of blank verse. Notice the metrical stresses on *but* in the passage. The pyrrhics are cleverly used to create the tension between sense and pretentiousness. The conservative Polonius reveals his character in his linguistic and metrical ambivalence here:

Yet here, Laertes? Aboard, aboard, for shame!
The wind sits in the shoulder of your sail,
And you are stay'd for. There; my blessing with you!
And these few precepts in thy memory
See thou character. Give thy thoughts no tongue,   5
Nor any unproportion'd thought his act.
Be thou familiar, but by no means vulgar.
The friends thou hast, and their adoption tried,
Grapple them to thy soul with hoops of steel;

But do not dull thy palm with entertainment   *10*
Of each new-hatch'd, unfledg'd comrade. Beware
Of entrance to a quarrel; but being in,
Bear 't that the opposed may beware of thee.
Give every man thine ear, but few thy voice;
Take each man's censure, but reserve thy judgement.   *15*
Costly thy habit as thy purse can buy,
But not express'd in fancy; rich, not gaudy;
For the apparel oft proclaims the man,
And they in France of the best rank and station
Are most select and generous in that.   *20*
Neither a borrower nor a lender be;
For loan oft loses both itself and friend,
And borrowing dulls the edge of husbandry.
This above all: to thine own self be true,
And it must follow, as the night the day,   *25*
Thou canst not then be false to any man.
Farewell; my blessing season this in thee!

        (Act I, sc. iii)

Blank verse is admirably suited to grand description, as you can see from Milton's description of Lucifer in *Paradise Lost:*

    . . . He, above the rest
In shape and gesture proudly eminent,
Stood like a tower. His form had yet not lost
All her original brightness, nor appeared
Less than archangel ruined, and the excess   *5*
Of glory obscured: as when the sun new risen
Looks through the horizontal misty air
Shorn of his beams, or from behind the moon
In dim eclipse, disastrous twilight sheds
On half the nations, and with fear of change   *10*
Perplexes monarchs. Darkened so, yet shone
Above them all the archangel; but his face
Deep scars of thunder had intrenched, and care
Sat on his faded cheek, but under brows
Of dauntless courage, and considerate pride   *15*
Waiting revenge; cruel his eye, but cast
Signs of remorse and passion, to behold
The fellows of his crime, the followers rather
(Far other once beheld in bliss), condemned
For ever now to have their lot in pain,   *20*

Millions of spirits for his fault amerced
Of heaven, and from eternal splendors flung
For his revolt, yet faithful how they stood,
Their glory withered; as, when heaven's fire
Hath scathed the forest oaks or mountain pines,   25
With singéd top their stately growth, though bare,
Stands on the blasted heath.

                                        (I, ll. 589-615)

Alliteration, consonance, assonance, simile, metaphor, shifting caesura—all combine with metrical variety within the iambic pentameter to reveal the physical majesty and the crippled spirituality of the dark prince.

The brief, lyrical statement in blank verse becomes lyrical in the same sense an organ is lyrical—not as the flute or violin are. The stately tread of iambs is not lightened by the lilt of rhyme; so blank verse is suited to the "important," short observation. In "Days," Emerson employs a sonnet structure; but, as the poet must do when violating the sonnet, he compensates for the omitted rhyme and lines by intensifying other elements in the poem. The octave is reduced to a sestet; the sestet, to five lines. Language is economical, however, and the division is sharp and clear. Caesuras are manipulated to provide a discernable rhythm. Assonance is richly employed throughout:

Days

Daughters of Time, the hypocritic Days,
Muffled and dumb like barefoot dervishes,
And marching single in an endless file,
Bring diadems and fagots in their hands.
To each they offer gifts after his will,   5
Bread, kingdoms, stars, and sky that holds them all.
I, in my pleached garden, watched the pomp,
Forgot my morning wishes, hastily
Took a few herbs and apples, and the Day
Turned and departed silent. I, too late,   10
Under her solemn fillet saw the scorn.

                                Ralph Waldo Emerson

In the following excerpt from *Macbeth,* repetition is the major, though certainly not the only, device raising Shakespeare's lines to blank verse greatness:

> To-morrow, and to-morrow, and to-morrow
> Creeps in this petty pace from day to day
> To the last syllable of recorded time;
> And all our yesterdays have lighted fools
> The way to dusty death. Out, out, brief candle!   5
> Life's but a walking shadow, a poor player
> That struts and frets his hour upon the stage
> And then is heard no more. It is a tale
> Told by an idiot, full of sound and fury,
> Signifying nothing.   10

(Act V, sc. v)

Diction has been a blessing and a curse to the poet from the beginning of poetic form. At times, critics have railed against the inappropriateness of language of writers, the inaccuracy of their language concepts, and the unreasonableness of their attitudes as displayed in their word-choices. Sir William Davenant, born ten years before Shakespeare's death, took umbrage with the above passage from *Macbeth* and rewrote it in what he considered an improved form. Compare the two versions, deciding which is superior. The changes, you will notice, lie in vocabulary and punctuation. The blank verse remains constant, and repetition is not disturbed except in alliteration:

> Tomorrow and tomorrow and tomorrow
> Creeps in a stealing pace from day to day,
> To the last minute of recorded time,
> And all our yesterdays have lighted fools
> To their eternal homes; out, out that candle!   5
> Life's but a walking shadow, a poor player
> That struts and frets his hour upon the stage,
> And then is heard no more. It is a tale
> Told by an idiot, full of sound and fury,
> Signifying nothing.   10

Young people or beginning poets can aspire to seriousness in blank verse—and achieve it. William Cullen Bryant was a teenager when he wrote the major portion of

Thanatopsis

> To him who in the love of Nature holds
> Communion with her visible forms, she speaks
> A various language; for his gayer hours
> She has a voice of gladness, and a smile
> And eloquence of beauty, and she glides   5

Into his darker musings, with a mild
And healing sympathy, that steals away
Their sharpness, ere he is aware. When thoughts
Of the last bitter hour come like a blight
Over thy spirit, and sad images   10
Of the stern agony, and shroud, and pall,
And breathless darkness, and the narrow house,
Make thee to shudder, and grow sick at heart;—
Go forth, under the open sky, and list
To Nature's teachings, while from all around—   15
Earth and her waters, and the depths of air—
Comes a still voice—Yet a few days, and thee
The all-beholding sun shall see no more
In all his course; nor yet in the cold ground,
Where thy pale form was laid, with many tears,   20
Nor in embrace of ocean, shall exist
Thy image. Earth, that nourished thee, shall claim
Thy growth, to be resolved to earth again,
And, lost each human trace, surrendering up
Thine individual being, shalt thou go   25
To mix for ever with the elements,
To be a brother to the insensible rock
And to the sluggish clod, which the rude swain
Turns with his share, and treads upon. The oak
Shall send his roots abroad, and pierce thy mould.   30

    Yet not to thine eternal resting place
Shalt thou retire alone,·nor couldst thou wish
Couch more magnificent. Thou shalt lie down
With patriarchs of the infant world—with kings,
The powerful of the earth—the wise, the good,   35
Fair forms, and hoary seers of ages past,
All in one mighty sepulchre. The hills
Rock-ribbed and ancient as the sun,—the vales
Stretching in pensive quietness between;
The venerable woods—rivers that move   40
In majesty, and the complaining brooks
That make the meadows green; and, poured round all,
Old Ocean's gray and melancholy waste,—
Are but the solemn decorations all
Of the great tomb of man. The golden sun,   45
The planets, all the infinite host of heaven,

Are shining on the sad abodes of death,
Through the still lapse of ages. All that tread
The globe are but a handful to the tribes
That slumber in its bosom.—Take the wings   *50*
Of morning, pierce the Barcan wilderness,
Or lose thyself in the continuous woods
Where rolls the Oregon, and hears no sound,
Save his own dashings—yet the dead are there:
And millions in those solitudes, since first   *55*
The flight of years began, have laid them down
In their last sleep—the dead reign there alone.
So shalt thou rest, and what if thou withdraw
In silence from the living, and no friend
Take note of thy departure? All that breathe   *60*
Will share thy destiny. The gay will laugh
When thou art gone, the solemn brood of care
Plod on, and each one as before will chase
His favorite phantom; yet all these shall leave
Their mirth and their employments, and shall come   *65*
And make their bed with thee. As the long train
Of ages glide away, the sons of men,
The youth in life's green spring, and he who goes
In the full strength of years, matron and maid,
The speechless babe, and the gray-headed man—   *70*
Shall one by one be gathered to thy side,
By those who in their turn shall follow them.

So live, that when thy summons comes to join
The innumerable caravan, which moves
To that mysterious realm, where each shall take   *75*
His chamber in the silent halls of death,
Thou go not, like the quarry-slave at night,
Scourged to his dungeon, but, sustained and soothed
By an unfaltering trust, approach thy grave,
Like one who wraps the drapery of his couch   *80*
About him, and lies down to pleasant dreams.

William Cullen Bryant

   The first sixteen and one-half lines of "Thanatopsis" create an introduction. Personified nature begins the monolog at that point, and the
first verse paragraph ends after an objective and unsentimental statement
of the inevitability of death. The second and longest verse paragraph

concerns itself with the compensations of death, making it seem majestic and impartial in its inclusiveness. The final verse paragraph becomes didactic. Its sane logic, however, makes it agreeable and a fit ending for the poem. Even though Bryant was only sixteen or seventeen when he wrote most of the poem, the metrical skill demonstrated is considerable. It is even more remarkable as you consider his success in fitting the pieces together. The original poem began with the words "Yet a few days and thee/The all-beholding sun shall see no more" (lines 17-18), and ended with "And make their bed with thee" (line 66). Several years later, he wrote the present opening and closing portions. Notice the skill employed in wedding sense and sound in the lines

$$\breve{} \ \_\ |\ \breve{}\ \_\ |\ \breve{}\ \_.\ ||\ \breve{}\ \breve{}\ \_\ |\ \_$$
And make|their bed|with thee.|| As the long|train∧

$$\breve{}\ \_\ \breve{}\ |\ \_\ \breve{}\ \breve{}\ \_\ |\ \breve{}\ \_\ |\ \_$$
Of a g e s|glide away,|| the sons|of men, . . .

In the first line, the caesura after the three iambs prepares the reader for the anapest and the truncated final foot. The words, as the eye beholds them, almost look like boxcars (*as the long*) and a locomotive (*train*) running off the page. The words fall on the ear with the decisiveness of the visual pattern. The truncated *train* rushes into the next line where the hovering accent in *of ages* slows it and the hardening of the *g* consonant glides it into *away.* A caesura restores the iambic pattern.

In such poetry as "Thanatopsis," theme (at its most simplified level) becomes painfully obvious. The basic attitudes presented in the poem are almost funneled into the final lines so the reader cannot possibly miss the paramount "message." Whether or not this simplicity is satisfactory to critics of poetic form, many readers reject poetry that does not conclude in a "message." Such readers frequently prefer the simpler verse of Edgar A. Guest or James Metcalf, thereby missing much of the very real enjoyment of poetry—an enjoyment that comes only to the reader who learns to examine metrics, literary devices, motion and countermotion, and so on, as they combine with language to reveal a theme which may defy reduction to a simple moral or message.

Suggested Activity. Since blank verse is used so successfully in Milton's *Paradise Lost,* examine the poem, reading it in its entirety or excerpting it as your mood suggests. It will reward you regardless of how little or how much time you spend with it. The plays of Shakespeare may hold little interest for you, but, with an awareness of poetry as you have learned to read it, examine *Romeo and Juliet* or *Macbeth.* If the plays still hold no interest, do not force yourself to read them. Poetry should be its own reward, not an imposed punishment. Later, perhaps, you will be ready to read those works you still find dull or difficult.

Suggested Assignment. "Tithonus" is a poem that can move you to understanding and sympathy. We live in a time and country where youth is considered especially precious, a fact which often results in a callous disregard for the aged and their problems. If you are young yourself, "Tithonus" can help you appreciate the tragedy of one who feels himself "Immortal age beside immortal youth,/And all I was, in ashes." The story of Tithonus can be recounted briefly: A son of Laomedon, king of Troy, Tithonus was loved by Aurora, goddess of the dawn, for his youthful beauty. Securing immortality for him, she failed to ask eternal youth. Aging, he grew helpless and wrinkled, finally sleeping in a cradle, like a child. Immortality became such a curse that he pleaded with Aurora for release. Because she could not grant him death, she turned him into a grasshopper.

After reading the poem, write an analysis of the form, or a defense of the poem as preparation for age, or a comparison of Tithonus and an old person you have known:

Tithonus

The woods decay, the woods decay and fall,
The vapors weep their burthen to the ground,
Man comes and tills the field and lies beneath,
And after many a summer dies the swan.
Me only cruel immortality   *5*
Consumes: I wither slowly in thine arms,
Here at the quiet limit of the world,
A white-haired shadow roaming like a dream
The ever-silent spaces of the East,
Far-folded mists, and gleaming halls of morn.   *10*

Alas! for this gray shadow, once a man—
So glorious in his beauty and thy choice,
Who madest him thy chosen, that he seemed
To his great heart none other than a God!
I asked thee, "Give me immortality."   *15*
Then didst thou grant mine asking with a smile,
Like wealthy men who care not how they give.
But thy strong Hours indignant worked their wills
And beat me down and marred and wasted me,
And though they could not end me, left me maimed   *20*

To dwell in presence of immortal youth,
Immortal age beside immortal youth,
And all I was, in ashes. Can thy love,
Thy beauty, make amends, though even now,
Close over us, the silver star, thy guide,   25
Shines in those tremulous eyes that fill with tears
To hear me? Let me go: take back thy gift:
Why should a man desire in any way
To vary from the kindly race of men,
Or pass beyond the goal of ordinance   30
Where all should pause, as is most meet for all?

A soft air fans the cloud apart; there comes
A glimpse of that dark world where I was born.
Once more the old mysterious glimmer steals
From thy pure brows, and from thy shoulders pure,   35
And bosom beating with a heart renewed.
Thy cheek begins to redden through the gloom,
Thy sweet eyes brighten slowly close to mine,
Ere yet they blind the stars, and the wild team
Which love thee, yearning for thy yoke, arise,   40
And shake the darkness from their loosened manes,
And beat the twilight into flakes of fire.

Lo! ever thus thou growest beautiful
In silence, then before thine answer given
Departest, and thy tears are on my cheek.   45

Why wilt thou ever scare me with thy tears,
And make me tremble lest a saying learnt,
In days far-off, on that dark earth, be true?
"The Gods themselves cannot recall their gifts."

Ay me! ay me! with what another heart   50
In days far-off, and with what other eyes
I used to watch—if I be he that watched—
The lucid outline forming round thee; saw
The dim curls kindle into sunny rings;
Changed with thy mystic change, and felt my blood   55
Glow with the glow that slowly crimsoned all
Thy presence and thy portals, while I lay,
Mouth, forehead, eyelids, growing dewy-warm

With kisses balmier than half-opening buds
Of April, and could hear the lips that kissed   60
Whispering I knew not what of wild and sweet,
Like that strange song I heard Apollo sing,
While Ilion like a mist rose into towers.

Yet hold me not for ever in thine East:
How can my nature longer mix with thine?   65
Coldly thy rosy shadows bathe me, cold
Are all thy lights, and cold my wrinkled feet
Upon thy glimmering thresholds, when the steam
Floats up from those dim fields about the homes
Of happy men that have the power to die,   70
And grassy barrows of the happier dead.
Release me, and restore me to the ground;
Thou seëst all things, thou wilt see my grave:
Thou wilt renew thy beauty morn by morn;
I earth in earth forget these empty courts,   75
And thee returning on thy silver wheels.

Alfred, Lord Tennyson

CHAPTER IX

Free Verse and the Creative Process

You should, by now, understand poetic convention well enough to read free verse intelligently. In many ways, it is easier to read than the fixed forms, for rhyme is sometimes used and sometimes not; meter may be used or not used—in short, the writer of free verse may employ all of the poetic devices of the fixed forms, or he may, for certain reasons, employ none.

All of which probably makes free verse sound unrestrained and lacking in conventions—effortless to write and effortless to read. But nothing could be less true. Ambiguity, ellipsis, telescoping—all lend their usefulness *and* their problems to this form as they ordinarily do not in fixed forms.

Ambiguity is the expression of ideas in language designed to create more than one possible meaning. It may be deliberately employed—for evasion, perhaps, as Juliet does in Act III, scene v of *Romeo and Juliet*. Romeo has killed her cousin Tybalt, and her mother mistakes Juliet's tears, thinking they are shed for the kinsman, while they are really for Romeo. In response to her mother's regret that Romeo "the traitor murderer lives," Juliet responds:

Aye, madam, from the reach of these my hands.
Would none but I might venge my cousin's death!

Could none but Juliet avenge that death, harm would never come to her beloved Romeo. Lady Capulet, unaware of Juliet's love, is misled by the ambiguity. Juliet almost immediately resorts to a second type of ambiguity, called *amphiboly*, resting on misunderstood grammatical structure. At her mother's suggestion that Romeo be poisoned and that such an act should satisfy Juliet, the girl replies:

> Indeed, I never shall be satisfied
> With Romeo, till I behold him—dead—
> Is my poor heart so for a kinsman vexed."

Her mother hears the adjective *dead* as a modifier of *him* (Romeo), but Juliet means it as a predicate adjective modifying *my poor heart.*

Such *squinting constructions* (another name for amphiboly) were so effectively used by John Dryden in "Absolom and Achitophel" that William Empson, in *Seven Types of Ambiguity,* noted of one passage: *"Sway'd, dissembl'd, delay'd* may each be either verb or participle independently . . . granting that at least one must be a verb." Indeed, the reader's understanding of the lines will vary as he reads the words as different parts of speech:

> Thus long have I by Native Mercy sway'd,
> My wrongs dissembl'd, my Revenge delay'd;
> So willing to forgive th' Offending Age;
> So much the Father did the King assuage.

The ubiquitous *pun* is, actually, another form of ambiguity, as it depends on the understanding of one word in more than one sense or suggests another word of very similar sound. A classic example is found in Thomas Hood's "Faithless Sally Brown": "They went and *told* the sexton, and/The sexton *tolled* the bell."

When such ambiguity is deliberately employed by the poet, the line becomes correspondingly richer as possible meanings multiply. When such ambiguity is unintentional, weakness results and the line may become impossible to understand. Undue brevity in telescoping of ideas, extreme compression of ideas, faulty sequence as a result of poetic inversion, unclear reference of pronoun or absence of antecedent, and the imprecise use of words with more than one meaning—all lead the poet into unintentional ambiguity and the reader into difficulty.

Ellipsis is the omission of words which are essential to the syntax of the sentence but which can be supplied by the careful reader. You use this figure of speech when you introduce two friends: "Jane, this is John. John, Jane." The words *this is* have been omitted in the second clause, but you still understand the sentence. The poet also uses ellipsis for emphasis of statement by eliminating needless words. You will remember ellipsis as a major device in haiku.

Free verse poets frequently use ellipsis to bridge ideas—ideas that are, to the poets, so closely and logically associated that intervening ideas are too apparent to need stating. This omitting of obvious ideas is called *telescoping.* If you picture a collapsible telescope and remember how one made of three sections can be reduced to two, you can see the origin of the term. The middle section of the partially opened telescope isn't removed; it still connects sections one and three; but you can't see it as it is concealed inside the visible sections.

Difficulty for the reader arises when he does not understand the telescoping process. If he fails to see the bridging idea (the transitional one which has been elided or folded into the telescope of words) the poem will lack coherence *for him.* This does not mean *the poem* lacks coherence. The reader's failure to follow the poet's logic creates the seeming incoherence. On the other hand, much contemporary poetry is so elliptical, the bridging ideas so concealed or obvious only to the poet, that even the good reader cannot make the intellectual jump between ideas. When such poets as T. S. Eliot and Ezra Pound include vague references from their vast knowledge of many literatures in many languages, the telescoping becomes so abstruse that elaborate research is required of the reader who wishes to understand the line. Such research is profitable for anyone, but the general reader is not an English scholar and he, quite understandably and defensibly, considers the reward inadequate for the effort. Modern poets are not unique in such practices, however. In "Il Penseroso," John Milton wrote:

> And let some strange, mysterious dream
> Wave at his wings, in airy stream
> Of lively portraiture displayed,
> Softly on my eyelids laid.

The ambiguity of these lines may result from poor syntax, ellipsis, or telescoping. Milton's grammar is usually impeccable; he is not ordinarily given to telescoping; his knowledge was, however, extensive. At any rate, scholars have disagreed about the cause of the difficulty of the lines, and they have offered many possible meanings. It is scarcely unreasonable, then, to understand a student's distress on meeting such lines.

Free verse is not a new form, though readers frequently think it is. Hebrew verse and Oriental poetry have never used the foot or line as the poetic unit. Each employs the entire stanza to create a total rhythm pattern resting on emphasis supplied by the natural modulations of the voice. The loosely-knit units of syllables result in an irregular spacing of accents to create cadences of sound that are pleasing to the ear in the same way speech is when vocabulary, syntax, and rhythm are highly organized. These cadences are musical in their phrasal groupings—not musical in the sense of being timed with a metronome (for that is metrical verse), but musical as lyrics are when a good singer rearranges word stress and tempo to create his own unique style. These cadences are easily discernible, even in translation, in

The Twenty-Third Psalm

The Lord is my shepherd; I shall not want.

He maketh me to lie down in green pastures: he leadeth me beside the still waters.

He restoreth my soul: he leadeth me in the paths of righteousness for his name's sake.

Yea, though I walk through the valley of the shadow of death, I will fear no evil: for thou art with me; thy rod and thy staff they comfort me.

Thou preparest a table for me in the presence of mine enemies: thou anointest mine head with oil; my cup runneth over.

Surely goodness and mercy shall follow me all the days of my life: and I will dwell in the house of the Lord forever.

A scansion of the psalm reveals many repeated iambs, but the English language, you remember, is iambic in structure. However, a careful survey of the metrics reveals no pattern emerging. The rise and fall of the rhythm depends on a symmetrical pattern of stressed and unstressed syllables compensating naturally and gracefully for each other much as they do in the speech of those speakers who delight us with their ease and fluidity of language.

You will notice that we said "A scansion of the psalm." Free verse can, indeed, be scanned. It may be forced into an observably repeated pattern of stressed syllables, but it is impossible to read it in the forced scansion rhythm.

In English, two kinds of accent exist. One is the musical *chromatic accent* created by pitch which can be consciously controlled. As you read the following sentences, stress the italicized words and you will hear pitch at work:

I love you.
I *love* you.
I love *you.*
I love *you.*
I love you.

The second kind of accent is *emphatic* or *stress accent* which results from the amount of breath employed in creating syllables—the greater the expenditure of breath, the longer the syllable. Notice the different breath expenditures in *entire* and *enter*. Traditional verse accent is based primarily on emphatic accent. Free verse, like conversational English, utilizes chromatic accent to a much greater degree.

You probably encountered difficulties in scanning "Spring and Fall: To a Young Child" (p. 103) because Hopkins relies on chromatic accent. Turn back to that poem and notice the acute accent marks (´) supplied by Hopkins as an indication of which syllables should receive the force of stress. Developing a theory he called "sprung rhythm," Hopkins rejected traditional meter wherein rhythm results from the combination of feet (with their limited number of possible substitutions and variations) within a given line. He heard poetry as he heard the number of beats to the measure in music. Phrasal groupings result as words are hyphenated to create clusters of unaccented syllables (which he called "slack") within a line. In one of his greatly admired poems, "The Windhover," Hopkins uses "falling" rhythm, so called because the stress comes at the beginning of each foot. Read the poem aloud, trying to find a dominant foot in the lines:

The Windhover:
To Christ Our Lord

I caught this morning morning's minion, king-
   dom of daylight's dauphin, dapple-dawn-drawn Falcon, in his riding
   Of the rolling level underneath him steady air, and striding
High there, how he rung upon the rein of a wimpling wing
In his ecstasy! then off, off forth on swing,   5
   As a skate's heel sweeps smooth on a bow-bend: the hurl and gliding
   Rebuffed the big wind. My heart in hiding
Stirred for a bird,—the achieve of, the mastery of the thing!

Brute beauty and valor and act, oh, air, pride, plume, here
   Buckle! AND the fire that breaks from thee then, a billion   10
Times told lovelier, more dangerous, O my chevalier!

   No wonder of it: shéer plód makes plough down sillion
Shine, and blue-bleak embers, ah my dear,
   Fall, gall themselves, and gash gold-vermilion.

In Hopkins' own scansion of the first four lines of the poem, you will see cadences forming from the rhythm pattern:

x⋮ ́ x ́ x ́ x ́ x ́
I caught this morning morning's minion, king-

x x ́ x ̋ x x x ́ x ̋ x x x x ́ x
dom of daylight's dauphin, dapple-dawn-drawn Falcon, in his riding

x x ̋ x x x ́ x ̋ x x x ́ x ́ x
Of the rolling level underneath him steady air, and striding

́ x x x ́ x x x ́ x x ́ x ́
High there, how he rung upon the rein of a wimpling wing * * *

Stressed syllables are marked with acute accent marks; unstressed syllables are marked x, and the curved line beneath a syllable indicates a
"hanger" or "outrider" which Hopkins defined as "one, two, or three
slack syllables added to a foot and not counted in the nominal scanning."
In traditional terms, the "hanger" would be a feminine rest syllable.
According to Hopkins, "The strong syllable in an outriding foot is always a great stress and after the outrider follows a short pause." Consequently, he marked the first syllable of *dauphin* and *Falcon* with a
double accent mark.

The uneven altitude created by updrafts is reproduced in the plunging
rhythms of the lines as the windhover, a sea bird, rises and falls. A sense
of forward motion in the bird's flight results from the hyphenation of
kingdom which is divided between two lines so the masculine syllable
may be rhymed with the feminine syllables of *riding* and *striding* and the
single syllable of *wing*. The clustered *dapple-dawn-drawn* hyphenation removes the necessity of conjunctions or commas and creates interesting
possibilities in the reading. Modification possibilities are added to each
word in the compounding. The effect is similar to that achieved in the
ambiguities of the line "Though worlds of wanwood leafmeal lie" in
"Spring and Fall: To a Young Child."

Scanned traditionally, "The Windhover" lines can be forced into the
following pattern:

Line 1: unrelieved iambic pentameter
Line 2: an initial anapest, six iambs, and one extra feminine syllable
Line 3: same as line 2
Line 4: an initial headless iamb, four iambs, an anapest, and a final
iamb

But read in such meter, the poem loses its music as well as its meaning.

Such attention to Hopkins' free verse is not a suggestion that the
twentieth-century use of the form originated with him. His lines are,
rather, as representative as any could be of a form that is as individual-

istic as its author can make it. Poetry in Old English was alliterative and accentual before Middle English imposed rhyme and the metrical stanza on it. The next major revolution came with blank verse in the sixteenth century, and Keats and Wordsworth penned lines that will not scan traditionally. Poe experimented with verse approaching the cadenced, and Walt Whitman was a pioneer in free verse form. It can not be argued that he merely revolted against the "tyrrany of the iamb," for such is not the case. He did attempt to discover the cadence of breath groups, to create the structure of thought as it is translatable into poetry. Emily Dickinson did not invent slant rhyme, certainly, but she did raise it to the level of poetic art. Her metrics may be a result of an indifference, a lack of craft, or deliberate intention, but they are effective forerunners of the cadenced verse of today. Hopkins' "sprung rhythm" influenced many of the twentieth-century poets, and Ezra Pound and T. S. Eliot were the most recent "great" innovators in the development of free verse.

A second misconception is that free verse is utterly formless. This, too, is far from true. While the form is not fixed, each poet must establish the pattern of his poem—actually structure it to work in conjunction with the meaning. As the poem is freed of conventions, it must create original approaches of its own. E. E. Cummings manages to weld visual form and content into a remarkable unit in

Chanson Innocent

in Just-
spring   when the world is mud-
luscious the little
lame balloonman

whistles   far   and wee   5

and eddieandbill come
running from marbles and
piracies and it's
spring

when the world is puddle-wonderful   10

the queer
old balloonman whistles
far   and   wee
and bettyandisbel come dancing

from hop-scotch and jump-rope and   15

```
it's
spring
and
    the


        goat-footed              20

balloonMan    whistles
far
and
wee
```

                                        E. E. Cummings

The upper and lower case letters are used effectively and deliberately here. Opposed to the conventional use of capitals, Cummings used them only when they seemed effective. The initial *i*'s lower case creates a feeling of timelessness in this poem. The reportage is without beginning (an upper case letter in an unwritten, earlier portion is suggested) and without end—notice the absence of final punctuation. The capital *J* of *Just-spring* establishes the time as a season of childhood and nature. On the other hand, *spring* is merely commonplace, therefore lower case *s*. The children, *eddieandbill* and *bettyandisbel,* are as inseparable as their names, as ubiquitous as small letters. These are collective nouns rather than proper names.

That abused conjunction, *and,* is employed brilliantly in this poem. Used twelve times, the word creates unity as it allows the run-on constructions to flow with unbroken movement. Spacing is also an integral part of the total poem. Lines 1, 2, and 3 employ saṁvegha, for the reader does not expect *spring* after *Just* or *luscious* after *mud.* Line 2 separates *spring* and *when* with white space in the same way haiku employs the ellipsis. Line 5 demands a spacious reading as a result of the use of separation. The sound seems to come from everywhere. The second use of *far and wee* narrows the space, limiting it so the children can run to the geographical point. The third use suggests a column or file of children marching away.

The arrangement is reinforced in the diction of the poem. At first, the baloonman is *little* and *lame*—an ordinary enough description. As he and spring work their magic in the localized geography, he becomes queer and old—as spring is queer in its inducements and old in its recurring pattern. In the final use of *balloonMan,* he retains his human qualities (notice the capital *M*) but the spell is cast utterly, and he becomes *goat-footed*—a Pan. He thereby becomes the spirit of man in nature

as well as nature itself, strong in its lure. The whistle becomes the Pied
Piper's hypnotic sound, and the parade to never-never land begins as the
words file out of the poem. The enchantments of *mud-luscious* and
puddle-wonderful overlay the *and it's spring* repetition to create the timelessness of myth. As the children disappear, the reader may note the first
syllable of *balloon* and recall Bal, the fertility god to whom children were
once sacrificed so spring would bring rebirth after the winter.

 A traditional scansion of the poem is scarcely possible, but the phrasal
groupings can easily be marked with Hopkins' symbols:

in Just-

spring   when the world is mud-

luscious the little

lame balloonman

whistles   far   and wee

and eddieandbill come

running from marbles and

piracies and it's

spring

when the world is puddle-wonderful

the queer

old balloonman whistles

far   and   wee

and bettyandisbel come dancing

from hop-scotch and jump-rope and

it's

spring

and

the

goat-footed

balloonMan   whistles

far

and

wee

Writing poetry which achieves such effects demands much more than a casual disregard for convention. It demands additional creativity because the reader is not conditioned to violations of form. He must be led into the desired reactions through clarity in the new form's intent. And a rhythm suitable to the progress of the poem must be established.

Can you hear the marching rhythm of the pioneers crossing endless plains in this excerpt from Walt Whitman's "Pioneers! O Pioneers!"?

> For we cannot tarry here,
> We must march my darlings, we must bear the brunt of danger,
> We the youthful sinewy races, all the rest on us depend,
> Pioneers! O Pioneers!

You can probably "feel" the gossamer threads unreeling from the spider and the soul in Whitman's

A Noiseless Patient Spider

A noiseless patient spider,
I mark'd where on a little promontory it stood isolated,
Mark'd how to explore the vacant vast surrounding,
It launch'd forth filament, filament, filament, out of itself,
Ever unreeling them, ever tirelessly speeding them.   5

And you O my soul where you stand,
Surrounded, detached, in measureless oceans of space,
Ceaselessly musing, venturing, throwing, seeking the spheres
   to connect them,

Till the bridge you will need be form'd, till the ductile
    anchor hold,
Till the gossamer thread you fling catch somewhere, O my soul.   *10*

Did you notice the comparisons, and the meticulousness with which Whitman built them? Did you notice the devices he used to establish echo? Did you notice the action of filament-throwing in stanza 2? The lines are like hurled gossamers, thrown further and further with each long vowel. How does the placement of *O my soul* create a different cadence each time in the first and last lines of the second stanza? Why?

Whitman's poetry frequently becomes wordy, obvious in intent, prosy; but, at its best, it recalls the structure of fixed forms, with the tightness of absolute control. Compare "Good-bye My Fancy" (p. 47) with Michael Drayton's "Idea 61" (p. 45) and Byron's "When We Two Parted" (p. 46) and assess the poets' choices of form for their communications. Structurally, Whitman's poem shares much with Drayton's sonnet. In Whitman's "free verse sonnet," the "octave" occupies the first ten lines. A pivotal transition (*yet*) begins the "sestet" which occupies eight lines. In both poems, the octave states a definite parting, the sestet is a reconsideration. Drayton suggests the outcome is in the hands of the loved one; Whitman assumes a personal responsibility, arrives at a more satisfactory conclusion in "Good-bye—and hail! my Fancy." Drayton separates his octave and sestet with a change in diction and idiom; Whitman employs more penetrating analysis and a carefully interwoven line to recapture the past, entwine it with the future. His hyphenation of *may-be* reshapes the word, you will notice, to make it serve a double function, and his repetition of words and ideas through the poem strengthens rather than weakens the idea. Each repetition has been faintly embroidered with new meanings—meanings which are cumulative in their impact. Three lines are noticeably longer than others in the poem—why? Compare the first line of the poem with the last one. How has the poem worked from one attitude to the other? Notice that the last line repeats the first, but it makes the addition which justifies the body of the poem. The rise and fall of the rhythm creates a cadence particularly suitable to the poem. And it establishes an echo through its rise and fall—an echo demanding a more finely attuned ear than rhyme demands. Drayton's sonnet structure warns the reader of a change in attitude at the beginning of the sestet. Whitman's free verse does not immediately reveal its sonnet structure, and the reader is involved in the countermotion, much as he is involved in the flow of his own thoughts as they weigh possibilities in other decisions. What does Byron's poem have in common with Whitman's and Drayton's, and how does it differ?

A third misconception about free verse is that it allows ease in telescoping ideas. This, too, is folly. While the form does allow the poet to
telescope material as fixed forms cannot, a clear logic must pervade the
line or, in the telescoping, ideas are lost. Notice, in "Love Lies A-
Bleeding," the use of sonnet conventions—conventions freed from fourteen lines of iambic pentameter and recast in contemporary idioms. The
ampersand would, ordinarily, not be acceptable in poetry, but here it is
completely appropriate:

Love Lies A-Bleeding

That they should quarrel
over garbage! Yet he *did*
fail to set it out, & now
it must fill the back porch
   with its putridness   *5*
for another three days.

There are no words
to reconcile this: a promise
forgotten, the passionate
   imbecility of love   *10*
slashed open. *Her* loss
as well—who, grieving,
slams the cupboard doors
while he sulks on the couch
   his heart drowning
   in that mortal stench.

          Frederick Eckman

Implicit in the poem is the knowledge that this argument did not really
concern garbage; it was merely triggered by it. Can you see why *did*
ends line 2? Why is it italicized? Why is *Her* italicized? Why are the
four lines indented? What are the *two* meanings of *this* in line 8? At
what points are hyperbole and understatement employed? Why? What
poetic devices do you notice in the poem? Would this be a "better"
poem if it were written in conventional sonnet form?

Free verse does allow for greater personal expression—but it imposes
restraints on the poet: vacuity becomes agonizingly apparent; ineptness in
form announces itself in loud, clear tones. No poem ever seems quite as bad
(even to the point of embarrassing the reader) as a weak free verse effort.

The insights, the imagery, the symbols of free verse must be intense,
clear, and vivid. Compare the next sonnet by Dante Gabriel Rossetti,

"The Portrait," with the free verse of Ezra Pound and William Carlos Williams which follows it. All three poets comment on a specific woman; each does it in a different way. Notice how each of the poems is granted freedom and yet how it is restricted by the author's choice of form. The sonnet and free verse both have unique limitations; yet both have compensating freedoms:

The Portrait

O Lord of all compassionate control,
   O Love! let this my lady's picture glow
   Under my hand to praise her name, and show
Even of her inner self the perfect whole:
That he who seeks her beauty's furthest goal,   *5*
   Beyond the light that the sweet glances throw
   And refluent wave of the sweet smile, may know
The very sky and sea-line of her soul.

Lo! it is done. Above the long lithe throat
   The mouth's mould testifies of voice and kiss,   *10*
     The shadowed eyes remember and foresee.
Her face is made her shrine. Let all men note
That in all years (O Love, thy gift is this!)
   They that would look on her must come to me.
                         Dante Gabriel Rossetti

Portrait D'une Femme

Your mind and you are our Sargasso Sea,
London has swept about you this score years
And bright ships left you this or that in fee:
Ideas, old gossip, oddments of all things,
Strange spars of knowledge and dimmed wares of price.   *5*
Great minds have sought you—lacking someone else.
You have been second always. Tragical?
No. You preferred it to the usual thing:
One dull man, dulling and uxorious,
One average mind—with one thought less, each year.   *10*
Oh, you are patient, I have seen you sit
Hours, where something might have floated up.
And now you pay one. Yes, you richly pay.
You are a person of some interest, one comes to you
And takes strange gain away: *15*

Trophies fished up; some curious suggestion;
Fact that leads nowhere; and a tale or two,
Pregnant with mandrakes, or with something else
That might prove useful and yet never proves,
That never fits a corner or shows use,   20
Or finds its hour upon the loom of days:
The tarnished, gaudy, wonderful old work;
Idols and ambergris and rare inlays,
These are your riches, your great store; and yet
For all this sea-hoard of deciduous things,   25
Strange woods half sodden, and new brighter stuff:
In the slow float of differing light and deep,
No! there is nothing! In the whole and all,
Nothing that's quite your own.
                    Yet this is you.   30

Ezra Pound

Portrait of a Lady

Your thighs are appletrees
whose blossoms touch the sky.
Which sky? The sky
where Watteau hung a lady's
slipper. Your knees   5
are a southern breeze—or
a gust of snow. Agh! what
sort of man was Fragonard?
—as if that answered
anything. Ah, yes—below   10
the knees, since the tune
drops that way, it is
one of those white summer days,
the tall grass of your ankles
flickers upon the shore—   15
Which shore?—
the sand clings to my lips—
Which shore?
Agh, petals maybe. How
should I know?   20
Which shore? Which shore?
I said petals from an appletree.

William Carlos Williams

A poet may decide to use free verse for a statement, only to find the final poem lacking poetic spark. Since the form is allowed privilege, he may decide to incorporate rhyme as Emerson did in

Fable

The mountain and the squirrel
Had a quarrel;
And the former called the latter "Little Prig."
Bun replied,
"You are doubtless very big;   5
But all sorts of things and weather
Must be taken in together
To make up a year
And a sphere.
And I think it's no disgrace   10
To occupy my place.
If I'm not so large as you,
You are not so small as I,
And not half so spry.
I'll not deny you make   15
A very pretty squirrel track;
Talents differ: all is well and wisely put;
If I cannot carry forests on my back,
Neither can you crack a nut."

Ralph Waldo Emerson

But, you will notice, the poet is equally free to use rhyme only where and if he feels it to be an asset.

Intensification of meaning and sharpness of imagery are often achieved in free verse in ways the fixed forms could not afford. The poet's *idiom* (language used in a stylistically unique way) may be more vividly realized in this form. Compare the next three poems to observe distinctive idiom. The first is free verse; the second, blank; the third, free:

Heat

O wind, rend open the heat,
cut apart the heat,
rend it to tatters.

Fruit cannot drop
through this thick air—   5
fruit cannot fall into heat
that presses up and blunts

the points of pears
and rounds the grapes.

Cut through the heat—   *10*
plow through it,
turning it on either side
of your path.

> H.D. *(Hilda Doolittle)*

from *The Seasons* (from *Winter)*

Where are your stores, ye powerful beings! say,
Where your aërial magazines reserved
To swell the brooding terrors of the storm?
In what far-distant region of the sky,
Hushed in deep silence, sleep you when 'tis calm?   *5*
    When from the pallid sky the sun descends,
With many a spot, that o'er his glaring orb
Uncertain wanders, stained; red fiery streaks
Begin to flush around. The reeling clouds
Stagger with dizzy poise, as doubting yet   *10*
Which master to obey; while, rising slow,
Blank in the leaden-colored east, the moon
Wears a wan circle round her blunted horns.
Seen through the turbid, fluctuating air,
The stars obtuse emit a shivering ray;   *15*
Or frequent seem to shoot athwart the gloom,
And long behind them trail the whitening blaze.
Snatched in short eddies, plays the withered leaf;
And on the flood the dancing feather floats.
With broadened nostrils to the sky upturned,   *20*
The conscious heifer snuffs the stormy gale.
E'en as the matron, at her nightly task,
With pensive labor draws the flaxen thread,
The wasted taper and the crackling flame
Foretell the blast. . . .   *25*

> *James Thomson*

Preludes
I

The winter evening settles down
With smell of steaks in passageways.
Six o'clock.
The burnt-out ends of smoky days.

And now a gusty shower wraps   5
The grimy scraps
Of withered leaves about your feet
And newspapers from vacant lots;
The showers beat
On broken blinds and chimney-pots,   10
And at the corner of the street
A lonely cab-horse steams and stamps.
And then the lighting of the lamps.

II

The morning comes to consciousness
Of faint stale smells of beer
From the sawdust-trampled street
With all its muddy feet that press
To early coffee-stands.   5
With other masquerades
That time resumes,
One thinks of all the hands
That are raising dingy shades
In a thousand furnished rooms.   10

III

You tossed a blanket from the bed,
You lay upon your back, and waited;
You dozed, and watched the night revealing
The thousand sordid images
Of which your soul was constituted;   5
They flickered against the ceiling.
And when all the world came back
And the light crept up between the shutters
And you heard the sparrows in the gutters,
You had such a vision of the street   10
As the street hardly understands;
Sitting along the bed's edge, where
You curled the papers from your hair,
Or clasped the yellow soles of feet
In the palms of both soiled hands.   15

IV

His soul stretched tight across the skies
That fade behind a city block,
Or trampled by insistent feet
At four and five and six o'clock;

And short square fingers stuffing pipes,   *5*
And evening newspapers, and eyes
Assured of certain certainties,
The conscience of a blackened street
Impatient to assume the world.

I am moved by fancies that are curled   *10*
Around these images, and cling:
The notion of some infinitely gentle
Infinitely suffering thing.

Wipe your hand across your mouth, and laugh;
The worlds revolve like ancient women   *15*
Gathering fuel in vacant lots.

                              T. S. Eliot

Subjects which the garden-club poet avoids are, not infrequently, explored in free verse. This is not to suggest free verse exploits the salacious or shocks the reader's senses in unrestrained delight. If it does, it is not poetry—it is exhibitionism devoid of poetic intent. In the next poem, the poet is not concerned with descriptions of a shocking nature, but the simile creates a graphic picture which will be merely natural or indecently vulgar as the reader's mind prefers to see the scene. A social comment pervades the lines as the homely symbols create a picture as sharp as oil on canvas:

East River Nudes[1]
They stand,
As if to take a dare,
At water's edge,
Boy bathers,
Bare,   *5*
Drawn up
To meet a city stare:

Long legs,
Round heads,
The span between   *10*
As spare as wood
And whittled clean,

They make
A river bank design
As lewd   *15*
As clothes-pins
On a line.
                    Mildred Weston

Violence in emotional moments is often explored in free verse, as ragged lines re-create ragged emotions:

The Taxi

When I go away from you
The world beats dead
Like a slackened drum.
I call out for you against the jutted stars
And shout into the ridges of the wind.   *5*
Streets coming fast,
One after the other,
Wedge you away from me,
And the lamps of the city prick my eyes
So that I can no longer see your face.   *10*
Why should I leave you,
To wound myself upon the sharp edges of the night?
                    Amy Lowell

And harsh reality becomes very harsh, indeed, in this form:

True Love at Last

The handsome and self-absorbed young man
looked at the lovely and self-absorbed girl.

The lovely and self-absorbed girl
looked back at the handsome and self-absorbed young man
and thrilled.   *5*

And in that thrill he felt:
Her self-absorption is even as strong as mine.
I must see if I can't break through it
and absorb her in me.

And in that thrill she felt: *10*
His self-absorption is even stronger than mine!
What fun, stronger than mine!
I must see if I can't absorb this Samson of self-absorption.

So they simply adored one another
and in the end they were both nervous wrecks, because   *15*
in self-absorption and self-interest they were equally matched.

                                                    D. H. Lawrence

But the eloquence of the Orient may find equally adequate expression in free verse:

Nocturne in a Deserted Brickyard

Stuff of the moon
Runs on the lapping sand
Out to the longest shadows.
Under the curving willows,
And round the creep of the wave line,   *5*
Fluxions of yellow and dusk on the waters
Make a wide dreaming pansy of an old pond in the night.

                                                    Carl Sandburg

Or symbolism may become almost palpable:

Oread

Whirl up, sea—
Whirl your pointed pines.
Splash your great pines
On our rocks.
Hurl your green over us—   *5*
Cover us with your pools of fir.

                    H. D. (Hilda Doolittle)

The most commonplace experience may be examined in a casual, seemingly effortless statement, as natural as a moment you have known:

The Fish

I caught a tremendous fish
and held him beside the boat
half out of water, with my hook
fast in a corner of his mouth.

He didn't fight.   5
He hadn't fought at all.
He hung a grunting weight,
battered and venerable
and homely. Here and there
his brown skin hung in strips   10
like ancient wall-paper:
and its pattern of darker brown
was like wall-paper:
shapes like full-blown roses
stained and lost through age.   15
He was speckled with barnacles,
fine rosettes of lime,
and infested
with tiny white sea-lice,
and underneath two or three   20
rags of green weed hung down.
While his gills were breathing in
the terrible oxygen—
the frightening gills,
fresh and crisp with blood,   25
that can cut so badly—
I thought of the coarse white flesh
packed in like feathers,
the big bones and the little bones,
the dramatic reds and blacks   30
of his shiny entrails,
and the pink swim-bladder
like a big peony.
I looked into his eyes
which were far larger than mine   35
but shallower, and yellowed,
the irises backed and packed
with tarnished tinfoil
seen through the lenses
of old scratched isinglass.   40
They shifted a little, but not
to return my stare.
—It was more like the tipping
of an object toward the light.
I admired his sullen face,   45
the mechanism of his jaw,

and then I saw
that from his lower lip
—if you could call it a lip—
grim, wet, and weapon-like,   *50*
hung five old pieces of fish-line,
or four and a wire leader
with the swivel still attached,
with all their five big hooks
grown firmly in his mouth.   *55*
A green line, frayed at the end
where he broke it, two heavier lines,
and a fine black thread
still crimped from the strain and snap
when it broke and he got away.   *60*
Like medals with their ribbons
frayed and wavering,
a five-haired beard of wisdom
trailing from his aching jaw.
I stared and stared   *65*
and victory filled up
the little rented boat,
from the pool of bilge
where oil had spread a rainbow
around the rusted engine   *70*
to the bailer rusted orange,
the sun-cracked thwarts,
the oarlocks on their strings,
the gunnels—until everything
was rainbow, rainbow, rainbow!   *75*
And I let the fish go.

Elizabeth Bishop

"The Fish" is, obviously, a symbol as well as a physical creature in nature; the poem is less concerned with the act itself than the revelation of character, the *I* of the poem. While she has not said as much, you know her life is bounded by a house and a frequent visit to the sea. Imagery and selection reveal far more than is indicatively stated.

Form may be unique in free verse, as unique as the author feels it should be to satisfy his purpose. At times, that uniqueness may be understood only by the author, but it is usually acceptable to the reader because, whether he can isolate the form variations or not, the successful variation adds dimension and depth of meaning to the poem. Marianne Moore's

"The Fish" establishes its own best form to communicate an emotional response to fragmented suggestion as well as to the physical imagery of the poem. As you read the work carefully, you should be able to see reasons for the "violations" in form, lines, and words:

The Fish

wade
through black jade.
   Of the crow-blue mussel-shells, one keeps
   adjusting the ash-heaps;
      opening and shutting itself like   *5*

an
injured fan.
   The barnacles which encrust the side
   of the wave, cannot hide
      there for the submerged shafts of the   *10*

sun,
split like spun
   glass, move themselves with spotlight swiftness
   into the crevices—
      in and out, illuminating   *15*

the
turquoise sea
   of bodies. The water drives a wedge
   of iron through the iron edge
      of the cliff; whereupon the stars,   *20*

pink
rice-grains, ink
   bespattered jelly-fish, crabs like green
   lilies, and submarine
      toadstools, slide each on the other.   *25*

All
external
   marks of abuse are present on this
   defiant edifice—
      all the physical features of   *30*

ac-
cident—lack
   of cornice, dynamite grooves, burns, and
   hatchet strokes, these things stand
      out on it; the chasm-side is   *35*

dead.
Repeated
   evidence has proved that it can live
   on what cannot revive
      its youth. The sea grows old in it.   *40*

                     Marianne Moore

Free verse demands vision, sensitivity, and penetrating language if it is to explore the emotions well, honestly, and freely. If the poet's intention is honest, if his statement is important to him, free verse may be intensely bold. In the following poem, the imagery is shocking, but the poet's intention is honest. His idiom is borrowed from that group of restless people searching for reason which his poem depicts. If confused values seem to permeate the lines, you should remember that poetry is not always the language of "the beautiful thought." It is also the language of the honest thought—however disagreeable that thought may be. Such honesty of thought lifts this poem and many others into importance:

Hotel Park (East 110 St.)

My fingers.
        popping with eyes
           touch you
       in a sea of foaming sheets

I beauty-mark your blubbery thighs   *5*
       mash thick kisses
         on your swollen lips
            your tongue puddles in my ear
      I'm king of the ceiling

The bed bee-hives with sighs   *10*
      my nose spiders
      in your mouse-tit hair
       baby-bottle breasts
    dance with the springs

your meshy bush   *15*
    drips with night-dew
      nailed to my loins
        like religion
Then
    grisly seconds clog   *20*
      the sand-clocks
    love's funk hangs
      in the room
        like a dirty shirt
we leave   *25*
    but life pools behind
      the hairy socket
        it smells like a miracle
we're sixteen.

Frank Lima

When such poetry as "Hotel Park (East 110 St.)" is attacked as "filthy, pornographic, depraved," and so on, the rational reader recognizes more than a concern for the poem at work in the attacker's mind. He recalls the criticism of such poems as Coleridge's "Christabel" on precisely the same grounds, and he recognizes the need of new statements for each generation—time lends respectability to all things, including poetry.

Contemporary poets are, as their forerunners were, critics of our society. It is they who manage to see it clearly. While we may not like the truth of such a poem as "Dolor," we know we cannot deny that truth—and we need to be reminded of it, frequently:

Dolor

I have known the inexorable sadness of pencils,
Neat in their boxes, dolor of pad and paper-weight,
All the misery of manila folders and mucilage,
Desolation in immaculate public places,
Lonely reception room, lavatory, switchboard,   *5*
The unalterable pathos of basin and pitcher,
Ritual of multigraph, paper-clip, comma,
Endless duplication of lives and objects.
And I have seen dust from the walls of institutions,
Finer than flour, alive, more dangerous than silica,   *10*
Sift, almost invisible, through long afternoons of tedium,
Dropping a fine film on nails and delicate eyebrows,
Glazing the pale hair, the duplicate gray standard faces.

Theodore Roethke

Accustomed to certain tragedies as we are, we fail to see them clearly. Living daily with the possibility of death on wheels, we assume ourselves safe, and are morbidly fascinated at the scenes of wrecks. Karl Shapiro reveals us to ourselves in

Auto Wreck

Its quick soft silver bell beating, beating,
And down the dark one ruby flare
Pulsing out red light like an artery,
The ambulance at top speed floating down
Past beacons and illuminated clocks   5
Wings in a heavy curve, dips down,
And brakes speed, entering the crowd.
The doors leap open, emptying light;
Stretchers are laid out, the mangled lifted
And stowed into the little hospital.   10
Then the bell, breaking the hush, tolls once,
And the ambulance with its terrible cargo
Rocking, slightly rocking, moves away,
As the doors, an afterthought, are closed.

We are deranged, walking among the cops   15
Who sweep glass and are large and composed.
One is still making notes under the light.
One with a bucket douches ponds of blood
Into the street and gutter.
One hangs lanterns on the wrecks that cling,   20
Empty husks of locusts, to iron poles.

Our throats were tight as tourniquets,
Our feet were bound with splints, but now,
Like convalescents intimate and gauche,
We speak through sickly smiles and warn   25
With the stubborn saw of common sense,
The grim joke and the banal resolution.
The traffic moves around with care,
But we remain, touching a wound
That opens to our richest horror.   30
Already old, the question Who shall die?
Becomes unspoken Who is innocent?
For death in war is done by hands;
Suicide has cause and stillbirth, logic;

And cancer, simple as a flower, blooms.   *35*
But this invites the occult mind,
Cancels our physics with a sneer,
And spatters all we knew of dénouement
Across the expedient and wicked stones.

Karl Shapiro

Irony, anger, rage move the poet:

War Is Kind

Do not weep, maiden, for war is kind.
Because your lover threw wild hands toward the sky
And the affrighted steed ran on alone,
Do not weep.
War is kind.   *5*

     Hoarse, booming drums of the regiment,
     Little souls who thirst for fight,
     These men were born to drill and die.
     The unexplained glory flies above them,
     Great is the battle-god, great, and his kingdom—   *10*
     A field where a thousand corpses lie.

Do not weep, babe, for war is kind.
Because your father tumbled in the yellow trenches,
Raged at his breast, gulped and died,
Do not weep.   *15*
War is kind.

     Swift blazing flag of the regiment,
     Eagle with crest of red and gold,
     These men were born to drill and die.
     Point for them the virtue of slaughter,   *20*
     Make plain to them the excellence of killing
     And a field where a thousand corpses lie.

Mother whose heart hung humble as a button
On the bright splendid shroud of your son,
Do not weep.   *25*
War is kind.

Stephen Crane

Nor does he see only one viewpoint:

The Goddess

When eyeless fish meet her on
her way upward, they gently
turn together in the dark
brooks. But naked and searching
as a wind, she will allow   5
no hindrance, none, and bursts up

through potholes and narrow flues
seeking an outlet. Unslowed
by fire, rock, water or clay,
she after a time reaches   10
the soft abundant soil, which
still does not dissipate her

force—for look! sinewy thyme
reeking in the sunlight; rats
breeding, breeding, in their nests;   15
and the soldier by a park
bench with his greatcoat collar
up, waiting all evening for

a woman, any woman
whose dress is tight across her   20
ass as bark in moonlight.
Proserpina! it is we,
vulnerable, quivering,
who stay you to abundance.

Thom Gunn

One of the areas where contemporary poetry is often most noticeably different is the poet's idiom. As poets do not confuse *diction* and *idiom,* you should not (see p. 147). Poetic diction is that great body of words, phrases, and constructions which seems peculiarly fitting to poetry. At its worst, it includes *o'er the briny deep;* at its best, it includes the graceful, bold, uncompromising lines from a poem that demand to be remembered. Idiom, on the other hand, is the unique expression in language that suggests a person. You know people who seem gifted with the ability to create phrases appropriate to the time, that express those people and their ideas "just right." The same phrases, borrowed and used by someone else, may seem "all wrong." Such phrases are right for the first, wrong for the second because they are the idiom of their creators. They establish the style of language peculiar to or characteristic of those people.

To clarify the difference between diction and idiom, think of the speech of teachers or ministers. You expect their diction (the language they use professionally) to be patterned in a definite fashion. It should be "correct" and "appropriate" to the subject at hand. When it is not, you are disappointed somehow. Now and again, however, a teacher or minister will stand out sharply in your memory because an additional ingredient pervades his diction. He seems capable of lucidity, appropriateness, great communicative power because he phrases his speech in a manner unlike others of his group. You remember his perceptive ability to get to the heart of meaning, to make you remember. It is his idiom that sets him apart. He has learned to express his insights and his personality in language you associate with him.

A poet must develop his own unique idiom if he is to express himself rather than merely repeat what other poets have said. This does not mean he will use language in an anguished, tortured fashion. Nor will he be deliberately obscure. He will seek out fresh combinations of language and appropriate imagery to bring awareness into being. His idiom will not be shocking if it is functional; nor will it be functional if it is deliberately shocking—either to the sensibilities of his readers or to their sense of language decorum. It will seem "right" for the occasion if it is *his* idiom.

In attaining this uniqueness with words, poets usually develop logically through influences from other poets. They do not consciously imitate the language and methods of other poets; they so admire them that they unconsciously emulate them.

Probably no American poet has had a greater poetic influence *on other poets* than Hart Crane. His is a name not always familiar to readers, but poets are very aware of it. More elegies, eulogies, and testimonials in poetry have been written to him than to any other American poet in an equal space of time. Although his poetic body is small, his influence has been great because of the power of his words. His idiom is clear and unique. And it is relatively traceable in its growth. The poetic influences in his development fall into three general groups. The first was an awareness of the French Imagists and Symbolists such as Laforgue, Vildrac, Mallarmé, and Rimbaud. Their method was, basically, to evoke a single, dominant mood in a poem through exploration of sensory imagery. Notice the method in

Legend

As silent as a mirror is believed
Realities plunge in silence by . . .

I am not ready for repentance;
Nor to match regrets. For the moth
Bends no more than the still   5
Imploring flame. And tremorous
In the white falling flakes
Kisses are,—
The only worth all granting.

It is to be learned—   10
This cleaving and this burning,
But only by the one who
Spends out himself again.

Twice and twice
(Again the smoking souvenir,   15
Bleeding eidolon!) and yet again.
Until the bright logic is won
Unwhispering as a mirror
Is believed.

Then, drop by caustic drop, a perfect cry   20
Shall string some constant harmony,—
Relentless caper for all those who step
The legend of their youth into the noon.

Later, Crane was to become profoundly interested in the Elizabethan poets with their careful attention to form and their employed *conceits* (striking modes of expression, such as Donne's "God's conduits" for preachers, or Herbert's "box where sweets compacted lie" for the season of spring). Notice his fusion of the richness of French imagery and symbolism with careful conceits and structure in

Black Tambourine

The interests of a black man in a cellar
Mark tardy judgment on the world's closed door.
Gnats toss in the shadow of a bottle,
And a roach spans a crevice in the floor.

Aesop, driven to pondering, found   5
Heaven with the tortoise and the hare;
Fox brush and sow ear top his grave
And mingling incantations on the air.

The black man, forlorn in the cellar,
Wanders in some mid-kingdom, dark, that lies,   10
Between his tambourine, stuck on the wall,
And, in Africa, a carcass quick with flies.

The second stanza apparently owes some small debt also to Edward
FitzGerald's

They say the Lion and the Lizard keep
The Courts where Jamshyd gloried and drank deep;
    And Bahrám, that great Hunter—the Wild Ass
Stamps o'er his Head, but cannot break his Sleep.

Contemporary imagery eventually replaced the language of his models,
and Crane was, in his third stage, to bring his idiom to full fruition,
making it uniquely his. Notice the originality of metaphor and language
in

Praise for an Urn
In Memoriam: Ernest Nelson
It was a kind and northern face
That mingled in such exile guise
The everlasting eyes of Pierrot
And, of Gargantua, the laughter.

His thoughts, delivered to me   5
From the white coverlet and pillow,
I see now, were inheritances—
Delicate riders of the storm.

The slant moon on the slanting hill
Once moved us toward presentiments   10
Of what the dead keep, living still,
And such assessments of the soul

As, perched in the crematory lobby,
The insistent clock commented on,
Touching as well upon our praise   15
Of glories proper to the time.

> Still, having in mind gold hair,
> I cannot see that broken brow
> And miss the dry sound of bees
> Stretching across a lucid space.   *20*
>
> Scatter these well-meant idioms
> Into the smoky spring that fills
> The suburbs, where they will be lost.
> They are no trophies of the sun.

The poem is apparently a statement of belief, couched in Crane's unique idiom and bearing the identifying marks of his style. That particularly elusive element, *style,* is a singularly difficult thing to describe. Various authors, critics, and teachers have attempted definitions, but no very satisfactory one exists. It encompasses within itself originality, ability to discipline oneself, craftsmanship, and temperament. Probably the best known definition was offered by the French naturalist Buffon. He said, "Style is the man himself." And, perhaps, that is as adequate a definition as one needs—if he understands the statement.

All of a man's life—his background, education, self-education, and aspirations—all somehow compound themselves into a body of attitudes and reactions and expressions that make the man. If he is to reveal himself through the communication of his work, he will somehow show facets of all those things. Certainly, Hemingway would not have used the phrase "dimity convictions" that Dickinson did. Crane would not have said, "O world, I can not hold thee close enough!" For any one of those authors to have written the line of another would have been to violate his own idiom, to weaken his own style. For style is *not* a deliberate attempt to achieve the readily apparent surface features of unusual writing. If the author courts cheapness in novelty of expression unsuitable to the content of a work, if he establishes precious or lavish figures of speech where none are needed, if he cultivates a writing habit that will reveal his cleverness while alienating his reader, he can be said to *lack* style.

How do poets cultivate that elusive necessity? If there is a formula, it is something like this: *awareness* (ability to see, hear, touch, taste, smell in distinct ways) + *selectivity* (ability to use what is pertinent and reject what is not) + *orderliness* (ability to arrange the retained details and elements in a comprehensible fashion) + *idiom* + *artistic presentation* (setting the details and elements forth in a fashion acceptable to the reader and vital to the work's intent) = *style.* There is no place in that formula for the florid, the pretentious, the overdone.

Poets usually attain style after learning to revise and revise and revise until they are sick of their projects, then beginning to revise seriously. Crane's "Praise for an Urn" that you have just read has been called the most successful elegy in the language. It did not spring from his pen in its finished form. We know this because some of the imagery was taken from an earlier, inferior work called "The Bridge of Estador." Coupling lines from that poem with what we know biographically of Crane, we can see the genesis and growth of "Praise for an Urn," which seems so effortless, so spontaneous, so "immediate."

In 1921, Crane wrote the Estador poem, subtitling it "An Impromptu, Aesthetic Tirade." He suggested the reader should walk on the bridge of Estador where no one had walked before. It rises above the world, above the sun. One walks there to find beauty. He suggests each man finds beauty in his own way—some not at all. Some may not be able to find it, he feels, though they look,

> But some are twisted with the love
> Of things irreconcilable,—
> The slant moon with the slanting hill. . .

These people are "Beauty's fool," according to Crane, but they will not forget what they have seen. The others, those who have found the beauty, are directed by the poet to go where beauty leads them, whether it be

> The everlasting eyes of Pierrot,
> Or, of Gargantua, the laughter.

In the winter of 1922, Crane met Ernest Nelson, an older man, a Norwegian immigrant who had, in his youth, been a painter and poet, but who had been defeated by the demands of making a living in America. His art had suffered, but his ideas, which he shared with Crane, were impressive. He influenced Crane's beliefs and, when Nelson died shortly after they had come to know each other, Crane wrote a letter stating, "He was one of many broken against the stupidity of American life in such places as here." ("Here" was Cleveland, Ohio.)

Working with the quotation from the letter and the quoted lines from "The Bridge of Estador," you can see how "Praise for an Urn" developed in 1923. Refinement of imagery, words used to their ultimate, best end— these are obvious in the completed poem. You should go back and re-read it now.

Readers frequently ask, hoping for a negative kind of answer, "But how much of the poet's achievement is conscious and how much of it is beyond his understanding?" While poets usually do not care to explicate their own works, Crane did find it necessary to do so once. The poem was

At Melville's Tomb

Often beneath the wave, wide from this ledge
The dice of drowned men's bones he saw bequeath
An embassy. Their numbers as he watched,
Beat on the dusty shore and were obscured.

And wrecks passed without sound of bells,   5
The calyx of death's bounty giving back
A scattered chapter, livid hieroglyph,
The portent wound in corridors of shells.

Then in the circuit calm of one vast coil,
Its lashings charmed and malice reconciled,   10
Frosted eyes there were that lifted altars;
And silent answers crept across the stars.

Compass, quadrant and sextant contrive
No farther tides . . . High in the azure steeps
Monody shall not wake the mariner.   15
This fabulous shadow only the sea keeps.

Harriet Monroe, editor of *Poetry* magazine, published the poem in the October, 1926 issue with an exchange of correspondence between her and Crane. That exchange is interesting because it reveals a poet's intention and suggests very valid arguments from the reader's standpoint (as presented by Miss Monroe) and from the poet's (as presented by Crane):

From the editor to Mr. Crane:

Take me for a hard-boiled unimaginative unpoetic reader, and tell me how *dice* can *bequeath an embassy* (or anything else); and how a *calyx* (*of death's bounty* or anything else) can give back a *scattered chapter, livid hieroglyph*; and how, if it does, such a *portent* can be *wound in corridors* (of shells or anything else).

And so on. I find your image of *frosted eyes lifting altars* difficult to visualize. Nor do compass, quadrant and sextant *contrive* tides, they merely record them, I believe.

All this may seem impertinent, but is not so intended. Your ideas and rhythms interest me, and I am wondering by what process of reasoning you would justify this poem's succession of champion mixed metaphors, of which you must be conscious. The packed line should pack its phrases in orderly relation, it seems to me, in a manner tending to clear confusion instead of making it worse confounded.

But pardon me—you didn't ask for criticism. Of course, I should not venture upon these remarks if I were not much interested.

From Mr. Crane to the editor:

Your good nature and manifest interest in writing me about the obscurities apparent in my Melville poem certainly prompt a wish to clarify my intentions in that poem as much as possible. But I realize that my explanations will not be very convincing. For a paraphrase is generally a poor substitute for any organized conception that one has fancied he has put into the more essentialized form of the poem itself.

At any rate, and though I imagine us to have considerable differences of opinion regarding the relationship of poetic metaphor to ordinary logic (I judge this from the angle of approach you use toward portions of the poem), I hope my answers will not be taken as a defense of merely certain faulty lines. I am really much more interested in certain theories of metaphor and technique involved generally in poetics, than I am concerned in vindicating any particular perpetrations of my own.

My poem may well be elliptical and actually obscure in the ordering of its content, but in your criticism of this very possible deficiency you have stated your objections in terms that allow me, at least for the moment, the privilege of claiming your ideas and ideals as theoretically, at least, quite outside the issues of my own aspirations. To put it more plainly, as a poet I may very possibly be more interested in the so-called illogical impingements of the connotations of words on the consciousness (and their combinations and interplay in metaphor on this basis) than I am interested in the preservation of their logically rigid significations at the cost of limiting my subject matter and perceptions involved in the poem.

This may sound as though I merely fancied juggling words and images until I found something novel, or esoteric; but the process is much more predetermined and objectified than that. The nuances of feeling and observation in a poem may well call for certain liberties which you claim the poet has no right to take. I am simply making the claim that the poet does have that authority, and that to deny it is to limit the scope of the medium so considerably as to outlaw some of the richest genius of the past.

This argument over the dynamics of metaphor promises as active a future as has been evinced in the past. Partaking so extensively as it does of the issues involved in the propriety or non-propriety of certain attitudes toward subject matter, etc., it enters the critical distinctions usually made between "romantic," "classic" as an organic factor. It is a problem that would require many pages to state adequately—merely from my own limited standpoint on the issues. Even this limited statement may prove onerous reading, and I hope you will pardon me if my own interest in the matter carries me to the point of presumption.

Its paradox, of course, is that its apparent illogic operates so logically in conjunction with its context in the poem as to establish its claim to another logic, quite independent of the original definition of the word or phrase or image thus employed. It implies (this *inflection* of language) a previous or prepared receptivity to its stimulus on the part of the reader. The reader's sensibility simply responds by identifying this inflection of experience with some event in his own history or perceptions—or rejects it altogether. The logic of metaphor is so organically entrenched in pure sensibility that it can't be thoroughly traced or explained outside of historical sciences, like philology and anthropology. This "pseudo-statement," as I. A. Richards calls it in an admirable essay touching our contentions in last July's *Criterion*, demands completely other faculties of recognition than the pure rationalistic associations permit. Much fine poetry may be completely rationalistic in its use of symbols, but there is much great poetry of another order which will yield the reader very little when inspected under the limitation of such arbitrary concerns as are manifested in your judgment of the Melville poem, especially when you constitute such requirements of ordinary logical relationship between word and word as irreducible.

I don't wish to enter here defense of the particular symbols employed in my own poem, because, as I said, I may well have failed to supply the necessary emotional connectives to the content featured. But I would like to counter a question or so of yours with a similar question. Here the poem is less dubious in quality than my own, and as far as the abstract pertinacity of question and its immediate consequences are concerned the point I'm arguing about can be better demonstrated. Both quotations are familiar to you, I'm sure.

You ask me how a *portent* can possibly be wound in a *shell*. Without attempting to answer this for the moment, I ask you how Blake could possibly say that "a *sigh* is a *sword* of an Angel King." You ask me how *compass, quadrant and sextant* "*contrive*" tides. I ask you how Eliot can possibly believe that "Every street *lamp* that I pass *beats* like a fatalistic *drum!*" Both of my metaphors may fall down completely. I'm not defending their actual value in themselves; but your criticism of them in each case was leveled at an illogicality of relationship between symbols, which similar fault you must have either overlooked in case you have ever admired the Blake and Eliot lines, or have there condoned them on account of some more ultimate convictions pressed on you by the impact of the poems in their entirety.

It all comes to the recognition that emotional dynamics are not to be confused with any absolute order of rationalized definitions; ergo, in poetry the *rationale* of metaphor belongs to another order of experience than science, and is not to be limited by a scientific and arbitrary code of relationships either in verbal inflections or concepts.

There are plenty of people who have never accumulated a sufficient series of reflections (and these of a rather special nature) to perceive the relation between a *drum* and a *street lamp—via* the *unmentioned* throbbing of the heart and nerves in a distraught man which *tacitly* creates the reason and "logic" of the Eliot meta- phor. They will always have a perfect justification for ignoring those lines and to claim them obscure, excessive, etc., until by some experience of their own the words accumulate the necessary connotations to complete their connection. It is the same with the "patient etherized upon a table," isn't it? Surely that line must lack all eloquence to many people who, for instance, would delight in agreeing that the sky was like a dome of many-colored glass.

If one can't count on some such bases in the reader now and then, I don't see how the poet has any chance to ever get beyond the simplest conceptions of emo- tion and thought, of sensation and lyrical sequence. If the poet is to be held com- pletely to the already evolved and exploited sequences of imagery and logic—what field of added consciousness and increased perceptions (the actual province of poetry, if not lullabyes) can be expected when one has to relatively return to the alphabet every breath or so? In the minds of people who have sensitively read, seen and experienced a great deal, isn't there a terminology something like short-hand as compared to usual description and dialectics, which the artist ought to be right in trusting as a reasonable connective agent toward fresh concepts, more inclusive evaluations? The question is more important to me than it perhaps ought to be; but as long as poetry is written, an audience, however small, is implied, and there re- mains the question of an active or an inactive imagination as its characteristic.

It is of course understood that a street-lamp simply can't beat with a sound like a drum; but it often happens that images, themselves totally dissociated, when joined in the circuit of a particular emotion located with specific relation to both of them, conduce to great vividness and accuracy of statement in defining that emotion.

Not to rant on forever, I'll beg your indulgence and come at once to the explana- tions you requested on the Melville poem:

> "The dice of drowned men's bones he saw bequeath
> An embassy."

Dice bequeath an embassy, in the first place, by being ground (in this connec- tion only, of course) in little cubes from the bones of drowned men by the action of the sea, and are finally thrown up on the sand, having "numbers" but no identifica- tion. These being the bones of dead men who never completed their voyage, it seems legitimate to refer to them as the only surviving evidence of certain messages undelivered, mute evidence of certain things, experiences that the dead mariners might have had to deliver. Dice as a symbol of chance and circumstance is also implied.

"The calyx of death's bounty giving back," etc.

This calyx refers in a double ironic sense both to a cornucopia and the vortex made by a sinking vessel. As soon as the water has closed over a ship this whirlpool sends up broken spars, wreckage, etc., which can be alluded to as *livid hieroglyphs,* making a *scattered chapter* so far as any complete record of the recent ship and her crew is concerned. In fact, about as much definite knowledge might come from all this as anyone might gain from the roar of his own veins, which is easily heard (haven't you ever done it?) by holding a shell close to one's ear.

"Frosted eyes lift altars."

Refers simply to a conviction that a man, not knowing perhaps a definite god yet being endowed with a reverence for deity—such a man naturally postulates a deity somehow, and the altar of that deity by the very *action* of the eyes *lifted* in searching.

"Compass, quadrant and sextant contrive no farther tides."

Hasn't it often occurred that instruments originally invented for record and computation have inadvertently so extended the concepts of the entity they were invented to measure (concepts of space, etc.) in the mind and imagination that employed them, that they may metaphorically be said to have extended the original boundaries of the entity measured? This little bit of "relativity" ought not to be discredited in poetry now that scientists are proceeding to measure the universe on principles of pure *ratio,* quite as metaphorical, so far as previous standards of scientific methods extended, as some of the axioms in *Job.*

I may have completely failed to provide any clear interpretation of these symbols in their context. And you will no doubt feel that I have rather heatedly explained them for anyone who professes no claims for their particular value. I hope, at any rate, that I have clarified them enough to suppress any suspicion that their obscurity derives from a lack of definite intentions in the subject-matter of the poem. The execution is another matter, and you must be accorded a superior judgment to mine in that regard.

From the editor to Mr. Crane:

No doubt our theories and ideals in the art differ more or less fundamentally, yet I would not deny to the poet the right to take certain of the liberties you claim. I think he can take as many as he succeeds with without mystifying his particular audience; for mystery is good, but not mystification.

I think that in your poem certain phrases carry to an excessive degree the "dynamics of metaphor"—they telescope three or four images together by mental leaps

(I fear my own metaphors are getting mixed!) which the poet, knowing his ground, can take safely, but which the most sympathetic reader cannot take unless the poet leads him by the hand with some such explanation as I find in your letter. I refer to such phrases as my letter quoted, except that I think I was over-exacting in criticizing the "quadrant and sextant" line. Accepting as I do much of what you say about "the illogical impingements of the connotations of words on the consciousness, and their combinations and interplay in metaphor," I must admit that these phrases in your poem are for me too elliptical to produce any effect but mystification (this until you explained them).

I don't get this effect from Blake or Eliot in the lines you quote or others that I have read. I am not familiar with Blake's symbolic poems but now, opening Prof. Pierce's volume of selections from them, I find in their use of metaphor a singular simplicity and clarity. He deals with magnificent mysteries, but presents them in flaming images like

"what time I bound my sandals
On to walk forward through eternity."

I find here no crowded and tortured lines.

My argument comes down, I suppose, rather to your practice than your theory. Or, more specifically, your practice strains your theory by carrying it, with relentless logic, to a remote and exaggerated extreme. You find me testing metaphors, and poetic concept in general, too much by logic, whereas I find you pushing logic to the limit in a painfully intellectual search for emotion, for poetic motive. Your poem reeks with brains—it is thought out, worked out, sweated out. And the beauty which it seems entitled to is tortured and lost.

In all this I may be entirely wrong, and I am aware that a number of poets and critics would think so. Yvor Winters, for example, in a recent letter, speaks of your *Marriage of Faustus and Helen* in *Secession 7* as "one of the great poems of our time, as great as the best of Stevens or Pound or Eliot." Well, I cannot grant it such a rank.

The editor would rather not have the last word, but as Mr. Crane contributes no further to the discussion, we must pass it on to our readers.

H. M.

So much for a poet's defense of his completed work. How does a poem "happen" for him in the first place? Various writers have left records of the beginnings of their poems. Samuel Taylor Coleridge recorded the birth of "Kubla Khan" as follows:

In the summer of the year 1797, the author, then in ill health, had retired to a lonely farmhouse between Porlock and Lynton, on the Exmoor confines of Somerset and Devonshire. In consequence of a slight indisposition, an anodyne had been prescribed, from the effects of which he fell asleep in his chair at the moment that he was reading the following sentence, or words of the same substance, in *Purchas's Pilgrimage:* "Here the Khan Kubla commanded a palace to be built, and a stately garden thereunto. And thus ten miles of fertile ground were inclosed with a wall." The author continued for about three hours in a profound sleep, at least of the external senses, during which time he has the most vivid confidence that he could not have composed less than from two to three hundred lines; if that indeed can be called composition in which all the images rose up before him as *things,* with a parallel production of the correspondent expressions, without any sensation or consciousness of effort. On awaking he appeared to himself to have a distinct recollection of the whole, and taking his pen, ink, and paper, instantly and eagerly wrote down the lines that are here preserved. At this moment he was unfortunately called out by a person on business from Porlock, and detained by him above an hour, and on his return to his room, found, to his no small surprise and mortification, that though he still retained some vague and dim recollection of the general purport of the vision, yet, with the exception of some eight or ten scattered lines and images, all the rest has passed away like the images on the surface of a stream into which a stone has been cast, but, alas! without the after restoration of the latter!

Edgar Allan Poe, on the other hand, reported in "The Philosophy of Composition" these deliberate considerations in his plans for "The Raven": 1) He realized a poem must make an immediate effect in a limited time. He, therefore, planned a poem of about one hundred lines. He noted it became one hundred and eight. 2) The effect or impression to be conveyed was the one "most intense, the most elevating, and the most pure"—contemplation of beauty. 3) "Regarding, then, Beauty as my province, my next question referred to the *tone* of its highest manifestation; and all experience has shown that this tone is one of *sadness.*" From this observation, Poe concluded, "Melancholy is thus the most legitimate of all the poetical tones." 4) He then sought a "pivot upon which the whole structure might turn," and he "did not fail to perceive immediately that no one had been so universally employed as that of the *refrain.*" What reader can forget the raven's "Nevermore"?

Robert Frost admits to "worrying" many of his poems into existence but preferring the ones which he "carried through like the stroke of a racquet, club, or headsman's ax."

William Wordsworth's sister Dorothy recorded in her journal for April 15, 1802, a walk she and her brother shared:

It was a threatening, misty morning, but mild. . . . The wind was furious, and we thought we must have returned. We first rested in the large boat-house, then under a furze bush opposite Mr. Clarkson's. Saw the plow going in the field. The wind seized our breath. The Lake was rough. There was a boat by itself floating in the middle of the bay below Water Millock. . . . When we were in the woods beyond Gowbarrow Park we saw a few daffodils close to the water-side. We fancied that the lake had floated the seeds ashore, and that the little colony had so sprung up. But as we went along there were more and yet more; and at last, under the boughs of the trees, we saw that there was a long belt of them along the shore, about the breadth of a country turnpike road. I never saw daffodils so beautiful. They grew among the mossy stones about and about them; some rested their heads upon these stones as on a pillow for weariness; and the rest tossed and reeled and danced, and seemed as if they verily laughed with the wind, that blew upon them over the lake; they looked so gay, ever glancing, ever changing. This wind blew directly over the lake to them. There was here and there a little knot, and a few stragglers a few yards higher up; but they were so few as not to disturb the simplicity, unity, and life of that one busy highway.

Two years later, Wordsworth was to compose "I Wandered Lonely As a Cloud." Turn to p. 182 and reread the poem under its alternate title, "Daffodils." Recalling the scene, Wordsworth exercises that selectivity so demanded of the poet. Dismissed is his sister. Compare his *I* with her *we*. In abstracting himself from the experience he shared with Dorothy, Wordsworth creates a new self through which "to see" the scene, for he must see it twice: as it *was* originally and as it *is* after the changes of the two-year storage in his memory. From the two views emerges still a third: the meaning of the actual and the recollected scenes. And from the third view emerges a fourth: the view the reader discovers on the page, a distillation of Wordsworth's three views. And still the process does not stop. The reader visualizes the Wordsworthian scene and application, changing it to correspond with his understanding of the words (both denotatively and connotatively). At this point, another change occurs. The reader too has stored memories of flowers and bodies of water. Wordsworth's poem triggers those memories into recall, possibly endowing them with meaning for the first time. They also exist at several levels. As Wordsworth's "revelation" merges with the "response" of the reader, the poem becomes a vital experience.

Who is the *I* of "I Wandered Lonely As a Cloud"? Certainly it is not simply Wordsworth, for he was merely a man walking with his sister on that April day. Nor is it the poet, for the reader replaces the poet at that moment when communication takes place. Nor is *I* the reader, for, at that moment of communication, he fuses into one unit with Wordsworth the man and Wordsworth the poet and, by extension, with all men who have shared or will share that communication. Such is the power of the poetic communication. Had Wordsworth selected the same details

Dorothy included in her account, the poem would be quite a different experience. Notice his omission of the boat-house, the furze bush, the plow, the boat. So grew his poem through recollection and selectivity.

This next poem, though by a student, followed a pattern not uncommon to accomplished poets. Miss Lynch was walking near her home one day when she saw a dog in the street. One car had struck it; others had been unable to avoid the dead beast. The sight became grim memory that worked itself out through the various revisions:

#1

This spot, this black, tire-treaded blot
That spreads here in the noisy indifferent street
Was once a cat—or dog—or some such beast.

He used the wrong equation,
Didn't balance it perhaps   5
A decimal to right or left
Means one significant figure or the other.

Nature's children do no wrong
They do just what they ought
It's man who sets these nasty traps   10
In which her work is caught.

#2

This spot, this black, tire-treaded blot
That spreads here in the noisy indifferent street
Was once a cat or dog or some such beast
Man tore him from his own, yet will not claim him.

#3

Lonely, flat, unclaimed, unwept,
This black, tire-treaded blot
Spreads here in the noisy street
Indifferent, unused to human ways, poor beast,
And pulled by natural curiosity   5
To go from place to place,
A dog or cat has not been blessed
(Or cursed) with thoughts and logic
As are needed to cross the street.
But man treats him as equal in the road   10
And strikes him down and
Leaves him there to rot.

#4

Fly blown, unclaimed, unwept,
A black, tire-treaded blot
Spreads in the street
Like life's corsage
Pressed useless.   5
It is crushed and left
To rot.

#5

Flyblown, unclaimed, unwept,
A black, tire-treaded blot
Spreads in the street.
A vital corsage pressed useless
To the ground.   5
Life crushed and left to rot.

The final version of this poem evolved from changing the punctuation and giving the lines form to establish an emotional response in the reader, complementing the meaning of the poem:

Dog in the Street

Fly-blown . . . unclaimed . . . unwept . . .
a black, tire-treaded blot
spreads in the street . . .
a vital corsage
pressed useless   5
to the ground:
Life crushed . . .
and left
to rot.

Mary Kelly Lynch (student)

Many manuscripts exist, revealing the tortured process the poet follows to find the right word, the right progression of ideas, the right form to make his poem worth your attention. Some are so heavily altered that little remains of the original idea. Studying such manuscripts, a reader becomes aware of one very real truth: inspiration, genius, spirituality may be involved in the genesis of the *idea* of the poem, but the construction of it is a craft, deliberately employed. The experience of the poem does not appear (despite Coleridge's statement on "Kubla Khan") from thin air; the experience is communicated through the poet's words, and he usually labors long and hard with the words to achieve that communication.

Suggested Assignment. Alfred, Lord Tennyson printed two versions of "The Lady of Shalott." He had worked with the poem until he was pleased enough with it to allow publication in 1833. As the critics attacked it, he revised it extensively before republishing it in 1842. The first stanzas of the 1833 and the 1842 editions appear below. In a brief paper, discuss which, in your opinion, is "better" poetry. Support your arguments.

1833

On either side the river lie
Long fields of barley and of rye,
That clothe the wold, and meet the sky.
And thro' the field the road runs by
        To manytowered Camelot.   *5*
The yellowleavéd waterlily,
The greensheathéd daffodilly,
Tremble in the water chilly,
        Round about Shalott.

1842

On either side the river lie
Long fields of barley and of rye,
That clothe the wold and meet the sky;
And through the field the road runs by
        To many-towered Camelot;   *5*
And up and down the people go,
Gazing where the lilies blow
Round an island there below,
        The island of Shalott.

Suggested Reading

Yvor Winters, *The Function of Criticism: Problems and Exercises*—the section on "scanning" free verse

John Livingston Lowes, *The Road to Xanadu*—a fascinating reconstruction of the "sources" of Coleridge's "Kubla Khan"

CHAPTER X

Reading Narrative and Dramatic Poetry

Lyric poetry is an integral part of narrative and dramatic poetry, for all poetry rests on its musical sound. But the focus in the latter forms is on larger elements, as their scope is larger than the lyric's "sung moment." Narrative poetry, as the name suggests, tells a story. Dramatic poetry reveals character, the narrative qualities being of secondary importance. As the basic purposes of such poems are different, we will consider the forms separately.

Narrative Poetry

Everyone enjoys a good story, whether it be a brief anecdote or an elaborate narrative of some length. The vast body of myth, legend, and folk tale that has survived from primitive man indicates such has always been true. *Epic poetry* (accounts of national heroes as explanation for the beginnings of nations or races) seems to be comprised of episodes recounted by various reporters and eventually organized by one poet or a group of poets working together. *The Iliad* and *The Odyssey* of the Greeks, *The Nibelungenlied* of the Germans, *Beowulf* of the Anglo-Saxons present daring men in exciting circumstances. Less spontaneous narratives such as Virgil's *Aeneid* and Longfellow's *Hiawatha* follow the same pattern, though more self-consciously.

In reading narrative poetry, you should follow five steps for maximum enjoyment:

Step 1: Read the poem for the story line (the plot) without conscious attention to other details.

Step 2: Reread the poem to see how the ingredients of narration work together. Is the structure chronological? If not, is the order rearranged to create suspense? How do setting and characters create believability?

Step 3: Examine the expository material of the poem. How is the setting created? What details create characters? How are the actions of characters explained?

Step 4: Read for more than the surface narrative. Is there a second level of meaning to be found? Do the characters represent unique individuals, or are they representative of large groups? Is it possible to find allegorical significance in the work? Frequently a narrative poem is an elaborate metaphor developed so cleverly that the casual reader misses the point completely.

Step 5: Examine the technical structure of the poem. How is sound wedded to sense? What does the metrical pattern contribute? How are figures of speech employed?

Now let's examine a short narrative to see the process at work:

Step 1: "Telling the Bees" should be read with the following folk belief in mind: New Englanders of Whittier's day believed domestic bees would leave their hives to seek new homes if they were not told of death in the family and their hives draped with mourning cloth.

Telling the Bees

Here is the place; right over the hill
   Runs the path I took;
You can see the gap in the old wall still,
   And the stepping-stones in the shallow brook.

There is the house, with the gate red-barred,   *5*
   And the poplars tall;
And the barn's brown length, and the cattle-yard,
   And the white horns tossing above the wall.

There are the beehives ranged in the sun;
   And down by the brink   *10*
Of the brook are her poor flowers, weed-o'errun,
   Pansy and daffodil, rose and pink.

A year has gone, as the tortoise goes,
   Heavy and slow;
And the same rose blows, and the same sun glows,   *15*
   And the same brook sings of a year ago.

There's the same sweet clover-smell in the breeze;
    And the June sun warm
Tangles his wings of fire in the trees,
    Setting, as then, over Fernside farm.   *20*

I mind me how with a lover's care
    From my Sunday coat
I brushed off the burrs, and smoothed my hair,
    And cooled at the brookside my brow and throat.

Since we parted, a month had passed,—   *25*
    To love, a year;
Down through the beeches I looked at last
    On the little red gate and the well-sweep near.

I can see it all now,—the slantwise rain
    Of light through the leaves,   *30*
The sundown's blaze on her window-pane,
    The bloom of her roses under the eaves.

Just the same as a month before,—
    The house and the trees,
The barn's brown gable, the vine by the door,—   *35*
    Nothing changed but the hives of bees.

Before them, under the garden wall,
    Forward and back,
Went drearily singing the chore-girl small,
    Draping each hive with a shred of black.   *40*

Trembling, I listened: the summer sun
    Had the chill of snow;
For I knew she was telling the bees of one
    Gone on the journey we all must go!

Then I said to myself, "My Mary weeps   *45*
    For the dead to-day:
Haply her blind old grandsire sleeps
    The fret and the pain of his age away."

> But her dog whined low; on the doorway sill,
>> With his cane to his chin,   *50*
> The old man sat; and the chore-girl still
>> Sung to the bees stealing out and in.

> And the song she was singing ever since
>> In my ear sounds on: —
> "Stay at home, pretty bees, fly not hence!   *55*
>> Mistress Mary is dead and gone!"
>>>> *John Greenleaf Whittier*

Step 2: Chronology is distorted. Stanza 4 tells us a year has passed since the main action occurred. Stanza 7 adds a month: in all, the narrative begins thirteen months before. The final line reveals the poet's reason for beginning *in media res* (in the midst of things) and employing the *flashback* (a recounting of events before the opening episode of the story). *Foreshadowing* (hints casually inserted to make the final revelation meaningful) exists in stanza 3 (the weed-o'errun flower beds), the last line of stanza 9, and stanza 13. The pivot follows stanza 12, and the climax occurs as the last line of the poem. Conflict exists in the lover's impatience to see Mary—an impatience that finds complication in what he fears (the summer sun had the chill of snow, stanza 11), and growing realization through the remaining stanzas. Setting provides the character a narrative frame as he describes it graphically. His powers of observation sharpen our understanding of his grief as we seem to realize the extent of the tragedy before he can reveal it.

Step 3: Stanza 1 creates the orderly rural setting. Stanza 2 colors it vividly. Stanza 3 introduces conflicting images. Time is established in stanza 4. The senses of touch and smell are evoked in stanza 5. Recollection passes on concrete imagery of *burr* and *beech* and *gate*. Color creates changed scene; and the beehives, so casually mentioned in stanza 3, are emphasized again. *Interior monolog* (the thoughts of a character) prepares us for the dialog between the chore-girl and the bees.

Step 4: A charming custom recounted, a delightful superstition recorded, a sudden, anguished moment shared—these are in the poem. To find allegorical depth would do violence to a work that needs no tortured interpretation. The shared emotion, however, should reveal something to the reader about himself.

Step 5: The $a^4b^2a^4b^2a^4b^4$ sestets are balladic in tone, and the varied metrics (primarily anapests and iambs) lyrically trip along as the reader is danced into a sorrowful understanding of the title. The tortoise simile, the lulling sound created by the soft assonance throughout the poem, repetition—all work to create a drowsy summer day. That day is shattered in the harsh sounds of the last line of the poem.

In some narrative poetry, the lyric quality is so apparent it dominates the work, causing the reader to concentrate on sound rather than sense or narrative flow. Edgar Allan Poe involves the reader in so many considerations in "Annabel Lee," for instance, that a sharply defined purpose escapes detection. As you read it, you will be caught up in the musical anapests, artfully varied, and the stanza pattern variations. Most of the techniques of poetry are to be found within the lines:

Annabel Lee

It was many and many a year ago,
  In a kingdom by the sea,
That a maiden there lived whom you may know
  By the name of Annabel Lee;—
And this maiden she lived with no other thought   *5*
  Than to love and be loved by me.

She was a child and *I* was a child,
  In this kingdom by the sea,
But we loved with a love that was more than love—
  I and my Annabel Lee—   *10*
With a love that the wingéd seraphs of Heaven
  Coveted her and me.

And this was the reason that, long ago,
  In this kingdom by the sea,
A wind blew out of a cloud by night   *15*
  Chilling my Annabel Lee;
So that her highborn kinsmen came
  And bore her away from me,
To shut her up in a sepulchre
  In this kingdom by the sea.   *20*

The angels, not half so happy in Heaven,
　　Went envying her and me:—
Yes! that was the reason (as all men know,
　　In this kingdom by the sea)
That the wind came out of the cloud, chilling　　　　　　　25
　　And killing my Annabel Lee.

But our love it was stronger by far than the love
　　Of those who were older than we—
　　Of many far wiser than we—
And neither the angels in Heaven above　　　　　　　　30
　　Nor the demons down under the sea,
Can ever dissever my soul from the soul
　　Of the beautiful Annabel Lee:—

For the moon never beams without bringing me dreams
　　Of the beautiful Annabel Lee;　　　　　　　　　　35
And the stars never rise but I see the bright eyes
　　Of the beautiful Annabel Lee;
And so, all the night-tide, I lie down by the side
Of my darling, my darling, my life and my bride,
　　In her sepulchre there by the sea—　　　　　　　40
　　In her tomb by the side of the sea.

Edgar Allan Poe

Balladic delight with the supernatural is clearly evident in this poem. Was the maiden's name "Annabel Lee," or did mortals call some unearthly creature by that name (lines 3-4) in the misty city by the sea? Why were the angels, ordinarily kind and loving, so envious and vindictive that they caused the death of the girl? Why were the townsmen so aware of the reasons (stanza 4), and how does the parenthetical inclusion in line 23 emphasize their knowledge? In what sense were the lovers children (note the emphasis in line 7), and *what* were the "highborn kinsmen"? Is there reason to believe, from internal evidence, that they were mortal nobility? From whence did they come (line 17)? What was the identity of those who were "older and wiser than we," and what is meant by the "love" of those elder sages? Time and place are only two elements of setting in this narrative. How does atmosphere provide a third? Poe's metrical virtuosity is so apparent in this poem that the narrative is beclouded; yet that misty veil allows the reader's speculations to fill out the suggested plot as he wishes. Such narrative poetry must be examined for sound, for sense, and for the nuances created by the combination of sound-sense before final evaluations become possible.

The most commonplace event often provides narrative possibility for a poet. In "Wild Grapes," Robert Frost employs conversational iambic pentameter to create an account so vivid it is as if the narrator speaks directly to the reader. To appreciate the conversational quality of Frost's blank verse, read this poem aloud, or listen as someone reads it to you:

Wild Grapes

What tree may not the fig be gathered from?
The grape may not be gathered from the birch?
It's all you know the grape, or know the birch.
As a girl gathered from the birch myself
Equally with my weight in grapes, one autumn,   5
I ought to know what tree the grape is fruit of.
I was born, I suppose, like anyone,
And grew to be a little boyish girl
My brother could not always leave at home.
But that beginning was wiped out in fear   10
The day I swung suspended with the grapes,
And was come after like Eurydice
And brought down safely from the upper regions;
And the life I live now's an extra life
I can waste as I please on whom I please.   15
So you see me celebrate two birthdays,
And give myself out as two different ages,
One of them five years younger than I look—

One day my brother led me to a glade
Where a white birch he knew of stood alone,   20
Wearing a thin head-dress of pointed leaves,
And heavy on her heavy hair behind,
Against her neck, an ornament of grapes.
Grapes, I knew grapes from having seen them last year.
One bunch of them, and there began to be   25
Bunches all round me growing in white birches,
The way they grew round Lief the Lucky's German;
Mostly as much beyond my lifted hands, though,

As the moon used to seem when I was younger,
And only freely to be had for climbing.   30
My brother did the climbing; and at first
Threw me down grapes to miss and scatter
And have to hunt for in sweet fern and hardhack;
Which gave him some time to himself to eat,
But not so much, perhaps, as a boy needed.   35
So then, to make me wholly self-supporting,
He climbed still higher and bent the tree to earth,
He put it in my hands to pick my own grapes.
"Here, take a tree-top, I'll get down another.
Hold on with all your might when I let go."   40
I said I had the tree. It wasn't true.
The opposite was true. The tree had me.
The minute it was left with me alone
It caught me up as though I were the fish
And it the fishpole. So I was translated   45
To loud cries from my brother of "Let go!
Don't you know anything, you girl? Let go!"
But I, with something of the baby grip
Acquired ancestrally in just such trees
When wilder mothers than our wildest now   50
Hung babies out on branches by the hands
To dry or wash or tan, I don't know which
(You'll have to ask an evolutionist)—
I held on uncomplainingly for life.
My brother tried to make me laugh to help me.   55
"What are you doing up there in those grapes?
Don't be afraid. A few of them won't hurt you.
I mean, they won't pick you if you don't them."
Much danger of my picking anything!
By that time I was pretty well reduced   60
To a philosophy of hang-and-let-hang.
"Now you know how it feels," my brother said,
"To be a bunch of fox-grapes, as they call them,
That when it thinks that it has escaped the fox
By growing where it shouldn't—on a birch,   65
Where a fox wouldn't think to look for it—
And if he looked and found it, couldn't reach it—
Just then come you and I to gather it.
Only you have the advantage of the grapes

In one way: you have more stem to cling by,   70
And promise more resistance to the picker."

One by one I lost off my hat and shoes,
And still I clung. I let my head fall back,
And shut my eyes against the sun, my ears
Against my brother's nonsense; "Drop," he said,   75
"I'll catch you in my arms. It isn't far."
(Stated in lengths of him it might not be.)
"Drop or I'll shake the tree and shake you down."
Grim silence on my part as I sank lower,
My small wrists stretching till they showed the banjo strings. 80
"Why, if she isn't serious about it!
Hold tight awhile till I think what to do.
I'll bend the tree down and let you down by it."
I don't know much about the letting down;
But once I felt ground with my stocking feet   85
And the world came revolving back to me,
I know I looked long at my curled-up fingers,
Before I straightened them and brushed the bark off.
My brother said: "Don't you weigh anything?
Try to weigh something next time, so you won't   90
Be run off with by birch trees into space."

It wasn't my not weighing anything
So much as my not knowing anything—
My brother had been nearer right before.
I had not taken the first step in knowledge;   95
I had not learned to let go with the hands,
As still I have not learned to with the heart,
And have no wish to with the heart—nor need,
That I can see. The mind—is not the heart.
I may yet live, as I know others live,   100
To wish in vain to let go with the mind—
Of cares, at night, to sleep; but nothing tells me
That I need learn to let go with the heart.

Robert Frost

Had the lines been written in prose paragraph form, you would almost
be unaware they are poetry. The rhythm would probably delight you,
however, as you are delighted with intensely poetic prose. The four
verse paragraphs of this poem might serve as a model for the well-de-

veloped essay. Verse paragraph 1 introduces the work, stating why the account is important. Verse paragraphs 2 and 3 recount the incident. Verse paragraph 4 reveals the précis of the poem and comments on the meaning of the experience to the old woman. The reader can make whatever application he wishes. Characters, setting, and dialog are employed here just as they would be in a short story. Two points of view emerge: the boy's and the girl's. However, because the narrative is a recalled experience, her point of view is ambivalent. Can you point out lines wherein she reveals that her early terror is humorous in retrospect? How does this ambivalence reveal character? As both poetry and prose fiction employ the pivot and climax, isolate them in this poem. You might find a poetic pivot and climax as well as a narrative pivot and climax. If you do, you have gained insight that allows you to understand the greater richness that poetry offers that prose does not. A variety of structural methods are employed in this narrative. You should be able to see chronological and example development as well as editorial. Are comparison and contrast ignored? Is the descriptive approach included? What do poetic devices contribute to the account? This poem is an extended metaphor, comparable in some ways to "The Twenty-Third Psalm." You might write a paper revealing your understanding of the comparative features.

Narrative poetry frequently relies on one element (character, action, description, dialog) more than it does on the other three. In Porphyria's Lover," the four elements are clearly observable. As you read the poem, be aware of their individual contributions to the total effect:

Porphyria's Lover

The rain set early in tonight;
   The sullen wind was soon awake—
It tore the elm-tops down for spite,
   And did its worst to vex the lake.
I listened with heart fit to break.   *5*
When glided in Porphyria; straight
   She shut the cold out and the storm,
And kneeled and made the cheerless grate
   Blaze up, and all the cottage warm;
Which done, she rose, and from her form   *10*
Withdrew the dripping cloak and shawl,
   And laid her soiled gloves by, untied
Her hat and let the damp hair fall,
   And, last, she sat down by my side

And called me. When no voice replied,   15
She put my arm about her waist,
    And made her smooth white shoulder bare
And all her yellow hair displaced,
    And, stooping, made my cheek lie there,
And spread, o'er all, her yellow hair,   20
Murmuring how she loved me—she
    Too weak, for all her heart's endeavor,
To set its struggling passion free
    From pride, and vainer ties dissever,
And give herself to me forever.   25
But passion sometimes would prevail,
    Nor could tonight's gay feast restrain
A sudden thought of one so pale
    For love of her, and all in vain;
So, she was come through wind and rain.   30
Be sure I looked up at her eyes
    Happy and proud; at last I knew
Porphyria worshiped me; surprise
    Made my heart swell, and still it grew
While I debated what to do.   35
That moment she was mine, mine, fair,
    Perfectly pure and good; I found
A thing to do, and all her hair
    In one long yellow string I wound
Three times her little throat around,   40
And strangled her. No pain felt she;
    I am quite sure she felt no pain.
As a shut bud that holds a bee,
    I warily oped her lids; again
Laughed the blue eyes without a stain.   45
And I untightened next the tress
    About her neck; her cheek once more
Blushed bright beneath my burning kiss.
    I propped her head up as before,
Only, this time my shoulder bore   50
Her head, which droops upon it still—
    The smiling rosy little head,
So glad it has its utmost will,
    That all it scorned at once is fled,
And I, its love, am gained instead!   55

> Porphyria's love—she guessed not how
>   Her darling one wish would be heard.
> And thus we sit together now,
>   And all night long we have not stirred,
> And yet God has not said a word!   60
>
> *Robert Browning*

Referring back to this poem, try to answer the following questions: Where does the narrative pivot occur? Where does the poetic pivot occur? What is the narrative climax? Where is the poetic climax? Why did Porphyria's lover kill her? Does setting lend *verisimilitude* (believability) to the narrative? (Examine lines 1-5 *carefully* before answering.) In what lines is the violence of lines 37-41 *foreshadowed* (suggested in advance to lend verisimilitude to a character's action)? Give *specific* examples. Explain how the metrics of lines 36-37 reveal character. Explain the metrics of line 50 in the same way. Understatement in line 60 is employed for what reason?

Sometimes narrative poetry can reveal human problems such as loneliness, fear, and hate better than the brief lyric, for its length allows *identification* (seeing oneself in a character, understanding motivation through self-knowledge) to occur. In "The Lady of Shalott," Tennyson tells a romantic story that charms the reader with its seeming remoteness from contemporary problems, but, on reflection, the reader realizes the problems are his too. Only the time and the place are different. The reader has been beguiled into understanding things he probably would have avoided, given a choice:

The Lady of Shalott
Part I

> On either side the river lie
> Long fields of barley and of rye,
> That clothe the wold and meet the sky;
> And through the field the road runs by
>   To many-towered Camelot;   5
> And up and down the people go,
> Gazing where the lilies blow
> Round an island there below,
>   The island of Shalott.
>
> Willows whiten, aspens quiver,   10
> Little breezes dusk and shiver
> Through the wave that runs for ever

By the island in the river
  Flowing down to Camelot.
Four gray walls, and four gray towers,   *15*
Overlook a space of flowers,
And the silent isle imbowers
  The Lady of Shalott.

By the margin, willow-veiled,
Slide the heavy barges trailed   *20*
By slow horses; and unhailed
The shallop flitteth silken-sailed
  Skimming down to Camelot;
But who hath seen her wave her hand?
Or at the casement seen her stand?   *25*
Or is she known in all the land,
  The Lady of Shalott?

Only reapers, reaping early
In among the bearded barley,
Hear a song that echoes cheerly   *30*
From the river winding clearly,
  Down to towered Camelot,
And by the moon the reaper weary,
Piling sheaves in uplands airy,
Listening, whispers " 'Tis the fairy   *35*
  Lady of Shalott.''

Part II

There she weaves by night and day
A magic web with colors gay.
She has heard a whisper say,
A curse is on her if she stay   *40*
  To look down to Camelot.
She knows not what the curse may be,
And so she weaveth steadily,
And little other care hath she,
  The Lady of Shalott.   *45*

And moving through a mirror clear
That hangs before her all the year,
Shadows of the world appear.
There she sees the highway near
  Winding down to Camelot;   *50*

There the river eddy whirls,
And there the surly village-churls,
And the red cloaks of market girls,
    Pass onward from Shalott.

Sometimes a troop of damsels glad,   55
An abbot on an ambling pad,
Sometimes a curly shepherd-lad,
Or long-haired page in crimson clad,
    Goes by to towered Camelot;
And sometimes through the mirror blue   60
The knights come riding two and two:
She hath no loyal knight and true
    The Lady of Shalott.

But in her web she still delights
To weave the mirror's magic sights,   65
For often through the silent nights
A funeral, with plumes and lights
    And music, went to Camelot;
Or when the moon was overhead,
Came two young lovers lately wed;   70
"I am half sick of shadows," said
    The Lady of Shalott.

Part III

A bow-shot from her bower-eaves
He rode between the barley-sheaves,
The sun came dazzling through the leaves,   75
And flamed upon the brazen greaves
    Of bold Sir Lancelot.
A red-cross knight for ever kneeled,
To a lady in his shield,
That sparkled on the yellow field,   80
    Beside remote Shalott.

The gemmy bridle glittered free,
Like to some branch of stars we see
Hung in the golden Galaxy.
The bridle bells rang merrily   85
    As he rode down to Camelot;

And from his blazoned baldric slung
A mighty silver bugle hung,
And as he rode his armor rung,
    Beside remote Shalott.   *90*

All in the blue unclouded weather
Thick-jeweled shone the saddle-leather,
The helmet and the helmet-feather
Burned like one burning flame together,
    As he rode down to Camelot;   *95*
As often through the purple night,
Below the starry clusters bright,
Some bearded meteor, trailing light,
    Moves over still Shalott.

His broad clear brow in sunlight glowed;   *100*
On burnished hooves his war-horse trode;
From underneath his helmet flowed
His coal-black curls as on he rode,
    As he rode down to Camelot.
From the bank and from the river   *105*
He flashed into the crystal mirror,
"Tirra lirra," by the river
    Sang Sir Lancelot.

She left the web, she left the loom,
She made three paces through the room,   *110*
She saw the water-lily bloom,
She saw the helmet and the plume,
    She looked down to Camelot.
Out flew the web and floated wide;
The mirror cracked from side to side;   *115*
"The curse is come upon me," cried
    The Lady of Shalott.

Part IV

In the stormy east-wind straining,
The pale yellow woods were waning,
The broad stream in his banks complaining,   *120*
Heavily the low sky raining
    Over towered Camelot;

Down she came and found a boat
Beneath a willow left afloat,
And round about the prow she wrote   *125*
    The Lady of Shalott.

And down the river's dim expanse
Like some bold seër in a trance,
Seeing all his own mischance—
With a glassy countenance   *130*
    Did she look to Camelot.
And at the closing of the day
She loosed the chain, and down she lay;
The broad stream bore her far away,
    The Lady of Shalott.   *135*

Lying robed in snowy white
That loosely flew to left and right—
The leaves upon her falling light—
Through the noises of the night
    She floated down to Camelot;   *140*
And as the boat-head wound along
The willowy hills and fields among,
They heard her singing her last song,
    The Lady of Shalott.

Heard a carol, mournful, holy,   *145*
Chanted loudly, chanted lowly,
Till her blood was frozen slowly,
And her eyes were darkened wholly,
    Turned to towered Camelot.
For ere she reached upon the tide   *150*
The first house by the water-side,
Singing in her song she died,
    The Lady of Shalott.

Under tower and balcony,
By garden-wall and gallery,   *155*
A gleaming shape she floated by,
Dead-pale between the houses high,
    Silent into Camelot.
Out upon the wharfs they came,
Knight and burgher, lord and dame,   *160*

And round the prow they read her name,
   The Lady of Shalott.

Who is this? and what is here?
And in the lighted palace near
Died the sound of royal cheer;   *165*
And they crossed themselves for fear,
   All the knights at Camelot;
But Lancelot mused a little space;
He said, "She has a lovely face;
God in his mercy lend her grace,   *170*
   The Lady of Shalott."

                                   Alfred, Lord Tennyson

The nonsense quality of Lewis Carroll's *Alice in Wonderland* may find
its way into narrative poetry, leaving the delighted reader with mixed
reactions. As you read Edward Lear's "The Dong with a Luminous
Nose," look for answers to these questions: Who is the narrator? From
whence comes his information? What is the Dong? Who are the
Jumblies? Where, from evidences in the poem, are the Gromboolian
plain and the Hills of the Chankly Bore located? Account for Lear's
varying meter, line length, and stanza pattern. If the poem is merely
nonsense verse, why are elements of reality (such as buildings, sieve,
oysters) included? In what ways does this narrative poem differ from
Lewis Carroll's "Jabberwocky"? In what ways is it similar?

The Dong with a Luminous Nose

When awful darkness and silence reign
Over the great Gromboolian plain,
   Through the long, long wintry nights;—
When the angry breakers roar
As they beat on the rocky shore;—   *5*
   When Storm clouds brood on the towering heights
Of the Hills of the Chankly Bore:

Then, through the vast and gloomy dark,
There moves what seems a fiery spark,
   A lonely spark with silvery rays   *10*
   Piercing the coal-black night,—
   A meteor strange and bright:
Hither and thither the vision strays,
   A single lurid light.

Slowly it wanders,—pauses,—creeps,— 15
Anon it sparkles,—flashes and leaps;
And ever as onward it gleaming goes
A light on the Bong-tree stems it throws.
And those who watch at that midnight hour
From Hall or Terrace, or lofty Tower, 20
Cry, as the wild light passes along,—
    "The Dong!—the Dong!
  The wandering Dong through the forest goes!
    The Dong! the Dong!
  The Dong with a luminous Nose!" 25

    Long years ago
  The Dong was happy and gay,
Till he fell in love with a Jumbly Girl
  Who came to those shores one day,
For the Jumblies came in a Sieve, they did,— 30
Landing at eve near the Zemmery Fidd
    Where the Oblong Oysters grow,
  And the rocks are smooth and gray.
And all the woods and the valleys rang
With the Chorus they daily and nightly sang,— 35
    "Far and few, far and few,
    Are the lands where the Jumblies live;
    Their heads are green, and their hands are blue,
    And they went to sea in a sieve."

Happily, happily passed those days! 40
    While the cheerful Jumblies stayed;
  They danced in circlets all night long,
  To the plaintive pipe of the lively Dong,
    In moonlight, shine, or shade.
For day and night he was always there 45
By the side of the Jumbly Girl so fair,
With her sky-blue hands, and her sea-green hair.
Till the morning came of that hateful day
When the Jumblies sailed in their sieve away,
And the Dong was left on the cruel shore 50
Gazing—gazing for evermore,—
Ever keeping his weary eyes on
That pea-green sail on the far horizon,—
Singing the Jumbly Chorus still
As he sat all day on the grassy hill,— 55

"Far and few, far and few,
Are the lands where the Jumblies live;
Their heads are green, and their hands are blue,
And they went to sea in a sieve."

But when the sun was low in the West,   60
   The Dong arose and said,—
   "What little sense I once possessed
   Has quite gone out of my head!"
And since that day he wanders still
By lake and forest, marsh and hill,   65
Singing—"O somewhere, in valley or plain
Might I find my Jumbly Girl again!
For ever I'll seek by lake and shore
Till I find my Jumbly Girl once more!"

   Playing a pipe with silvery squeaks,   70
   Since then his Jumbly Girl he seeks,
   And because by night he could not see,
   He gathered the bark of the Twangum Tree
      On the flowery plain that grows.
      And he wove him a wondrous Nose,—   75
   A Nose as strange as a Nose could be!
Of vast proportions and painted red,
And tied with cords to the back of his head.
   —In a hollow rounded space it ended
   With a luminous lamp within suspended,   80
      All fenced about
      With a bandage stout
      To prevent the wind from blowing it out;—
   And with holes all round to send the light,
   In gleaming rays on the dismal night.   85

And now each night, and all night long,
Over those plains still roams the Dong;
And above the wail of the Chimp and Snipe
You may hear the squeak of his plaintive pipe
While ever he seeks, but seeks in vain   90
To meet with his Jumbly Girl again;
Lonely and wild—all night he goes,—
The Dong with a luminous Nose!
And all who watch at the midnight hour,
From Hall or Terrace, or lofty Tower,   95

Cry, as they trace the Meteor bright,
Moving along through the dreary night,—
"This is the hour when forth he goes,
The Dong with a luminous Nose!
Yonder—over the plain he goes;   *100*
He goes!
He goes;
The Dong with a luminous Nose!"

Edward Lear

Family relationships often serve the narrative poet's purpose, for readers are concerned with human behavior. Wordsworth, in a letter to a friend, explained that his purpose in writing "Michael" was to reveal a man "agitated by two of the most powerful affections of the human heart; the parental affection and the love of property, *landed* property, including the feelings of inheritance, home, and personal and family independence." As you read "Michael," you should be aware of the verse paragraphs, since they serve to reveal narrative breaks just as chapters do in novels. The opening verse paragraph not only introduces the narrative, it indicates the tale is based on truth. The misfortunes of Michael are a reportorial account of a family at Grasmere, England, where the ruins of the sheepfold mentioned in the poem still existed in Wordsworth's lifetime. The closing verse paragraph serves as *denouement* (a tying up of loose ends, an explanation, or statement of outcome):

Michael
A Pastoral Poem

If from the public way you turn your steps
Up the tumultuous brook of Greenhead Ghyll,
You will suppose that with an upright path
Your feet must struggle; in such bold ascent
The pastoral mountains front you, face to face.   *5*
But, courage! for around that boisterous brook
The mountains have all opened out themselves,
And made a hidden valley of their own.
No habitation can be seen; but they
Who journey thither find themselves alone   *10*
With a few sheep, with rocks and stones, and kites
That overhead are sailing in the sky.
It is in truth an utter solitude;
Nor should I have made mention of this dell
But for one object which you might pass by,   *15*

Might see and notice not. Beside the brook
Appears a straggling heap of unhewn stones!
And to that simple object appertains
A story—unenriched with strange events,
Yet not unfit, I deem, for the fireside,   20
Or for the summer shade. It was the first
Of those domestic tales that spake to me
Of Shepherds, dwellers in the valleys, men
Whom I already loved—not verily
For their own sakes, but for the fields and hills   25
Where was their occupation and abode.
And hence this Tale, while I was yet a Boy
Careless of books, yet having felt the power
Of Nature, by the gentle agency
Of natural objects, led me on to feel   30
For passions that were not my own, and think
(At random and imperfectly indeed)
On man, the heart of man, and human life.
Therefore, although it be a history
Homely and rude, I will relate the same   35
For the delight of a few natural hearts;
And, with yet fonder feeling, for the sake
Of youthful Poets, who among these hills
Will be my second self when I am gone.

    Upon the forest side in Grasmere Vale   40
There dwelt a Shepherd, Michael was his name;
An old man, stout of heart, and strong of limb.
His bodily frame had been from youth to age
Of an unusual strength: his mind was keen,
Intense, and frugal, apt for all affairs,   45
And in his shepherd's calling he was prompt
And watchful more than ordinary men.
Hence had he learned the meaning of all winds,
Of blasts of every tone; and oftentimes,
When others heeded not, he heard the South   50
Make subterraneous music, like the noise
Of bagpipers on distant Highland hills.
The Shepherd, at such warning, of his flock
Bethought him, and he to himself would say,
"The winds are now devising work for me!"   55

And, truly, at all times, the storm, that drives
The traveler to a shelter, summoned him
Up to the mountains: he had been alone
Amid the heart of many thousand mists,
That came to him, and left him, on the heights.   60
So lived he till his eightieth year was past.
And grossly that man errs, who should suppose
That the green valleys, and the streams and rocks,
Were things indifferent to the Shepherd's thoughts.
Fields, where with cheerful spirits he had breathed   65
The common air; hills, which with vigorous step
He had so often climbed; which had impressed
So many incidents upon his mind
Of hardship, skill or courage, joy or fear;
Which, like a book, preserved the memory   70
Of the dumb animals, whom he had saved,
Had fed or sheltered, linking to such acts
The certainty of honorable gain;
Those fields, those hills—what could they less? had laid
Strong hold on his affections, were to him   75
A pleasurable feeling of blind love,
The pleasure which there is in life itself.

His days had not been passed in singleness.
His Helpmate was a comely matron, old—
Though younger than himself full twenty years.   80
She was a woman of a stirring life,
Whose heart was in her house; two wheels she had
Of antique form: this large, for spinning wool;
That small, for flax; and, if one wheel had rest,
It was because the other was at work.   85
The Pair had but one inmate in their house,
An only Child, who had been born to them
When Michael, telling o'er his years, began
To deem that he was old—in shepherd's phrase,
With one foot in the grave. This only Son,   90
With two brave sheep dogs tried in many a storm,
The one of an inestimable worth,
Made all their household. I may truly say,
That they were as a proverb in the vale
For endless industry. When day was gone,   95

And from their occupations out of doors
The Son and Father were come home, even then,
Their labor did not cease; unless when all
Turned to the cleanly supper board, and there,
Each with a mess of pottage and skimmed milk,   100
Sat round the basket piled with oaten cakes,
And their plain homemade cheese. Yet when the meal
Was ended, Luke (for so the Son was named)
And his old Father both betook themselves
To such convenient work as might employ   105
Their hands by the fireside; perhaps to card
Wool for the Housewife's spindle, or repair
Some injury done to sickle, flail, or scythe,
Or other implement of house or field.

    Down from the ceiling, by the chimney's edge,   110
That in our ancient uncouth country style
With huge and black projection overbrowed
Large space beneath, as duly as the light
Of day grew dim the Housewife hung a lamp;
An aged utensil, which had performed   115
Service beyond all others of its kind.
Early at evening did it burn—and late,
Surviving comrade of uncounted hours,
Which, going by from year to year, had found,
And left, the couple neither gay perhaps   120
Nor cheerful, yet with objects and with hopes,
Living a life of eager industry.
And now, when Luke had reached his eighteenth year,
There by the light of this old lamp they sate,
Father and Son, while far into the night   125
The Housewife plied her own peculiar work,
Making the cottage through the silent hours
Murmur as with the sound of summer flies.
This light was famous in its neighborhood,
And was a public symbol of the life   130
That thrifty Pair had lived. For, as it chanced,
Their cottage on a plot of rising ground
Stood single, with large prospect, north and south,
High into Easedale, up to Dunmail Raise,
And westward to the village near the lake;   135

And from this constant light, so regular,
And so far seen, the House itself, by all
Who dwelt within the limits of the vale,
Both old and young, was named The Evening Star.

    Thus living on through such a length of years,   *140*
The Shepherd, if he loved himself, must needs
Have loved his Helpmate; but to Michael's heart
This son of his old age was yet more dear—
Less from instinctive tenderness, the same
Fond spirit that blindly works in the blood of all—   *145*
Than that a child, more than all other gifts
That earth can offer to declining man,
Brings hope with it, and forward-looking thoughts,
And stirrings of inquietude, when they
By tendency of nature needs must fail.   *150*
Exceeding was the love he bare to him,
His heart and his heart's joy! For oftentimes
Old Michael, while he was a babe in arms,
Had done him female service, not alone
For pastime and delight, as is the use   *155*
Of fathers, but with patient mind enforced
To acts of tenderness; and he had rocked
His cradle, as with a woman's gentle hand.

    And in a later time, ere yet the Boy
Had put on boy's attire, did Michael love,   *160*
Albeit of a stern unbending mind,
To have the Young-one in his sight, when he
Wrought in the field, or on his shepherd's stool
Sate with a fettered sheep before him stretched
Under the large old oak, that near his door   *165*
Stood single, and, from matchless depth of shade,
Chosen for the Shearer's covert from the sun,
Thence in our rustic dialect was called
The Clipping Tree, a name which yet it bears.
There, while they two were sitting in the shade,   *170*
With others round them, earnest all and blithe,
Would Michael exercise his heart with looks
Of fond correction and reproof bestowed

Upon the Child, if he disturbed the sheep
By catching at their legs, or with his shouts   *175*
Scared them, while they lay still beneath the shears.

    And when by Heaven's good grace the boy grew up
A healthy Lad, and carried in his cheek
Two steady roses that were five years old;
Then Michael from a winter coppice cut   *180*
With his own hand a sapling, which he hooped
With iron, making it throughout in all
Due requisites a perfect shepherd's staff,
And gave it to the Boy; wherewith equipped
He as a watchman oftentimes was placed   *185*
At gate or gap, to stem or turn the flock;
And, to his office prematurely called,
There stood the urchin, as you will divine,
Something between a hindrance and a help;
And for this cause not always, I believe,   *190*
Receiving from his Father hire of praise;
Though nought was left undone which staff, or voice,
Or looks, or threatening gestures, could perform.

    But soon as Luke, full ten years old, could stand
Against the mountain blasts, and to the heights,   *195*
Not fearing toil, nor length of weary ways,
He with his Father daily went, and they
Were as companions, why should I relate
That objects which the Shepherd loved before
Were dearer now? that from the Boy there came   *200*
Feelings and emanations—things which were
Light to the sun and music to the wind;
And that the old Man's heart seemed born again?

    Thus in his Father's sight the Boy grew up:
And now, when he had reached his eighteenth year,   *205*
He was his comfort and his daily hope.

    While in this sort the simple household lived
From day to day, to Michael's ear there came
Distressful tidings. Long before the time
Of which I speak, the Shepherd had been bound   *210*
In surety for his brother's son, a man

Of an industrious life, and ample means;
But unforeseen misfortunes suddenly
Had pressed upon him; and old Michael now
Was summoned to discharge the forfeiture,   215
A grievous penalty, but little less
Than half his substance. This unlooked-for claim,
At the first hearing, for a moment took
More hope out of his life than he supposed
That any old man ever could have lost.   220
As soon as he had armed himself with strength
To look his trouble in the face, it seemed
The Shepherd's sole resource to sell at once
A portion of his patrimonial fields.
Such was his first resolve; he thought again,   225
And his heart failed him. "Isabel," said he,
Two evenings after he had heard the news,
"I have been toiling more than seventy years,
And in the open sunshine of God's love
Have we all lived; yet, if these fields of ours   230
Should pass into a stranger's hand, I think
That I could not lie quiet in my grave.
Our lot is a hard lot; the sun himself
Has scarcely been more diligent than I;
And I have lived to be a fool at last   235
To my own family. An evil man
That was, and made an evil choice, if he
Were false to us; and, if he were not false,
There are ten thousand to whom loss like this
Had been no sorrow. I forgive him—but   240
'Twere better to be dumb than to talk thus.

"When I began, my purpose was to speak
Of remedies and of a cheerful hope.
Our Luke shall leave us, Isabel; the land
Shall not go from us, and it shall be free;   245
He shall possess it, free as is the wind
That passes over it. We have, thou know'st,
Another kinsman—he will be our friend
In this distress. He is a prosperous man,
Thriving in trade—and Luke to him shall go,   250
And with his kinsman's help and his own thrift
He quickly will repair this loss, and then

He may return to us. If here he stay,
What can be done? Where everyone is poor,
What can be gained?"
                    At this the old Man paused,   *255*
And Isabel sat silent, for her mind
Was busy, looking back into past times.
There's Richard Bateman, thought she to herself,
He was a parish boy—at the church door
They made a gathering for him, shillings, pence,   *260*
And halfpennies, wherewith the neighbors bought
A basket, which they filled with peddler's wares;
And, with this basket on his arm, the lad
Went up to London, found a master there,
Who, out of many, chose the trusty boy   *265*
To go and overlook his merchandise
Beyond the seas; where he grew wondrous rich,
And left estates and monies to the poor,
And, at his birthplace, built a chapel floored
With marble, which he sent from foreign lands.   *270*
These thoughts, and many others of like sort,
Passed quickly through the mind of Isabel,
And her face brightened. The old Man was glad,
And thus resumed: "Well, Isabel! this scheme
These two days has been meat and drink to me.   *275*
Far more than we have lost is left us yet.
We have enough—I wish indeed that I
Were younger—but this hope is a good hope.
Make ready Luke's best garments, of the best
Buy for him more, and let us send him forth   *280*
Tomorrow, or the next day, or tonight:
If he *could* go, the Boy should go tonight."

    Here Michael ceased, and to the fields went forth
With a light heart. The Housewife for five days
Was restless morn and night, and all day long   *285*
Wrought on with her best fingers to prepare
Things needful for the journey of her son.
But Isabel was glad when Sunday came
To stop her in her work; for, when she lay
By Michael's side, she through the last two nights   *290*
Heard him, how he was troubled in his sleep;
And when they rose at morning she could see

That all his hopes were gone. That day at noon
She said to Luke, while they two by themselves
Were sitting at the door, "Thou must not go;   *295*
We have no other Child but thee to lose,
None to remember—do not go away,
For if thou leave thy Father he will die."
The Youth made answer with a jocund voice;
And Isabel, when she had told her fears,   *300*
Recovered heart. That evening her best fare
Did she bring forth, and all together sat
Like happy people round a Christmas fire.

   With daylight Isabel resumed her work;
And all the ensuing week the house appeared   *305*
As cheerful as a grove in spring; at length
The expected letter from their kinsman came,
With kind assurances that he would do
His utmost for the welfare of the Boy;
To which requests were added that forthwith   *310*
He might be sent to him. Ten times or more
The letter was read over; Isabel
Went forth to show it to the neighbors round;
Nor was there at that time on English land
A prouder heart than Luke's. When Isabel   *315*
Had to her house returned, the old Man said,
"He shall depart tomorrow." To this word
The Housewife answered, talking much of things
Which, if at such short notice he should go,
Would surely be forgotten. But at length   *320*
She gave consent, and Michael was at ease.

   Near the tumultuous brook of Greenhead Ghyll,
In that deep valley, Michael had designed
To build a Sheepfold; and, before he heard
The tidings of his melancholy loss,   *325*
For this same purpose he had gathered up
A heap of stones, which by the streamlet's edge
Lay thrown together, ready for the work.
With Luke that evening thitherward he walked;
And soon as they had reached the place he stopped,   *330*
And thus the old Man spake to him: "My son,
Tomorrow thou wilt leave me: with full heart

I look upon thee, for thou art the same
That wert a promise to me ere thy birth,
And all thy life hast been my daily joy.   335
I will relate to thee some little part
Of our two histories; 'twill do thee good
When thou art from me, even if I should touch
On things thou canst not know of. After thou
First cam'st into the world—as oft befalls   340
To newborn infants—thou didst sleep away
Two days, and blessings from thy Father's tongue
Then fell upon thee. Day by day passed on,
And still I loved thee with increasing love.
Never to living ear came sweeter sounds   345
Than when I heard thee by our own fireside
First uttering, without words, a natural tune;
While thou, a feeding babe, didst in thy joy
Sing at thy Mother's breast. Month followed month,
And in the open fields my life was passed   350
And on the mountains; else I think that thou
Hadst been brought up upon thy Father's knees.
But we were playmates, Luke; among these hills,
As well thou knowest, in us the old and young
Have played together, nor with me didst thou   355
Lack any pleasure which a boy can know.''
Luke had a manly heart; but at these words
He sobbed aloud. The old Man grasped his hand,
And said, "Nay, do not take it so—I see
That these are things of which I need not speak. 360
Even to the utmost I have been to thee
A kind and a good Father: and herein
I but repay a gift which I myself
Received at others' hands; for, though now old
Beyond the common life of man, I still   365
Remember them who loved me in my youth.
Both of them sleep together; here they lived,
As all their Forefathers had done; and, when
At length their time was come, they were not loath
To give their bodies to the family mold.   370
I wished that thou shouldst live the life they lived,
But 'tis a long time to look back, my Son,
And see so little gain from threescore years.
These fields were burthened when they came to me;

Till I was forty years of age, not more   *375*
Than half of my inheritance was mine.
I toiled and toiled; God blessed me in my work,
And till these three weeks past the land was free.
It looks as if it never could endure
Another master. Heaven forgive me, Luke,   *380*
If I judge ill for thee, but it seems good
That thou shouldst go.''
                              At this the old Man paused;
Then, pointing to the stones near which they stood,
Thus, after a short silence, he resumed:
"This was a work for us; and now, my Son,   *385*
It is a work for me. But, lay one stone—
Here, lay it for me, Luke, with thine own hands.
Nay, Boy, be of good hope—we both may live
To see a better day. At eighty-four
I still am strong and hale; do thou thy part;   *390*
I will do mine. I will begin again
With many tasks that were resigned to thee:
Up to the heights, and in among the storms,
Will I without thee go again, and do
All works which I was wont to do alone,   *395*
Before I knew thy face. Heaven bless thee, Boy!
Thy heart these two weeks has been beating fast
With many hopes; it should be so—yes—yes—
I knew that thou couldst never have a wish
To leave me, Luke; thou hast been bound to me   *400*
Only by links of love; when thou art gone,
What will be left to us!—But I forget
My purposes. Lay now the cornerstone,
As I requested; and hereafter, Luke,
When thou art gone away, should evil men   *405*
Be thy companions, think of me, my Son,
And of this moment; hither turn thy thoughts,
And God will strengthen thee; amid all fear
And all temptation, Luke, I pray that thou
May'st bear in mind the life thy Fathers lived,   *410*
Who, being innocent, did for that cause
Bestir them in good deeds. Now, fare thee well—
When thou return'st, thou in this place wilt see
A work which is not here: a covenant
'Twill be between us; but, whatever fate   *415*

Befall thee, I shall love thee to the last,
And bear thy memory with me to the grave.''

   The Shepherd ended here; and Luke stooped down,
And, as his Father had requested, laid
The first stone of the Sheepfold. At the sight   *420*
The old Man's grief broke from him; to his heart
He pressed his Son, he kissed him and wept;
And to the house together they returned.
Hushed was that House in peace, or seeming peace
Ere the night fell; with morrow's dawn the Boy   *425*
Began his journey, and, when he had reached
The public way, he put on a bold face;
And all the neighbors, as he passed their doors,
Came forth with wishes and with farewell prayers,
That followed him till he was out of sight.   *430*

   A good report did from their kinsman come,
Of Luke and his well-doing; and the Boy
Wrote loving letters, full of wondrous news,
Which, as the Housewife phrased it, were throughout
"The prettiest letters that were ever seen."   *435*
Both parents read them with rejoicing hearts.
So, many months passed on; and once again
The Shepherd went about his daily work
With confident and cheerful thoughts; and now
Sometimes when he could find a leisure hour   *440*
He to that valley took his way, and there
Wrought at the Sheepfold. Meantime Luke began
To slacken in his duty; and, at length,
He in the dissolute city gave himself
To evil courses; ignominy and shame   *445*
Fell on him, so that he was driven at last
To seek a hiding place beyond the seas.

   There is a comfort in the strength of love;
'Twill make a thing endurable, which else
Would overset the brain, or break the heart;   *450*
I have conversed with more than one who well
Remember the old Man, and what he was
Years after he had heard this heavy news.
His bodily frame had been from youth to age

Of an unusual strength. Among the rocks   455
He went, and still looked up to sun and cloud,
And listened to the wind; and, as before,
Performed all kinds of labor for his sheep,
And for the land, his small inheritance.
And to that hollow dell from time to time   460
Did he repair, to build the Fold of which
His flock had need. 'Tis not forgotten yet
The pity which was then in every heart
For the old Man—and 'tis believed by all
That many and many a day he thither went,   465
And never lifted up a single stone.

   There, by the Sheepfold, sometimes was he seen
Sitting alone, or with his faithful Dog,
Then old, beside him, lying at his feet.
The length of full seven years, from time to time,   470
He at the building of this Sheepfold wrought,
And left the work unfinished when he died.
Three years, or little more, did Isabel
Survive her Husband: at her death the estate
Was sold, and went into a stranger's hand.   475
The Cottage which was named The Evening Star
Is gone—the plowshare has been through the ground
On which it stood; great changes have been wrought
In all the neighborhood; yet the oak is left
That grew beside their door; and the remains   480
Of the unfinished Sheepfold may be seen
Beside the boisterous brook of Greenhead Ghyll.

Trace the character development of Michael as it is revealed in the poem, finally explaining the line "And never lifted up a single stone."

Dramatic Poetry

Dramatic poetry differs from its narrative counterpart primarily in its method of telling a story. As it is used in plays, dramatic poetry functions against a background of stage directions and settings and is spoken by actors. In its shorter forms, however, stage directions and settings are merely implied by the dialog. The character's speech, then, must reveal attitudes, indicate physical details, and forward the narrative—all at the same time. Concurrently, it must re-create speech, complete with its ellipsis and lack of transitional words. To read dramatic poetry, then, as opposed to hearing it read, is more difficult for the reader—he must actively participate by "seeing" the undescribed scene, supplying the gestures of the speaker, and responding to the undescribed actions (such as facial twitchings) of the character being spoken to. As the reader so actively participates in the action, he intuitively understands the character through identification, and the essential purpose of dramatic poetry (the revelation of character) is realized.

In the *dramatic monolog,* lyric poetry is employed to reveal a dramatic incident in the life of a character. A second person (often only the reader) is present, but he does not respond. Any words of his must be revealed through the monolog of the speaker. Character thus reveals itself in the language, selection of details, and the speaker's response to the unrecorded words of the implied listener.

Amy Lowell's dramatic monolog, "Patterns," resembles the *soliloquy* (a speech revealing the thought processes of a character in a play, delivered out of hearing of the other characters). A young woman walks down her garden-path, lost in her thoughts, and we are allowed to eavesdrop as thought leads into thought and the final anguished question is asked:

Patterns

I walk down the garden-paths,
And all the daffodils
Are blowing, and the bright blue squills.
I walk down the patterned garden-paths
In my stiff, brocaded gown.   *5*
With my powdered hair and jewelled fan,
I too am a rare
Pattern. As I wander down
The garden-paths.

My dress is richly figured,   *10*
And the train
Makes a pink and silver stain
On the gravel, and the thrift
Of the borders.
Just a plate of current fashion,   *15*
Tripping by in high-heeled, ribboned shoes.
Not a softness anywhere about me,
Only whalebone and brocade.
And I sink on a seat in the shade

Of a lime tree. For my passion   20
Wars against the stiff brocade.
The daffodils and squills
Flutter in the breeze
As they please.
And I weep;   25
For the lime tree is in blossom
And one small flower has dropped upon my bosom.

And the plashing of waterdrops
In the marble fountain
Comes down the garden-paths.   30
The dripping never stops.
Underneath my stiffened gown
Is the softness of a woman bathing in a marble basin,
A basin in the midst of hedges grown
So thick, she cannot see her lover hiding,   35
But she guesses he is near,
And the sliding of the water
Seems the stroking of a dear
Hand upon her.
What is Summer in a fine brocaded gown!   40
I should like to see it lying in a heap upon the ground.
All the pink and silver crumpled up on the ground.

I would be the pink and silver as I ran along the paths,
And he would stumble after,
Bewildered by my laughter.   45
I should see the sun flashing from his sword-hilt and the buckles on his shoes.
I would choose
To lead him in a maze along the patterned paths,
A bright and laughing maze for my heavy-booted lover.
Till he caught me in the shade,   50
And the buttons of his waistcoat bruised my body as he clasped me,
Aching, melting, unafraid.
With the shadows of the leaves and the sundrops,
And the plopping of the waterdrops,
All about us in the open afternoon—   55
I am very like to swoon
With the weight of this brocade,
For the sun sifts through the shade.

Underneath the fallen blossom
In my bosom,
Is a letter I have hid.
It was brought to me this morning by a rider from the Duke.
"Madam, we regret to inform you that Lord Hartwell
Died in action Thursday se'nnight."
As I read it in the white, morning sunlight,
The letters squirmed like snakes.
"Any answer, Madam?" said my footman.
"No," I told him.
"See that the messenger takes some refreshment.
No, no answer."
And I walked into the garden,
Up and down the patterned paths,
In my stiff, correct brocade.
The blue and yellow flowers stood up proudly in the sun,
Each one.
I stood upright too,
Held rigid to the pattern
By the stiffness of my gown.
Up and down I walked,
Up and down.

In a month he would have been my husband.
In a month, here, underneath this lime,
We would have broke the pattern;
He for me, and I for him,
He as Colonel, I as Lady,
On this shady seat.
He had a whim
That sunlight carried blessing.
And I answered, "It shall be as you have said."
Now he is dead.

In Summer and in Winter I shall walk
Up and down
The patterned garden-paths
In my stiff, brocaded gown.
The squills and daffodils
Will give place to pillared roses, and to asters, and to snow.
I shall go
Up and down,

In my gown.
Gorgeously arrayed,   *100*
Boned and stayed.
And the softness of my body will be guarded from embrace
By each button, hook, and lace.
For the man who should loose me is dead,
Fighting with the Duke in Flanders,   *105*
In a pattern called a war.
Christ! What are patterns for?

                                                              Amy Lowell

Robert Browning is credited with developing the dramatic monolog. One of his poems, "My Last Duchess," is set in Ferrara, Italy, a setting established in the title. Time is indefinite, but a general period is suggested. Frà (a religious title: "Brother; a monk") Pandolf and Claus of Innsbruck are imaginary artists. Read the poem to discover everything you can about the speaker:

My Last Duchess
Ferrara

That's my last Duchess painted on the wall,
Looking as if she were alive. I call
That piece a wonder, now: Frà Pandolf's hands
Worked busily a day, and there she stands.
Will 't please you sit and look at her? I said   *5*
"Frà Pandolf" by design, for never read
Strangers like you that pictured countenance,
The depth and passion of its earnest glance,
But to myself they turned (since none puts by
The curtain I have drawn for you, but I)   *10*
And seemed as they would ask me, if they durst,
How such a glance came there; so, not the first
Are you to turn and ask thus. Sir, 't was not
Her husband's presence only, called that spot
Of joy into the Duchess' cheek: perhaps   *15*
Frà Pandolf chanced to say "Her mantle laps
Over my lady's wrist too much," or "Paint
Must never hope to reproduce the faint
Half-flush that dies along her throat"; such stuff
Was courtesy, she thought, and cause enough   *20*
For calling up that spot of joy. She had
A heart—how shall I say?—too soon made glad,

Too easily impressed; she liked whate'er
She looked on, and her looks went everywhere.
Sir, 't was all one! My favour at her breast,   25
The dropping of the daylight in the West,
The bough of cherries some officious fool
Broke in the orchard for her, the white mule
She rode with round the terrace—all and each
Would draw from her alike the approving speech,   30
Or blush, at least. She thanked men,—good! but thanked
Somehow—I know not how—as if she ranked
My gift of a nine-hundred-years-old name
With anybody's gift. Who'd stoop to blame
This sort of trifling? Even had you skill   35
In speech—(which I have not)—to make your will
Quite clear to such an one, and say, "Just this
Or that in you disgusts me; here you miss,
Or there exceed the mark"—and if she let
Herself be lessoned so, nor plainly set   40
Her wits to yours, forsooth, and made excuse,
—E'en then would be some stooping; and I choose
Never to stoop. Oh, sir, she smiled, no doubt,
Whene'er I passed her; but who passed without
Much the same smile? This grew; I gave commands;   45
Then all smiles stopped together. There she stands
As if alive. Will 't please you rise? We'll meet
The company below, then. I repeat,
The Count your master's known munificence
Is ample warrant that no just pretence   50
Of mine for dowry will be disallowed;
Though his fair daughter's self, as I avowed
At starting, is my object. Nay, we'll go
Together down, sir! Notice Neptune, though,
Taming a sea-horse, thought a rarity,   55
Which Claus of Innsbruck cast in bronze for me!

Robert Browning

That a court's emissary is the silent second person is not revealed until
near the end of the poem. How does this heighten suspense? What does
last imply in line 1? Explain the irony of line 5. Explain the intentional
ambiguity of lines 9-10. Explain the understatement in line 36. If you
have difficulty understanding lines 35-43, remember the trouble you find
with demanded responses in your own life. If you have ever asked some-

one "Do you like me?", you know the pain of the rest of such a conversation: "Yes." "Well, *tell* me so." "O.K. I *like* you." Now reread the lines. Why does the Duke insist they descend abreast of each other? Why does he point out a second art treasure? How many possessions has he discussed in this poem? Why?

In other poems, Browning employed dialog *within* the monolog. In "A Toccata of Gallupi's," an Englishman, all science and objectivity, has heard Gallupi's toccata, which has forced him to reconsider his attitudes. Never out of England, he has been imaginatively transported to Venice. Reason is disturbed (stanzas 4-6) and he hears voices in the music as a young couple discuss its meaning to them (stanzas 7-9). As he relinquishes the lovers (stanza 10), the music still insists love is more important than reason, regardless of love's fleeting nature (stanzas 11-14). Rationalizing wildly, he is defeated by the music and, as he realizes what he has missed (stanza 15), he feels "chilly and grown old."

Sound creates much of the sense in this monolog, sound you can hear if you read the poem aloud. The toccata is a musical composition for organ or clavichord, unrestrained in form but utilizing vibrant, full chords and running, lilting passages. Often speeding to brilliance, at times it slows to stateliness or lingers happily in sweet passages. Baldassare Galuppi was a Venetian composer of the eighteenth century, famous for his toccatas. Read the monolog aloud to hear the toccata rhythms in the lines:

A Toccata of Galuppi's

1

O Galuppi, Baldassaro, this is very sad to find!
I can hardly misconceive you; it would prove me deaf and blind;
But although I take your meaning, 'tis with such a heavy mind!

2

Here you come with your old music, and here's all the good it brings.
What, they lived once thus at Venice where the merchants were the kings,   5
Where St. Mark's is, where the Doges used to wed the sea with rings?

3

Ay, because the sea's the street there; and 'tis arched by . . . what you call . . .
Shylock's bridge with houses on it, where they kept the carnival:
I was never out of England—it's as if I saw it all.

4

Did young people take their pleasure when the sea was warm in May?   *10*
Balls and masks begun at midnight, burning ever to mid-day,
When they made up fresh adventures for the morrow, do you say?

5

Was a lady such a lady, cheeks so round and lips so red,—
On her neck the small face buoyant, like a bell-flower on its bed,
O'er the breast's superb abundance where a man might base his head?   *15*

6

Well, and it was graceful of them—they'd break talk off and afford—
She, to bite her mask's black velvet—he, to finger on his sword,
While you sat and played Toccatas, stately at the clavichord?

7

What? Those lesser thirds so plaintive, sixths diminished, sigh on sigh,
Told them something? Those suspensions, those solutions—"Must we die?"   *20*
Those commiserating sevenths—"Life might last! we can but try!"

8

"Were you happy?"—"Yes."—"And are you still as happy?"—"Yes. And you?"
—"Then, more kisses!"—"Did *I* stop them, when a million seemed so few?"
Hark, the dominant's persistence till it must be answered to!

9

So an octave struck the answer. Oh, they praised you, I dare say!   *25*
"Brave Galuppi! that was music! good alike at grave and gay!
I can always leave off talking when I hear a master play!"

10

Then they left you for their pleasure; till in due time, one by one,
Some with lives that came to nothing, some with deeds as well undone,
Death stepped tacitly and took them where they never see the sun.   *30*

11

But when I sit down to reason, think to take my stand nor swerve,
While I triumph o'er a secret wrung from nature's close reserve,
In you come with your cold music till I creep through every nerve.

12

Yes, you, like a ghostly cricket, creaking where a house was burned:
"Dust and ashes, dead and done with, Venice spent what Venice earned!   *35*
The soul, doubtless, is immortal—where a soul can be discerned.

13

"Yours for instance: you know physics, something of geology,
Mathematics are your pastime; souls shall rise in their degree;
Butterflies may dread extinction—you'll not die, it cannot be!

14

"As for Venice and her people, merely born to bloom and drop,   *40*
Here on earth they bore their fruitage, mirth and folly were the crop;
What of soul was left, I wonder, when the kissing had to stop?

15

"Dust and ashes!" So you creak it, and I want the heart to scold.
Dear dead women, with such hair, too—what's become of all the gold
Used to hang and brush their bosoms? I feel chilly and grown old.   *45*

Robert Browning

T. S. Eliot's "Journey of the Magi" combines a simple narrative with a subtle monolog to offer comment that is as timeless as the story itself. As you read, ask yourself the following questions: Did the Magi arrive at the stable? At Golgotha? Were the three trees (line 24) symbols of life or symbols of death? Were they trees at all? What accounts for the repetition of *Set down this* (lines 33-35)? (Consider the age of the narrator before you answer.) And, finally, whose death does the narrator refer to in the last line of the poem?

Journey of the Magi

"A cold coming we had of it,
Just the worst time of the year
For a journey, and such a long journey:
The ways deep and the weather sharp,
The very dead of winter."   *5*
And the camels galled, sore-footed, refractory,
Lying down in the melting snow.
There were times we regretted
The summer palaces on slopes, the terraces,
And the silken girls bringing sherbet.   *10*

Then the camel men cursing and grumbling
And running away, and wanting their liquor and women,
And the night-fires going out, and the lack of shelters,
And the cities hostile and the towns unfriendly
And the villages dirty and charging high prices: *15*
A hard time we had of it.
At the end we preferred to travel all night,
Sleeping in snatches,
With the voices singing in our ears, saying
That this was all folly.   *20*

Then at dawn we came down to a temperate valley,
Wet, below the snow line, smelling of vegetation;
With a running stream and a water-mill beating the darkness,
And three trees on the low sky,
And an old white horse galloped away in the meadow.   *25*
Then we came to a tavern with vine-leaves over the lintel,
Six hands at an open door dicing for pieces of silver,
And feet kicking the empty wine-skins.
But there was no information, and so we continued
And arrived at evening, not a moment too soon   *30*
Finding the place; it was (you may say) satisfactory.

All this was a long time ago, I remember,
And I would do it again, but set down
This set down
This: were we led all that way for   *35*
Birth or Death? There was a Birth, certainly,
We had evidence and no doubt. I had seen birth and death,
But had thought they were different; this Birth was
Hard and bitter agony for us, like Death, our death.
We returned to our places, these Kingdoms,   *40*
But no longer at ease here, in the old dispensation,
With an alien people clutching their gods.
I should be glad of another death.

                                                    T. S. Eliot

How much of setting is indicated in this poem? To whom does the narrator speak? How characteristic is this poem of the "inspired" writings of the Bible? Can you find reasons to justify your answers?

Suggested Assignments. 1. In "The Ballad of the Oysterman," Oliver Wendell Holmes combines the narrative poem and the ballad form to create a melodramatic, romantically sentimental tale. Delightful humor emerges. In a brief paper, account for your sympathy or lack of sympathy for the lovers. Make some reference to the metrics and line length and their contribution to the tone of the poem. Also include a brief comment on allusion and simile:

The Ballad of the Oysterman

It was a tall young oysterman lived by the riverside,
His shop was just upon the bank, his boat was on the tide;
The daughter of a fisherman, that was so straight and slim,
Lived over on the other bank, right opposite to him.

It was the pensive oysterman that saw a lovely maid,   5
Upon a moonlight evening, a-sitting in the shade;
He saw her wave her handkerchief, as much as if to say,
"I'm wide awake, young oysterman, and all the folks away."

Then up arose the oysterman, and to himself said he,
"I guess I'll leave the skiff at home, for fear that folks should see;   10
I read it in the storybook, that, for to kiss his dear,
Leander swam the Hellespont,—and I will swim this here."

And he has leaped into the waves, and crossed the shining stream,
And he has clambered up the bank, all in the moonlight gleam;
Oh, there were kisses sweet as dew, and words as soft as rain,—   15
But they have heard her father's step, and in he leaps again!

Out spoke the ancient fisherman,—"Oh, what was that, my daughter?"
" 'Twas nothing but a pebble, sir, I threw into the water."
"And what is that, pray tell me, love, that paddles off so fast?"
"It's nothing but a porpoise, sir, that's been a-swimming past."   20

Out spoke the ancient fisherman,—"Now bring me my harpoon!
I'll get into my fishing boat, and fix the fellow soon."
Down fell that pretty innocent, as falls a snow-white lamb,
Her hair drooped round her pallid cheeks, like seaweed on a clam.

Alas for those two loving ones! she waked not from her swound,   25
And he was taken with the cramp, and in the waves was drowned;
But Fate has metamorphosed them, in pity of their woe.
And now they keep an oyster shop for mermaids down below.

Oliver Wendell Holmes

2. Thomas Love Peacock was a close friend of Percy Bysshe and Mary Shelley. His famous novels, *Headlong Hall* and *Nightmare Abbey,* are in the Gothic tradition (tales of terror and the supernatural), as is Mary Shelley's *Frankenstein.* "The War Song of Dinas Vawr" is included in Peacock's novel *The Misfortunes of Elphin.* Poets of the Romantic Movement (of which Peacock and the Shelleys were a part) delighted in writing lengthy metrical romances (see p. 115), pseudohistorical in nature. In forty lines, Peacock devastates the fashionable form. In a brief paper, explain why his poem is effective:

The War Song of Dinas Vawr

The mountain sheep are sweeter,
But the valley sheep are fatter;
We therefore deemed it meeter
To carry off the latter.
We made an expedition;   5
We met a host, and quelled it;
We forced a strong position,
And killed the men who held it.

On Dyfed's richest valley,
Where herds of kine were browsing,   10
We made a mighty sally,
To furnish our carousing.
Fierce warriors rushed to meet us;
We met them, and o'erthrew them:
They struggled hard to beat us;   15
But we conquered them, and slew them.

As we drove our prize at leisure,
The king marched forth to catch us:
His rage surpassed all measure,
But his people could not match us.   20
He fled to his hall pillars;
And, ere our force we led off,
Some sacked his house and cellars,
While others cut his head off.

We there, in strife bewild'ring,   25
Spilt blood enough to swim in:
We orphaned many children,
And widowed many women.

The eagles and the ravens
We glutted with our foemen;   *30*
The heroes and the cravens,
The spearmen and the bowmen.

We brought away from battle,
And much their land bemoaned them,
Two thousand head of cattle,   *35*
And the head of him who owned them:
Ednyfed, king of Dyfed,
His head was borne before us;
His wine and beasts supplied our feasts,
And his overthrow, our chorus.   *40*

                    Thomas Love Peacock

CHAPTER XI

Writing About the Poem

By now, you doubtless recognize that the humorous couplet can be as valuable as the epic poem of extended length and serious intent. Each has its purpose, and the purpose of the epic is no more important in the final analysis than the purpose of the couplet. Each is designed to create some awareness in the reader, that he may be amused or entertained, instructed, or improved in some way. If you assume that poetry of serious intent is more *important* than humorous works, you have missed the marvelous communication of poetry. Man has his serious moments, he has his tragic hours. But they are no more important than the delightful moments he prefers. As life itself is structured on a combination of such moments, poetry also concerns itself with them, singly and in combination. The poet's aims and techniques will vary from poem to poem, from poet to poet; but they will often be blended in one poem. Even the elegy may have its bittersweet, if not humorous, sections—the tragic is compounded of many elements, even in life. And the humorous almost always contains some tragic element—even if it is no more than the tragedy of *needing* to laugh.

To reveal your new poetic knowledge, both to yourself and to others, you will find it necessary to analyze poems of various lengths, discovering something about them that makes them worth reading, worth discussing. You should, then, learn the basic steps involved in writing a theme, essay, or interpretation of a poem. The following short list of steps will serve as a beginning for you. Your own repeated efforts with it will suggest modifications and variations which, if followed, will allow you to discuss a poem with comfort in the knowledge that you have reasons for your stated beliefs about the work at hand.

Step 1: Read the poem without concentrating on anything except the impact of the total work. Make notes of your first impressions without referring back to the poem.

Step 2: Reread the poem to verify those impressions. If they change, what subtlety did you miss in the first reading? That subtlety may be the central point of your analysis. Was the language deceptive because of ambiguities or connotations? Did you mistake humor for irony, irony for didacticism? Revise your notes to include new revelations.

Step 3: Reduce the poem to the best précis (see pp. 27-28) you can extract.

Step 4: With your précis firmly in mind, reread the poem. Does examination of the parts verify your précis? If not, paraphrase the poem; then reduce your paraphrase to a précis. Check that précis against the poem. Continue the process until you are satisfied your précis is adequate.

Step 5: From the basic idea or ideas of the poem, you can speculate on the poet's intention. And you can compare his intention to your reaction. Remember: you may react in a way that would not occur to the poet. If such is the case, do not assume that either you or the poet has failed. After all, a poem becomes successful when it creates a reaction in you. The poet does not say you must have any particular reaction—he will be satisfied if you have one at all.

Step 6: You are now ready to find a general theme for your discussion. What insights gained from reading the poem do you wish to share? The answer will be a précis of your paper and will control the development of it just as the poet's précis controlled the development of his poem. Anything that does not contribute to the logical development of your précis should be discarded as ruthlessly as the poet probably discarded lines of his work when they failed to contribute to the total effect.

Step 7: With précis in mind, begin to make notes from the poem. They will probably be illogical in sequence, but you can unify them later. Your notes should cite specific examples as a result of answering the following questions:

    A. Language: Is the language primarily denotative? Does the poet say what he means at the simplest level? Is it primarily connotative? Is it a combination of denotative and connotative? Why is one level used more than the other, or does the poet strike a balance? If so, why?

How much reliance is there on imagery? How do the associated images create meaning? What specific literary devices (simile, personification, paradox, etc.) are included? How do grammar, syntax and punctuation work with vocabulary choice (both diction and idiom) to make the imagery effective? Do images build into symbols? Are established symbols employed without the need of imagery?

B. *Prosody:* Is a metrical pattern readily obvious? How does the metrical pattern contribute to the total effect of the poem? If an elegy is predominantly iambic or anapestic, why is the lilting meter used? What effect is achieved? If free verse is employed, why is it more effective than measured verse would be? Do conventions of the form limit the poet? What liberties does he take with the form? How does enjambment of lines affect the rhythm? How are caesuras employed? To what purpose? Is rhyme employed? Does it result in fixed forms or does it create innovation in stanza patterns? Is the rhyme masculine, feminine, triple, slant, outrageous? How do such choices serve the poem? If rhyme is not used, why not? Is internal rhyme employed? Why? What aids to rhyme (assonance, alliteration, consonance, etc.) are employed? What do they contribute to the mood and tone of the work?

C. *Structural Development:* How is the poem developed? If the editorial method is used, why? Does chronology seem paramount? How does the development contribute to the total effect? Is the poem unified? Do coherence and logic seem apparent? Does the absence of either contribute anything to the poem?

D. *Reason for the Poem:* With what areas is the poet concerned? Is he commenting, judging, or observing? Is he examining abstract ideas? Justifying the ways of God to man? Of man to God? Creating a mood? Being amusing through irony or satire? Is he posing a resolvable paradox? How does the structural development serve the poem?

Step 8: Every question you ask, every answer you discover, every observation you make about the total poem will, in some way, be related to the theme of the poem. They should, then, help you see the relationship between the poet's theme and the theme of your essay. You might read a biographical note on the poet to see if an insight can be gleaned there. As the poet's theme was developed from selected principles, so must the interpreter's be. You are ready now to decide on your method. Examine your notes in relation to the précis of your paper. Choose the order of presentation you think best.

Step 9: Establish the main ideas of your paper, rejecting material you cannot accommodate if you have been given a maximum word-age. The main ideas will be the roman numerals of your outline.

Step 10: From your notes, select those points which best support and illustrate your main points. Fill in the letters and arabic numerals of your outline.

Step 11: Examine the outline for errors in logic. Is the order of ideas the best order? Can you visualize the impact of the argument from the outline?

Step 12: Write your paper, remembering that you too can employ the techniques you have learned. Your paper should express you, and, therefore, reveal style.

Experiment with the following poem, following steps 1 through 11. (Do not write the paper.) Do not assume you are ready to take short-cuts yet. As you become more proficient, you will learn to do several things at once. However, until such time, be content to plod slowly.

Read the poem, but do not read beyond it until you have completed the 11 steps. When you have done so, check your answers against those which are suggested below:

Song

I make my shroud, but no one knows—
So shimmering fine it is and fair,
With stitches set in even rows.
I make my shroud, but no one knows.

In door-way where the lilac blows,   *5*
Humming a little wandering air,
I make my shroud and no one knows,
So shimmering fine it is and fair.

Adelaide Crapsey

Step 1: Melancholia might have been your first response to this poem. It is concerned with awareness of approaching death, but there is a pride in the workmanship of the shroud. That "no one knows" seems tragic, as the maker of the shroud seems so alone in the knowledge. Self-pity on the speaker's part may have suggested itself to you.

Step 2:   In your second reading, you should have noticed that the first line is repeated as line 4. With one word changed, it is repeated as line 7. Line 2 is repeated as line 8. Two lines, then, make up five-eighths of the poem. Such repetition is either poor poetry or else it is done deliberately to establish a definite effect. Reevaluate step 2 of your notes in light of these facts if they escaped you. The poem is a triolet in form.

Steps 3–4:   Your précis may be as simple as "I'm dying, but no one knows it." Or it might be, "I know I'm dying; so I'm preparing a fine burial garment." Or, "One should prepare for death without public display." If it is any of these, you have missed the point! Double-check!

Step 5:   If, upon reevaluation, you cannot see another précis, are you satisfied with the "message"? Is it a new awareness? If it is an old one, is it more understandable or acceptable in this form? If the answers to these questions are "Yes," you have profited from the poem even if you have missed its greater complexities.

Step 6:   We'll return to this step later.

Step 7:

    A. Language: The language seems to function at a denotative level. However, *shroud* has more than one meaning. A shroud may be a fragment or shred. It may also be a burial garment. It may also be a veil, shelter, or screen, something that covers and protects. *Shimmering* means "to shine with an unsteady light," but it does connote brilliance. *Stitches* suggests that the burial garment denotation for *shroud* is correct. But can a burial garment shimmer? Are not such garments usually somber in color? A paradox suggests itself at this point. Are the words more connotative than they seemed at first glance? *Fine* includes, among its meanings, "containing a specified proportion of pure metal (in gold and silver)." Does this suggest the shroud is of cloth containing gold or silver threads? *Fine* also means "not coarse"; silk is a fine cloth which shimmers in a certain light. The word also means "subtle or discriminating." And it means "highly disciplined in training—as 'a fine athlete'."

The punctuation in the first three lines is interesting. Line 1 contains a compound sentence properly punctuated internally with a comma, but ending with a dash. As dashes indicate a break in thought, or make an abrupt separation between clauses, or enclose a parenthetical expression, the usage here is not immediately apparent. However, if *so* were a conjunction, it would introduce a third clause which would demand at least a comma after *knows*. Therefore, *so* functions as an adverb of degree to modify the predicate adjective *fine*. The poet employs the dash to break the thought, making the unspoken remainder of line 1 an elliptical "it is my shroud because." Line 2 becomes an adverbial clause modifying *knows* and the implication is that no one knows it is a shroud because it does not resemble the usual dark burial garment. The period after line 3 stops the statement abruptly. Line 4 (a repetition of line 1) seems even more abrupt because it concludes with a period which changes the meaning as it was built in line 1. Line 4 says simply, "No one knows it is my shroud," and pride in the assertion attends the line.

In the second stanza, there seems no immediately apparent reason to hyphenate *door-way*. Also, commas after lines 5 and 6 create ambiguity. Line 6 is a participial phrase. Does it modify *lilac* of line 5 or *I* of line 7—or both? Line 7 creates a new problem. The meaning changes subtly as the word *but* in lines 1 and 4 becomes *and*. The punctuation after *knows* is not the dash used earlier, though line 8 is exactly the same as line 2. The comma changes the word *so* to a conjunction meaning "and, as a result," or "therefore."

B. *Prosody:*

line 1 = iambic tetrameter

line 2 = iambic tetrameter with "*-mering*" combining two very weak feminine syllables into 1 feminine syllable. The foreshortening makes *shimmering* visual onomatopoeia.

line 3 = iambic tetrameter

line 4 = iambic tetrameter

line 5 = iambic tetrameter. However, had *door-way* not been hyphenated, the first foot would read *in doorway,* and the spondaic quality would be very grim. This proves to be an important point: *-way where* becomes alliteration as a result, making *-way* seem to go with *where* rather than with *door-.*

line 6 = either iambic tetrameter with an initial trochee or

$$\bar{}\; \smile\; \smile\; \bar{}\smile\; \smile\; \bar{} \qquad \bar{}$$

Humming a | little wan | dering air,

a dactylic trimeter line of great melancholy ending in a stark spondee.

line 7 = iambic tetrameter unless the second scansion possibility of line 6 is accepted. The initial trochee of line 6 would cause the reader to accent *I* in line 7 as parallel scansion, creating an initial trochee emphasizing the subject rather than the verb.

line 8 = iambic tetrameter unless initial trochee readings of lines 6 and 7 create an initial trochee in this one, a possibility reinforced by the punctuation and grammar.

The indicated subtleties suggest veiled imagery, and, as the imagery seems to extend through the poem, it may be assuming the status of a symbol.

As this is a "Song," the iambic tetrameter is well chosen for its light, happy quality. The grim shroud symbol works against it to create a paradoxical tone. Enjambment in lines 1-3 is very effective since it isolates line 4 so completely, thereby creating its effect. Caesuras exist after *shroud* each time the word is used, emphasizing it. They are not employed anywhere else in the poem. The hyphenation of *door-way* avoided the necessity of a caesura following that word. Duplicate rhyme is used in each stanza. However, both stanzas must be read together as a unit of 8 lines to establish the rhyme scheme *abaaabab*—a curious, haunting rhyme, twisting always back on itself. Masculine rhyme throughout establishes a strong determination in tone.

Assonance in *no one knows* creates a mournful tone. The alliterative *s*'s of *shroud-shimmering-stitches-set* create a visual image of darting, small needles. The consonance of *lilac blows* is evocative of Whitman's "When Lilacs

Last in the Dooryard Bloom'd," and sadness results. Consonantal *r*'s in *wandering air* add weight to the heavy spondee.

C. *Structural Development:* The structure of this poem rests on description (the scene of a woman sewing a shroud in a doorway overlooking a plot where lilac blooms). The grammatical ambiguity of lilacs blooming *in* a doorway is resolved as editorial structure becomes apparent in a second level of meaning—the poem becomes autobiographically allegorical. The motion of the poetic idea in stanza 1 becomes countermotion in stanza 2 as editorial structure becomes obvious.

D. *Reason for the Poem:* What can the poem be presumed to say as a result of your answers? You will remember Adelaide Crapsey as the inventor of the delicate and exact (or fine) cinquain (pp. 75-81). In the final year of a short life, she was forced to abandon a study of metrics she was writing, and, from her room at Saranac, New York, she looked out over a graveyard which she called "Trudeau's Garden," Trudeau being her nickname. The ironic insights of this frail woman of bittersweet temperament are revealed by close examination of this poem which she wrote during that grim year.

Now to return to step 6.

Step 6: The seeming ambiguities of the poem work magically to establish at least four possible levels of meaning in the eight lines.

At the most obvious level, a woman sews her burial shroud, defying conventional colors and fabrics as she defies the human urge to share knowledge of her activity. She takes great pains to set the stitches in even rows, revealing a pride in her work. As she sews, she sits where she can enjoy the lilacs in the spring air when thoughts of death are painful, but she hums, obviously content.

At a less obvious, second level, that shroud may be the poetry (fragments and shreds) such a person leaves behind at her death. Time alone, however, reveals its shimmering fine and fair quality; so no one would now know it represents the fragments to be left. The "fine" quality results from the study of prosody; the stitches in even rows are words. If the poetry is valuable, the poems contain pure gold and silver, and are, therefore, fine. The imagery has become symbol.

At a third level, the possibilities combine. As one considers a poet's sensitive awareness of death, the poem becomes a universal statement of Everyman as he attempts to leave something behind. In this sense, his conduct, actions, ambitions are his protective shield, ensuring his memory once he is gone. The symbol has become allegory.

At a fourth level, the poem may be a very personal statement. A paraphrase might be:

> line 1: I create my poetry (including the cinquain I invented), but no one recognizes it
> line 2: because it is too controlled and disciplined, offering sensitive, glimmering insights
> line 3: in its 2-4-6-8-2 pattern so evenly paced—
> line 4: a pattern as measured as gauged stitches.
> line 5: At the entrance to the cemetery (*door-way*) where death flowers bloom in spring
> line 6: calling me with their tune as I hum happily at my work while I yet have time,
> line 7: I use the time even though no one knows,
> line 8: and because even I (*no* one) do not know the value of the work, it is especially shimmering fine and fair.

Such paraphrasing does great damage to the poem, but it allows you to see the possibilities.

In this poem, Miss Crapsey obviously did not make one definite statement; there are many. Within the editorial framework, there is the implication that the reader who still has life might use it well if he considers the nearness of the door-way to the graveyard. And therein rests a fifth level of meaning: what personal use or application should the reader make?

Combining language, figures of speech, metrics, motion and countermotion, literary devices, structure and idea—all compressed into eight lines of 66 syllables—the poet evokes a poem bittersweet in tone, grimly gay in mood. And, in combining the art of poetry with her craft, Adelaide Crapsey furnishes you much food for spiritual thought and a great deal to work with in writing your essay on the poem.

Every poem, no matter how simple it may be, exists at a minimum of two levels. You may read the poem, assuming it is addressed directly to you by the poet. But, notice, "by the poet." It is not the man who speaks; it is the singer. How often have you heard someone observe, "Shakespeare says life "is a tale told by an idiot, full of sound and fury, signifying nothing"? In the same breath, the person may say, "Of course, Shakespeare wasn't Shakespeare; he was Sir Francis Bacon." Two levels are clearly revealed in the observation. To the speaker, "Shakespeare" is the singer of the line; "Bacon," to that speaker, is the man who lived, breathed, and wrote the line. As "Shakespeare," the man had no existence beyond his poetic craft as far as the speaker is concerned. As "Bacon," the man, he lived a life—even as the speaker. And when the poet wrote sonnets, he was a singer; when he praised England, he was a patriot; when he narrated "Venus and Adonis," he was a story teller. At no time, in the speaker's mind, was he more or less than his role demanded. And whatever he observed, he observed from that single facet. Simultaneously, however, the speaker is aware that the poet, free of his craft, was a man. As a human, rather than as a literary figure, he might have held quite different views from those he penned. Did Shakespeare-Bacon really think life signifies nothing? Had he held such a view, as a human, would he have tried to communicate the idea in the first place? Obviously, then, two possibilities emerge: the singer comments in his art on what the man has observed in his life. Two meanings emerge. And, in this particular instance, a third level becomes instantly apparent—you realize that Macbeth, a character in a play, makes the observation as a result of the fateful events of *his* poetic life. So this third level appears; and yet the possible ambiguities and connotations of the language have not been mentioned at all. A textual examination might reveal several additional levels of meaning. Nor will any of them be in conflict. Each one discovered will illuminate and enrich the others. As a result, several *personae* (characters speaking) manifest themselves in the poetic lines—a *person* will almost never emerge. If one seems to, he is a persona, at best.

You can see the difference in the persona and the person in the following poem, one of the rare examples in literature when a man does emerge from the line to become a man speaking for himself alone—not as poet or poetic character:

The Argument of His Book

I sing of brooks, of blossoms, birds, and bowers,
Of April, May, of June and July flowers;
I sing of May-poles, hock-carts, wassails, wakes,
Of bridegrooms, brides, and of their bridal cakes;

I write of youth, of love, and have access   5
By these to sing of cleanly wantonness;
I sing of dews, of rains, and piece by piece
Of balm, of oil, of spice and ambergris;
I sing of times trans-shifting, and I write
How roses first came red and lilies white;   10
I write of groves, of twilight, and I sing
The Court of Mab, and of the Fairy King;
I write of hell; I sing (and ever shall)
Of heaven, and hope to have it after all.

Robert Herrick

In the last seven words, the total man, the human with fears and aspirations to eternal life, intrudes his wish. He is not the singer, joying in his song; he is the man aware of his mortal flesh and eternal soul. As such, his lines as a singer are touched and changed. Are they as joyous, as emphatic as they seem? Certainly not from the second level. They become deliberately assertive—a little loud in their protestations. (For a more complete analysis of the speaker of the poem, see *The Poet in the Poem,* by George T. Wright, University of California Press, 1960.)

Another effective approach to poetic examination is the comparison of two works on a similar subject. You will remember Adelaide Crapsey's "Susanna and the Elders." Reread the poem and the discussion of it (pp. 76-77). Adelaide Crapsey's cinquain compresses attitude into twenty-three syllables. The extra syllable in line 3 focuses attention on the countermotion of the poem. As *that* is an expletive, it serves no grammatical necessity and would not, if omitted, change the literal meaning of the lines. *For* is a conjunction here, meaning "because," the same number of syllables as in *For that.* However, the tone of the chosen words is biblical, indicative of the scholarly minds of the elders, and suggestive of the small confusions of age. The remainder of the unstated argument is telescoped into possibility by *Therefore,* and the reader is left to reconstruct the scene, the meaning, and to understand the elders' rationalizations, as well as his own judgments of their behavior and attitudes.

In "Peter Quince at the Clavier," Wallace Stevens employs the same subject matter. In this longer treatment, however, the poet includes details of the biblical story, reconstructed in extensive metaphor. The didactic fourth section weaves the metaphor's meaning into the complexities of Peter Quince's observation. As you read the poem, you should be aware of Quince's identity. In Shakespeare's comedy *A Midsummer Night's Dream,* a play is presented. It is *Pyramus and Thisbe,* a story of two lovers who reach faulty conclusions on too little evidence and kill themselves needlessly. Peter Quince is a rustic carpenter who manages the play, employing such paradoxical language as "laughable tragedy, lamentable comedy, and tragical mirth," to describe it. A clavier is the keyboard of a piano or organ. As you read the poem, remember the toccata rhythms as they were woven into Browning's "A Toccata of Galuppi's" (p. 318). Musical phrasings are also obvious in

Peter Quince at the Clavier
I

Just as my fingers on these keys
Make music, so the selfsame sounds
On my spirit make a music, too.
Music is feeling, then, not sound;
And thus it is that what I feel,   5
Here in this room, desiring you,

Thinking of your blue-shadowed silk,
Is music. It is like the strain
Waked in the elders by Susanna.

Of a green evening, clear and warm,   10
She bathed in her still garden, while
The red-eyed elders watching, felt

The basses of their beings throb
In witching chords, and their thin blood
Pulse pizzicati of Hosanna.   15

II

In the green water, clear and warm,
Susanna lay.
She searched
The touch of springs,
And found   20
Concealed imaginings.
She sighed,
For so much melody.

Upon the bank, she stood
In the cool   25
Of spent emotions.

She felt, among the leaves,
The dew
Of old devotions.

She walked upon the grass,   30
Still quavering.
The winds were like her maids,
On timid feet,
Fetching her woven scarves,
Yet wavering.   35

A breath upon her hand
Muted the night.
She turned—
A cymbal crashed,
And roaring horns.   40

III

Soon, with a noise like tambourines,
Came her attendant Byzantines.

They wondered why Susanna cried
Against the elders by her side;

And as they whispered, the refrain   45
Was like a willow swept by rain.

Anon, their lamps' uplifted flame
Revealed Susanna and her shame.

And then, the simpering Byzantines
Fled, with a noise like tambourines.   50

IV

Beauty is momentary in the mind—
The fitful tracing of a portal;
But in the flesh it is immortal.
The body dies; the body's beauty lives.
So evenings die, in their green going,   55
A wave, interminably flowing.
So gardens die, their meek breath scenting
The cowl of winter, done repenting.

So maidens die, to the auroral
Celebration of a maiden's choral.   60
Susanna's music touched the bawdy strings
Of those white elders; but, escaping,
Left only Death's ironic scraping.
Now, in its immortality, it plays
On the clear viol of her memory,   65
And makes a constant sacrament of praise.

Wallace Stevens

The choice of Quince as singer of these lines is interesting. While the poem is lyric, it is also a dramatic monolog. The recognizable personae are Stevens (as poet and man), Quince (as narrator and man), and the reader (as receiver and man). The *you* of the sixth line may be present, but the tone of enjambed lines 4-8 suggests she is absent. Reverie pervades the poem, creating the mood. Rhythms change much as tempos do when a piano player amuses himself idly at the keyboard. Unconsciously, he chooses at random from his repertory, but a pattern emerges. Quince's subconscious is also given the latitude of such selection, and musical choice combines with memory as a composition emerges. Orchestration is provided in such words as *music, strain, basses, chords, pizzicati, melody, cymbal, horns, tambourines, choral, strings,* and *viol.* Alliteration, assonance, consonance, occasional rhyme—all bind the rhythms into one harmonious whole.

Section I begins in conscious thought as simile and metaphor introduce the extended metaphor of the poem. The statement "Music is feeling" extends through the lines to become, in Section IV, a statement of realization. As thought leads on to thought, Quince considers his immediate occupation, the loved one, and the nature of passion. Iambs dominate, providing the underlying melody, but themes are introduced with varied metrics, cleverly interwoven. Notice the anapest introducing line 3; however, lest the lilting quality become too joyous, a solemn trochee introduces the profound statement of line 4. Joy returns iambically, only to be tempered with the trochaic *Thinking* of line 7. Line 9 is hypercatalectic, as *waked* is inserted abruptly, jarringly, and followed by a rest to create a spondee. The lost syllable is returned to the line to create the youthful amphibrach, *Susanna,* spirited in this one line only. Used four more times in the poem, the name never again suggests the proud, highbred Susanna unsullied by knowledge of the aged eyes. Visual color overlays the tonal color also. *Blue-shadowed silk, green evening,* and *red-eyed elders* create a progression from the cool to the fertile to the passionately hot. And sound vibrates as assonance, consonance, and alliteration re-create the bass section of an orchestra in line 13. The pizzicati (notes produced by plucking musical strings rather than bowing them) is shrill in the *p, t,* and *th* alliteration of lines 14-15. The effect of the pyrrhic leading into the amphibrach of *Hosanna* leaves the reader's emotions suspended in a high intensity of response.

Section II opens with a line that is sensual in both imagery and rhythm. While it is possible to scan it as iambs, it is impossible to read it as such. "Sprung rhythm" creates a cadenced phrasing almost onomatopoetic in its lithe and languorous presentation of Susanna. The iambic dimeter of line 17 is utterly relaxed. The next six lines of iambic dimeter and alternating trimeter read as quick, impassioned breathing. Tonal words such as *touch, springs, imaginings,* and *sighed* heighten the sense of scene. (No wonder the elders were red-eyed!) This vibrancy is intensified in lines 24-29 as the passionate rhythm subsides erratically in a pattern of iambic trimeter, anapestic monometer, iambic dimeter, iambic trimeter, iambic monometer, and iambic dimeter. Rhyme is incorporated to heighten the erratic pulsations as the feminine *emotion-devotions* add their unstressed syllables to the iambs to create amphibrachs with their measured haste.

Lines 30-35 allow Susanna's ecstatic moment to subside in further rhythmical pleasantries as triple rhyme is employed in *quavering-wavering* and pyrrhics signify complete exhaustion.

Iambs comprise the next three lines, but each is shortened to reveal growing anxiety as the rhythm drops from trimeter to dimeter to monometer, and the assonance of *u*'s is employed with the tonal words *muted-turned.* Lines 39-40 erupt as the monometer line gives way to lengthening dimeter reinforced with the onomatopoeia of *crashed-roaring,* the assonance of *a*'s in *cymbals crashed* and *o*'s in *roaring horns,* which also harshens in the consonantal *r*'s. So ends the second movement of the symphony. But what has the paradoxical Peter Quince achieved in this section? Merely a tour de force with sound? Hardly. Has he not also suggested that Susanna, however innocently, has contributed to the arousal of the elders by conduct which is unseemly—no matter how private?

Section III creates a lavish ballet beginning and ending with the entrance and exit of exotic oriental dancers, accompanied by tambourines. The headless iamb *Soon* opens the poetic curtain on the colorful scene. As the tonal quality of *tambourines* creates visual imagery in the metal discs, *Byzantine* builds a mosaic richness. Couplets combine with the rapidly paced iambic tetrameter to create a whirling dance tempo. Lines 45-46 sweep like rain to draw music from the string section as *w*'s wash the line with onomatopoeia. *L*'s and *m*'s in lines 47-48 reveal more than Susanna naked. *And* becomes heavily accented in line 48. And then, as suddenly as they appeared, the dancers depart on the headless iamb of line 50. Their passing closes the section with the music of their entrance as the simile is repeated.

The subtle humor and the gentle indirection of the rustic Peter Quince delight the clever reader as he visualizes the scene on several levels. At its serious best, it suggests that point at which the elders must charge Susanna before she is forced to bring charges against them. Largely innocent of evil, she is compromised by her nudity even though the elders have no reason to be in her garden. At a more sympathetic level, the scene causes the reader to avert his eyes modestly from the nude Susanna so cruelly revealed in the merciless lamplight and unspoken doubts of her maids. At the delightfully theatrical level, he suspends disbelief and merely enjoys the spectacle of ballet. At the level of "lamentable comedy" or "laughable tragedy," the reader can be forgiven if he chuckles at the ludicrous spectacle of Susanna, clad only in a horrified blush, watching helplessly as her maids pirouette and assume the postures demanded by ballet. The elders, already worked up to a froth, are treated further to this stylized display of eastern flesh, but they are too concerned with their compromising position to enjoy it. Peter Quince, that rustic carpenter, would be aware of all such possibilities.

Section IV opens with a line of prose in sharp countermotion to the sprightly music of the third movement. The harshness of the prose is tempered by alliterative *m*'s, but it is deliberate prose nonetheless. Contrast achieved and the observation firmly imprinted, the poem returns to scannable lines employing feminine rhyme to recall Susanna to serious intent. A series of profound observations follows, building, in their feminine rhyme, always on the memory of Susanna. The profundity of the observations seems, on the surface, impressive—but a disquieting tone pervades the lines. The amphibrachs of the feminine rhymes seem in a hurry, however stately their stride. And the reader becomes faintly aware he has heard these sentiments before. A pervasive triteness becomes apparent, and the reader suddenly realizes that Polonius could have delivered these lines with happy vacuity. However, they do get where Quince wishes them to go. The awareness of the pleasant clichés is shattered by lines 59-60, as the memory of the ballet and Susanna's helplessness is recalled. The hyperbolic suggestion is: "She could just have died as they danced around her with their lamps creating a false dawn."

The musical reverie of Quince at the keyboard returns to solemnity, however, in lines 61-63, as the judgment is made. The musical metaphor is sharp and clear. The symphony ends on the board of the soloist with a final flourish in masculine rhyme, leaving no doubt that the personal recital is complete. However, as "music, when soft voices die, vibrates in the memory," the reader wonders at Quince's employing the feminine rhyme in lines 62-63 and the ambiguity in *ironic scraping*. If ambiguity is employed by the rustic carpenter, can *viol* be read "vile"? And is Susanna's praise elevated to become a religious service, or is her praise a constant re-sacrificing of the elders? If so, are they scapegoats for her sensuality in section II? Once again, the reader is reminded it is Peter Quince, rustic carpenter and manager of the drama, who sits at this clavier. But the persona of the poet is also present in the poem, and in his poem, "Thirteen Ways of Looking at a Blackbird," Stevens admitted:

> I do not know which to prefer,
> The beauty of inflections
> Or the beauty of innuendoes. . . .

Adelaide Crapsey's cinquain approached the subject of Susanna from a smaller poetic unit, leaving many unstated possibilities. Stevens approached it from a much longer free verse form, but his unstated possibilities are also numerous. Such discovery is one of the very real delights of poetic examination.

Compare the treatments of the following poems in the same way:

On Seeing Weather-Beaten Trees

Is it as plainly in our living shown,
By slant and twist, which way the wind hath blown?

Adelaide Crapsey

Lovers in Winter

The posture of the tree
    Shows the prevailing wind;
And ours, long misery
    When you are long unkind.

But forward, look, we lean—   5
    Not backward as in doubt—
And still with branches green
    Ride our ill weather out.

Robert Graves

Sometimes it is desirable to study one subject as it is treated by several different authors. In the following group of poems, observe the various forms, treatments, and themes. Subject each poem, as you read it, to the questions of language, rhythm, development, theme, and so on, on pp. 326-327. If you like a poem, discover why. Is it a good poem? On what grounds is it good?

Invictus

Out of the night that covers me,
   Black as the Pit from pole to pole,
I thank whatever gods may be
   For my unconquerable soul.

In the fell clutch of circumstance   *5*
   I have not winced nor cried aloud.
Under the bludgeonings of chance
   My head is bloody, but unbowed.

Beyond this place of wrath and tears
   Looms but the Horror of the shade,   *10*
And yet the menace of the years
   Finds, and shall find, me unafraid.

It matters not how strait the gate,
   How charged with punishments the scroll,
I am the master of my fate;   *15*
   I am the captain of my soul.

                         William Ernest Henley

John Ciardi has called "Invictus" "the most widely known bad poem in English," and few—if any—will disagree. Taken point by point, however, evaluative questions will not reveal the reason for the charge. The metrics are ragged in spots, but the rhythm is adequate to its purpose. The poem will scan as unrelieved iambic tetrameter with definite forcing; it scans naturally with several pyrrhics, anapests, trochees, and cadenced feet that save it from a singsong tiresomeness. The optimism of melody has made it, in its orchestrated form, a favorite lyric of baritones. It will, definitely, "sing." The language is clear and obvious—a little *too* obvious in its didacticism; yet the poet has a message which he delivers without ambiguity. Nor does he include any element which might suggest the poem functions at more than the simple, obvious level. That trite phrases seem to abound in the poem is an invalid criticism, for, while the Roman historian and politician Sallust (86-34 B.C.) stated, "The soul is the captain and rules of the life of mortals," Henley rephrases the line into its popularly quoted form. Other phrases inextricably reminiscent of the worst of Victorian sentiment are *fell clutch of circumstance, bludgeonings of chance,* and *head is bloody but unbowed.* They appear too often nowadays as sententious mouthings of the insincere, and therefore are trite. However, they originated with Henley, and were, therefore, not trite mouthings by *him.*

Still, that such lines have been adopted by the pompous, the melodramatic, and the insincere, suggests the reason for the poem's lack of merit. It sounds *insincere.* The assertive ego stands naked before the reader, and he is embarrassed at the insensitive display. Whatever else a poem is, it must be a communication, and the first responsibility inevitably rests with the poet, for he opens the conversation. Henley's opening gambit in the first quatrain is, by all odds, the most acceptable portion of the poem. A striking image is created in the first two lines, and an admirable humility is combined with a defensible assertion in the second two. But, from the opening line of the second stanza, the braggart, the declaimer, the possessor of a superiority complex assumes command. The reader is forced to do one of several things: 1) identify with the loud protester; 2) reject him as aesthetically vulgar; or 3) read on with growing embarrassment because it is rude to leave a half-finished conversation without excusing oneself. And Henley plunges ahead so rapidly on his iambs and anapests that the reader can't wedge in an "Excuse me."

Henley, like all such purveyors of absolute statement, is his own prosecutor. Few readers, once offended, will allow him a second chance. Unfortunately, as a result, they might miss such lines as the following from his "In Memoriam Margaritae Sorori":

> So be my passing!
> My task accomplished and the long day done,
> My wages taken, and in my heart
> Some late lark singing. . . .

In these lines, the imagery is less bold, more subtle, quite sincere in tone. So different is the attitude, in fact, a reader might question the seeming reversal. Poets, even as you, are subject to mood and the temperings of time, but the reader, uncommitted to statement preserved in print, is not inclined to grant the charitable benefit of doubt.

Reread and notice your reaction to Walter Savage Landor's "Death Stands Above Me" (p. 167). Landor's metrics are similar to Henley's in "Invictus." Unrelieved iambs can be extracted forcibly. Personification in the first word induces dread in the reader, and the quiet terror of connotation extends into the frightening *stands above me.* Memory of night-fears is always close to conscious thought. The tone of language softens with *whispering low,* but it is still unsettling. The second line is intimate in tone, suggestive of shared secrets. Line 3 introduces the adventurous note of distant, exciting places which enjambs into the comfortable re-assurance of line 4. The experience is familiar to the reader; he associates the poem with memory of being awakened unexpectedly to leave on pleasant journeys. From that memory springs his belief in Landor's sincerity—and the poem seems "good" rather than aesthetically "bad." Landor has tried to prove nothing except his kinship with all men.

Emily Dickinson achieves the same effect in

[Because I Could Not Stop for Death]

Because I could not stop for Death—
He kindly stopped for me—
The Carriage held but just Ourselves—
And Immortality.

We slowly drove—he knew no haste   *5*
And I had put away
My labor and my leisure too,
For His Civility—

We passed the School, where Children strove
At Recess—in the Ring—   *10*
We passed the Fields of Gazing Grain—
We passed the Setting Sun—

Or rather—He passed Us—
The Dews drew quivering and chill—
For only Gossamer, my Gown—   *15*
My Tippet—only Tulle—

We paused before a House that seemed
A Swelling of the Ground—
The Roof was scarcely visible—
The Cornice—in the Ground—   *20*

Since then—'tis centuries—and yet
Feels shorter than the Day
I first surmised the Horses' Heads
Were toward Eternity—

Emily Dickinson

Ordinarily, when a poet chooses a metrical pattern, he assumes the pre-rogative of adhering to it only as it will establish a dominant beat which

LIVING THE
REIKI
WAY

LIVING THE
REIKI
WAY

Reiki Principles for
Everyday Living

PENELOPE QUEST

Jeremy P. Tarcher/Penguin
a member of Penguin Group (USA) Inc.
New York

JEREMY P. TARCHER/PENGUIN
Published by the Penguin Group
Penguin Group (USA) Inc., 375 Hudson Street,
New York, New York 10014, USA

USA · Canada · UK · Ireland · Australia
New Zealand · India · South Africa · China

Penguin Books Ltd, Registered Offices:
80 Strand, London WC2R 0RL, England
For more information about the Penguin Group visit penguin.com

First published in Great Britain in 2008 by Piatkus Books Ltd
First Tarcher/Penguin edition 2013
Copyright © 2008 by Penelope Quest
Most Tarcher/Penguin books are available at special quantity discounts for bulk purchase for
sales promotions, premiums, fund-raising, and educational needs. Special books or book excerpts
also can be created to fit specific needs. For details, write Penguin Group (USA) Inc.
Special Markets, 375 Hudson Street, New York, NY 10014.

Library of Congress Cataloging-in-Publication Data

Quest, Penelope.
Living the reiki way : reiki principles for everyday living / Penelope Quest.
p.   cm.
Includes index.
ISBN 978-0-399-16221-3 (pbk.)
1. Reiki (Healing system)   I. Title.
RZ403.R45Q475   2013   2013009658
615.8'52—dc23

Printed in the United States of America
1 3 5 7 9 10 8 6 4 2

Neither the publisher nor the author is engaged in rendering professional advice or services
to the individual reader. The ideas, procedures, and suggestions contained in this book are not
intended as a substitute for consulting with your physician. All matters regarding your health
require medical supervision. Neither the author nor the publisher shall be liable or responsible
for any loss or damage allegedly arising from any information or suggestion in this book.

While the author has made every effort to provide accurate telephone numbers, Internet addresses,
and other contact information at the time of publication, neither the publisher nor the
author assumes any responsibility for errors, or for changes that occur after publication.
Further, the publisher does not have any control over and does not assume any
responsibility for author or third-party websites or their content.

ALWAYS LEARNING   PEARSON

This book is dedicated to my mother,
Irene Monica Harris (1913–1999), who taught
me to appreciate life and live it my way.

CONTENTS

ACKNOWLEDGMENTS

I would like to express my heartfelt gratitude to the many people who have helped, directly or indirectly, with this book, especially to my friend the Reverend Simon John Barlow, for allowing me to adapt some of the material we wrote together for our workshops on consciousness, meditation and visualization. I would also like to thank my son, Chris, and daughter, Kathy, for their unfailing love and support in everything I do, and my many Reiki friends and students for the love and learning they have brought me. In addition, thank you to Helen, Gill, Krystyna and Rebecca from Piatkus, for their enthusiasm and help, and to my readers for all the wonderful e-mails you send me, which are always greatly appreciated and very inspiring.

Of course, special thanks go to my Reiki teachers Kristin Bonney, William Lee Rand, Andrew Bowling and Richard Rivard, who have been so instrumental in my own Reiki journey. Thanks also go to the many other teachers and writers who have advanced my knowledge and experience in various other subjects, such as psychology, NLP, EFT, abundance theory, meditation and spiritual development, which have been such a useful foundation for writing this book.

INTRODUCTION

Reiki has been an essential part of my life since 1991 when I attended my first Reiki course, and I have been trying to "live the Reiki way" ever since. I worked part-time as a Reiki practitioner for a number of years, alongside my work as a lecturer and senior manager in a college, and in 1994 I qualified as a Reiki Master—the term that describes a teacher of Reiki. By 1996 I knew that practicing and teaching Reiki was what I really wanted to do, so I left my job in order to devote more time to teaching and writing about Reiki.

However, along the way, in addition to learning more and gaining further qualifications in Reiki and writing a number of books on the subject, I have followed many other interests and gained knowledge and experience in a wide range of topics, including psychology, meditation and visualization, Neuro-Linguistic Programming (NLP), Emotional Freedom Technique (EFT), Native American and Celtic shamanism, abundance theory and cosmic ordering, and other areas of study that promote under-standing, personal growth and a holistic view of the person. My special interest in healing has also led me to learn a number of other healing methods, such as Hawaiian Huna and Karuna Reiki®, and recently I added to my academic qualifications by gaining a master's degree in Health and Healing Science.

It was this wide-ranging background that led me to want to write a book about living with the Reiki principles in today's hectic world. For me, living the Reiki way hasn't just been about Reiki, although Reiki has certainly been the most important aspect of my personal spiritual and healing journey for nearly twenty years. But I believe that Reiki has also been instrumental in guiding me to other methods for personal growth and spiritual development, as well as to various self-help techniques for my own healing, and this is why I have incorporated some of these into this book. While I think Reiki is fantastic, I am aware that it isn't the only way forward, so I wanted to present some other methods for people to explore. Sometimes Reiki is all you need, and at other times another method, such as NLP, EFT, or working through a visualization, will help to produce the shift in perception or energy you need to help you to deal with a problem.

Nearly a century ago Dr. Mikao Usui, the founder of the healing system we call Reiki, encouraged his students to live by the following precepts:

> Just for today, do not anger, do not worry, be filled with gratitude, devote yourself to your work, and be kind to people.

Reiki students today are advised to live by the same principles, but perhaps these present even more of a challenge in the twenty-first century. Nevertheless, I believe they can be a great help and support to people in their everyday lives, as well as offering a way to a more spiritual path of personal growth.

Living the Reiki Way isn't just intended for people who already use Reiki, although I hope they will find plenty within its pages that is both helpful and inspiring. It is a book for anyone interested in personal growth and spiritual development—so whether you've just done your first Reiki course, or have practiced or taught Reiki for years, or even if this is the first you've heard about Reiki, you will find something here for you.

Living the Reiki Way includes suggestions for using Reiki (or healing energy) to help you to cope with strong emotions like anger, or to understand how being grateful can bring a lot of joy and happiness into your life—although these methods can only be employed by those who have undertaken at least one Reiki course. However, there are plenty of other techniques that anyone can use, whether they have learned Reiki or not. These include meditations, visualizations and self-help techniques utilizing NLP and EFT, all of which you will find beneficial.

For those who may not know very much about Reiki, chapter 1 covers the Reiki basics, including what Reiki is, where it originated, how it works, what a Reiki treatment consists of, what effects Reiki can have and how you can learn to do Reiki yourself. If you need more detailed information about Reiki, you will find it in my other books—*The Basics of Reiki, Reiki for Life, The Reiki Manual* and *Self-healing with Reiki* (see Further Reading, page 255).

While this is a book based on Reiki, it embraces a great deal more than Reiki alone: it provides information, advice and useful techniques to help you navigate through strong emotions, negative thinking habits, fear, worry, lack of self-belief and other issues that might be holding you back from achieving your true potential. It offers principles for living today that are every bit as vital as they were when Dr. Usui was alive, and that can help you to change, let go of destructive patterns of thinking and feeling, and develop your own positive attitudes, beliefs, concepts and philosophy for life.

Living the Reiki Way is about living thoughtfully, kindly, generously, gratefully, calmly, confidently, considerately, diligently, conscientiously and happily. If those are aspects you would like to demonstrate in your life, read on!

part one

REIKI BASICS

The secret method of inviting happiness;
The wonderful medicine for all diseases.
                                    Mikao Usui

chapter one
WHAT IS REIKI?

This book is about living the Reiki way, or, in other words, living with the Reiki Principles in today's modern world. Anyone who has taken part in a Reiki course or workshop will know what the Reiki Principles are, but there may be readers of this book who haven't heard of them before, and perhaps, more to the point, don't really know what Reiki is. To set the scene, in this chapter I describe briefly what Reiki is and where it came from—this will make other chapters in this book easier to understand. However, if you have already read one of my other books, especially *The Basics of Reiki, Reiki for Life* or *The Reiki Manual,* or have taken part in a Reiki course, you can probably skip this chapter and go straight to chapter 2. For anyone else, please read on!

THE ORIGINS OF REIKI

We may never know the exact origins of Reiki as a healing system, but it probably dates back at least 2,500 years, as we know that the Buddha used something similar, and it is likely to be even older than that. However, the healing system we use today in the West, which we call Reiki, was developed initially in the 1920s by Dr. Mikao Usui (1865–1926), a Buddhist scholar in Japan, and further developed by one of his students, Dr. Chujiro Hayashi (1879–1940), who passed his teachings on between 1936 and 1938 to a Hawaiian woman of Japanese parentage, Mrs. Hawayo Takata (1900–1980). She was responsible for bringing the teachings to the West, initially to Hawaii, the U.S.A. and Canada, and through the 22 teachers (Reiki Masters) she taught between 1972 and 1980 to the rest of the Western world.

WHAT IS REIKI?

The way in which Reiki is seen in the West today is primarily as a form of complementary therapy—a safe, gentle, nonintrusive, hands-on healing technique that uses spiritual energy (the Japanese word *reiki* means spiritual energy or universal life-force energy) to treat physical ailments. It is, however, much more than a physical therapy; it is a holistic system for balancing, healing and harmonizing all aspects of the person—body, mind, emotions and spirit—promoting relaxation and a sense of well-being.

It is therefore healing in its most all-encompassing sense—healing the physical, emotional, psychological and spiritual aspects enables a person to become whole, or "holy" in what was possibly the original sense of the word. Unlike other complementary or alternative therapies, the practice of Reiki is also a spiritual discipline that includes meditation, energy-cleansing techniques and spiritual principles for living, and practitioners are encouraged to

4

use Reiki on themselves daily not only for self-healing but also to increase self-awareness, personal growth and spiritual development.

THE WAY REIKI WORKS

Life-force energy (Ki or Chi) flows within the physical body through energy centers called chakras and pathways called meridians, as well as flowing around the body in a field of energy called the aura. This energy field responds to everything we think, say, feel and experience, and it becomes disrupted or blocked whenever we consciously or unconsciously accept and absorb negative words, thoughts, feelings or experiences. If these blockages are not dispersed, their energy can gradually become more dense, which is when they can transform into physical illnesses. Reiki is a spiritual energy vibrating at a very high rate that helps to break through these blockages, flowing through all the affected parts of the aura and the physical body, charging them with positive energy and raising the vibratory level of the whole energy field. It clears and balances the chakras, and straightens the energy pathways (meridians), allowing the life force to flow in a healthy and natural way around the whole body. This strengthens and accelerates the body's own natural ability to heal itself, and opens the mind, emotions and spirit to an acceptance and understanding of the causative issues that have led to "dis-ease" in both the physical and energy bodies.

Because Reiki is guided by a Higher Intelligence (God, the Universe, your Soul or Higher Self, or whatever description you feel comfortable with), it always finds its way to the areas of the physical body and/or the energy body most in need of healing, without any conscious direction from either the healer or the person being healed, and it adjusts to suit the recipient, so that each person receives as much or as little healing as he or she needs.

A REIKI TREATMENT

Many people first experience Reiki when they receive a Reiki treatment from a holistic practitioner. Reiki treatments take about an hour, and are usually carried out with you lying comfortably on a massage table, covered with a soft blanket. You remain fully clothed (except for shoes and coat), and the practitioner's hands are placed and held still for 3–5 minutes in each of about 12 specific positions over your head and body. There is no pressure, manipulation or massage, and no sensitive or intimate areas of the body need to be touched.

The most usual hand positions are:

- Four on the head—the back of the head, over the ears or temples, over the eyes and on either side of the neck.
- Four on the front of the body—the upper chest, solar plexus, navel area and pelvic area.
- Four on the back of the body—the shoulders, middle of the back, waist level and buttocks.

You usually feel very relaxed, warm and peaceful as the energy flows through you—people often fall asleep during the treatment—although sometimes you might feel heat, coolness or tingles where the practitioner's hands are placed (this is quite normal). It is also quite normal for people to feel a bit emotional sometimes, as the Reiki releases blocked energy and brings to the surface old issues and patterns to be released, so memories might come flooding back. After a treatment some people feel super-energized, while others feel very tranquil and sleepy.

TREATING YOURSELF WITH REIKI

Once you have learned how to use Reiki, being able to treat yourself is one of its great advantages, because it encourages you to take responsibility for yourself and your own health and well-being, and most Reiki practitioners use it on themselves every day. A full self-treatment involves the same 12 or more hand positions on your head and body as those described above, but you can also give yourself Reiki at other times—while watching television, for example—by simply placing your hands on any part of your body and holding them there for as long as it feels comfortable.

Reiki can also be successfully incorporated into many of the healing arts practiced by health professionals, such as reflexology, aromatherapy, shiatsu, osteopathy, etc., because the Reiki energy can simply flow out of the practitioner's hands during the treatment, to promote even greater healing effects.

THE EFFECTS OF REIKI

Most people who go for a Reiki treatment want help with a specific physical problem, from frequent headaches or a frozen shoulder, to more serious complaints, although some simply want to be able to relax and cope better with the stresses of modern life—you don't have to be ill to benefit from Reiki! The potential with Reiki is unlimited, so anything can be treated, but it is important to rid yourself of specific expectations of what it will do, and how fast it will perform. Many physical symptoms can be eased very quickly, while others may need a lot of Reiki before starting to respond, but it is essential to remember that it is *your own body* that is actually doing the healing.

The human body has an amazing ability to regenerate itself, as most of the cells in your body are replaced each year, which is why physical healing can happen—as an example, if you cut yourself, new skin cells are produced to heal the cut. Some people report amazing, even miraculous, effects from Reiki treatments, but "healing" is not *always* the same as "curing," although we tend to use the words interchangeably, which creates misunderstanding. Healing doesn't always occur on the physical level first. Because Reiki works holistically, it may be that healing needs to happen first at the emotional level, with the releasing of anger, guilt or hatred, or it may be required first at the mental level, releasing negative thoughts, concepts or attitudes, or at the spiritual level, developing self-awareness, self-understanding and self-love, before the physical symptoms can be addressed.

If you are open-minded and willing to receive the

8

Reiki (belief in it is not a prerequisite), healing *will* take place, although it may not always be in quite the way you expect—Reiki goes where it is needed, not always where you want it to go! Ultimately, if you want the healing to be permanent, you have to take responsibility for healing the cause. This may mean changing how you think or the way you relate to other people, or even altering your whole lifestyle, from your diet and home environment to your close relationships, job or career. Surprisingly, perhaps, Reiki can help with these adjustments too, allowing you to approach the changes in a relaxed way.

LEARNING HOW TO USE REIKI

Reiki is probably the simplest and easiest holistic healing method available to us, so anyone can learn to use it, whatever their age or gender, religion or origin. No specific previous knowledge or experience is required— only a desire to learn, a willingness to let this healing energy flow through you and a little time to attend your first course. The ability to channel Reiki can only be acquired by being transferred to the student by a qualified Reiki Master (Teacher) in a special ceremony during a Reiki course, called an attunement, which is a form of spiritual empowerment based on ancient Buddhist techniques. This attunement process makes Reiki unique and is the reason why the ability to heal can be developed so quickly yet so permanently. It activates a Reiki channel through which the Reiki healing energy can flow, and once you have been attuned you will be able to use Reiki for the rest of your life—the ability to channel Reiki

9

doesn't wear off or wear out. From then on, whenever you intend to use Reiki, simply thinking about it, or holding your hands out in readiness to use it on yourself or someone else, will activate the flow of Reiki energy.

There are three levels of training, usually referred to as "degrees." These do not refer to (or confer) any academic level or qualification; they are just used to describe the different training levels.

- At First Degree, which can be a one- or two-day course, you normally receive four "attunements," which gradually open up your inner healing channel, allowing Reiki to flow through. The emphasis at this level is on self-healing, although you will also be taught how to carry out a treatment on family, friends and animals.

- The Second Degree course usually takes one or two days, and includes another attunement that enables you to access even more Reiki. You learn three sacred symbols (shapes that you draw in the air with your hand) and their mantras (sacred names). These are the Distant (Connection) symbol, which allows you to connect with anyone or anything in any time or space; the Harmony (Mental and Emotional) symbol, which helps to bring peace and harmony to a person, animal or situation; and the Power (Focus) symbol, which brings extra Reiki energy into whatever it is focused upon. You will also learn some special ways of using them, including a form of distant healing that enables you to "send" a Reiki treatment to anyone, anywhere, with the same effectiveness as if that person was with you. This is sometimes referred to as practitioner level, although it is possible to practice Reiki professionally at First Degree level.

◆ The Third Degree is the level of a Reiki Master (Teacher), and involves essentially making a lifelong commitment to the mastery of Reiki, which requires a lot of personal and spiritual development and learning, in addition to working with Reiki every day. Reiki Master training can be a short course, or it may be an apprenticeship over a longer period of time with an experienced Master. At this level you learn another symbol and mantra, some advanced healing techniques and how to attune others to the Reiki energy.

In the rest of this book you will find many techniques that will help you to "live the Reiki way," but I should point out that if you haven't yet undertaken at least a Reiki First Degree (Reiki 1) course, you won't be able to carry out any of the Reiki techniques, as you won't yet have established a flow of the Reiki energy, which can only be acquired by receiving a Reiki attunement from a qualified Reiki Master. However, the other self-help methods that are described in the following chapters are open to anyone, whether you have learned about Reiki or not, so I hope you will give them a try.

The next chapter details the Reiki Principles that Dr. Usui passed on to his students to help them to live a good life, which are the major focus of this book: just for today, don't get angry, don't worry, be grateful, work hard and be kind to others.

chapter two

THE ORIGINS OF THE REIKI PRINCIPLES

The Reiki Principles are a set of guidelines for living a fulfilled life. They were probably originally written by Emperor Mutsuhito of Japan during the Meiji period (1868–1912), although they are very similar to precepts used for hundreds on years in the Tendai Buddhist sect of Shugendo. They were then adopted—and possibly adapted—by Dr. Mikao Usui (1865–1926), the founder of the Usui Reiki Ryoho (Usui Spiritual Energy Healing Method), a holistic healing system that originated in Japan, but which is now in use all over the world.

There are a number of translations of the Principles, but my favorite is: just for today, don't get angry, don't worry, be grateful, work hard and be kind to others.

WHICH SET OF PRINCIPLES?

You may have first come into contact with the Reiki Principles, sometimes called the Reiki Ideals, when you attended your Reiki First Degree course, or on a website or in a book about Reiki. You may have been confused because you came across different versions of the Principles, although they all still seemed pretty similar. The wording you learn or read depends on how particular Reiki Masters were taught. For example, when I did the first level of Reiki training in 1991 I was taught the following:

1. Just for today, do not anger.
2. Just for today, do not worry.
3. Honor your parents, teachers and elders.
4. Earn your living honestly.
5. Show gratitude to every living thing.

Another form of the Reiki Principles was also in common use in the 1980s and '90s:

1. Just for today, I will let go of anger.
2. Just for today, I will let go of worry.
3. Today I will count my many blessings.
4. Today I will do my work honestly.
5. Today I will be kind to every living creature.

These two versions were taught by two different branches of Reiki, the first by Reiki Masters who joined the Reiki Alliance, an organization formed in 1982 under the direction of Mrs. Takata's granddaughter, Phyllis Lei Furumoto, and the second by Radiance Technique Reiki Masters under the direction of Dr. Barbara Ray, another of the 22 Reiki Masters taught by Mrs. Takata; there may well have been other slightly different versions around at the time. However, in the late 1990s the author and Reiki Master Frank Arjava Petter, who was living and working in Japan at the time, gave us access to the original version from a document written in Dr. Usui's own hand, which he translated with the help of his Japanese wife, Chetna Kobayashi, like this:

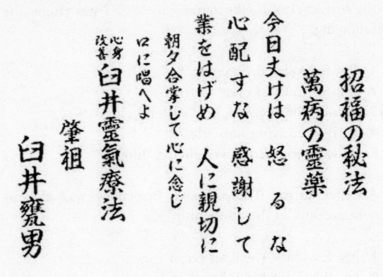

(Japanese is read from right to left.)

JAPANESE	ENGLISH TRANSLATION
Shoufuku no hihoo	The secret method of inviting happiness
Manbyo no ley-yaku	The wonderful medicine for all diseases (of the body and the soul)
Kyo dake wa	Just today
1 Okoru-na	1 Don't get angry
2 Shinpai suna	2 Don't worry

14

3 Kansha shite	3 Be grateful (or show appreciation)
4 Goo hage me	4 Work hard (on yourself)
5 Hito ni shinsetsu ni	5 Be kind to others
Asa yuu gassho shite, koko-ro ni nenji, Kuchi ni tonaeyo	Mornings and evenings, sit in the gassho★ position and repeat these words aloud and in your heart
Shin shin kaizen, Usui Reiki Ryoho	(For the) improvement of body and soul, Usui Spiritual Energy Healing Method
Chosso Usui Mikao	The founder, Mikao Usui

★Gassho means to sit quietly with your hands together in the prayer position, with your thumbs pointing to the center of your chest, as in the illustration below.

These Principles also appear on Mikao Usui's memorial, a large inscribed monolith erected in 1927 next to his grave in the public cemetery at the Saihôji Temple in the Suginami Ko district of Tokyo. There they are described as the five principles of the Meiji Emperor (Emperor Mutsuhito).

The Meiji Emperor came to the throne in Japan when Usui was only three years old, and as Usui grew up he was undoubtedly influenced by the expansiveness that was characteristic of the reign of this progressive emperor. During the Meiji Restoration period, between 1868 and 1912, a new wave of openness began, as Japan's previously closed borders were opened for the first time in many centuries. Japan went from an agrarian economy to an industrial one during that time, and this resulted in an eagerness to explore the benefits of Western influences, with a consequent freedom for Japanese nationals to travel outside their own country.

Many Japanese scholars were sent abroad to study Western languages and sciences, and this relaxing of restrictions allowed Dr. Usui to pursue his studies by traveling widely. It states on his memorial that he visited China, the United States and Europe, and that he was fond of reading, acquiring knowledge of medicine, history, psychology and world religions. I expect Usui had absorbed Mutsuhito's principles for living, and lived by them for many years, so using them with his students was probably quite natural for him, and showed the level of respect and admiration he had for his country's emperor and his teachings.

Perhaps it isn't surprising that in the West our form of the Principles isn't exactly the same as the recently revealed version from Japan. Mrs. Takata was taught Reiki in the late 1930s, and taught it herself for over 40 years as an oral tradition, so perhaps the wording changed slightly over all that time. Or maybe the way she was taught by Hayashi wasn't quite the same. Or perhaps some of the Masters she taught didn't remember it accurately. The reason doesn't really matter, because there are great similarities between all of the versions, although the second of the Western versions seems a bit closer to the original. It is a bit of a challenge, though, to see where the Principle "honor your parents, teachers and elders" has come from, yet it is probably just another way of interpreting "be kind to others." Moreover, although it may sound like it, I don't think it was ever meant to suggest that you should only be kind to older people! It's really about honoring and respecting everyone we meet for the part they play in our lives—parents, siblings, partners, friends, neighbors, colleagues, children, salespeople bus drivers, and so on. Also, of course, if you honor (or are kind to) others, and treat them well, they will honor and respect you. What goes around, comes around.

LIVING WITH THE REIKI PRINCIPLES TODAY

Although Dr. Usui asked his students to live by the Principles in the early part of the twentieth century, they are just as relevant to Reiki students—and others—today. Working more closely with the Reiki Principles is a valuable part of Reiki practice, and as you gradually absorb them into your everyday life and make them a

17

part of you, you will inevitably find that you develop a deeper understanding of their meanings, and this is one of the purposes of this book. Here are some ideas to get you started, which are developed much further in later chapters.

Today, do not anger

Anger is usually tied to responses in the past that are of little use to us as we grow personally and spiritually, and it is generally triggered when someone or something fails to meet our expectations—or sometimes, even more important, when we don't come up to our own expectations. However, although it may feel uncomfortable to realize it, anger is a conscious choice, and it is often just a habitual reaction to a given set of circumstances, so we *can* choose not to be angry—just for today!

Today, do not worry

In the same way, we can choose not to worry. Worry is linked to our fear of the future and the unknown, and our lack of self-belief that we can cope, and it often centers around a "what if?" scenario—a future event that is unrealized and possibly never will be. Worrying can also be a habit we get into, but it is inappropriate for people who are "living in the moment," so we *can* choose not to worry—just for today!

Be grateful

It is important to value and appreciate many things in our lives and to be grateful for our many blessings—to develop an "attitude of gratitude," rather than just taking things for granted, or thinking with regret about what we haven't got. Reiki is a consciousness-raising tool (as a high spiritual energy it raises our vibrations), and as our consciousness is raised, we know instinctively that every living thing is a part of us, and we are a part of it, and everything is a part of the Divine, God, the Source or whatever we choose to call it. It is therefore right to give thanks for everyone and everything in this wonderful world.

Devote yourself to your work

We need to respect whatever "job" we have chosen for ourselves, and to honor ourselves by doing our best to create a feeling of satisfaction in that work. *All* work is valuable to the extent that we choose to value it. Also, Dr. Usui's intention with Reiki was that it should be a tool for spiritual growth, so this Principle is about working toward personal growth and spiritual development each day with Reiki, and perhaps also with meditation, energy cleansing, reading self-help books, and so on. Remember that *you* are your life's work!

Be kind to others

This is about being kind to everyone we meet, under any circumstances. We make conscious choices when we make contact with people, choosing those from whom we wish to learn, those we want as friends, those we work with. But we need to honor and respect *all* the people we interact with in our lives, not just those in our inner circle, because everyone we meet is in some way one of our teachers, whether we love them or loathe them, because they are all helping us to learn and grow spiritually. We also need to extend this kindness to ourselves, because we are important, too. I am also sure this Principle is encouraging us to be kind to every living thing—animals, birds, fish and other creatures, and even to plants and the planet itself.

CHANTING THE PRINCIPLES

What Usui advised his students to do was to place their hands in gassho—palms together, fingers pointing upward, hands held at midchest height (see page 15)—and repeat the Principles twice a day, once in the morning and once in the evening, as part of their spiritual practice, and of course you can do the same thing. You can choose the version you were taught, or the one you like best from those given above, or say the Principles in Japanese. They have a mantra-like quality when you do this, and I find I go into a beautifully quiet, meditative state after repeating them a few times, so perhaps you would like to try this. You might like to have a go at the phonetic pronunciation I've given below. It's unlikely to make you sound really Japanese, as this language is quite complex in its stresses and intonations, and of course the phonetics I have used are based on English sounds, but have a go anyway. It's only for your own satisfaction, and it can be fun.

Kyo dake wa	Kee oh dah kay wah
Okoru-na	Oh koh roo nah
Shinpai suna	Shin pie soo nah
Kansha shite	Kan shah she tay

Goo hage me   Gyo oh hah gay may
Hito ni shinsetsu ni   Hee toe nee shin set soo nee

In the next section I look at the first part of the Reiki Principles—"just for today," which is about living in the moment, and the art of mindfulness and meditation.

part two

LIVING IN THE "NOW"

Yesterday is but today's memory,
and tomorrow is today's dream.
Kahlil Gibran

chapter three
JUST FOR TODAY

I want to emphasize in this chapter that one of the most important aspects of the Reiki Principles is the phrase "just for today." This is notable for several reasons. First, if you were to promise yourself, when repeating the Principles, that you would never again be angry, or never again worry, or always and forever be kind to others—well, that's a pretty tall order, and quite hard to live up to. We are all human, with all the human failings and foibles, so it's unlikely that any of us can keep permanently to the spirit of the Principles, at least at first. Making a promise to ourselves that we won't get angry today, or won't worry today, means we only have to try one day at a time, which is an achievable goal. If on occasion we don't quite manage to live up to the Principles, well, tomorrow is another day, so we can just start again—one day at a time.

The other reason why the words "just for today" are important is that they highlight the need to live in the moment and be aware of what is going on around you; to live in the present, in the now. One of my favorite phrases is:

Yesterday is history, tomorrow is a mystery;
Today is a gift—that's why it's called the present!

Most people spend the majority of their time with their minds somewhere else. Their thoughts are perpetually on what happened an hour ago, or yesterday, or last week or last year: what they wish they had said to their partner last night; why they didn't buy that bargain-price TV when they had the chance; whether they left some essential paperwork at home—and so on. Or their thoughts are constantly on what might be in the future: what's in the freezer that they can cook for dinner tonight; where to go on holiday; how to get their child to swimming practice in time; how they are going to get the money together to pay that bill, etc. Then there are always the "what if?" scenarios to fill the mind—What if I mess up? What if I lose this job? What if my partner fancies someone else? Or even bigger things, like: If there's a recession, how will we cope? What if our house burns down or is flooded? What if I catch some awful disease? While such thoughts are spinning through your mind, you are not living life as it really is—you're on auto-pilot.

Eckhart Tolle, in his book *The Power of Now*, states "Wherever you are, be there totally." He suggests that some people try to escape the present with thoughts of the future and memories of the past because their "here" is never good enough. His suggestion is that if you find your "here and now" intolerable and it makes you unhappy, you basically have only three options:

- Remove yourself from the situation.
- Change the situation.
- Accept the situation totally.

A fairly stark response, maybe, but it is about taking responsibility for your life and accepting the consequences. Choose one of those options, and choose it now, is his proposition. And then get on with living, *in the present*.

TAKING TIME TO BE IN THE "NOW"

There are some simple things you can do to practice "being in the now." Try this on a day when you have some time to yourself.

Use an alarm clock or cooking timer or something similar, and set it to go off once every hour for 8 hours. Then when it rings, pause for 3–5 minutes, and practice being fully aware, using all your senses:

- Look around you, noticing colors, shapes, light and shadow.
- Listen to any sounds and notice their effects on you.
- Touch things around you, noticing different textures and temperatures.
- Really breathe in the scents and smells around you.
- If the alarm goes off while you're eating or drinking, really allow yourself to appreciate the taste and texture of whatever is in your mouth.

This may seem to be a very simple exercise, and you may question why you need to do it more than once a day, but it can be profound to do it every hour, because you become more sensitive to the various sensations as the day progresses. It's a good thing to repeat when life isn't going too well, or when you know you've been rushing around for days on end, because it brings things to a full stop. And it helps you to remember that you are a human *being*, not a human *doing*!

BEING PRESENT

The present moment is the one you are living in now, the only moment over which you have any control, so to be present is to be alive, right now, this very minute. You may already have experienced moments of total presence, in sports or creative activities, perhaps, or when reading a good book, when the boundary between yourself and your thinking and feeling processes has dissolved or disappeared. You are completely absorbed in what you are doing at that moment in time, so you are not *doing*, but *being*. This state has been described at various times as:

- Being in the zone
- Peak experience
- Going with the flow

There isn't really any new or special technique you need to learn to be mindful, or in other words, live in the "now," in your daily life, as it is part of what happens when you concentrate fully on what is happening to you at that moment. Moreover, even though our minds are often flitting between the past and the future, we do usually have some lucid moments of being totally in the present, especially if we begin to meditate, and meditation and mindfulness is discussed more fully in the next chapter.

chapter four

MINDFULNESS AND MEDITATION

Mindfulness is a Buddhist precept, meaning having your mind right here, right now, and not allowing your thoughts to wander into memories of time gone by or imaginings of time to come.

MINDFULNESS—MEDITATION IN ACTION

Part of what Dr. Usui asked us to do was to be mindful and live in the present (just today) and to work hard on ourselves, by which I believe he meant working on our personal growth and spiritual development through medi-tation, such as the Reiki meditation and cleansing technique called Hatsurei-ho (see chapter 15). However, the ideal of meditation practice is to be aware in every moment of your waking life, not just in those moments when you are sitting quietly, deliberately meditating. There is no more joyful place in the world than exactly where you are, right now—because you cannot experience real joy when your mind is elsewhere, thinking of what has happened in the past, or what might happen in the future.

It is possible to turn even the most mundane and potentially boring tasks into a form of meditation, to experience them fully and to learn to wonder at that experience. Try it with washing dishes. You can really experience washing dishes in a completely new way if you pay real attention to it, instead of letting your mind wander, which is probably what you normally do.

- ◆ Pay attention to the feeling of the warm water on your skin.
- ◆ Pay attention to the rainbow colors in the bubbles.
- ◆ Pay attention to the rhythmic movement of your hand as it cleans a plate.
- ◆ Pay attention to the slight squeaky sounds, as the plate becomes clean.
- ◆ Pay attention to the sparkle as you place the plate on the dish rack.
- ◆ ... and so on.

I'm not suggesting that you slow down your washing dishes to this pace every time you do it, but it's an interesting experiment, so do try it, because it can be really valuable to take time with everyday tasks. Being more in touch with your experiences helps you to realize that you are *living*, rather than just *existing*, and that is part of the benefit of meditation.

This doesn't mean that you should perform common meditative practices all the time, such as shutting your eyes and counting your breaths while driving (please don't!), or sitting in a half-lotus position and starting to chant "om" in the middle of the office! It does mean, however, that the awareness you develop in your daily meditation practice can naturally expand to encompass your day. It just takes a bit of practice, and it makes life much more fun because you begin to notice things that have passed you by before. You will start to see and sense more beauty around you, like the way the sun catches the edge of a cloud, or the way a smile lights up someone's face, or the softness of rain against your skin or the smell of honeysuckle.

MINDFUL LIVING

Being mindful means staying in touch with everything that is going on with us on a physical, emotional, psychological or spiritual level. Our bodies are perhaps the best benchmark we have for developing mindfulness in daily life, but most of us are not very aware of our bodies. Try the following exercise.

BEING IN TOUCH WITH YOUR BODY

Right at this moment, as you are reading this, become really aware of your body. Take an inventory.

- How are you holding your head? Is it straight up, or leaning to the left or right?
- Is your mouth relaxed, or are your lips stretched in a tense line, or slightly curved in a smile?
- Are your shoulders slightly hunched, or are you

sitting straight up? If you are sitting very straight, allow your shoulders and body to relax, and see if that feels different. If you're hunched over a little, sit up really straight, and see how your body feels like that.

◆ Maybe some parts of your body feel warm, while others feel cold? Perhaps you can feel a draft?

◆ Sense the chair beneath you.

◆ Sense your feet on the floor.

◆ Become aware of where your hands are—perhaps resting on your lap, or on the arm of the chair.

◆ Feel the breath being drawn in through your nose and hear the sound it makes.

◆ Hear the other sounds in the room. Maybe you can hear other people breathing? Perhaps you can hear traffic noise outside, or someone playing a musical instrument, or the hum of conversation from a nearby TV or radio, or the clattering of dishes in the kitchen?

◆ Now that you've become more aware of your surroundings, let yourself move into a few minutes of sitting quietly, just concentrating on your breathing, letting your breaths become slow and deep. Let each in-breath become slightly slower, deeper and longer.

◆ Let there be a pause before you breathe out again, and let the air out slowly, until you're sure your lungs are really empty. Then let there be another pause, before you breathe in again.

◆ As you adopt this slow, calm breathing, notice how

your body begins to feel more relaxed. Perhaps you can sense your heart rate slowing down, too.

You may not realize it, but this is a fairly classic method of meditation—becoming fully aware of something, or in other words, being mindful. Continue the exercise in silence for a while—for as long or as short a time as you feel comfortable. It could be just 2–3 minutes, or 10–20 minutes, or half an hour. Choose what feels right for you.

WHY MEDITATE?

Meditation is really a holistic discipline. It creates change at all levels of being, including the physical, emotional and psychological. It also has the power to awaken us to the spiritual levels of our being, and enables us to discover who we really are and what we might achieve. It brings us to a state of self-realization that is the highest expression of human nature.

Why do people meditate? What would be *your* main reason to meditate? Would it be for improved health, relaxation, stress prevention or reduction, self-realization or spiritual inspiration? Hopefully this chapter will give you various ideas that will help you to choose the most appropriate way for you to meditate, and will take away some of the myths about meditation that tend to frighten people off, or make them believe they can't do it. First let's look at what meditation is, and what methods are available to us.

What Is Meditation?

"Meditation" is an umbrella word that encompasses a multitude of techniques aimed at achieving an altered state of consciousness, resulting in a deeply relaxed state that can eventually bring about a state of enlightenment or ecstasy or both. There are two major types of meditation.

1. Most Christian, Sufi and yoga meditation techniques are based on heightened concentration, where you give your undivided attention to a single idea or perception, seeking the total absorption that leads to understanding. If this is successful it leads to a trance-like state where external awareness dims and the effects of competing external stimuli fade away. This is probably the oldest type of meditation, and it is found in most cultures in some form.

2. The other type of meditation is Buddhist, which is itself divided into two strands—samatha, which means calm, and vipassana, which means insight. Both involve the passive examination, and then letting go, of whatever content drifts into the individual's awareness. Samatha is designed to bring peaceful awareness and acceptance, and vipassana to bring mindfulness and understanding.

That may make it sound quite difficult, but it doesn't have to be. The myth about meditation is that you have to completely empty your mind, preferably while sitting in the lotus position—and if that's your starting point then it's no wonder people give up quite quickly! Certainly, the aim is to quiet the mind, but to totally empty it is probably only possible for those with many years of practice. It is estimated that we have at least 60,000 thoughts each day, and our minds are busy even when we're asleep, so achieving a quieter, more peaceful state is all you really need to aim for. You can start with just a few minutes, and gradually build up the time you spend in meditation. Don't jump straight in and aim for half an hour, because you will probably feel frustrated and uncomfortable, start fidgeting and give up the whole process. Try 5 minutes—or even 2–3—to start with.

My view is that meditation allows you to experience and enjoy a feeling of being at one with yourself and with the Universe. It brings an acceptance of yourself and your part in "the grand scheme of things," and leads to a deepening of "inner knowing," as opposed to simply having acquired knowledge. Meditation is a mental and spiritual discipline that is open to anyone who is willing to try it. Successful meditation does require some practice and self-discipline, but after a while you will find it quite easy, and it will become a natural part of daily life.

In all forms of meditation, therefore, there is a focus and a quieting of the mind. This aims, at first, simply to reduce, and eventually to eliminate, the chatter of daily life, the stresses of the environment in which we live, and so provide a haven within which we are free to connect with our inner being. It helps us to overcome the problems and illusions we create for ourselves and that we allow others to create for us, and also to overcome habits we have formed that hold us back. Meditation allows us to go beyond the everyday, into who we really are. The art of focusing, and awareness of being in the moment, changes brain activity, which leads to a psychological opening up of ourselves to compassion, joy, contentment and fulfillment.

The Physiological Effects of Meditation

Lots of research has been done into the effects of meditation on the body, particularly on the activity of the brain, nervous system and immune system. As mentioned, meditation is an altered state of consciousness, and some researchers have suggested that there are various stages of consciousness, from deep sleep to highly active wakefulness. Various brain activities can be measured, and tracing these patterns has produced waves of different frequencies:

- Beta waves (the highest frequency), associated with active wakefulness
- Alpha waves, associated with relaxed wakefulness
- Theta waves, associated with dreaming
- Delta waves (the lowest frequency), associated with sleep

Meditation has been shown to increase alpha-wave activity, which has led to the suggestion that it acts as a form of self-hypnosis and relaxation. The alterations in brain activity caused by meditation apparently have profound effects on the autonomic nervous system—the part of the nervous system that controls digestion, breathing, heart rate and blood pressure, and that enables our body to respond to everyday stresses. It appears that, particularly with the increase in alpha waves produced by some forms of meditation, the autonomic nervous system responds by reducing activity in the "fight-or-flight" response, reducing heart rate and blood pressure, calming

37

the breathing and thus generally reducing the stress on the body.

A relatively new topic for research is in the area of psychoneuroimmunology, which examines the effect of the mind on the nervous system and immune systems. Again, there is the suggestion that meditation reduces the stresses on the immune system, thus allowing the body to defend itself more easily against infection, and to promote healing by responding to, and overcoming, invading microorganisms and cancerous and other rogue cells.

Meditation is therefore seen by many health professionals to be an aid to stress reduction, to have beneficial effects on the body and to promote good health in general.

Methods of Meditation

A variety of methods can be used for meditation:

- Chanting or singing, using repeated simple phrases or mantras
- Transcendental meditation (going beyond the individual)
- Seeking the "great void" or Nirvana (as in Buddhism)
- Meditation on objects, such as feathers or stones
- Meditation on symbols, such as icons or mandalas
- Meditation on a flame, such as a candle flame
- Meditation on nature—trees, plants, water or a landscape
- Meditation on the four elements—earth, air, fire and water (this occurs in both Eastern and Western spiritual traditions)

- Meditation with sound, such as Tibetan gongs or the sounds of nature
- Meditation on color
- Meditation on qualities—loving-kindness, compassion, happiness and joy
- Meditation on the body and its natural activities—breathing, walking, moving and resting
- Guided meditation, usually called visualization, which takes you on an inner journey to your deeper self

All methods of meditation are equally valid, so you might want to try out quite a few in your search for the technique that fits you best, or you may find that using a combination of meditation forms is the way for you to develop. Later in this chapter there are examples of several types of meditation for you to try.

Preparing to Meditate

Anyone can learn to meditate, but there are some things that make it easier and more effective. Meditation does require a level of self-discipline, and in terms of producing permanent changes and helping with your spiritual journey of personal growth and development, regular meditation is seen as an essential practice. By all means start off with just a few minutes a day to help you develop the habit of regular meditation, but you should ideally aim after a while to do at least 20 minutes a day.

When meditating you will need to be in a safe, quiet environment, one in which you feel comfortable and where you will either be undisturbed, or where disturbances will be as few as is possible, although when you are more experienced you will find you can enter a meditation state almost anywhere, regardless of the noises around you—a railway station, a busy park or while sitting with a coffee in a café.

Bright light stimulates the body and can make meditation more difficult, whereas complete darkness tends to promote sleep, so soft lighting, such as candlelight, is usually best, and many people find candles with their flickering flames to be an aid to meditation in their own right. Some people like to burn incense or essential oils such as lavender, or a scented candle, and you will need to ensure that the room is at an appropriate temperature— too cold and it will prevent concentration, too warm and it is likely to make you sleepy. It is also a good idea to remove glasses, large pieces of jewelry and your watch, and some people like to remove their shoes as well.

Posture is important, as having a straight back will help your inner energies to flow better, and this is best accomplished sitting in a supportive chair or on a cushion on the floor with your back against a wall, with your hands loosely relaxed in your lap or resting on your knees, or in a classic prayer position (although this can be a bit tiring after a while). Of course, it is possible to meditate while lying on the floor or on a bed, but this often induces sleep. Crossing the legs or arms can make meditation more difficult unless you can assume a completely cross-legged posture such as the lotus position, which if you are agile enough is a very satisfying position in which to meditate—but don't force the issue. Only try this if you feel reasonably comfortable.

It can be very helpful to establish a meditation routine, by meditating for a certain length of time at a particular time of day. Some people find meditation best in the early morning, while others prefer to meditate during the evening, so choose a time that's convenient for you. Bear in mind that it is difficult to enter a proper meditative state after a heavy meal, and even more so after drinking alcohol, so it is best to wait at least 2 hours after eating, or to meditate beforehand, otherwise you may become too sleepy.

Meditation on the Breath

Perhaps the easiest and best way to begin meditation is with the breath. Breathing is essential to life. We start our lives with an in-breath, and end them with an out-breath, and breathing is something that we mostly take for granted, unless we are unfortunate enough to have an illness or some other reason that causes breathing difficulties. Yet it is really a miraculous process, which continues thousands of times a day without any conscious effort or control from us.

- To begin with, close your eyes and concentrate on your breathing.
- Let your breathing become slower and deeper, allowing the breath to be inhaled to its fullest extent, and allowing it to be exhaled completely.
- Try to be aware of where the air is going, how far down your chest it is traveling. Perhaps place a hand on your chest and feel it rising up and down.
- Place a hand on your solar plexus (your midriff), and feel it going up and down.
- Move your hand down to your abdomen. Is it also

going up and down? Can you deepen your
breathing to make your abdomen move?

◆ Start to count your breaths, counting each in-
breath until you reach the number nine. Then start
again at one, and just enjoy some silent meditation
for a few minutes, continuing to concentrate and
counting your breaths from one to nine for as long
as you feel comfortable.

The Four-fold Breath

This is a slightly different form of breathing meditation,
where the in-breath, out-breath and the spaces between
breaths are given equal time.

◆ Breathe in with a deep but comfortable breath
from the diaphragm to the count of four (about
four seconds).
◆ Hold your breath for the count of four.
◆ Breathe out slowly to the count of four.
◆ Hold the lungs empty to the count of four.
◆ Start again.

This exercise has a very relaxing effect on the body, and
when you are quite practiced you will find that you can
increase the length of time for each stage to five, six or
seven seconds, although I wouldn't advise lengthening it
beyond about nine seconds, as it then becomes more a
state of endurance than a state of meditation.

Meditation Using Mantras

A mantra is a sound, phrase or prayer that is repeated over and over again, either aloud (spoken or sung) or as a thought, which is believed to bring meditational benefits to the person chanting it. You may have heard of people chanting "om," which is a Sanskrit mantra that might also be incorporated into a phrase such as "om ah hum," where "om" represents the body, "ah" the speech and "hum" the mind. The chanting of these words is believed to be a prayer that purifies negativity produced by the body, speech and thought, as well as bringing a blessing to the person chanting it.

- Sit in a comfortable posture with your eyes closed.
- Bring the mantra "om ah hum" (or another phrase or word you have chosen, such as "love and compassion") into your consciousness, and begin repeating it slowly, either silently in your mind, or aloud, speaking as distinctly as possible. (If you wish, you can use musical tones for chanting, singing rather than speaking, either the same note three times, i.e., once each for "om," "ah" and "hum," or three different notes.) You may feel the need to gradually increase the speed of repetitions—or not. If you are chanting aloud you may run out of breath, but this is quite natural. Just breathe deeply for a few moments, then continue with the chant.
- Stop whenever you need to. With practice you will find it easier to incorporate your inhalations and exhalations with the repetitions of the mantra, but

there is no need to try too hard; just let it happen naturally. As you recite the mantra you may find that you naturally relax into the sound, your breath and your attention combining effortlessly and powerfully.

◆ Repeat the mantra for 3, 5, 7, 9 or 11 minutes—whichever feels best to you. (I would suggest 3 minutes to start with, until you're more practiced at this technique.)

◆ As you reach the end of your mantra meditation period, it is good practice to gently slow down the repetitions, rather than coming to an abrupt stop.

◆ When you've finished, sit quietly and explore your awareness. Take note of the feelings in your body and mind. You might feel relaxed and at peace, receive an insight into some area of your life, experience colors in your inner vision or sense that some form of cleansing or healing has taken place.

Meditation on Sound

People react to sounds in very different ways. For example, some people enjoy listening to loud rock or pop music with a strong beat, while others prefer classical, jazz or folk music. For meditation purposes, rock, pop, jazz and folk are probably not the best inspirations, as they are rarely calming and relaxing, but some people enjoy listening to classical or "New Age" music playing in the background as they meditate.

Traditional sounds for meditation include Tibetan bowls made of seven different metals, which have a special resonance, depending upon their size; or ting-sha, which are pairs of small, flat, cymbal-shaped pieces of metal, usually joined together at either end by a piece of thin leather or cord; or Tibetan gongs that can vary in size from about 12 inches to 48 inches in diameter. Other sounds that encourage meditation are recordings (or live perform-ances) of monks chanting, or soft, rhythmic drumming, such as a combination of three-beat, five-beat and seven-beat drumming in the Celtic tradition.

There are plenty of recordings on the market, from Tibetan monks chanting "om" and chanting special rhythms to link to each of the seven chakras, to Native American drumming and "New Age" music from flutes and guitars, to whale songs and other natural sounds, so this might be something you would like to try. Some of my favorite titles are given on page 259.

A Relaxation Practice

Two great tools to aid meditation are relaxation and breathing control, and as part of the process of meditation you may wish to develop the habit of relaxing your body by visualizing and feeling it relax.

- Sit in a comfortable position.
- Feel your feet on the floor, then tense the muscles of your toes, feet and heels, and then relax them completely.
- Tense the muscles of your calves, knees and thighs, and then let them relax.
- Tense the muscles of your hips, abdomen and

chest, then let them relax, and then slow your breathing to an even rate.

◆ Tense, then relax the muscles in your shoulders, arms, hands and fingers.

◆ Tense, then relax the muscles in your neck, jaw, face and scalp.

This method is useful because we tend to store a lot of tension in our muscles, particularly in our shoulders and legs, so you might like to tense and relax those areas 3–4 times. When you're feeling relaxed—with practice this will only take 2–3 minutes—become aware of your breathing, and perhaps count the breaths. Allow yourself to fall into a slow, regular pattern of breathing—then you can choose which method of meditation to use.

Dealing with Distractions

One of the major problems encountered in meditation is difficulty in getting rid of the thoughts, sounds and activities of daily life. However, if you try too hard concentrating on getting rid of these distractions, you will actually make it more difficult for yourself, because you will generate even more thoughts. If you work on the principle that all our thoughts and activities are worthy of acknowledgment, just acknowledge them, then let them go.

There are many techniques for letting go, and here are three for you to try:

1. If a thought, or recognition of a sound such as a car, or the humming of central heating, comes into your mind, try to visualize that thought or sound, and surround it with a bubble of light, or a balloon, then watch it float up and up and out of your mind.
2. You may see thoughts as birds flying across the sky. Acknowledge their presence. Visualize each thought or noise as a bird, then allow it to fly away, out of the scene in your mind.
3. Some people like to visualize intruding thoughts in a candle flame. The thought may float up with the heat and smoke of the candle, or it may be imagined within the flame and the candle snuffed out. The candle can always be relit (in your imagination) should another intruding thought drift by.

There may be occasions when you want to remember a thought for later use. In this case you could visualize a box or basket into which the thought bubble can be placed, then the lid can be put on the box to hold the bubble inside until later. Such thoughts can be retrieved after the meditation has finished, if you wish.

WHAT IS VISUALIZATION?

Visualization, sometimes called guided meditation, is a method of meditation in which your soul or spirit, some-times called your "Higher Self," allows images to develop within the mind. These images can be symbols, objects, landscapes, people, animals, plants or colors, which may be familiar or new to you. Although these images may initially seem to be unrelated, they will often form a story, which may be allegorical, or more directly understandable as an exploration of your personal truth, the knowledge and insight you are seeking, an understanding of your desires and needs, or a spiritual awareness of some kind.

Visualizations can have a variety of purposes—they can be used for self-development, healing, relaxation, relieving stress or seeking greater union with the Divine/Source/Universe. They are also often good fun!

In visualizations, you allow your soul or spirit to influence your mind and present you with new ideas, or maybe a different way of looking at things. Often some natural object, or a word someone says, allows our mind to go somewhere else, a state we might describe as "daydreaming," which is usually a pleasant and occasionally helpful activity. Visualization is a much more structured, supportive and effective vehicle for doing this.

When you begin visualizations, you may see only part of an image, or you may see an image for only a few moments. "Seeing" may seem more "knowing" what is there, or imagining what is there, or a feeling, or it may even appear in words. All of these "sensings" are valid parts of visualization, and the more often you take yourself on visual inner journeys, the more the focus of what you "see" will become clearer, more defined and more definite. Thus your visualizing will potentially begin to lead you and expand you out of a set visualization, and bring you deeper and broader understanding.

One problem with visualization is that some people believe they can't do it, and this is usually because they have unrealistic expectations of what they should "see."

Granted, some people are very visual, and do see things very clearly in their visualizations, but others do not.

◆ Try this. Can you remember, by "seeing" it in your mind, what your bedroom looks like? In your imagination, can you "move" around the room and see it from different angles? That's the type of image you might have when you are visualizing.

◆ Try something else. Here's a short list of things that will probably trigger visual images in your mind: elephant, cat, tree, flower. The way you see each of these things might be different from the way others see it—for instance, you might see a black cat, while someone else might see a ginger cat; you might see a rose, but another person may see a daffodil. That's quite natural, because the images which come to mind are usually familiar ones, so you will "see" something you know.

◆ The same is true, initially, if you visualize a landscape. You will probably see a countryside, seaside or woodland scene that you have seen in real life. However, after a bit of practice your mind will present you with "new" landscapes that are no less real to you, but which exist only as imaginings—and that can be quite exciting!

The Visualization Process

In this book there are a number of visualizations that are obviously given in print, and it is useful to read each one through 2–3 times before you start, to enable you to become familiar with its pattern. Alternatively you might choose to let someone read it to you slowly, or you could prepare a recording for yourself so that you can play it back whenever you wish. Eventually you can try creating your own visualizations—if you do so, be clear what you want to focus on, or what question you want answered, before you start.

Initially try to follow each visualization the way it is set out, but if your soul or spirit directs you to a different place or different things, or if within your visualization someone comes to greet you, that is what you need at that time, and you should go along with the new "route." However, if you're following your own visualization, try not to let it continue too long, because the benefit lies in taking note of the emotions and the knowledge that it brings—it isn't a good idea to overload yourself with detail, especially when you're just beginning to visualize on a regular basis. It is also very important, if you're following your own visualization, to always bring yourself back to the point where you started the visualization (i.e., the first scene you imagined) before your awareness fully returns to the room you are in.

After a Visualization

At the end of a visualization, give yourself a minute or two to become aware of your surroundings once again, and when you are ready, open your eyes. It is helpful to note down straightaway as much as you can remember of the visualization, so keep a notebook and pen nearby. Don't worry if at first you don't see much detail, or you don't remember very much. You can always return to the visualization at another time, and, indeed, repeat it again and again if you want to, and gradually the fuller picture will develop.

One idea you could try is to do the same visualization every day for a week, then collate a list of the symbols and gifts to explore in meditation over the following week. For this you will need to keep a journal or diary of your visualizations to record what you experience—this can be a very helpful document in its own right, especially when you look back in it from sometime in the future, as it can be a record of your spiritual progress and personal growth.

Feeling Safe When Visualizing

As previously mentioned, it is important to feel safe and secure when meditating, and one of the best ways of promoting a feeling of safety is by using the power of your mind to create a protective barrier of white light (or Reiki). This first visualization allows you to fill yourself with white light, bringing it down from the Divine Source into the crown of your head and moving it throughout your whole body, finally spreading the white light out around you to fill the space in which you are sitting, to provide a protective screen around you. You also anchor yourself into the earth with roots of white light, and this gives a further feeling of security. With practice, the visualization of white light becomes easier and quicker, and takes perhaps only 30 seconds or a minute. Many people like to carry out this visualization every time they meditate, as the feeling of protection allows them to relax more deeply.

BRINGING IN THE LIGHT

◆ Sit in a comfortable position and allow your body to relax. Begin to be aware of your breathing, and follow your breath in and out, in and out; with each breath you are becoming more and more relaxed.

◆ Visualize an opening at the top of your head, and see a thin thread of white light passing up through the ceiling, through the roof and up into the sky above.

◆ See this thread of light going through the edge of the Earth's atmosphere and out into space, moving farther and farther out until you feel it connecting with the Divine Source, a huge mass of brilliant white light, and allow that white light to flow back down the thread, making it bigger and brighter, and allow the light to flow right down into your head.

◆ The brilliant light now fills your head, and moves down into your neck, shoulders and arms, and right down into your hands to the very tips of your fingers.

◆ You see it flowing through your chest and back, and down into your abdomen and hips, and then into your thighs, knees, calves, ankles and feet, right to the tips of your toes.

◆ You feel your feet becoming heavier and more solid, feel the connection with the floor beneath you, then allow the white light to flow out of your feet into the earth.

- ◆ Imagine the white light forming roots growing from your feet down into the earth, anchoring you and making you feel very secure.
- ◆ Now the whole of your body is flooded with white light—you can use this light to form a protective barrier around you.
- ◆ Imagine that the light is coming out of your hands and visualize yourself moving your hands over all of your body so that a cloak of white light surrounds you.
- ◆ Now allow that light to spread out, filling the room to create a safe and sacred space, and watch the light swirl into all the corners, from floor to ceiling, from wall to wall, from door to window, until the whole room is bathed in white light.
- ◆ Just enjoy the peace and tranquillity of your protected space, and allow any stray thoughts that come into your mind to simply drift across. Remain in a relaxed, meditative state for 5 or 10 minutes, or as long as you feel comfortable.

In the rest of this book we look at the Reiki Principles in more depth. In Part 3 we concentrate on the first of Dr. Usui's Principles: "Just for today, do not anger."

part three

LIVING WITHOUT ANGER

Your emotions can guide you, but you don't have
to let them control you.

Penelope Quest

chapter five

UNDERSTANDING EMOTIONS

"Living without anger" is the theme of Part 3, which might seem a difficult thing to do—surely everyone feels angry sometimes? But "just for today, do not anger" is the first of the Reiki Principles Dr. Usui passed on to us, so in this and the next chapter I show you why you might get angry, what anger does to you, and how to cope with it and heal it. However, anger is only one of the many distressing emotions we experience that can potentially produce harmful reactions in us—and I feel sure that the essence of what Dr. Usui was guiding us to do was to live more equably. Therefore before we look at anger specifically, in this chapter I want to explore the theory of emotions and how they can either help or hinder us in our attempt to "live the Reiki way."

WHAT ARE EMOTIONS?

We have over 600 words in the English language to describe emotions, and we use up to 42 muscles in our faces to express them, but the six most common emotions are happiness, sadness, surprise, disgust, fear and anger.

Emotions are thought to arise in the part of the brain known as the limbic system, which is a primitive system that also exists in all other mammals and some reptiles, and it represents a part of our survival mechanism. What was once perhaps just a mechanism that allowed us to react to danger—feelings of fear release adrenaline in our bodies to get us ready for "fight or flight"—has evolved over millions of years into a delicate and sophisticated internal guidance system. Our emotions basically help us to:

◆ Identify when our basic human needs are, or are not, being met.
◆ Identify whether our choices or decisions "feel" good or bad.
◆ Identify whether we feel safe or unsafe with someone's behavior so that we can set comfortable boundaries.
◆ Provide verbal and nonverbal communication (e.g., facial expressions) to signal to others how we feel, to facilitate interpersonal interaction.
◆ Potentially provide a way of uniting us as a species (e.g., empathy, compassion, cooperation, forgiveness).
◆ Identify what makes us happy or unhappy.

So, for example, if you feel fear, you will try to escape from the danger; if you feel disgusted, you might move away from whatever makes you feel like that; if you're feeling happy, you will relax; so your emotions influence your behavior. We use our emotions for making decisions to help us in our daily lives. For instance, when we meet people we look at their faces to assess whether we know them, to judge their gender and age, and to see what mood they are in.

Most of us are pretty good at identifying the facial expressions that indicate the six basic emotions described above—happiness, sadness, surprise, disgust, fear and anger—and we are therefore able to react appropriately.

GENERATING EMOTIONS

Emotions result when feelings are filtered through our beliefs, when we develop judgments about what we should, or should not, be feeling. So, for example, if someone in back of you cuts in line in a shop and gets served before you, you could either accept the situation, shrug your shoulders and wait your turn, which would not generate any specific emotion or, if you were in a hurry and believed that person would make you late for something important, you might react with anger, even possibly challenging him or her verbally to reinstate your place in the line. However, emotions are not caused by outer events. They are an internal reaction to an external event. They represent a choice you have made. We choose what emotion to feel. *Always*. So emotions aren't automatic reactions to situations or events; they form a part of our complex responses to life—our personalities. They are based on our life experiences so far, which is why people—each person being individual—react in diverse ways to the same situations.

EMOTIONAL PROGRAMMING

All of your experiences since you were a small child have had an impact on you, and although your emotions are always generated within you, you learn your particular range of emotions from the people who were influential in your life, especially when you were young. Effectively, you have been receiving emotional programming since you were old enough to discern facial, verbal and physical expressions, and in your early years this would have been from your parents or caregivers, siblings, teachers and friends. Scientists believe that, even if you don't remember an actual emotional event from childhood, you will remember what you felt, which becomes an emotional memory that can be triggered by something you saw, heard or even smelled at the time, and those memories might still affect you as an adult.

In the modern world your emotional programming can also come from TV, films and even computer games, because these reflect images of emotions to which we are susceptible, especially when we're young. Think of the huge range of emotions, from intolerable grief to overwhelming happiness, sexual desire to violent anger, demonstrated in any of TV's soap operas, for example. It is this emotional programming that is one of the foundations for our belief system, which we integrate into our subconscious, and which then provides us with our patterns of behavior and habitual emotional responses.

Psychological research has shown that if either or both of your parents showed little emotion, laughing or crying infrequently, and rarely or never hugging or holding you, you are likely to grow up suppressing your emotions, because you believe it is the way to be. Alternatively, you may have been exposed to a parent who was overly emotional, crying easily or losing his or her temper regularly, so this would be the "norm" to you, and you are likely to follow in his or her footsteps. We all learn by example, and what we learn eventually becomes absorbed into our own personalities, so that pattern continues from one generation to another.

Of course, we do have other choices. Sometimes people react against their programming, and if their childhood was miserable because of harsh or restrictive and unloving parents, they will behave in the opposite way when they are adults, becoming loving, tolerant and demonstrative. But that only goes to show that our emotions, and the way we express them, are choices. Just because we have formed a subconscious habit and react to certain situations in a certain way doesn't mean we have to continue doing so forever. We can change our reactions.

Positive and Negative

Perhaps this sounds as though having emotions is pretty undesirable? Not so. We have a huge range of emotions that we can enjoy, as well as those which aren't so much fun. Of course, extremes of emotion can cause problems. Sadness can become depression, anger can become unprovoked aggression, and pleasure can lead to addiction. Feeling afraid in a dangerous situation is natural and useful, but being too fearful can cause unhelpful anxiety, phobias and panic attacks. However, there are many more positive emotions we can choose to feel as well. How about feeling elated, ecstatic or enthralled? Or enlivened, energetic or enthusiastic?

61

EMOTIONS AS GUIDANCE

I've already mentioned that our emotions were originally part of our survival instinct, and that in our modern world we use them to guide us in our everyday interactions with other people. However, there is another, more innovative, metaphysical viewpoint—that emotions are actually part of our spiritual guidance system—a way in which our Soul, sometimes referred to as our Higher Self, can communicate with us.

From this perspective, if you are feeling fearful, depressed or pessimistic, this indicates that something is "wrong" in your life, or you are not going in the "right" direction, whereas if you are feeling enthusiastic, optimistic or content, then you are on the "right path"—doing what you need to do, being who you really are. The most comprehensive explanation of the relationship between emotions and their effect on our lives can be found in a book I highly recommend—*Ask and It Is Given* by Esther and Jerry Hicks, who report the channeled spiritual teachings of Abraham. (Abraham is not a living person; he is a highly evolved entity—a collection of souls who may or may not have lived physical lives—who lives in the spiritual realm, whose wisdom and insight is "channeled" through Esther Hicks, a psychic medium who lives in the United Stares.) I will try to explain, briefly, some of the theories described in this book.

The Emotional Hierarchy

Abraham explains that all emotions can be classified on a hierarchy from the lowest, darkest feelings such as fear, grief or despair, up to the highest, lightest feelings such as love and joy.

love, joy, enthusiasm, passion, trust, freedom, empowerment, gratitude, eagerness

happiness, optimism, contentment, hope, positive expectation

boredom, pessimism, frustration, impatience, irritation

feeling overwhelmed, disappointment, doubt, worry

blame, discouragement, anger, revenge

rage, hatred, jealousy

insecurity, guilt, lack of self-worth

fear, grief, depression,
despair,
powerlessness

At the top of the scale, when you're feeling full of love, joy and gratitude, you are said to be in alignment with who you truly are, and are fully connected with the Source (or God or the Universe). At this level your life feels good, you're having fun, with nice people around you, and you seem to attract good things to you, so you feel enthusiastic about life, and you're happy to be alive.

Down at the bottom of the scale, though, when you're consumed with grief, or full of fear, you are out of alignment with the real you, and less connected with the Source, so the people around you reflect depressing feelings and confirm your sense of powerlessness, and you feel you are on a never-ending spiral of despair.

MOVING UP THE EMOTIONAL SCALE

Fortunately there is a way out of that spiral of despair, but it doesn't take you straight up to the top. The way up the emotional scale is usually taken one or at the most two steps at a time. Let's take one emotional example—grief— which has a classic recovery schedule that, psychologists tell us, normally takes about three years. If you're feeling in the depths of despair because you're grieving over the death of a loved one, having people tell you to cheer up, or suggest happy affirmations to "bring you out of it," or plan fun, exciting things for you to do, is absolutely the last thing you can stand. But then you might feel guilty, because you know your friends or relatives are trying to help you, or you may even sink into feelings of unwor- thiness, not believing you deserve their help because you're so unwilling to accept it—but actually, guilt and feelings of unworthiness are one stage up the hierarchy, so that can be a step in the right direction.

Later, as you begin to get over the shock of your loved one's death, you might react to outsiders' suggestions with rage—how dare they interfere? Why can't they leave you alone? Or you might feel rage toward the person who has died, for leaving you, but that's actually a natural reaction, and it's another step upward on the emotional hierarchy. The next step might be to blame someone or something for your loss—perhaps the doctors who didn't save your loved one, or the driver of the car who injured him or her, but again, that's a very normal response, and you've stepped up the scale again.

That doesn't mean that rage and blame are good places to be, of course, but they do indicate that you are starting to engage with your situation, which is a more positive reaction than being right down in the depths of despair, where your feelings tend to overwhelm you so that you don't feel able to do anything. Although rage and blame are negative emotions, they are more active than passive, which means they are a little higher up the emotional scale—and they may also make you more likely to be a bit more receptive to positive suggestions from those who care about you. However, there's still quite a way to go before you begin to recognize that your situation has improved—and although it's a cliché, they do say that time is a great healer. You may need to work your way through some worry and doubt and frustration, perhaps wondering how you will cope without your loved one, before you can start to feel more content, hopeful or optimistic. Eventually, however, you will regain your passion and enthusiasm for life; you will feel happy and joyful, and wake up each morning eager to face a new day. It just takes some time.

The idea of a hierarchy of emotions may seem a bit complicated, but hopefully the example I've given shows that with time we can—and do—move out of depressing and negative emotions into more satisfying and enjoyable feelings. That is perhaps as far as I can go with this theory in this chapter, so if you would like to learn more about the hierarchy of emotions, do read *Ask and It Is Given*. In Part 5 I return to another aspect of Abraham's theory, about the power of thought and the Law of Attraction, so hopefully it will become a bit clearer—and you will learn how to use your thoughts and emotions to create the kind of life you want. Here I suggest a few techniques that can prove invaluable in changing your emotions for the better, and getting you up the emotional hierarchy at a much faster pace. The first two are Reiki techniques, naturally, but then I introduce you to an innovative method called Emotional Freedom Technique, or EFT, which I have found to be an effective and interesting way of dealing with negative emotions. As I mentioned in the Introduction, *Living the Reiki Way* isn't only about using Reiki—it can encompass other methods which help you to cope with overwhelming emotions or problems of any kind.

USING REIKI TO HEAL YOUR EMOTIONS

One way of carrying out emotional healing is to use Reiki, of course, and there are advantages to being able to use the Reiki symbols for this, if you have already done a Reiki Second Degree course, but if not, you can simply let the Reiki flow and it will do its job, although it may take just a little longer. In case you are not familiar with the term "chakra," which I use in the technique below, it is a Sanskrit word meaning wheel or vortex, and it is used to describe some energy centers in the body. The seven main chakras are located near the perineum (base), the navel (sacral), the midriff (solar plexus), the chest (heart), the throat (throat), the brow (third eye) and the top of the head (crown).

1. Decide which emotions you want to work on. You can work on more than one at a time, or link similar types of emotions together. You may choose to deal with fear, nervousness, depression, anger, sadness, grief, impatience, stress or any other emotion that you feel needs healing.

2. Decide where you generally feel these emotions. For example, anger, fear or problems with self-esteem are often felt in the solar plexus; loneliness, grief or rejection in the heart area; money or job worries in the base chakra; jealousy about sexual relationships in the sacral chakra, and so on.

3. Next, if you have Reiki Second Degree, draw, or imagine, a large Harmony (Mental and Emotional) symbol over what seems to be the most appropriate chakra (if you're not sure, draw the symbol over your crown chakra), then visualize the symbol expanding until it encompasses the whole of you, say its mantra three times, and ask and *intend* that it bring its gentle, healing, peaceful and restorative energy to fill your physical and energy bodies, to bring greater harmony and balance to your life, and to heal your feelings of . . . (*name whatever emotions you want to work on*).

4. If you don't have Reiki Second Degree, place both your hands over the appropriate chakra, and imagine and *intend* that Reiki be flowing out of your hands, and ask and *intend* that Reiki heal, harmonize and balance your physical and energy bodies, to bring greater harmony and balance to your life, and to heal your feelings of . . . (*name the emotions you want to work on*).

5. Let yourself stay in a meditative state, giving yourself Reiki, and imagine being surrounded and encompassed by Reiki for at least 5 minutes, but preferably for about 15 minutes, until you feel much calmer and more content; then, either take your hands away

and place them in the gassho (prayer) position, giving thanks to Reiki with a little bow, or if you have Reiki Second Degree, draw a Power symbol to seal in the peaceful energies, saying its mantra three times, then gassho and give thanks.

6. Finally, clap your hands or shake them vigorously to break the energy connections.

Repeat this exercise on a daily basis, working with one or more emotions, until you sense that they have changed and feel less strong or less troublesome. A good check for this is to think of some situation that would normally trigger the type of emotion you are working on, let yourself imagine it as vividly as possible and see if you get any reaction in the appropriate chakra. If you don't, then at least some healing has occurred, but of course you can always repeat the process anytime those emotions resurface—if they ever do.

A SIMPLE REIKI TECHNIQUE

If you are feeling churned up, anxious or irritated, and all you want to do is feel calmer or more centered, then a simple way of using Reiki is to place one hand on your heart chakra (roughly over your breastbone) and the other on your solar plexus (midriff), and allow the Reiki to flow, intending that it help you to become calm and centered. Stay like this for 5–10 minutes, or until you feel that your emotional state has become more composed.

EMOTIONAL FREEDOM TECHNIQUE (EFT)

Although my first reaction is always to turn to Reiki to help me feel better, there are other techniques that I have found useful and would like to share with you. One of the most effective is called the Emotional Freedom Technique (EFT). This was developed by Gary Craig, based on a system of psychological healing called Thought Field Therapy (TFT), which was originally developed by a clinical psychologist, Dr. Roger Callahan. He based his system on acupuncture points and kinesiology, and his most famous case was a patient named Mary who had such a severe water phobia that she couldn't go out in the rain, or even look at water on TV. Having tried everything else he could think of, he eventually tapped on her stomach meridian (the end of one of the energy lines running throughout the body, used in acupuncture, acupressure and reflexology), below the eye, and astonishingly, 20 seconds later, the phobia was completely gone, and she was able to stand by a swimming pool and splash her face with water.

EFT is therefore a form of Energy Psychology that uses the energetic pathways through the body, the meridians. These relay information to the entire energy system, as well as channeling vital energy to the organs and tissues of the physical body, and the energy within each meridian also registers emotions, feelings and sensations. Each time we experience an emotion, the body's energy system is influenced to some degree, so the meridian system and our psychology are closely linked. EFT is designed to directly interact with the energy system, rebalancing and stabilizing the disruption that occurs when a distressing emotion is experienced, thus enabling our energies to flow freely again.

An EFT session involves gently tapping with the finger-tips on specific meridian points on the body, in a set sequence. This simple yet powerful technique rebalances the energies of the body, releasing unwanted emotions and allowing an inner sense of calm to return. Perhaps one of the most amazing effects of EFT is the speed with which emotional distress can be resolved, sometimes in little more than minutes, creating freedom from emotional problems or issues that might have troubled you for years. There are several excellent books that describe this tech-nique in detail—notably *Emotional Healing in Minutes* by Valerie and Paul Lynch, and *The Healing Power of EFT and Energy Psychology* by David Feinstein, Donna Eden and Gary Craig. I highly recommend them if you are inter-ested in learning more. However, as this is such a simple technique, I have included the instructions below. Although it looks quite lengthy, that's just because describing it in writing requires rather more explanation— actually, it only takes a few minutes.

The technique is divided into ten steps, split into four stages, and it is important to remember to follow them in progression in order to achieve the desired results. (You may find it useful to write the various stages and your results in a notebook.)

The four stages are:

1. The Setup
2. The Sequence
3. The Gamut
4. The Second Sequence

1. The Setup

Step 1, Identify the Problem

Identify the emotion you want to work on, and spend a few moments tuning in to the thoughts and feelings it causes.

Step 2, Formulate a Statement

To establish the intention of what needs to be cleared, you need to create a statement that encompasses these feelings, being as specific, honest and realistic as possible about how you are feeling. The more exact you can be, the deeper the healing can be, because the statement you use needs to have impact and register a disruption within your energy system. So, for example, it is better to be truthful and say something like, "I am afraid of being hurt if I get involved in a relationship," rather than "I want to have a loving relationship," because the former statement will generate more emotion.

Therefore to formulate the perfect statement, you need to be as specific as possible, and use the present tense and describe how you feel right now, rather than what you are hoping to achieve. For instance, if you wanted to work on the emotion of anger, you could just say "I feel angry," but it would be better to be more precise and state why you feel angry, for example, "I feel angry that my partner won't listen to me" or "I feel angry that Tom (or Jenny) let me down."

Next, place the words "Even though I ... " in front of your chosen statement, followed by " ... I deeply and completely accept myself." For example: "Even though I feel angry that my partner wouldn't listen to me, I deeply and completely accept myself," "Even though I am frightened of flying, I deeply and completely accept myself" or "Even though I am afraid to speak up and say how I feel, I deeply and completely accept myself."

This type of affirmation promotes acceptance of the problem, and of yourself, and it overrides any part of you that does not want to change, or that has a hidden agenda to keep you the way you are. The statement really needs to be said aloud for the best results, and as emphatically as possible, putting some emotion into it, but if you need to work on something when you're with other people, you can say it silently to yourself.

Step 3, Score Chart

Now you need to get to what is called the SUDS level—the Subjective Unit of Distress—by giving your emotion a score from one to ten, relating to its intensity and to how disturbing the memory is, ten being the highest intensity of feeling and zero being the lowest, meaning the problem has gone. The score helps you to check and record your progress after the first round, and after any succeeding rounds. As an example, a dreadful trauma or a deeply ingrained fear might be described as an intense "ten out of ten" reaction, whereas a mild irritation or a slight anxiety might only score a three.

Write down the emotion you want to deal with:

_____

Then mark the number you feel is appropriate, in the Initial Intensity column:

Initial Intensity	After 1st Round	After 2nd Round	After 3rd Round
10	10	10	10
9	9	9	9
8	8	8	8
7	7	7	7
6	6	6	6
5	5	5	5
4	4	4	4
3	3	3	3
2	2	2	2
1	1	1	1
0	0	0	0

You may not need to go through three rounds, but it's still a good idea to give yourself that number of columns, just in case.

Step 4, Affirmation Linkup
To make the affirmation more effective and give it more energy, *one* of the following two procedures needs to be performed, so experiment and see which you prefer:

A. LOCATING THE TENDER POINTS
Just below your collarbone are the K27 points (see diagram, page 75). You'll probably feel a slight

indentation there, and they may feel tender or sore (lymphatic congestion often occurs at these points). Gently rub the two sore spots in a circular motion while repeating your affirmation aloud three times.

B. THE KARATE CHOP POINT

The karate chop points are located on the side of each hand, roughly an inch below the little finger (see diagram, page 76). Gently tap either point with your fingertips for as long as it takes to repeat your affirmation aloud three times.

2. The Sequence

This is the part of the EFT process when the energetic disruption from the body is cleared by tapping all the major meridian points.

Step 5, Reminder Phrase

You need a short reminder phrase to keep your attention focused on the problem, which is said aloud each time you tap every one of the meridian points. This is a shortened version of your affirmation, so it might be "This nervous feeling," or "This anger" or "This hurt."

Step 6, Tapping Points

Using two fingers, gently but firmly tap each of the meridian points approximately seven times, from 1 through 12 in sequence, while repeating your reminder phrase. You can tap with either hand, on either side of the body—or even switch halfway through if you want.

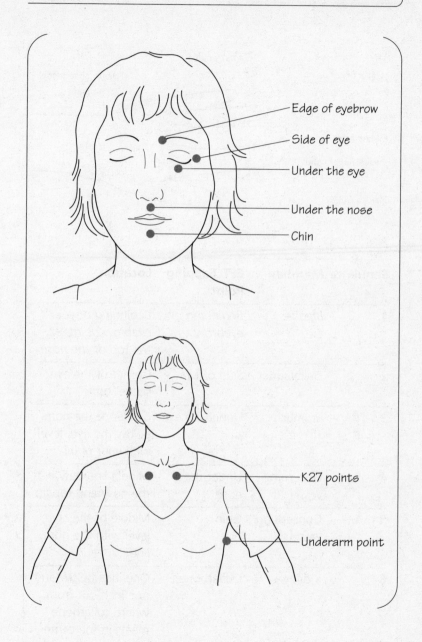

Edge of eyebrow

Side of eye

Under the eye

Under the nose

Chin

K27 points

Underarm point

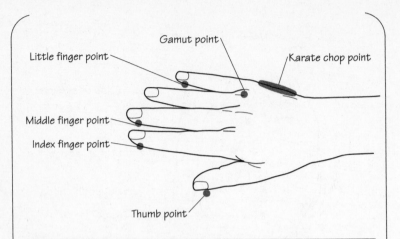

Sequence	Meridian	EFT Tapping Point	Location
1	*Bladder*	*Beginning of eyebrow*	*Beginning of your eyebrow point, at the top of the nose*
2	Gallbladder	Side of eye	Corner of the eye socket bone
3	Stomach	Under the eye	Center of the bone below the eye, level with your pupil
4	Governing vessel	Under the nose	Middle line between the nose and top lip
5	Conception vessel	Chin	Middle of the chin, level with the gum line
6	Kidney	Collarbone	One inch below and one inch out from where collarbone meets in the center, just below the neck

7	Spleen	Underarm	On the torso, under the arm, level with nipple (men) or seam of bra (women)
8	Lung	Thumb	Outside edge of thumb, level with base of thumbnail
9	Large intestine	Index finger	Side edge of index finger (nearest to thumb), level with base of fingernail
10	Circulation/ sex	Middle finger	Side of middle finger (nearest to thumb), level with base of fingernail
11	Heart	Little finger	Side of little finger (nearest to thumb), level with base of fingernail
12	Small intestine	Side of hand	Karate chop point, on side of hand, one inch below little finger

When you have completed this sequence, close your eyes and take a deep breath in and out.

13	Triple warmer	Back of hand (Gamut)	On the back of the hand, half an inch below the knuckles, between the ring and little fingers
14	Liver	Under breast	The liver point is not used in EFT

3. The Gamut

Step 7, The Gamut

The Gamut point is on the back of the hand, half an inch below the knuckles, between the ring finger and little fingers. Tap this point at the same time as performing the eye movements below:

EYE MOVEMENTS
1. Close your eyes.
2. Open your eyes.
3. While holding your head still, look hard down right.
4. While holding your head still, look hard down left.
5. While holding your head still, look hard down right again.
6. While holding your head still, look hard down left again.
7. Keeping your head still, roll your eyes in an anti-clockwise direction.
8. Keeping your head still, roll your eyes in a clock-wise direction.

Take a deep breath in and out, and allow a few moments for your energy to reconfigure.

(These eye movements may seem a strange thing to do, but research suggests that our thoughts, memories, feelings, sensations, sounds and visual images all have their individual storage areas in the brain, and that these different mental functions can be accessed by means of certain eye positions.)

4. The Second Sequence

Step 8, Second Sequence

When you have completed the Gamut procedure, the tapping sequence is repeated a second time, starting from the eyebrow point, through to the karate chop point, repeating the reminder phrase as before.

Step 9, Reassessment

The first round of EFT is now complete, so it is time to check how you are feeling about your original problem by again giving it a score out of ten (in the first round column), to see if there is any difference. Sometimes there will be a huge change, say from ten down to three or two or even zero, but at other times less difference is noted, say from a starting point of eight, down to six or five.

Step 10, Round Adjustments

Depending on the depth of the problem, the emotional intensity level may drop a few points, so if your original feelings are slightly improved but still present, you will need to repeat the EFT round until the feelings resolve, which may take one or two or more further rounds. When performing repeat round adjustments, you need to make slight changes to your initial statement, which tells the unconscious mind that you now wish to clear the remaining feelings that are connected to the problem, rather than the original feelings you had. You can do this by adding the word "still." For example: "Even though I still feel anger, I deeply and completely accept myself," "Even though I still feel afraid, I deeply and completely accept myself" or "Even though I still feel hurt, I deeply and completely accept myself."

Then repeat the whole process from Step 1 through to Step 9, only this time when tapping use a reminder phrase that includes the word "remaining," such as: "This remaining anger," "This remaining fear" or "This remaining guilt."

At this stage you may also find that a completely new aspect or feeling about the same problem surfaces, which is quite common. If this does happen, you may need to formulate a new statement that takes the new feeling into account, and start a whole new EFT round.

Effects During EFT

As you work through the tapping positions you may get a range of physical indications that there is an energy shift going on, such as a need to sigh or yawn or burp (embarrassing but beneficial!), or a feeling of sleepiness or light-headedness. Alternatively, you may experience some emotional indications, such as a feeling of elation or calmness, or sometimes momentary bewilderment or confusion (this soon passes).

A typical EFT session might go like this:

Intensity Score	Reaction	EFT Rounds
10	Terror	1st round
8	Fear	2nd round
6	Apprehension/nervousness	
4	Uncertainty	3rd round
2	Aversion/dislike	
0	Indifference	

If relief doesn't happen immediately after a few rounds of EFT, the changes may still take place over the following few hours or days, which can be because the body needs extra time to incorporate the adjustments that have been made before any of the benefits become apparent. According to Valerie and Paul Lynch, people often achieve insight into their limitations, situations or emotions, and discover where they originated. This is probably because, once the emotional charge is reduced, it is possible to see your circumstances more clearly, and with a more balanced outlook, so you might suddenly realize why you feel a certain way, or recognize the original cause of your problem.

Working with EFT

What Gary Craig believed was that the cause of all negative emotions was a disruption in the body's energy system, so using EFT takes away the pain of negative emotions, but leaves insights and memories. Although a specific problem may really need only one or two meridians activating, his reasoning was that if you tap on all the relevant points, then you're bound to do the ones you need. Essentially, this works because your body probably received programming, e.g., fear of spiders or fear of rejection, when you were small or at another time when you were under severe stress or going through trauma, but it is possible for you to reprogram it. Basically the process is to tap out the negative, and then (if necessary) tap in the positive.

Complete beginners can usually achieve 50 percent success, and experienced practitioners between 80 percent and 98 percent success, because the wording is important, and that's what needs practice. If you follow the process above, you can do it on yourself, but you might also consider going to an EFT practitioner, or taking a course in EFT. There are some contact addresses given in Resources, page 251.

Having examined emotions in general, in the next chapter we look in more detail at anger and how to cope with it.

chapter six

DEALING WITH ANGER

At the beginning of the last chapter, I referred to Dr. Usui's first Principle, "just for today, do not anger," and as I mentioned, initially this may seem an almost impossible request. What I hope to show you in this chapter is that it is possible to handle your anger in different ways, and even to reduce the number of times you feel angry, until you reach a stage where you are calm and centered enough not to feel anger in any but the most extreme circumstances.

WHAT IS ANGER?

Anger is "an emotional state that varies in intensity from mild irritation to intense fury and rage," according to Charles Spielberger, PhD, a psychologist who specializes in the study of anger. An angry response may sometimes feel like the only option, but anger can be a very destructive emotion, and often it hurts us almost as much as it hurts those against whom we direct it, as they are often the people we care about the most. Anger is usually triggered when someone or something fails to meet our expectations, and sometimes—even more important—

when we don't live up to our own expectations. However, like any other emotion, anger is actually a conscious choice, a habitual response you have developed, as mentioned in chapter 5. Expressing anger toward someone rarely achieves anything other than to make you both feel bad, but you *can* break the cycle and choose a different response instead. You can find healthier and safer ways of expressing the frustration that usually lies behind the anger by turning the emotion into creativity, going for a brisk walk or doing that very old-fashioned thing: counting to ten before you speak! Sometimes a short pause is all it takes to defuse a situation and allow you to talk calmly, in an assertive and adult way, rather than sliding into belligerence and aggressiveness.

The next time you feel angry, pause for a moment and ask yourself "why?" What is going on? Is this a replay of something that has happened over and over again? Are you angry about the thing you think you're angry about—such as a partner's insulting comment in front of your friends—or is there something deeper going on, like a general dissatisfaction with your relationship? It's only by asking yourself these sorts of questions that you will begin to unravel the issues which are triggering the emotion of anger and begin the healing process.

A Reiki Technique for Revealing Causes
This technique can generate insight and intuition about the causes of problems, and also helps to calm you down and promote healing of the situation.

1. Decide what situation you want to work on that is generating feelings of anger in you. Continue to think about it throughout the treatment, and let yourself be open to receiving intuition or insight into the causes.

2. Sit or lie down and place one hand at the back of your neck and one hand on the front of your throat, and let Reiki flow for your greatest and highest good for about 5 minutes, or longer if you feel this is necessary.

3. Place one (or both) hands on your crown, and let Reiki flow for 5 minutes or more.

4. Place one hand on your stomach (solar plexus) and the other over your intestines (navel area), and hold your hands there for 5 minutes or more.

5. Remove your hands, gassho (i.e., place your hands in the prayer position in front of the center of your chest, see page 15), give thanks for the Reiki and end with a bow of respect.

6. Spend a few minutes sitting quietly, contemplating any insight or intuition you discovered, and thinking about how this might help you to resolve the situation.

THE PHYSIOLOGY OF ANGER

Like other emotions, anger is accompanied by physiological and biological changes similar to those our prehistoric ancestors experienced as a reaction to danger—what is known as the "fight-or-flight" response. When you get

angry, your body can experience any of the following reactions, depending on the level of emotion you're feeling:

◆ Increase in heart rate and blood pressure
◆ Constriction of blood vessels in some areas of the
  body
◆ Increase in blood sugar levels
◆ Redirection of blood flow away from extremities
  toward major organs
◆ Faster and deeper breathing
◆ Digestion stops or slows down
◆ Increased sweating

These transformations are the result of neurohormonal
changes, especially the production in the adrenal glands
of adrenaline and noradrenaline, which circulate in the
bloodstream and target various organs, such as the heart,
to increase its rate of beating. Another neurohormonal
system also located in the adrenal glands stimulates
increased secretion of corticosteroids, especially cortisol,
which help to prepare the body for action by increasing
the release of glucose and other fuels from stores within
the body. This is one of the reasons why an angry
response can sometimes escalate into physical action—
fighting or brawling—because (literally) your "blood is
up" and you are ready for anything.

The instinctive, natural way to express anger is thus to
respond aggressively. Anger is a natural, adaptive response
to threats, which inspires powerful, often aggressive, feelings and behaviors that allow us to fight and defend
ourselves when we are attacked. A certain amount of
anger, therefore, is necessary to our survival.

Of course, in our ancestors these reactions were always meant to be a short-term answer to an emergency, like running away from a saber-toothed tiger or fighting off an enemy tribe, but in Western society we are rarely in extreme physical danger, so our "stressors" or "anger triggers" are more likely to be psychological in origin. Again, these might be of short duration, but the kind of stress that many people can identify with in modern society tends to be ongoing, chronic and long-term, and this often results in decreased tolerance and increased frustration, and a consequent "short fuse" for our tempers.

If your body is constantly on the alert because of chronic stress—and frequent episodes of anger actually add to the stress load—this ceases to be an adaptive condition and can lead to health problems. The state of heightened physical arousal that anger can induce puts considerable strain on our bodies, and chronic sustained anger can cause or exacerbate digestive disorders such as ulcers and gastritis, create hypertension, raise cholesterol levels, aggravate heart disease, exacerbate bowel conditions and affect the immune system, among other things. Anger therefore isn't a very healthy emotion to have, at least if it is experienced frequently.

EXPERIENCING ANGER

Some of the most common causes of anger include hurt or indignation, frustration or irritation, harassment or persecution, disappointment or regret, and perceived threats. However, the source of all of these feelings is based on unfulfilled expectations, and if you can let go of

87

your expectations, you will be able to let go of your anger. Before you can get to that stage, you might need some help just handling the feelings you are already experiencing.

There are basically two ways of experiencing anger:

1. You can feel angry with yourself in a variety of ways. Perhaps you haven't done as well as you had hoped in a job interview or qualifying exam, or you feel you've let someone down, or you've let yourself down by being late again for an important meeting, or you've lost something, and so on.

2. You can have the other kind of anger which is directed at someone else or some object—so you might be angry with your partner as a result of an argument, or as a reaction to something he or she has done, or you could be angry with a salesperson for not being helpful enough, with a work colleague because he or she has "messed up" in some way or even with the dishwasher because it has broken down.

Some people describe these two ways as:

1. Internal anger that is directed at yourself for something that you have done, or have not done.

2. External anger that is the result of an interaction with another person.

However, these aren't accurate descriptions—both types of anger are actually internally generated, and no one has ever *made* you angry. It has all been your own work! Anger is just one of a whole range of responses you could have to a given set of circumstances, which means it is a choice you have made, even if it doesn't feel like it. That's quite empowering, because if you can choose anger as a response, it also means you can choose some other response instead. There's a phrase I was introduced to many years ago by a colleague, and I've never forgotten it: "If you always do what you've always done, you will always get what you've always gotten."

In other words, if your habitual response to a given set of circumstances is always the same—such as always reacting angrily when your partner does something you don't like—you will always get the same sort of response from him or her, which will probably be defensive, or perhaps mirror your own anger because he or she feels threatened by it. See what I mean? If you can change *your* reaction by perhaps being more understanding of the other person's position because you realize his or her perception of it is different to yours, or feeling less threatened by someone's actions by developing more self-confidence and greater self-esteem, or simply by listening to his or her explanation rather than instantly "sounding off," then you'll get a whole new set of reactions from the people around you.

EXPRESSING ANGER

When we experience anger, we can't always physically or verbally lash out at every person or object that irritates or annoys us—laws, social norms and common sense place limits on how far our anger can take us. People use a variety of both conscious and unconscious processes to deal with their angry feelings, the three main approaches being:

- Expressing
- Suppressing
- Calming

Expressing your angry feelings in an assertive—not aggressive—manner is the healthiest way. To do this, you have to learn how to make clear what your needs are, and how to get them met, without hurting others. Being assertive doesn't mean being pushy or demanding; it means being respectful of yourself and others.

I am not advocating that you should always vent your feelings directly on the person who has triggered angry emotions in you. That can be unwise and even unhealthy—especially if his or her reaction is likely to be to punch you on the nose! Anger can be suppressed at the moment it is experienced, then converted or redirected. You can do this by holding in your anger, ceasing to think about it and focusing on something positive. The aim is to inhibit or suppress your anger, at least for a while, and convert it into more constructive behavior. The problem with this type of response is that if it isn't allowed outward expression at some point, your anger can turn inward, which can potentially cause high blood pressure, or even depression. It can also lead to passive-aggressive behavior, such as getting back at people indirectly, without telling them why, rather than confronting them head-on. People who are constantly putting others down, criticizing everything and making cynical comments almost certainly haven't learned how to constructively express their anger.

However, it is possible to cool down, which means not only controlling your outward behavior, but also controlling your internal responses and taking steps to lower your heart rate, calm yourself down and let the feelings subside.

COPING WITH ANGRY FEELINGS

The goal of anger management is to allow you to deal with your anger at a comfortable pace, in a way that helps to resolve the situation and doesn't create worse problems. I suggested earlier that it would be a good idea to ask yourself why you're feeling angry, but of course at the moment that emotion is aroused, you might think you are much less able to be objective, and certainly less able to be reflective. However, the human thought process is incredibly fast, so it is possible to think through the following stages in a matter of seconds. Before you speak or do anything else:

- Recognize and admit your feelings of anger.
- Identify the target and cause of your anger.
- Consider as many options as possible for responding to the situation, together with their possible results.
- Choose the best option—and follow it through.

Let's look at these stages one at a time. Firstly, recognizing and admitting to yourself that you feel angry is important because it means you are actually considering how you feel, rather than just reacting as if on "autopilot." You are thinking through what is happening, not just going with your first instinctive (habitual) response. Maybe using an example would be helpful here.

Your boss has just dumped a huge load of work on your desk, saying it all has to be done today, but there's only half an hour left of your normal workday, so you know you're being asked to work late again, and it's the third time this week. You feel angry.

Now let's identify the target and cause of your anger.

The immediate target is obviously your boss (although it might be that they have only just had the work dumped on them by their boss!), but the causes might be a lot harder to identify. You might feel resentful because you had other plans, or hurt because you feel you're being taken advantage of, or disgusted because you know your boss is disorganized and could have given you the work earlier, or furious because you don't think you're being paid enough to take this level of responsibility. Identifying what underlies your anger is a really useful step, because it will help you to realize what to do about it.

Then you need to consider what your options are in terms of responding to the situation, and theorize about what results they might have.

◆ You could react angrily, shout at your boss, refuse to do the work and storm out, throwing the words "I quit" behind you, if he or she hasn't already said, "You're fired." Not the most productive reaction, as you've just lost your job!

◆ You could swallow your anger, not say anything to your boss about your plans, and work as fast as you can, not really caring too much if you make mistakes, and leave an hour late, all the time feeling resentful, angry, put upon and generally wishing your boss would fall down a big hole. Again, not very productive, because you haven't gotten rid of the angry feelings: you've just pushed them down, so they're still simmering away, waiting to erupt— which they'll probably do as soon as you get home, which isn't going to be nice for your partner/ family/dog/cat! Also, you've ended up doing something you don't want to do, which is unsatisfactory and will just add to the burden the next time you're called upon to work late.

◆ You could do whatever you can in your last half hour, then just pick up your coat and leave, without saying anything to the boss. However, then you have to face up to the boss the next morning, so you'll probably worry about that all night.

◆ You could do whatever you can in the time, or stay and finish the work, but recognize that this is an ongoing situation and plan to complain to someone about the amount of work you are expected to do. Perhaps your company has a human resources department or union you can turn to, or maybe you could get other staff members on your side, as it's unlikely you're the only one who is having to do more work than is possible in a day. Any of those possibilities could have repercussions, of course, and you wouldn't be making yourself popular with your boss, but sometimes someone needs to stand up for what he or she believes is right, and that someone may have to be you.

◆ You could say quietly but firmly that you have to leave on time today as you have plans for the evening, so you will get done as much as you can in the next half hour. You might also suggest that your boss could prioritize the most urgent work in the pile, and you'll start immediately on that, and maybe some of the work could be passed over to other staff members if there are any. Being assertive, rather than aggressive, is often the best response, and surprisingly often engenders much more respect from employers than submissive behavior. Of course, it is a risk—some employers won't react favorably, but standing up for yourself will usually make you feel better about yourself than meekly giving in. There is really no excuse for bosses who take advantage of their employees' good nature— it's exploitative.

◆ And of course, you could send Reiki to the situation. See the simple method below.

These are just a few ideas for dealing with one situation, but your situation may be completely different and need alternative ways of coping, but hopefully you'll find something helpful in the process I've illustrated.

SENDING REIKI TO A SITUATION

The easiest way to do this is to write down your circumstances on a piece of paper, such as: "Let Reiki flow to the situation of my boss giving me extra work too late in the day," and hold the paper between your hands, allowing Reiki to flow into it for at least 5–10 minutes, or until you begin to notice a change in the way you feel about it. (If you have Reiki Second Degree, you can draw the Distant symbol in the air over the paper to connect to the situation, then draw the Harmony symbol to bring peace and harmony to the situation and finally draw the Power symbol to bring the Reiki in.) Sometimes using Reiki in this way actually produces insight into the best way to deal with the situation, but because the Reiki will also flow to your boss's Higher Self, it can impact the way he or she behaves, too. Try it—it can be amazingly powerful!

SAFER WAYS OF EXPRESSING ANGER

Basically you have choices to make. You can express your anger directly and verbally, which is sometimes risky, but if you are polite, don't shout, and own the anger, that is you don't blame the other person, and don't just "blow up," it can sometimes work well. By "owning" the anger, I mean saying "I am feeling angry about what you've just said/done," rather than saying "You've really made me angry now"—because the other person hasn't made you angry, you've just chosen to react that way. You can then go on to discuss in a calmer and more adult way what it is about what he or she has said or done that you don't like, so there's then a chance to resolve the state of affairs.

Sometimes using humor will help to defuse a situation, or you might want to let whatever it is pass this time, giving yourself time to think it through properly so you know how to face up to it next time it happens. Often it's a good idea to look at the situation in a different way. Try putting yourself in the other person's place to see if you can understand why he or she is doing or saying something; no one's perspective on the world is the same as anyone else's, so maybe there are things going on in that person's life that you don't know about, and that are making him or her behave that way.

Perhaps you need to talk over your feelings with someone you trust—a friend or counselor—to get a different perspective on the issue, because if bad situations go on for a long time, it's easy to blow things out of proportion, but not easy to see that that's what we've done, so a neutral third party can really help us to "see the forest for the trees."

Sometimes just letting out a scream of frustration (obviously somewhere private!) or slamming a door can help to release the tension. If you've had a bad day at work and traveled in your own car, use the drive home as an opportunity to say aloud all those things you wish you'd been able to say, as if the source of the aggravation was with you, so that by the time you get home you've "gotten it off your chest" and can get on with the rest of your day with a smile. If you're traveling home on public transportation where talking aloud wouldn't be an option, you could close your eyes and imagine yourself saying what you wanted to say, and imagine the situation being resolved happily. Or maybe you need to let out the day's annoyances by doing something physical, like jogging, cycling or swimming. You can of course also choose to let go of the issue, and decide that it isn't worth getting angry about—another version of this Principle is "just for today, I will let go of anger!"

There are other things you can do to help cope with anger, such as deep breathing (see page 41), giving yourself Reiki for a few minutes to help to calm yourself (see page 68), going somewhere private and carrying out a Reiki Shower, a technique for imagining Reiki flowing over your whole body to flush away negativity and unwanted emotions (see below), or meditating quietly until you receive some insight on the problem. They might not be the first things you think of when anger strikes, but as you get better at coping with it, you'll find it easier to be more accepting of other people's attitudes and behavior, and it will then be easier to take a calmer and more centered approach.

THE REIKI SHOWER

This is a technique from the Japanese tradition that is suitable for anyone with any level of Reiki. It consists of activating and cleansing your whole energy body (within your physical body and outside it throughout your aura) by absorbing Reiki energy like a shower. You can use this technique almost anywhere for cleansing and calming yourself, and it also helps to center you, raising your consciousness and bringing you into a pleasantly meditative state. It can be carried out either sitting in a chair or standing.

1. Stand or sit, and make yourself comfortable, place your hands in the gassho (prayer) position, with your palms together, fingers pointing upward, and your hands held close to your body at the level of the heart chakra. Stay like this for a few moments, letting your breathing become slower and deeper, and *intend* to carry out a Reiki Shower.

2. Then separate your hands and lift them above your head, as high as possible, keeping them about 12–15 inches apart. Wait for a few moments until you begin to feel the Reiki building up between your hands, then turn your palms downward so that they are facing the top of your head.

3. Visualize Reiki flowing out of your hands, and *intend* that you be receiving a shower of Reiki energy, which flows over and through your whole physical and energy body, cleansing you and removing any negative energy or emotions.

4. When you sense the vibration of the Reiki energy flowing over and through you, move your hands, palms still facing toward you, and begin to draw them slowly down over your face and body, keeping your hands about 12–15 inches away from your body. *Intend* that Reiki be flowing from your hands, and continuing to cleanse and revitalize you as

98

you draw your hands all the way down your body, and then down your legs to your feet, eventually turning your palms to face the floor, and either touching the floor or gently throwing the energy off your hands so that any negative energy flows out and into the earth below, for transformation.

5. Repeat this exercise a few times—I find three times to be ideal—and you should feel cleansed, calm and relaxed.

6. Place your hands together again in the gassho position, and spend a few moments experiencing gratitude for the Reiki, and then finish. You may find it helpful to clap your hands once or twice, to help you to return to a more wakeful state if you feel a bit "spacey."

OTHER HELPFUL TECHNIQUES

If you have access to the Internet you'll find lots of information on anger management, and there are some good ideas out there. Some of them are old standards, like deep breathing and meditation, but others are newer techniques that are gaining popularity, like forms of acupressure such as EFT (see chapter 5). There are many books around nowadays on positive psychology and achieving happiness—there are beneficial effects on brain chemistry of being positive, smiling and laughing, so you might choose to read up on that. I would recommend *The Endorphin Effect* by William Bloom, or any of the books by Robert Holden.

Talking about your feelings to someone you know and trust, and who will take you seriously but be supportive, is often a good choice, but sometimes talking directly to the person who triggers your anger is a necessary part of healing the situation between the two of you, because if you never clear the air the situation usually just gets worse. Many people fear hurting someone else's feelings if they share their angry feelings with that person, but holding on to anger often makes you behave differently, so the other person ends up feeling hurt anyway, and that can damage the relationship. You just need to be careful how you say things—it's important not to be accusatory or judgmental, and to give the other person a chance to have his or her say, without you reacting angrily to that person's thoughts or beliefs.

Each of us has the right to be ourselves, and sometimes huge fights can be the result of very small differences of opinion that could be sorted out quite easily if we could just feel safe with each other. Agreeing to spend time talking things over is the first step toward solving the problem, although sometimes it helps to have a "neutral" person around as a potential arbiter, such as a relationship counselor.

Another possibility is to write down your feelings, which is a good way of getting them "out there," rather than keeping them stuck inside. I would, however, advise that it is *not* a good idea to let the person you're writing about see what you've written. By all means, write him or her a letter and put in it all the stuff you'd like to say— but don't send it. Instead, hold a little ceremony where you burn the letter (in a safe place, like a metal saucepan so you can put the lid on afterward to make sure the flames go out properly) and let the smoke take your anger with it, to be healed and transformed, so you know you have truly let go of the issue.

INDIVIDUAL PERCEPTION

The problem we all have is that we generally only see things from our own perspective, and often assume that the way we see things is the way others see things. This is often at the root cause of problems with other people, which in turn can lead to the development of negative emotions like anger. Given the same trigger, under the same conditions, some people will laugh off frustration, others will express mild irritation and others still will get into a rage, stamping their feet and shouting. Each person will have perceived the situation differently, and will have reacted in a different way according to how that person has individually learned to manage and demonstrate his or her feelings. There is a Neuro-Linguistic Programming (NLP) technique called Perceptual Positions which can help you to consider other viewpoints on an issue or situation.

Neuro-Linguistic Programming (NLP)

I trained to became an NLP practitioner in the 1990s, and have found many of the techniques to be really helpful as an addition to my Reiki practice, so this is something I'd like to introduce to you. NLP was developed in the midseventies by a linguist, John Grinder, and a mathematician, Richard Bandler, who had strong interests in successful people, psychology, language and computer programming. They developed a range of communication and persuasion techniques, including self-hypnosis, to help people to motivate and change themselves, and to create greater self-esteem, by reprogramming their brains. At another level, NLP is about self-discovery, exploring identity and relating to the "spiritual" part of human experience that reaches beyond us as individuals to our family, community and global systems.

PERCEPTUAL POSITIONS TECHNIQUE

Most NLP techniques are deceptively simple—that is, they create change quickly and easily by reprogramming the way you think. In this technique you are asked to look at a particular situation, such as one that could potentially become an angry exchange between you and a colleague or family member, from three perspectives—Self, Other and Observer—using your imagination to gather information and explore your feelings. This may sound a bit strange, but I can assure you it really works.

Place three pieces of paper on the floor, or just imagine three distinct spaces, as below:

SELF   OTHER

OBSERVER

1. Decide what situation you are going to consider—something that might trigger anger in you—including who the interaction is with, and what subject or situation the two of you might be discussing.

2. First, stand on the SELF space, and think about the situation and get as much information as possible—what do you see, what do you hear, what do you feel?

3. Then move to the OTHER space, and imagine that you are the other person. Now what do you see, what do you hear, what do you feel?

4. Then move to the OBSERVER space, and consider the interaction between SELF and OTHER. As an impartial and benevolent observer, you make no judgments, but simply gather information about the relationship between SELF and OTHER. What do you see, what do you hear, what do you believe is going on?

5. Finally, move back to the SELF space, and allow the insights from the other two perspectives to be integrated into your own perceptions. How have they altered how you see things? How have they altered how you hear things? How have they altered how you feel?

6. Step into a neutral space (i.e., not in one of the three positions), and spend some time assimilating what has happened, perhaps by writing it down, or by sitting quietly and thinking about it. Become aware of new possibilities of behavior and language that may enable you to achieve your desired outcome and enhance the relationship between the two of you.

STRATEGIES TO KEEP ANGER AT BAY

Learn to be More Tolerant, Compassionate and Accepting

When we get angry, it is usually because we are intolerant of other people's views, beliefs or behavior, and therefore cannot accept something that someone has said or done—or perhaps his or her age or gender or sexual orientation, or anything else that is in some way different. Developing tolerance could help us, potentially, to live without anger.

The point is, people who demonstrate what we might call intolerant behavior generally don't think, feel or believe that they are being intolerant. They see nothing wrong in what they are doing or saying, because it accurately reflects their own values and life experience. It is all they know. Every person's life involves developing a value system by which he or she lives. We form our value systems based on our life experiences, and that naturally starts with what we see and hear as children, and goes on developing as we become teenagers and then adults. The main problem is that most of us don't realize that other people don't necessarily think or feel the same way we do. However, if we could respect the rights of individuals to be who they are, and develop a strong and positive acceptance of other people's differences, and an appreciation of why those differences exist, we could become more tolerant.

◆ If we could generate a climate of understanding, perhaps people wouldn't feel they had to stick so rigidly to their own ideas, but would instead recognize that other people's ideas had value too, so some sensible compromises could be reached.

◆ If we could generate a climate of compassion, perhaps we would recognize that everyone becomes the person they are because of the sum of their experiences so far, so maybe then we wouldn't judge others so harshly.

◆ If we could generate a climate of acceptance, perhaps we wouldn't need to feel challenged by people's differences, but instead could all learn to accept that each person is unique, with his or her own unique way of thinking, feeling and seeing the world, so we wouldn't always expect that person to think and behave like us, but instead could accept the strength in variety and diversity.

Learn to Be More Forgiving

Forgiveness is the mental and/or spiritual process of ceasing to feel resentment, indignation or anger toward another person for a perceived offense, difference or mistake, or ceasing to demand punishment or restitution. In order to forgive someone, you first have to judge that what he or she has said or done is wrong. Of course, I can almost hear the reactions from some readers—that there are awful things that some people do, which must be considered wrong. However, we *all* do what we believe is right, at least most of the time, and under certain circumstances we could *all* do things that we currently wouldn't contemplate. For example, however "civilized" you might think you are, if you are a parent, you would probably be prepared to kill to protect your children if they were under serious threat—it's a basic instinct. If your children were starving and there was no other way, you would probably be prepared to steal food, or money to buy food. You would justify to yourself that those actions were not wrong, under those circumstances. "There but for the grace of God go I" is a phrase that comes to mind.

Sometimes we do need to "forgive and forget" to help us to move on. *Beliefs divide us. Emotions can unite us.* While the ideal might be to view everyone as just living their lives the best way they can, and seeing them as "spirits having a human experience" and just learning whatever they need to learn in this life, we are still human. Sometimes it's tough to try to understand someone else's motivation if he or she does or says something that hurts us, or hurts those we love. But we can try it just for today. You might find the following visualization helpful.

FORGIVENESS VISUALIZATION

Try this by thinking of one person to start with, although when you've practiced it for a while you could visualize a small group of people, such as some members of your family or several work colleagues.

♦ Settle yourself comfortably and relax by breathing deeply and evenly, and when you are ready, imagine yourself on one side of a fast-flowing river.

♦ Take some time to make the image as real as you can—it can be a river you know, or one you just imagine—but try to see, feel and smell the whole scene, the grass or sand or pebbles on the river-bank, the blue sky and warm sun, the smell of wild flowers, the sound of the running water and bird-song.

◆ When you have the picture firmly in mind, look across to the other side of the river, and see or sense a person standing there. This is a person with whom you have felt angry, and whom you have decided to connect with in this visualization.

◆ Let the picture fill out so that you see what he or she is wearing, and maybe see the expression on his or her face.

◆ Now ask Reiki and your Higher Self to help you to develop understanding and forgiveness of this person, and of yourself, and see or sense a bridge beginning to form between you, over the river.

◆ It may be very wispy to begin with, but gradually a good, strong bridge is created. It may appear to be made of brick or stone, wood or metal, or it may even consist of stepping-stones, but now there is a connection between the two sides of the river.

◆ If it still doesn't look solid, ask Reiki and your Higher Self to help again by giving you confidence and allowing you to trust the process. (If you have Reiki Second Degree, you can imagine the Distant symbol stretching out in front of you to create the bridge.)

◆ Next, step onto the bridge, and begin to walk across it, but pause in the middle. Hopefully the person on the other side has also started to walk across it toward you, but if not, just wait a little longer.

◆ Then imagine Reiki flowing out of your hands and filling your aura, and spreading out in front of you across the bridge to encompass and enfold the other person in Reiki, and ask Reiki to heal the differences between you, to create harmony and calm. (You can imagine the Harmony symbol for this, too.)

◆ When you can meet in the middle of the bridge, which is a neutral space for you both, allow the other person to say whatever he or she needs to say, without judging it. You are talking soul to soul, so what the other person says is the truth as he or she knows it, even if it is not the same as the truth as you see it.

◆ When the other person has finished talking, speak your truth to him or her, and ask that Reiki flow into the situation to help you to create an atmosphere of forgiveness and trust. This may take a few minutes, but be patient, and eventually you will feel a spread of calmness throughout your body, and you will know that you have forgiven each other at a soul level.

◆ Imagine yourselves shaking hands, or hugging each other, as appropriate, and smile, thanking him or her for being present, and thanking Reiki and your Higher Selves for being present and helping in this situation.

◆ Turn and walk back to your side of the river, step off the bridge and let the bridge slowly dissolve.

- Wave and smile at the person on the other side of the bank, then gradually let your awareness of the present return as you feel the chair or bed beneath you and hear the sounds in the room.
- Finally, write down what you have experienced, so that you can reach even greater insight and understanding at a later date.

Learn to Calm Down and Relax

If you feel yourself getting angry, don't let the feeling build up until you have a violent outburst; try to calm down and relax instead. If you find it difficult to relax, there are books and courses that can help, but simple relaxation tools, such as deep breathing and relaxing visualizations, can be an aid to calming angry feelings. Here are some simple steps you can try. If you practice them regularly, you'll be able to use them automatically when you're in a tense situation.

- Breathe deeply, into your diaphragm, hold your breath for as long as is comfortable, then release it quite quickly, and you will find that your whole body relaxes.
- Visualize yourself in a beautiful place, like a woodland glade, or sitting beside a lake, or on a mountaintop with wonderful views around you, and hold that image in your mind until you feel yourself calming down.
- Do some nonstrenuous, slow stretching (yoga exercises), which can relax your muscles and make you feel calmer.

Learn to Express Yourself Calmly and Assertively

Try to express angry feelings in an assertive manner, using calm, logical words rather than violence. If you are having, or expecting to have, a heated discussion, slow down—think carefully about what you want to say, be clear about what you are asking and how it can be achieved and listen carefully to the other person, remembering that everyone is entitled to his or her own opinion. We all have our own communication style, which can be just a habit, or could be something we've copied from the way our parents or other adults spoke when we were children.

Most communication styles can be classified as aggressive, nonassertive or assertive.

Aggressive

Anger often results in aggressive behavior, but whether this is expressed directly or indirectly, it always communicates an impression of superiority and disrespect. By being aggressive we put our wants, needs and rights above those of others, and we attempt to get our way by not allowing others a choice, so it is often seen as bullying.

Examples: "That was a stupid thing to do." "You're always interrupting me."

Nonassertive

This is passive and indirect, and it communicates a message of inferiority. By being nonassertive we allow the wants, needs and rights of others to be more important than our own.

Examples: "I'm not very good at this sort of thing." "Well, all right, if that's what you want to do."

Assertive

Being assertive, rather than aggressive, communicates an impression of self-respect and respect for others. By being assertive we view our wants, needs and rights as equal with those of others. We work toward "win–win" outcomes (i.e., those that are successful for each party). An assertive person wins by influencing, listening and negotiating, so that others choose to cooperate willingly. This behavior leads to success without retaliation, and encourages honest, open relationships.

Examples: "I'm sorry I can't go, I have other plans." "That idea might not work, so perhaps we could look at some other options together."

Assertiveness requires us to accept responsibility for our thoughts, feelings and behavior, and requires us to respect the thoughts, feelings and behavior of others. You cannot be solely responsible for the feelings of others because you do not "make them feel." You are responsible for what you say and do because your words and actions invite others to feel certain emotions, but what they feel is up to them. When an individual accepts these responsibilities and stops blaming others for his or her feelings, that person has taken a giant step toward communicating in a sensible, adult way.

To communicate thoughts, feelings and opinions assertively, you need to choose words that are direct, honest, appropriate and respectful.

◆ Use "I statements" rather than "you statements," and own your own feelings rather than blaming someone else. Example: "I felt unhappy when you said that" rather than "what you said made me feel unhappy."

111

- Use factual descriptions instead of judgments or exaggerations. Example: "this letter needs retyping because some punctuation is missing" rather than "this work is terrible."
- Use clear, direct requests or directives (commands) when you want others to do something, rather than hinting, being indirect or presuming. Example: "please make three copies of this document" rather than "I need three copies of this document."

Learn a New Lifestyle

Some aspects of our lifestyles can lead to more frequent problems with anger, so by making some helpful changes you can reap great benefits:

- Exercise regularly—walking, cycling, swimming—to help to work off tension and stress.
- Take part in yoga or meditation classes to help to release tension in a controlled, healthy way.
- Eat healthfully, including plenty of fresh vegetables and fruits in your diet, and cutting out as many additives and preservatives as you can, as these can have detrimental effects on your mood.
- Keep your alcohol consumption within the daily recommended intake of one drink for women and two drinks for men. Alcohol lowers your inhibitions, which can trigger violent behavior.
- Spend as little time as possible in stressful environments or with people who affect you negatively, and schedule some time for relaxation and unwinding.
- Express your feelings in healthy ways, either by talking to a friend or creatively through painting or writing.

SEEKING HELP FOR ANGER
OR AGGRESSION

Some people need more help than others to address their anger or aggression problems, but if that includes you, don't feel embarrassed about seeking professional help. People who are angry and aggressive do need to take responsibility for their actions—blaming others isn't helpful—but looking back at your past might help you to understand your current angry behavior. For example, if your parents or other family members set bad examples and resolved conflicts angrily or aggressively, you might not have learned to deal with anger constructively. It is possible to change your anger patterns, and professional services can help to improve anger management.

You might consider taking a course to learn more about how to be assertive, rather than aggressive, and your local library or college might have details of suitable classes.

Counseling or Cognitive Behavioral Therapy (looking at how you think and behave) can help you to consider your thinking and behavior associated with anger, and you could find a suitable therapist through your doctor. He or she might also direct you to an anger management program, which could be a weekend course or regular evening sessions including both one-to-one and group work.

USE THE REIKI PRINCIPLES
AS AFFIRMATIONS

If you keep repeating the phrase to yourself "just for today, do not anger," when you feel yourself becoming irritated, that can help. You can also turn it into a positive affirmation, and keep telling yourself "today I will be cool, calm and relaxed," and that can be even more beneficial.

To conclude, you will always come across situations that could potentially provoke anger, but the key is to take responsibility for your own reactions and behavior by addressing angry feelings with new coping mechanisms and responses, using the various Reiki techniques and other methods described in this chapter and chapter 5, which I hope will, eventually, lead to you "living without anger."

In Part 4, we look at the second of Dr. Usui's Principles, "just for today, do not worry," and consider the power of thought, and how it is possible to stop worrying and start living.

part four

LIVING WITHOUT WORRY

Worry wounds the body,
Contemplation heals the mind,
Meditation unites the spirit.
Reverend Simon John Barlow

chapter seven

UNDERSTANDING THOUGHTS AND THE POWER OF WORDS

"Just for today, do not worry" is the second of the Principles passed on to us by Dr. Usui, and for many this also may seem a difficult, if not impossible, request. Some people are described as "born worriers," and the way they react to life is to agonize about almost everything—even to the extent of worrying that they haven't got anything to worry about! What I hope to show you in this and the next chapter is that worrying can be a habit, and like any habit, it is possible to break it, so you can change your thinking patterns to be more positive, which is a happier and healthier alternative. Chapter 8 examines worry in more depth, but worry is just one form of thinking that can disturb our mental state and make it more difficult to "live the Reiki way," so first we look at the process of thinking, as it controls so much of what we say and do.

THE BRAIN AND THINKING

Thought or thinking is a mental process that allows you to model the world, or, in other words, to bring the world into focus in a way that you can make sense of, which helps you to deal with it effectively. A thought may be an idea, image, sound, smell or touch, or even an emotional feeling that arises from the brain, because it is usually your thoughts that generate your emotions. When you are thinking, your brain is manipulating information, which is what is happening when you form concepts and engage in problem solving, reasoning and making decisions. Other brain functions include arousal, attention, concentration, consciousness, language, learning, memory, motor coordination, perception and planning. There are three parts to your brain:

1. The brain stem, or physical (reptilian) brain, which acts on a subconscious level and controls such things as breathing, heart rate, muscles and sleep, and any instinctive processes, such as reacting to danger.
2. The limbic or emotional brain, which controls emotions and motivation, and also acts as a filter for all the information your brain receives (which is why it is easier to remember things that happened when your emotions were aroused, either positively, when you were happy or successful, or negatively, when you were sad or frightened).
3. The cerebral cortex, or thinking brain, which is divided into two halves: the left hemisphere, which is responsible for logic, analysis, fact, language, mathematics and sequence thinking; and the right

hemisphere, which is responsible for creative thinking, rhyme, rhythm, music, pictures, daydreaming and visualizing.

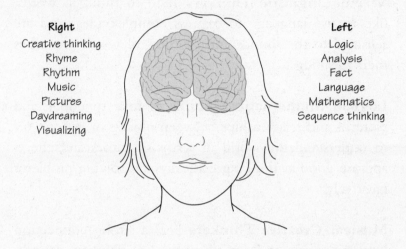

Right
Creative thinking
Rhyme
Rhythm
Music
Pictures
Daydreaming
Visualizing

Left
Logic
Analysis
Fact
Language
Mathematics
Sequence thinking

There has been a lot of research into the different functions of the two halves of your thinking brain, and people sometimes describe themselves as either "left brain thinkers" or "right brain thinkers." While this can certainly be a useful image to use, in reality it's not correct, because everyone has the ability to use both parts of his or her brain, although each of us does seem to have one side that is slightly more dominant.

Thinking Styles

Whichever hemisphere of our brain we consider might be dominant, we don't all think in the same way. An important aspect of our personalities and the way we react to the world is our thinking style, and you might like to have a guess at which style of the following nine you feel most at home with, although most of us probably

119

reflect two or three styles, with one being more frequently used.

Verbal/Linguistic Thinkers Tend to think in words, like to use language to express complex ideas and are sensitive to the sounds and rhythms of words as well as their meanings.

Logical/Mathematical Thinkers Like to understand patterns and relationships between objects or actions, try to understand the world in terms of causes and effects and are good at thinking critically and solving problems creatively.

Musical/Creative Thinkers Feel a strong connection between music and emotions, tend to think in sounds, may also think in rhythms and melodies and are sensitive to the sounds and rhythms of words as well as their meanings.

Spatial/Visual Thinkers Tend to think in pictures, think well in three dimensions, have a flair for working with objects and can develop good mental models of the physical world.

Body/Kinesthetic Thinkers Tend to think in movements, so they like to use their bodies in skillful and expressive ways, and have an aptitude for working with their hands.

Interpersonal Thinkers Like to think about other people and try to understand them, so they recognize differences between individuals and appreciate that different people have different perspectives, and usually make an effort to cultivate effective relationships with family, friends and colleagues.

Intrapersonal Thinkers Spend a lot of time thinking about and trying to understand themselves, so they reflect on their thoughts and moods, work to improve them and try to understand how their behavior affects their relationships with others.

Naturalist Thinkers Like to understand the natural world and the living beings that inhabit it, often have an aptitude for communicating with animals and try to understand patterns of life and natural forces.

Existential Thinkers Like to spend time thinking about philosophical issues such as "What is the meaning of life?" so they consider moral and ethical implications of problems as well as practical solutions, try to see beyond the "here and now" and understand deeper meanings.

I think I'm mostly a mix between Spatial/Visual, Interpersonal and Existential thinking styles, with perhaps a touch of Verbal, since I'm a writer, but maybe the people who know me best might not agree. The point is that your style of thinking may be quite different from that of another person, so when you're having a conversation, you might "hear" things differently, or in other words, you'll mentally highlight different things. This often shows up in your language. Someone who thinks visually will often use words like "see," "look" and "examine," whereas someone who thinks kinesthetically might frequently use "feel," "in touch" and "handle." That doesn't mean the rest of us can't use those words, of course, but we do tend to emphasize words that sum up the way we relate to life.

Another important aspect of your thinking process is whether you generally view things from a positive or a negative perspective. This is often described as seeing things from a "glass half full" or "glass half empty" viewpoint, but from a metaphysical perspective, each thought has an energetic vibration, so it does actually matter whether you think optimistically or pessimistically.

THE ENERGETIC CONNECTION

Scientists have proved that everything in the Universe is energy—planets, people, animals, birds, fish, insects, plants, rocks, crystals and even manufactured goods like refrigerators and TVs (because they are made from things that were once natural materials). All energy is part of a continuum from dense, slow-moving energy with low vibrations at one end, which is things we can see—that is, physical matter—to light, fast-moving energy with high vibrations at the other end—which is spiritual energy, or consciousness—which we can't see, and everything that exists has its place somewhere on this continuum.

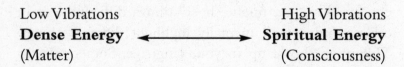

Low Vibrations   High Vibrations

Dense Energy ⟷ **Spiritual Energy**

(Matter)   (Consciousness)

This includes thoughts, which are fast-moving, high-vibrational energy. We may not be able to see them, but their energies can be detected by sensitive scientific equipment. Each thought has a different vibrational frequency, and there is a theory that these frequencies attract people, situations and experiences toward you that have a similar frequency. For example, if you are thinking pessimistic thoughts, they have a fairly low vibration, so you are likely to attract situations, such as being unsuccessful when applying for a job, which "prove" that your pessimism was accurate. However, if you are thinking in an optimistic way, that has a slightly higher vibration which will attract more success into your life, thus "proving," again, that your thoughts and expectations were valid.

You may have heard of this theory recently as something called "cosmic ordering," and there are now lots of self-help books expounding the theory, such as *The Secret* by Rhonda Byrne and *Life Is a Gift* by Gill Edwards. According to the theory, everything you think, feel, say or do produces energetic vibrations that attract toward you whatever you are thinking about or feeling. Basically, *you get what you focus on*. Therefore thoughts and emotions with higher vibrations—positivity, joy, love—attract much more of what you want in life, whereas thoughts and emotions with lower vibrations—fear, doubt, worry—block whatever you are yearning for, and keep you in the same fearful, doubting, worrisome situations.

YOU ARE WHAT YOU THINK

From this perspective, "you are what you think." If your thoughts are energy, vibrating at different rates, each attracting to you those things to which you give most of your attention, this means that you are constantly creating your own reality, and what you think about yourself is what you become; how you think life is, is what it turns out to be for you.

Above I referred to the energy continuum, which spreads at one end from dense physical matter to the other end, which is spiritual energy or consciousness. Human consciousness is made up of a person's subconscious self, his or her conscious self, or ego/personality, and a super-conscious, sometimes referred to as the Higher Self, or spiritual insight and guidance. The "self" can therefore be defined as a continuum of awareness, and every thought or emotion you have is a tiny fragment of that awareness.

Subconscious   Conscious Self   Super-conscious

1. The **Super-conscious**, or Higher Self, is the part of us that we might call our soul or spirit; our true self that is fully connected to the God/Goddess consciousness and that has full knowledge of our life purpose and the lessons and experiences we have chosen for this life. It is the very wise part of ourselves that is totally loving and supportive, and always working with us for our greatest and highest good by subtly guiding us and providing us with intuition and

deep insight, whether we choose to acknowledge and act on this wisdom or ignore it. (This is the level through which we channel the pure, loving, healing Reiki energy.)

2. The **Conscious Self**, sometimes referred to as the ego, is who we think we are, in other words, our thinking, speaking, acting self, our personality, beliefs, attitudes, concepts, likes, dislikes and so on—everything that makes us recognizable as ourselves. The Conscious Self is not necessarily aware of the helpful insights provided by either the Higher Self or the Subconscious, but can operate independently until such time as a person is ready to begin to discover more about themselves, developing and growing personally and spiritually so that they become more "in tune" with the other aspects of their consciousness.

3. The **Subconscious**, which works with the Higher Self to provide intuition and insight to the Conscious Self through dreams, visualizations, instinctive "feelings" or "gut reactions," and other aspects of the mind–body connection.

Your consciousness, or thinking, feeling self, is constantly creating thoughts—as mentioned earlier, more than 60,000 thoughts each day—but unfortunately your consciousness is often locked in the past, so it keeps re-creating the same old patterns, based on the same old thoughts and beliefs about yourself, your abilities, your body and the world around you. This can result in what is termed "Faulty Thinking."

Faulty Thinking

At the beginning of this chapter I said that your thoughts generate your emotions, and of course your emotions demonstrate how you feel about life. "Faulty thinking" contributes to or creates the most upsetting emotions, including anger, guilt, anxiety, resentment and poor self-esteem. Some examples of faulty thinking are:

◆ **Black-and-white thinking** You see things in a polarized way—good or bad, positive or negative, success or failure—rather than considering that most things probably fall in the middle ground.

◆ **Blaming** You refuse to accept disappointment or human failings if other people let you down, and become bitter or resentful.

◆ **Comparing** You compare yourself unfavorably with other people, either those you know, or famous people you've never met, such as those who exist in the celebrity culture of the Western world today.

◆ **Filtering** You filter out or ignore the positives and home in on the negatives of a situation.

◆ **Jumping to conclusions** You assume the worst or interpret other people's motives, actions or comments negatively.

◆ **Labeling** You live with an uncomplimentary label for yourself, such as thinking you're stupid or lazy, or you label others in an equally uncomplimentary way.

◆ **Mind reading** You think you know what other people are thinking, basing your ideas on what you might think under similar circumstances.

◆ **Overgeneralizing** You draw negative conclusions

about yourself, other people or life situations, based on limited evidence.

♦ **Personalizing** You incorrectly assume that other people's reactions are directed at you, or you feel responsible for things that are not your fault.

♦ **Predicting catastrophe** You focus on negative outcomes such as potential failure, rejection or loss, and therefore make yourself anxious.

Each person's mind is filled with an internal dialogue most of the time—what we call the "monkey mind"—as thoughts, judgments and feelings ceaselessly swirl around it, and these beliefs and assumptions create your reality, your perception of the world you live in. Each person's reality is different from every other person's reality. In effect, no two people share exactly the same world, because no two people share exactly the same thoughts and beliefs, since no two people have shared exactly the same life experiences—even identical twins.

PSYCHOLOGICAL PROGRAMMING

Just as with the emotional programming referred to in chapter 5, your beliefs and ways of thinking are the product of programming that began when you were a small child. The way you think about yourself, and your beliefs about everything in your life—from money, work and status through to love, sex and relationships, and even whether you are mostly "laid-back" about things or tend to be a "worrier"—have all been founded on how your parents, teachers and other significant adults behaved, and what they thought and believed. If as a child you experienced a lot of negative programming from parents or other adults who believed that "life is a struggle," or "nothing ever works out right" or "people can't be trusted" and other such judgmental beliefs, then these beliefs will probably inform your attitudes and concepts now. However, just as with your emotional programming, you can let go of your psychological programming, the ways of thinking that no longer serve you, and make up your own mind. You can give yourself permission to change.

I use the word "permission" deliberately, because changing your beliefs, concepts and thinking patterns can be quite a challenging process. You may have had these ways of thinking for many years, so they have become an essential part of you, but if they are now limiting you or holding you back, then it is time to let them go.

Whatever our thinking style, when we look at the way we live our life, we usually have only one perspective on it—our own—and that isn't generally very objective. Your perspective on yourself and your life is limited by your personal view of the world, your own experiences, the concepts, attitudes and beliefs you have. It's therefore hardly surprising that we sometimes (or most times!) limit ourselves and stop ourselves from doing things we want to do, because often we have formed well-scripted reasons why we shouldn't, couldn't, mustn't, oughtn't, etc. What would it be like if you could look at things from other perspectives? What new ideas or thoughts or beliefs could you explore? This exercise is designed to help you to do just that.

CHANGING PERSPECTIVES

Spend a few minutes deciding what you want to work on—think of something you want to do and think you could do, but something is stopping you, and you would like to respond differently. It is helpful to write down your responses as you go through the exercise, so that you can think about them later on.

1. Write down what it is you would like to do, and what seem to be the things (or people or situations, etc.) that limit you.
2. Ask yourself how the situation would be from the following perspectives, and what you believe these people would say to you, and write down your ideas:
   (a) A friend who is accepting and respectful
   (b) A mentor or guide
   (c) A curious, adventurous five-year-old child
   (d) An alien—from any planet of your choice!
   (e) A person who would think the opposite of you about the situation
3. Ask yourself how you would respond differently if you were 10 or even 20 years younger than you are now (i.e., not 10 years ago, but in the present, at a younger age).
4. Ask yourself how you would respond differently if you were 10 or 20 years older than you are now (not in 20 years time, but now, at an older age).
5. If the situation was humorous, what would you be laughing at?

6. What is the "bigger picture" of which this situation is only a part?
7. Consider your viewpoint now that you have looked at the situation from other perspectives.
   (a) How do you perceive the situation differently? Has your own perspective shifted?
   (b) What new and different possibilities are there now as a result of looking at the situation from multiple points of view?
8. Spend a little time thinking about how the whole exercise has affected you, then perhaps give yourself some Reiki for a while, either a full self-treatment, or simply place your hands on your chest or solar plexus and let the Reiki flow into you.

THE POWER OF WORDS

The words you say to yourself, the words that other people say to you (especially in childhood) or that you hear on TV or in films, and the words you read in newspapers, magazines and books, all have an effect on you and on your life-force energy, or Ki. As an example of how words can affect you, try this exercise in front of a mirror.

WORD POWER

Stand up straight and look at yourself in the mirror. Now begin to say aloud the words "I am sad," repeating the phrase at least 10, but not more than 20 times, and watch what happens to your body and listen to what happens to your voice. Your shoulders and back may begin to slump, you will probably find it a bit difficult to keep eye contact with yourself in the mirror, your breathing will become slower, you may begin to feel quite emotional and your voice will drop and become quieter.

Now reverse the process, continuing to watch and listen to yourself, and begin to say aloud the words "I am happy," repeating them 10 to 20 times. You will find that your body straightens up, your eyes become sparkly, a smile appears on your face—you may even laugh—and your voice lightens. And all from a few words!

What this demonstrates is how important it is to monitor what you say about yourself. Like the words of a well-known song, you need to "accentuate the positive, eliminate the negative, and latch on to the affirmative." I often overhear people saying really negative things about themselves, calling themselves stupid, or saying that they can't do things or that they'll never be able to achieve something. If you keep telling yourself that, you'll believe it and it will become a self-fulfilling prophecy. Just try really listening to what you say for one day, and you'll be astonished at how many negative statements you make, especially as you'll probably be trying to be particularly positive that day. Once you've identified the problem, however, the situation can be changed. You've probably been brought up to be modest, but it really pays to say nice things about yourself, and if at first you feel a bit awkward about saying good things about yourself to other people, then say them aloud when you're alone. They still work that way, and it will be good practice for being positive about yourself to others.

WHAT DO YOU SAY ABOUT YOURSELF?

- ◆ Take a pen and paper and write a description of yourself. Be as honest as you can, so it's okay to put what you perceive to be negative traits as well as positive things. You might find it easiest to list some words. They can be descriptive of you (e.g., tall, blond, plump), but try to include personality traits (e.g., kind, generous, grumpy), thinking processes (e.g., logical, a bit slow), skills (e.g., good cook) and abilities, attitudes, beliefs, etc.
- ◆ Put a check mark next to all the words that are positive and affirming, and an X next to all the words that are disapproving and negative.
- ◆ Add up your scores. Do you have more positive than negative traits, or the other way around, or is your list fairly balanced?
- ◆ Finally, cross out *all* the negative words—you don't need to be self-critical, you need to be self-affirming!

OPTIMISM VERSUS PESSIMISM

Once you've identified that the way you think doesn't seem to be working in your favor, you can change it. Instead of being a pessimist, someone who always sees the glass as "half empty," you can turn yourself into an optimist who always sees the glass as "half full," someone who believes that lots of good things will happen to them and that they can live happily.

I know that some people believe that even *thinking* that something good might happen will jinx it, but that really isn't true. If you look into theories of universal abundance, which are covered in some detail in Chapter 10, you will see that thinking, feeling and acting positively can have really beneficial effects on your life. If you can replace negative thoughts and worries with positive thoughts and hopes, you will not only feel better, but the energies around you will be lighter and you'll be much more likely to attract those good results you've been hoping for. Even if you're a bit skeptical about energy theories and the abundant universe, thinking positively will still have a good effect on your body language, and you'll find that people around you will respond to you better, which in turn will help you to be more confident, and so on.

A REIKI TECHNIQUE FOR CHANGING YOUR THINKING

Here's a Reiki technique to help you rid yourself of negative thinking, old belief patterns and worries, and change your thinking to a more positive and optimistic frame of mind.

1. Sit comfortably, and spend a few moments breathing deeply to help you to become centered, with your hands in the gassho (prayer) position, and allow your mind to become calm. Then *intend* that the Reiki flow to remove any negative beliefs, worries, pessimistic thinking or unhelpful habits from your mind, and if you wish, you can say silently to yourself "let Reiki remove any toxic thoughts or beliefs now."

2. Place one hand on your sacral chakra, which is 1–2 inches below your navel, and the other hand on your forehead, over the brow or third eye chakra, and wait for the Reiki to build up. Sense the energy in your hands and hold this position for about 5 minutes, or until you feel the energy has balanced in both hands (sometimes it is better to hold the hands slightly away from the body, in the aura, as this makes it easier to feel the change in energies).

3. Remove your hand from your forehead and place it on top of the other hand on your sacral chakra. Silently ask the Reiki to remove from your mind

any negative beliefs, worries, pessimistic thinking or unhelpful habits that are holding you back and preventing you from living life to your fullest potential. Keep both hands in place, and let Reiki flow into your sacral chakra for as long as you feel is necessary, which will probably be between 10 and 30 minutes.

4. Finish by placing your hands at midchest height in the gassho position and mentally give thanks for the Reiki, bowing slightly as a mark of respect.

Having looked at our thinking processes, and at how various ways of thinking can interfere with living the Reiki way, in the next chapter we look more specifically at worry, and what worries are based on—fear—and how to overcome both.

chapter eight

DEALING WITH FEAR AND WORRY

The second of Dr. Usui's Principles was "just for today, do not worry," and as we've seen in the previous chapter, worry is just one of the thought patterns that can be detrimental to us.

WORRY AND FEAR

Worrying means spending a lot of time thinking about negative possibilities, and people who worry too much:

- ◆ Find it difficult to concentrate
- ◆ Feel helpless and unable to cope
- ◆ Experience disturbed sleep and eating patterns
- ◆ Lose confidence
- ◆ Develop obsessive behaviors
- ◆ Get headaches, stomach upsets or other physical symptoms
- ◆ Feel emotionally drained

Worry is linked to fear of the future and the unknown, and is often a response to a "what if?" scenario; to something that might happen, but that nine times out of ten doesn't. If you think about it, you didn't start life worrying—tiny babies don't worry—so being a worrier is a habit we can get into, a thinking pattern that we've probably copied from our parents and that gets us nowhere. No matter how much worrying we do, it never achieves anything or changes anything; it just makes us feel awful. Basically, whatever problem or situation you are worried about, if there is some action you can take to improve matters, such as asking for help, then take it, but if there is nothing you can do about it, then the best thing to do is to "let go and let flow." Easy to say, I know, and maybe difficult to do, but what alternative is there?

Fear is often based on negative beliefs about life or the world, so, for example, if you have a general belief that life is a struggle, or that the world is a dangerous place, it will color your judgment about what happens to you and will become a focus for worrying about lack of money, losing your job, being alone or having your home burglarized. The trouble is that we like to be in charge of our lives, but very few things are really under our direct control. One of my favorite phrases is: "If you want to give God a good laugh, tell him/her your plans!"

Life doesn't always turn out the way we expect, but as long as we continue to struggle and strive to bring things under our control, we are just creating an energy cycle that makes things worse. However, there's no point in just squashing your fears and worries down. Instead, try to become aware of what you're really afraid of or worrying about, then send love and Reiki to that fearful part of yourself.

GIVING REIKI FOR COMFORT

Sometimes it's just nice to give ourselves Reiki as something loving, gentle and comforting when we're feeling fearful or worried. The easiest way to do this is to place both hands over your heart chakra—roughly over your breastbone—and to *intend* that Reiki flow into you for your highest and greatest good. (If you have done Reiki Second Degree, you can also draw the Harmony symbol and the Power symbol on each hand before placing it on your chest, to enhance the peaceful effects.) Even 5 minutes like this will be helpful, but if you have 15 or 20 minutes to spare, that's even better. By the end of that time, you should find that your heart rate and breathing pace have become slower, and that you feel more relaxed and peaceful.

WHAT IS FEAR?

If our worried thoughts are caused by things we're afraid of, what exactly is fear? The dictionary definition is: an unpleasant emotion caused by exposure to danger, expectation of pain, etc.; a state of alarm; dread or fearful respect toward; anxiety or apprehension about. Another way of looking at it is to use each of the letters in the word:

False
Expectations
Appearing
Real

Fear is sometimes divided into two types—*fear of the unknown*, because we don't know what to expect, and *fear of the known* because we *think* we already know what to expect, and we don't want to repeat it. However, all fear is really of the unknown, because we cannot accurately anticipate what the future will bring.

Fear, worry, dread, anxiety and apprehension are all wasted thoughts and emotions, because they don't change anything. Okay, some fears keep us safe—for example, knowing that crossing a road without due care and attention could get us killed makes us more wary—but some fears keep us from experiencing life in all its fullness and wonder. Some of the fears many people experience are:

◆ Fear of the future—of bad things that might happen to you
◆ Fear of getting old and being alone
◆ Fear of illness, especially cancer
◆ Fear of being a failure—in relationships or at work
◆ Fear of not having enough money, now or in the future
◆ Fear of losing your job
◆ Fear of death

In her book *Feel the Fear and Do It Anyway*, one of my favorite authors, Susan Jeffers, describes several different levels of fear:

Level 1 Fears are situation-oriented, and they can be divided into two categories. First there are those that "happen"—i.e., those over which we have no control, such as aging, reaching retirement, losing a loved one or dying. Second, there are those requiring action, which might include a fear of flying, driving, public speaking, ending or beginning a relationship, or making mistakes.

Level 2 Fears are ego based, and they include such things as rejection, success, failure, being vulnerable, being conned, helplessness, disapproval or loss of image. These have to do with inner states of mind rather than external situations. They reflect your sense of self and your ability to handle this world, so if you are afraid of being rejected, this fear will affect almost every area of your life—friends, intimate relationships, job interviews, etc. The way in which you begin to protect yourself from this fear is simply to avoid any situation that might invite rejection, and as a result you greatly limit yourself and your life. You have less potential for happiness.

Level 3 Finally, Susan Jeffers says Level 3 fear is the basis of *all* fear: it is an inner belief that "I can't handle it!"

Level 1 fears therefore include: I can't handle illness, making a mistake, losing my job, getting old, being alone or making a fool of myself, etc. Level 2 fears include: I can't handle the responsibility of success, failure or being rejected, etc.

Susan Jeffers believes that all you have to do to diminish your fear is to develop more trust in your ability to handle whatever comes your way. Try this next exercise when you're not feeling particularly worried or fearful, and the next time those thoughts and feelings arise, you will hopefully have a better coping mechanism.

140

COPING WITH FEARS AND WORRIES

A powerful way of dealing with fears is to visualize what it is you're worried about or afraid of—such as a visit to the dentist, losing your job or even something like the death of a parent or partner, if that is something constantly on your mind—and in your imagination, see yourself coping with it.

See yourself at the various stages of the event, dealing with the difficulties or challenges it presents, perhaps getting help from family, friends, colleagues or officials, then see yourself at the conclusion of the event—you've survived!

Your life may have changed because of that event, but most challenges really can be overcome, either by adopting a new approach or by getting help from the right people. If you use Reiki on yourself every day to help to calm yourself (see page 138), and you also imagine the energy of Reiki surrounding you and the thing you are worried about, like a bubble, to bring its healing energies into it for your greatest and highest good, then hopefully the issue won't appear so difficult or frightening.

Whenever you have a fearful thought, try smiling, because psychology can follow physiology—or in other words, change your body and you can change your mind. Try it. It's really hard to worry or to be afraid with a smile on your face! If you can just let go and stop being fearful about the situation, you'll feel better—and very few things will turn out to be as bad as you've anticipated.

HOW TO HANDLE FEAR

Methods for dealing with chronic fear or worry fall into two areas:

◆ Changing how you *think* about the problems that worry you
◆ Changing what you *do* about the problems that worry you

This is what the suggestions and exercises in this chapter are all about—helping you to change how you think and what you do, so that you can let go of your fears and worries.

First Steps

Facing up to your fears can often show you that there wasn't that much to be afraid of after all—sometimes the fear of something is actually worse than the thing itself. Talking to someone you trust can be helpful too, and usually you will find that he or she has had similar feelings—we often think we're the only one who is facing some fear, but that's rarely the case. There are some sensible things you can do to help yourself. Make sure you eat well and get some exercise, which fills the body with endorphins that help to improve your mood. Moreover, going for a walk, bike ride or swim will get you out of your usual surroundings, which is also a good thing. Get involved in some activities that take your mind off your fears, especially things that help other people, such as doing shopping for an elderly neighbor, or helping at a day-care center or hospice. Hobbies that involve you physically are good too, such as gardening or painting.

Try not to worry about things late at night when you're in bed, because fears always seem bigger then. Read a book or watch a film (something romantic or funny, no horror or violence) on TV until you're tired enough to fall asleep—if you wake up at night and the worrying starts again, get up and do something instead. Drinking something soothing like chamomile tea (not tea or coffee, which contain stimulants) can be helpful, and put 2–3 drops (no more than that) of lavender oil on your pillow to help you to get back to sleep, and perhaps listen to some soothing music. You'll find that doing a Reiki self-treatment on yourself—the 12 hand positions referred to in chapter 1—will help you to fall asleep again too, often by the time you've reached hand position number five! However, if fears or worries are affecting your health or making you feel depressed, do talk things over with your doctor.

MOVING OUT OF WORRY

Breaking the cycle of worry is important. By recognizing how you behave physically when you worry (for instance, you might bite your nails, grind your teeth or tense your jaw) and how you behave emotionally (you might avoid other people or feel worthless), you can begin to make some changes that can help you to control your worrying.

♦ If you notice yourself grinding your teeth, for example, you can deliberately relax your jaw and the

143

rest of your facial muscles—and if possible yawn. Yawning makes you take a deep breath, and it acts to relax you.

◆ If you recognize feelings of worthlessness, do something physical to improve your mood. Put on some music and dance around the room, and sing along with the lyrics—even if you feel silly—or go for a brisk walk or do some yoga stretching.

Worrying is often a habit, a "way of being," so it can be helpful to figure out when you first started worrying and why you may have taken on that "role" and gotten into the cycle of worry. Did your family worry a lot? Were your friends at school worriers? Was there an event that made you start worrying, such as a member of your family becoming seriously ill, or dying? If you can find the trigger, you can bring a more realistic view to bear on it, and realize that you don't have to follow that habit anymore.

IDENTIFYING NEGATIVE THOUGHTS, BELIEFS OR ATTITUDES

Choose one area of your life that you are worried about— for example, money, a relationship, your job—and ask yourself the following questions to find out some of the negative thoughts, beliefs or attitudes you have about it. Many of the words or phrases you come up with will probably be those you heard in childhood, but some will have become influential because of experiences you've had as an adult. Either way, it can be quite a revelation to find out the kinds of negative (and some positive) opinions you have incorporated into your beliefs, and which are now potentially holding you back. For instance, a negative belief about money might be "money doesn't grow on trees," meaning it's difficult to come by, or "you have to work hard for a living," which is a limiting belief meaning there's no other way for money to come to you other than working for it.

1. It's better not to have this because?
2. I'm afraid of having this because?
3. People who have this are?

You might find that you come up with lots of answers, or just one or two, but it's a good idea to write them down so that you can think about them afterward.

DISCOVERING AND TALKING TO YOUR FEAR(S)

You could select one of the areas of your life that you've just answered questions on above, now that you've found some of the beliefs that could be blocking you, and use Reiki and visualization to help you discover and calm your fears, and to develop hope and trust. Try this visualization.

- You are going on an inner journey to discover and talk to one or more of your fears or worries, so take a few moments to imagine yourself in a bubble of light and fill it with Reiki, intending that it protect you from any harm at all levels.

- Next, imagine yourself on a path at the edge of some woodland, with the sunlight filtering through the trees, warming you and lighting the path. On either side of the path is a carpet of bluebells, and they look and smell beautiful, and you begin to walk along the path into the wood.

- As you continue walking, ahead of you there is something blocking your path. At first you can't quite see what it is, but as you draw closer it becomes identifiable. It may be an object like a large boulder or a tree trunk across the path, or a person, mammal or bird, or a being of light, but it is not threatening in any way, and you feel quite safe, because you know you are protected by Reiki, and you know it is appearing in this visualization in order to help you.

- When you get quite close to whatever is blocking your path, pause for a few moments, and mentally ask the blockage what fear or worry it symbolizes. Whether it is a person, a creature or an inanimate object, it will be able to communicate with you at an energetic level, so wait until you begin to get impressions and information. These may be words or images, sounds or symbols, but allow yourself to accept whatever is said without judgment or denial.

◆ When you are no longer getting any answers to your question, ask the blockage for guidance on what you can do to overcome this fear or worry, and listen and watch again for any answers.

◆ When you have finished receiving impressions, thank the blockage for its help, and ask it if it would like some Reiki in return. If it says yes, then imagine and intend that Reiki flow out of your hands to encompass the blockage in its healing, harmonizing energy, and you will notice that the blockage begins to fade and become fainter, until it finally disappears and your path is clear again.

◆ If the blockage did not wish to receive any Reiki, then ask it to please move aside and let you pass, and it will usually do so. If it refuses to move aside, you have further healing to do on this issue, but you will have received information to help you with this, so thank it again and turn back along the path to where you first began, at the edge of the woods.

◆ Let your awareness begin to return, feeling the chair or bed beneath you and the sounds in the room, and write down what you have just experienced, together with any insights that occur to you as you are writing, and any information, advice or symbols you were given by the blockage you encountered.

◆ Finish by giving yourself some Reiki, either over the heart chakra or the solar plexus chakra, for 5 or 10 minutes.

MORE NLP TECHNIQUES

There are several NLP techniques you can use to work on fears and worries, and I've adapted a couple of them here, presenting you with a number of questions to answer. You will probably find it helpful to write down the questions and answers, so that you can think about them afterward. Try not to "filter" your answers—just write the first thing that comes into your mind, as this will be the most revealing and truthful.

Step 1
Think of something that you are worried about, which is therefore a problem for you in your life right now.

Step 2
Answer each of the following questions:

1. What's wrong?
2. Why do you have this problem?
3. How long have you had this problem?
4. How does this problem limit you?
5. What does this problem stop you from doing?
6. Whose fault is it that you have this problem?

Step 3
Breathe deeply for a few moments to center and calm yourself, before moving on to the next step.

Step 4

Consider the same worry or problem, and answer each of the following questions in the same truthful and uncensored way:

1. What do you want?
2. Where, when and with whom do you want it?
3. How will you know, specifically, that you have gotten there?
4. What positive things, in any way, do you get out of your current behavior or situation?
5. How will you maintain these things in your new outcome?
6. How will your desired outcome affect other aspects of your life?
7. When you get what you want, what else will improve in your life?
8. Under what conditions would you not want to achieve your new goal?
9. What stops you from having your desired outcome already?
10. What resources do you have to help you to achieve your desired outcome?
11. What are you going to *do* to achieve your outcome?

Step 5

Breathe deeply for a few moments to center and calm yourself, then look back at all of your answers. Working through them in this way should help you to feel more resourceful, less worried and better able to cope with the situation, now that you understand more about your own reactions to it and have identified some things you can do to change it.

USING VISUALIZATION

One way of coping with fear and worry is to feel safe, and this visualization allows you to create a safe environment in your inner world, a place of shelter or retreat. The Cave of Sanctuary described in the exercise below is within you: a place that *is* you; that only you know; that only you have access to. This is a place where you can go to think, to be, a place that you might like to retreat to before or after any of the other visualizations, and a place that is always with you, if you choose to access it, no matter what is going on around you.

This cave is infinitely adaptable—different images, objects, pictures on the walls, signs and symbols, will come to you at different times to help you to discover more about yourself, and to deal with current aspects of your life. Various details within the visualization, such as the speed of the flow of the river, how clear it is, whether the river is young or mature, fast or slow, deep or shallow, will help you to identify how you feel about your life at that particular moment. The interpretation of such features is for you to decide but, for example, a raging torrent could mean that life is going faster than you want, so it could be time to slow down.

In order to experience a visualization fully, it is important to engage all your senses, so the walk along the river and the scenes that follow allow you to focus your mind on the visualization—hearing sounds, feeling the coolness of the water on your feet. Touching the cave wall helps to give you a sense of solid security—and of course you are always in the beam of the universal light to give you inspiration and love.

THE CAVE OF SANCTUARY
You are safe, always were safe and always will be safe

◆ When you feel happy and relaxed, either sitting or lying down, visualize yourself on a riverbank and look down at your feet. If you are wearing shoes or socks, take them off and feel the grass or earth underneath your feet.

◆ Now look all around you—at the grass, the flowers, the trees and bushes nearby. See the river, watch it flowing by and notice the speed of flow and the depth and width of the river, its clarity and color.

◆ Look across to the opposite bank to see the vegetation there, the grassy bank, the trees and bushes, and raise your eyes and look up to the sky. Notice the color of the sky, and whether there are any clouds floating by overhead.

◆ Listen to the sound of the river flowing past, the rustling of leaves, the birdsong, then sit on the riverbank and put your feet in the water.

◆ Feel the water on your skin and notice its temperature—is it cool and refreshing, or icy cold?

◆ You may like to spend some time here on the bank, taking in everything around you. When you're ready, stand up and start to walk along the side of the river.

◆ Notice everything around you—the scent of flowers, the sound of rustling leaves and birdsong. Soon you come to a small stream that feeds into the river. You can either splash through the stream or jump over it, and continue to walk along the riverbank.

◆ A little farther along, you see some bushes. You walk toward them, and as you reach them you spend some time examining their leaves and flowers. Then you notice that behind the bushes there is an entrance to a cave.

◆ You feel quite happy about going into the cave, because you know you're safe, so you begin to walk into it. As you walk, feel the ground under your feet, and notice its texture and whether it is damp or dry.

◆ You walk farther along the passage into the cave, noticing that there is still plenty of light, then pause for a moment and put out your hand to feel the rock at the side of the passageway, before continuing to walk along it.

◆ Now you notice that the passageway opens out into a huge cavern, and light streams from above into the center of this cavern. For a moment you pause and take in the majesty and beauty of the cavern, before moving into the center.

◆ You stand in the beam of light and look around the whole of the cavern—at the walls, the floor, the roof, and begin to feel familiar with this place.

◆ Here in your sanctuary you will find many things, many resources. You'll find a stream of water, of ideas running through; you'll find pools of water, of knowledge; and rocks for strength; and crystals for healing.

- Take some time to explore the cavern and familiarize yourself with the parts that are now open to you. As you do so, realize that you may visit this cavern as often as you wish, and the more often you visit it, the more resources you will find, and the more help will be available to you.
- When you have explored enough, return to the center and the beam of light, and you will find a number of objects there.
- Pick up as many objects as you want and examine them; see what shape they are, what color, what size. If you want to bring them back with you, you can do so, or you may leave them in the cavern where they will always be there for you.
- When you have spent enough time examining the objects, stand up in the beam of light. If you would like some time to relax and be still and quiet in this place of sanctuary, find a comfortable chair, daybed or large cushion to sit on for as long as you wish.
- When you are ready to leave, turn to the passage that led into the cavern and walk slowly out of the cavern.
- As you walk along the passage back to the outside, pause for a moment and put out your hand to feel the rock on the left, then walk out into the sunshine once again.
- Pause for a moment by the bushes, then walk back along the riverbank, noticing what's around you, splashing through or jumping over the little stream,

until you arrive back at the point where you began
the visualization.

◆ You may wish to pause here for a moment and feel
the sunlight on your face and hear the rushing of
the water, before finally putting on your socks and
shoes or sandals.

◆ Now you begin to notice other sounds and feelings—
the floor or chair or bed beneath you, the sounds in
the room, any noises outside and the soft sound of
your own regular breathing, as your awareness fully
returns.

◆ When you are ready you can open your eyes and
find yourself back in the room where you began
your visualization.

Hopefully the ideas and techniques in Part 4 will help
you to "live without worry." In Part 5, we look at the
third of Dr. Usui's Principles, "just for today, be grateful,"
and at the power of gratitude, abundance theory and the
Law of Attraction, to help you to create an even better
life for yourself.

part five

LIVING WITH GRATITUDE

Be thankful for everything you have now,
have had in the past, and will have in the future.
Being actively grateful will bring
even more good things into your life.

Penelope Quest

chapter nine

DEVELOPING AN ATTITUDE OF GRATITUDE

"Just for today, be grateful," sometimes translated as "show appreciation," is the third of the Reiki Principles passed on to us by Dr. Usui, and for many people this will seem a fairly obvious statement. Of course, we know we should be grateful, and most of us are brought up to be polite and say "thank you" whenever someone gives us a gift or does something nice for us. But in order to "live the Reiki way," I believe this Principle goes much further than that, and what I hope to show in this chapter is that being grateful can add a wonderful, joyous element that can enrich your life immeasurably, so that it is well worth developing an "attitude of gratitude."

BE GRATEFUL

Society today, at least in Western countries, seems to have a culture of wanting bigger, better and more, especially of material things—a bigger house, a better car, more money, the latest electronic gadget, more luxurious holidays, and so on—and one of the consequences of this is that it's easy to forget just how much we already have. It is important to value and appreciate many things in our lives and to be grateful for our many blessings—to develop an "attitude of gratitude," rather than just taking things for granted. Few, if any, people reading this book will have no roof over their head at night, no clothes on their backs and no food in their bellies, so even on your very worst day, you still have plenty to be thankful for.

One of the problems is that we get our "wants" and our "needs" mixed up. Few of us have everything we want, and sometimes the things we don't have can become a reason for depression, grumbling and comparison with other people who seem "luckier" than ourselves. Advertisements for everything from expensive cars, houses and holidays to cosmetics, perfumes and luxury goods are specifically designed to make us want them, to feel less of a person if we don't have them, so we can become obsessed with our "need' for them, without realizing that we've been "hooked" into our feelings of lack. But by their very nature, "luxury" goods aren't necessities—we don't actually "need" them at all.

To help us to lead happy, contented, fulfilled lives, it is important to distinguish between our wants and our needs, and to recognize and appreciate what we already have. Often we may not reach this realization until some crisis or emergency comes along, and then it can become very clear indeed. Ask yourself what you would try to save if your home was burning down, or what would be important to you if you found you were facing a life-threatening situation, or had only a short time to live? Such questions can often concentrate the mind wonderfully, making you understand that few material goods really matter, and that it is life itself that is precious, and the people and animals you care about that count.

The famous psychologist Abraham Maslow (1908–70) came up with what he termed our "hierarchy of needs," which is often depicted as a pyramid, with our most basic needs at the bottom.

5. Need for
Self-actualization

4. Need for Esteem

3. Need for Love and Belonging

2. Need for Safety

1. Physiological Needs Related to Survival

1. He saw our first major needs as physiological, related to our survival, so that refers to such things as food, drink, sleep and the need to procreate to continue the species.
2. The second need is for safety, which includes physical well-being, a safe place to live, enough money to live on and psychological security.
3. Once those basic needs have been met, we can concentrate on our needs for love and belonging, such as affection, intimacy and roots in the family or group.
4. The fourth level of need is for esteem, which is about our belief in our competence and adequacy, our sense of self-respect and getting respect from others.

5. Only when all of these needs have been met can we begin to satisfy our need for self-actualization, or in other words, our ability to become what we are capable of becoming, the stage at which we feel confident and safe enough to explore ideas beyond our everyday lives, such as philosophy or spirituality. (The stage you are likely to be at if you've taken a Reiki course, or you feel ready to read this book.)

You will notice that there's no reference in the list to cars, computers, cosmetics, mobile devices or any other material goods! Of course, there's nothing wrong with having a comfortable home and some of the luxuries that make life interesting and fun—it's just that we could do without many of what we consider to be "essentials" if we had to, and whether they're basics or extras, they all represent things to be grateful for.

THE NATURE OF GRATITUDE

Although gratitude is something that anyone can experience, some people seem to feel grateful more often than others. These people also tend to be happier, more helpful and forgiving, and less depressed than their less grateful counterparts. There are a few quotes I would like to share that make salient points about gratitude. The first is from Buddha: "Let us rise up and be thankful, for if we didn't learn a lot today, at least we learned a little, and if we didn't learn a little, at least we didn't get sick, and if we got sick, at least we didn't die; so, let us all be thankful." The second is from John F. Kennedy: "As we express our gratitude, we must never forget that the highest appreciation is not to utter words, but to live by them."

Well, that is what Dr. Usui wanted us to do—to live with appreciation, and Zen Buddhists have a ritual of kneeling for a few minutes, with eyes closed, to think about what and whom they are grateful for, and it apparently evokes a feeling of happiness, so that might be something you would like to try.

REASONS TO BE GRATEFUL

Apart from the fact that potentially it makes you feel happy, why should you be grateful? What benefits does it have?

- It reminds you about what's really important. If you are grateful that your children are alive and well, you don't need to bother about the little things. If you're grateful that you have a roof over your head, you might not need to feel so stressed out about paying bills.
- It reminds you about the positive things in your life—your family and friends, feeling warm and cozy at home, seeing a beautiful sunset or the kindness shown by a stranger.
- It turns negatives into positives. If you're having a bad time at work, be grateful that you have a job. If you're short of money, be grateful there's still just enough to put food on your table. If life just seems full of problems at the moment, be grateful that adversity makes you a stronger person.

HOW TO LIVE A LIFE OF GRATITUDE

The thing is, simple acts of gratitude don't cost you much (especially once you get over the initial discomfort some people feel about thanking others). But they can make a huge difference. The simple act of expressing gratitude to someone can make a big difference to that person's life. People like to be appreciated for who they are and what they do, yet it costs you so little to say "thank you." And because it makes them happy, it will make you happy too, and that's no bad thing.

Here are a few suggestions for living a life of gratitude:

◆ Whenever anyone does something nice for you, remember to say thank you, either in person, or on the phone, by e-mail or by letter. When I was a child I always had to write thank-you letters to my aunts and uncles when they sent me birthday or Christmas presents, but that idea seems to have gone out of fashion. So reinvent the fashion!

◆ Have a morning gratitude session. Before you start your day, take a few minutes to give thanks for everyone and everything in your life, either silently or aloud—or in writing in a gratitude journal (see page 164).

◆ Be thankful to your body for all the amazing things it does—breathing, seeing, hearing, smelling, tasting, feeling, moving—even if you're not completely healthy right now.

◆ Remember to be thankful for "negative" things in your life, too. Problems can be opportunities to grow, be creative, look at things differently and learn from your experience.

◆ Be thankful that you're alive, and for the chance to start again on another new day.

There's a wonderful prayer of gratitude I found on the Internet recently, and I think it sums things up perfectly.

Be Thankful
(Author Unknown)

Be thankful that you don't already have everything you
   desire.
If you did, what would there be to look forward to?
Be thankful when you don't know something
For it gives you the opportunity to learn.
Be thankful for the difficult times;
During those times you grow.
Be thankful for your limitations
Because they give you opportunities for improvement.
Be thankful for each new challenge
Because it will build your strength and character.
Be thankful for your mistakes
They will teach you valuable lessons.
Be thankful when you're tired and weary
Because it means you've made a difference.
It is easy to be thankful for the good things.
A life of rich fulfilment comes to those who are also
   thankful for the setbacks.
Gratitude can turn a negative into a positive.
Find a way to be thankful for your troubles and they can
   become your blessings.

If you like it, why not keep a copy of this quotation somewhere nearby so that you can refer to it whenever you want a touch of inspiration—on the fridge is my favorite place.

THE JOY OF GRATITUDE

Deep feelings of gratitude can bring about states of bliss and joy similar to those many of us experience when we are using Reiki. Something that Wayne Dyer says in his book *Manifest Your Destiny* is that: "The nature of gratitude helps dispel the idea that we do not have enough, that we will never have enough, and that we ourselves are not enough. When your heart is filled with gratitude, it is grateful for everything and cannot focus on what is missing." Wise words!

KEEPING A GRATITUDE JOURNAL

As mentioned earlier, most people reading this book will have many, many things to be grateful for, so one of the activities I suggest to my Reiki students is to keep a "gratitude journal" in which to write down, every evening, at least five things you can be grateful for that day. Even if you've had an appalling day, there will still be enough to appreciate—even if one of those entries is being grateful to have gotten through that day! At the end of a week you'll have 35 things to be grateful for, and at the end of 10 weeks you'll have 350 things to be grateful for, give or take a few repetitions.

This may sound like a very simple exercise, but it can really change the way you view your life. When you develop the capacity to appreciate all you have, you become more content with your life the way it is, and less likely to cultivate the craving for lots of "new" things. You just view things differently. That's not to say you don't want to improve things—often the appreciation for something makes you want to make it even better. For example, if you begin to really appreciate and feel grateful for the home you live in, instead of wanting to move to somewhere bigger or different in some other way, you will often want to carry out home improvements to make your current home feel cozier and more comfortable—perhaps doing a really good "clutter clear," or some decorating, or making new curtains or buying fresh flowers for some of the rooms. That way you build in even more things to be grateful for.

It isn't just "things" we can be grateful for. What about the beauty of a sunset, the perfume of a flower, the joy and laughter of a child at play, the warmth of a loving hug, the delicious taste and aroma of something as simple as a piece of fruit? Taking pleasure in the many simple things that are part of our lives is a fundamental step toward developing that "attitude of gratitude." Perhaps we could learn a lesson or two about gratitude and simplicity from the Shakers, the religious communal sect that flourished in America during the mid-nineteenth century. They prayed each morning for the grace that would enable them to express their love and appreciation of God through their daily tasks, however simple and mundane those tasks might be. This helped them to be content with their lives.

Listing Your Blessings

Imagine how empty your life would be without the people and pets you care about, the home you live in, the everyday objects that make your life easier or the hobbies and activities that fill your life with interest. Maybe you could make a list of the people and things in your life you most care about, and just spend a few moments actually visualizing what your life would be like without them. If you get upset just thinking about it, think how awful it would be if it really happened. That's reason enough to develop an attitude of gratitude, to be fully appreciative of everything and everyone in your life.

HOW TO BE GRATEFUL

Being grateful is like most other things—if it isn't currently central in your life, it might take a bit of practice, so here are some ideas on how to cultivate that attitude of gratitude.

1. Be willing to express your gratitude and appreciation to the people you care about: tell them regularly that you love them; thank them for the things they do for you; enjoy giving them little gifts that will please them and show them how much you care.
2. Practice small acts of kindness to other people too, as an expression of gratitude for the part they play in your life. Say something complimentary to the waitress who brings your coffee; take a home-baked cake to a neighbor for no particular reason; smile at the bus

driver when you pay your fare; say "thank you" when the salesperson hands you your goods.

3. When you notice yourself about to complain, stop for a moment and realize that most people are doing the best they can, it's just that at this moment in time they're not fulfilling your expectations. And sometimes we find fault with others because we're ashamed of the same kinds of faults in ourselves, so instead, appreciate that maybe this is just one of the lessons you have to learn, and just "grin and bear it."

4. Develop an awareness that everything you "own"— your home, clothes, car, etc.—owes its existence to other people: the builders, tailors, mechanics and so on. Appreciate the web of life that brings you the things you need, and be grateful for it.

5. Take notice of what is happening in your life, and be grateful for all the little miracles that can make up any day: the beauty of a rainbow, the smell of freshly baked bread as you walk past the bakery, an overheard joke, the fact that you managed to catch that train when you thought you would miss it.

6. Learn from and be grateful for the hard lessons, too— because each time you encounter difficulties and over-come them, you grow. There are ups and downs, happi-ness and sadness, in everyone's life, but every experience is valuable because it helps to make you who you are.

7. Begin and end every day with an expression of grati-tude and thanksgiving for the precious gift of another day of life on this amazing, wondrous planet. We live in a world where there are so many opportunities, so many possibilities, where we are surrounded by so

much beauty, so much love. Sure, we could remember the negative side of life, but it's so much better, and so much more fun, to be positive. This is about developing an awareness of life and what it means to live it.

THE UNIVERSAL LAW OF ABUNDANCE

According to metaphysical thinking, despite indications to the contrary, the Universe is actually totally abundant, and we can all share in that abundance, if we choose to believe in it and bring it into our lives with our thoughts and actions. It isn't the only reason why we should become grateful and appreciative, but the Law of Abundance says that the more gratitude you demonstrate, the more abundance the Universe will shower on you, because you are thinking positively, and positive thought energy attracts positive things.

- Try writing "thank you" on the back of every check you write; pay your bills willingly, with a sense of gratitude, rather than grumbling about the cost.
- Give generously of your time and money to charities you want to support.
- Say "thank you" every time you eat, to the Earth, the plants and creatures, and the people who have helped to supply your food (and maybe offer an energy exchange by giving Reiki to your food as part of that act of gratitude).

One of the good things about developing the habit of being grateful is that you will naturally begin to feel happier and less concerned about what you haven't got, so when the Universe does shower you with its abundance it feels even more special.

Using Reiki

You can use Reiki and affirmations to help you to learn to trust in the abundance of the Universe and to develop your own belief in your deservingness of love, beauty, peace and anything else you need or desire.

Sit quietly and center yourself, breathing deeply and evenly, and intend to draw in Reiki through your crown chakra until it fills the whole of your body, and you can feel it tingling in your hands. Place your hands on or near your base chakra and begin to speak any of the following affirmations aloud (or come up with some of your own). Repeat the same affirmation at least 20 times, *intending* that Reiki's healing energy flow into the affirmation to bring its energetic vibrations into harmony with your own vibrations, for your highest and greatest good; that is, to attract what you desire, providing it is for your highest and greatest good.

- I deserve love and I attract loving respect from everyone I meet.
- My life is filled with love, beauty and peace.
- The Universe is totally abundant, and it showers me with good.

- ◆ I love myself, I love my life and all is well in my world.
- ◆ I now attract to myself all that I need and all that I desire, for my highest good.
- ◆ I love and appreciate all that I have, and I recognize that I already have so much to be grateful for.
- ◆ I am grateful for all the people in my life, and for all the lessons they help me to learn.
- ◆ End with a gassho (hands in prayer position in front of your chest), and of course remember to thank Reiki for its help.

So just for today, show appreciation and give thanks for your many blessings. I hope this chapter has given you a few ideas to try, to help you to live with Usui's Principle "just for today, be grateful." In the next chapter we look in greater detail at abundance theory—or cosmic ordering—and expand on the idea of the Universal Law of Attraction.

chapter ten

COSMIC ORDERING AND THE UNIVERSAL LAW OF ATTRACTION

You've probably heard about the cosmic ordering service—a number of celebrities reportedly believe it is working for them, and several books have recently been published about it. Well, it's all about abundance thinking and the Law of Attraction. It ties in with "living the Reiki way" because Dr. Usui wanted us to learn to be grateful and appreciate what we have, and as you will see later in this chapter, the more grateful you are, the more abundant your life can become.

I've been working with abundance thinking—or cosmic ordering—for about twenty years, and I'm definitely getting better at it. I've manifested (brought into my life) lots of things, often within just a few days of asking for them, so I'm convinced that the ideas I discuss in this chapter really work. Let me give you a few examples:

♦ When I became a Reiki Master, I felt I needed a really good massage table, but didn't think I could afford one, so I "put out to the Universe" for one. A few days later someone called to say they would like to take

Second Degree training with me, but they didn't have much money, so would I take a massage table in exchange? Naturally, I said, "Yes, thank you!"

- ◆ When I left work, I only had an old computer and needed a more up-to-date one, and a good printer, to help me run my Reiki practice, but with far less money coming in I wasn't sure I could buy them. A few days later my son called me and said he realized I needed more modern equipment, and he had a spare computer and a laser printer, which I could borrow. Again, I said "yes, thank you."

- ◆ More recently, when I wanted to move to the country, I "put out to the Universe" for a three-bedroom house so that I could have a spare room and an office, plus a nice kitchen and bathroom, a conservatory, a secluded garden and views of hills. The very first place I looked at was exactly what I wanted, so that's where I now live. It's not absolutely perfect—I forgot to specify space for a freezer and a dishwasher in the kitchen—but I love it!

I could give you many more examples, but that's probably enough for now—and the point is, everything was achieved easily and effortlessly.

THE LAW OF ATTRACTION

I introduced this idea in chapter 5, when I mentioned the teachings of Abraham in the book *Ask and It Is Given*, and again in chapter 9. We know there are universal laws that govern the way the Universe works, like the Law of

Gravity, for instance. Well, you may not have heard of it before, but the Law of Attraction is one of the universal laws that is working in your life right now—and always has been. It's as impartial and as constant as the Law of Gravity. You wouldn't expect only a few of us to be affected by the Law of Gravity—it would be a bit strange if the rest of humanity floated off into space! Equally, the Law of Attraction works for everyone, at all times, attracting into their lives whatever they focus on most, whether that is positive or negative.

As mentioned in Chapter 7, everything in the Universe vibrates and is moving, and according to the Law of Attraction, when something vibrates at a particular frequency, it attracts and resonates with other things vibrating at the same frequency. Thoughts as well as objects have their own vibrations, so you attract particular events toward you, according to the frequency of the vibration of your thoughts. The energy of everything you think, say or do draws the corresponding vibration to you. Thoughts become things.

You are basically a magnet. You attract with both conscious and unconscious thoughts, so you draw to yourself the people in your life, your home, job, car, wealth or debt, etc. So people who think negatively attract negative things. A relative of mine is convinced that everything electrical, electronic or mechanical he buys will stop working—and guess what, it does. Another friend is always saying that she has disastrous holidays—and she comes back with tales of dreadful accommodations, meals that gave her an upset stomach, and often a bandaged arm or a leg in a cast as evidence of a fall.

Working with the Law of Attraction

Because the Law of Attraction grants our every command, the process of working with it is fairly simple:

ASK → BELIEVE → RECEIVE

ASK   Decide, in as much detail as possible, what you want to have, be or do, and get a clear picture of it in your mind.

BELIEVE It is important to believe that you will receive, and that what you want is yours already, on an energetic level. You must imagine, pretend, speak and think as though you have already received what you've asked for. When you give out the frequency of having received it, the Law of Attraction moves people, events and circumstances for you to receive.

RECEIVE It is equally important that you feel good about yourself, believe that you deserve to have what you have asked for and think about all the advantages it will bring you. Feel the way you will feel once your desire has manifested, and be ready for it. Be grateful, *feel* grateful, for it in advance.

How to Send Your Cosmic Order

So if the cosmic ordering process is Ask, Believe, Receive— how do you go about asking?

- State your intention verbally: say aloud what you wish for, then "I intend that this cosmic order be now realized in the most positive way possible."
- Visualize yourself in the future, as fully as possible, with whatever you want already realized.

- Write down your cosmic order on a piece of paper and place it on an "abundance board"—a small cork board will do, decorated with a few attractive pictures or postcards, or colored ribbons.

- Alternatively, write down your cosmic order and burn the paper (safely!), and see the Universe taking care of the ash and smoke, turning it into what you want in your life.

- You can ask your guardian angel to deliver it to you, if you believe in angels.

- Make an altar somewhere in your home—just a small space with a candle, some fresh flowers, perhaps a few crystals and an incense stick will be fine—and place your written order on it.

- Write your cosmic order on something like a Post-it note, and hold it between your hands for at least 5 minutes a day, allowing Reiki to flow into it, for your highest and greatest good.

- Clean a quartz crystal by holding it under running water, hold the crystal in your hands and fill it with Reiki for a few minutes, then place the crystal on your Post-it note with your cosmic order written on it. Recleanse the crystal and refill it with Reiki about once a week, until what you want has manifested—or until you've changed your mind and decided you don't actually need it anymore.

There are several things I need to point out. First, once you have placed your cosmic order, apart from sometimes visualizing yourself as if you've already achieved it, leave it to the Universe to sort out—don't let any doubtful thoughts come into your mind, because as soon as you do, you halt the process. Also, "God helps those who help themselves," or in other words, to get what you want takes some effort from you, too. Yes, the Law of Attraction will work for you, but just sitting at home waiting for a lottery win won't work if you haven't bought a ticket! Energy flows where your attention goes, so don't just *think* about what you want, *do* something, too. If you want to go on a world cruise, get the brochures and plan your trip. (This doesn't mean you should book an expensive trip using your credit card, unless you can be reasonably sure you can pay the bill—with the Law of Attraction, things should come easily and effortlessly, not put you into debt.) If you want to live in the countryside, take a few trips to the area you like best, browse through ads for property in local newspapers and online, and imagine yourself living there, shopping locally, eating in local restaurants, and so on. That's living "as if" you already have what you want, and that will activate the Law of Attraction to bring it to you.

Taking Advantage of Synchronicity

What you will often find is that the Universe gives you signals that you're on the right track—something we call synchronicity. Maybe you see a competition where the prize is a world cruise. Enter it! Or you see a free course offered that would help you to get the qualifications you need for the job you've always wanted. Go for it! Or the company you work for offers you a transfer to the very place you want to live. Take it! Because sometimes the Law of Attraction brings you things in stages, rather than all at once, be prepared to be flexible. Don't turn down something because it isn't absolutely "perfect," because it just might be the stepping-stone you need.

As I've said, cosmic ordering is really quite a simple process, but perhaps you need to practice it? Here is an NLP exercise to help.

STEP INTO THE FUTURE

1. Spend a few moments deciding on something you would like in your life. It could be something material, like a new car, a holiday or a big refrigerator. Or it could be a new loving relationship, a successful Reiki practice or anything else.
2. Now stand up, close your eyes and think about what your life is like *without* what you'd like to manifest. Get a real picture of how that is in your head.
3. Step to your left and think about what your life will be like when you have manifested what you want. Really *feel* it. Get as vivid a picture in your head as possible. Imagine everything you can about having this. Use all your senses to connect with it. See it, hear it, touch it, even smell and taste it, if that's possible. Really be with it now. Allow yourself to be filled with excitement and happiness because you have created what you wanted to have, do or be.
4. Open your eyes and step to your right, back where you started, in the present. Close your eyes again for a moment, and remember what your future life was like. Does it seem more possible now? Does it

make you feel happier, or more contented, knowing that it is there, somewhere in the future?

5. Open your eyes again, and spend a few moments thinking about what you have just experienced, and *know* for certain that now that you have placed your "cosmic order," it *will* come, in time, provided you still want it.

Timing

That brings up another point. How long does it take before your cosmic order is delivered? Well, it takes no time at all for the Universe to manifest what you want, because although we live a temporal existence as physical beings, in terms of the Universe, all time is now, so the moment you place your cosmic order, it is ready to be delivered. Any time delay you experience is due to your delay in getting to the place of believing, knowing and feeling that you already have it. You need to get yourself on the frequency of what you want, and then it will appear—so this can take hours, days, weeks, months or even years.

Alternatively, it might simply not be the right time for you. About twelve years ago I had a dream to develop my own Reiki training center, and at the time, I was living in the UK's Lake District. One day I was driving along a country road and saw a large barn with a realtor's sign outside. I walked around the building and looked inside the only window that I could access easily, and thought it looked ideal to develop into my center—it was in a beautiful, peaceful location with fabulous views across the

Lune Valley. I drove straight to the agents who were dealing with it, but discovered that it had already been rented. While I was very disappointed, I believe that "everything is as it should be," so I decided that perhaps the timing wasn't right—I had other commitments and responsibilities at that time—so I just shrugged my shoulders and got on with life. However, every time I drove past it, I kept thinking what a wonderful place it would be to use for teaching Reiki (so I was putting that thought out to the Universe). Three years later I found that it was available again, and yes, that time I was able to get it. I moved in and ran it as the Quest Centre for four years, until I decided that, although I loved it, it was time to move on. I now live in the Cots-wolds, and use other people's premises for teaching purposes, because that is what feels right for me now.

Another aspect of that success was that the building was worth about three-quarters of a million pounds sterling, which was far more money than I have ever had (so far!), but I didn't put any limits on how I could live and work in such a beautiful place. I didn't wonder how I could get the money to buy a suitable building—I let the Universe sort that out, which it did. The barn conversion wasn't available for purchase as it was part of a large estate, so it was offered on a business and residential rental lease. Initially that lease was more money than I felt I could reasonably afford, so I made a cheeky offer—and it was accepted!

Basically, it's as easy for the Universe to manifest $10 as it is to manifest $1,000,000, so while I haven't won the lottery yet, I always have enough to live a lovely life—because I believe I deserve it, and that whatever I want or need will come to me.

DON'T THINK NEGATIVELY

One thing to be aware of is that the Law of Attraction doesn't recognize the words "don't" or "not" or "no," so if you constantly think about things you don't want, it will continue to deliver what you're concentrating on, i.e., more of what you don't want. If you're thinking "I don't want to catch a cold," the Universe reads that as "I want to catch a cold," or if you're thinking "I need more money," the Universe will oblige by making sure you continue to need more money. This applies to every area of your life, so if you think there aren't any nice men or women out there for you to have a relationship with, you'll continue to meet people you don't really like, or if you believe you have no prospects in your job, you won't get that promotion. If you have thoughts that are in conflict with one another you will attract a jumble of experiences—the kind of chaos that is what most of us call "reality."

You are basically a human transmission tower, transmitting a frequency with your thoughts. If you want to change anything in your life, change the frequency by changing your thoughts. Your past thoughts have created the life you are living today, and your current thoughts are creating your future life. What you think about or focus on the most will appear as your life—so if you constantly think about the past, you will re-create those situations. As previously mentioned, we all have tens of thousands of thoughts each day, so that's a lot of creative potential.

The cosmic ordering process enables you to work with the Law of Attraction and become a deliberate thinker and creator of what you want to attract into your life. You get what you concentrate on, and you can have, do or be anything you want. There's a well-known saying by Henry Ford: "Whether you think you can, or think you can't, either way you are right." Another important quote is something attributed to Buddha: "All that we are is a result of what we have thought."

The Law of Attraction is really the Law of Creation. Quantum physics theory tells us that the entire Universe emerged from thought. You create your life through your thoughts and the Law of Attraction, and this doesn't just work if you know about it. It has always been working in your life, and every other person's life, throughout history. But when you become *aware* of this great law, then you become *aware* of how incredibly powerful you are to be able to *think* your life into existence. It works on a global dimension, too. The world we collectively create reflects the mass consciousness, the overriding beliefs, concepts, attitudes, fears and desires of the majority of people. The world we individually create— what we think, say, do, experience, who we meet and relate to, where we live, and so on—reflects our *personal* beliefs, concepts, attitudes, fears and desires.

I know these can be pretty mind-blowing concepts, especially if you've never come across them before, and some people find them very frightening, because it turns the responsibility for our lives well and truly over to us. No one else is responsible. No one else is to blame. Equally, no one else deserves the credit. However, once you get used to the idea, this viewpoint is incredibly empowering, because it puts you in the driver's seat of your life and gives you the power to change, to become who you really want to be and to live the life you really want to live. This belief allows people to fulfill their potential, make a unique and positive contribution to the world, enjoy life and also have dreams of how life will be even better.

THE IMPACT OF EMOTION

One of the important aspects of this idea is that in order to speed up the possibility of creation, you need to add feelings to thoughts, and as explained in chapter 5, the vibration of lower emotions, such as anger and resentment, actively blocks your potential to create, while the vibration of higher emotions, such as love, enhances your ability to create. So it is important to begin to *feel* healthy, *feel* prosperous, *feel* loved, *feel* successful, or anything else you want to manifest. When you feel good, you are powerfully attracting more good things to you—similarly, when you feel bad, you're attracting the frequency of more bad things. Love is the highest frequency—the more love you feel and give out, the greater the power of creation you are harnessing, so feeling *happy* and feeling *love* are the best ways to put out the good vibrations that will attract more good things to you.

THE IMPACT OF BELIEFS

Your beliefs also have a tremendous impact on your creative ability. If you believe you don't deserve something, then you won't allow yourself to get it. If we take one example, money, by using the exercise I suggested on page 145 you can see what your limiting beliefs about money might be. To attract money you must focus on wealth, not on your need for money—otherwise you will continue to need it. Focusing on an exact amount can be helpful, too. As I am self-employed, last year someone asked me how much income I thought I would need to live comfortably for the rest of the year, and I specified an amount. Just a few days later, I received an offer of an unexpected contract for exactly that amount of money!

Therefore, according to the Law of Attraction, if a person doesn't have enough money, that is because they are blocking money from coming to them with their thoughts. Every negative thought, feeling or emotion is blocking good things from coming to you, and that includes money. When you *need* money, it is a powerful feeling, so of course through the Law of Attraction you will continue to attract *needing* money. When you focus on lack and scarcity and what you *don't* have, you moan about it to your family and friends and are always saying "I can't afford that," so you'll never be able to afford it, because you begin to attract more of what you don't have. If you want abundance, if you want prosperity, focus on abundance and prosperity. It's as simple as that.

CREATING MONEY VISUALIZATION

♦ Close your eyes and imagine a door in front of you. Take a few moments to examine the door. Does it look old or new? Is it made of wood or some other material? What sort of handle does it have?

♦ When you have really connected with where you are, in your imagination, move forward and open the door. Behind the door is a beautiful room lit by candles, and the candlelight is reflecting on the piles of gold and jewels on the floor. As you look around the room, you see that there are also piles of banknotes—so many that you can't even begin to count them.

♦ This is your room of abundance, and everything in this room belongs to you—all the gold, all the jewels, all the banknotes. As you look around, begin to *feel* what it is like to be rich. The gold and jewels are beautiful, and you could get them made into gorgeous jewelry if you wished, or sell them to make more money—although the banknotes are worth an amount of money that should ensure you would never want for anything again, enough money to give you the freedom to go wherever you want to go, do whatever you want to do and have whatever you want to have.

♦ Spend some time just absorbing these feelings, and know that you can return to this mind-picture at any time, and feel these feelings again, whenever you have thoughts of lack and want to return to the thoughts and feelings of wealth and abundance.

THE IMPACT OF GRATITUDE

Gratitude is a powerful process for shifting your energy and bringing more of what you want into your life, so being grateful for what you already have will attract more good things. However, we do need to acknowledge that we're human, and it isn't always easy to feel grateful for what is going on in our lives. When things are going wrong, or we're encountering difficulties, or simply having a bad day, it's easier to grumble about it. Sometimes having a good old moan about things can feel pretty good, and at least it gets it off our chests. However, if you want to attract more good into your life, you need to adopt an "attitude of gratitude," as mentioned in the last chapter. One of the good things I've found about developing the habit of being grateful is that you will naturally begin to feel more joyful and less concerned about what you haven't got.

Something else you can do is to create your day in advance by thinking the way you want it to go. You will then be creating your life intentionally, rather than leaving it to chance with a few stray thoughts. Just spending a few minutes in the morning visualizing the day ahead, perhaps while still lying in bed, can make a world of difference.

A MORNING ABUNDANCE MEDITATION

At the start of each day, decide what you want that day—and in future days too, if you like. Believe you can have it. Believe you deserve it and believe it's possible for you. Then close your eyes for several minutes and visualize having what you want, feeling the feelings of already having it. Come out of that and focus on what you're grateful for already, and really enjoy it. Then go into your day and release it to the Universe and trust that the Universe will figure out how to manifest it.

When you visualize, you generate powerful thoughts and feelings of having it now. The Law of Attraction then returns that reality to you, just as you saw it in your mind. Many athletes and sportsmen and women use this technique to good effect, visualizing their best performance and seeing themselves as winners. If it can work for them, it can work for you.

THE POWER OF EXPECTATION

Expectation is a powerfully attractive force. Expect the things you want, and don't expect the things you don't want. Carl Jung, the famous psychologist, once said, "What you resist, persists." In other words, from the perspective of the Law of Attraction, what you resist, you attract, because you are powerfully focused on it with emotion, so if there are things you don't want in your life, and you keep resisting them by constantly thinking you don't want them, you'll actually be either bringing them into your life, or keeping them there.

THE LAW OF ATTRACTION AND HEALTH

The placebo effect is an example of the Law of Attraction in action. There has been plenty of scientific research which has shown that when patients truly believe that a particular tablet will make them feel better or even cure them, they receive what they believe, even if what they are really taking is a sugar pill.

It is therefore important to focus on perfect health, rather than on the illness you may have. If you don't feel well, don't talk about it—unless you want more of it! And don't take on the identity of an illness by saying things such as "I'm a diabetic." If you need to refuse foods that you know could raise your blood glucose levels too much, you could just say "no, thank you." Don't feel you always need to explain yourself.

Beliefs about aging are also negative, so release those thoughts and focus on health and feeling and looking youthful. You don't need to listen to society's messages about diseases and aging, because they aren't good for you.

Laughter is one of the higher emotions, as it attracts joy, releases negativity and can even lead to miraculous cures. There is scientific evidence that cancer patients who think positively and believe that they can get well have a 75 percent chance of surviving more than five years after diagnosis, whereas patients who don't believe they can get well only have a 25 percent chance of surviving for more than five years. That's surely a big enough difference to convince you that positive thinking is worthwhile.

Whether you find this approach easy to accept, or think it is absolute nonsense, it is at the root of mind–body

187

healing techniques such as affirmations and visualizations, and many medical centers use these methods and find them helpful. Try the following and see how they feel for you:

1. Visualize yourself in a protective bubble, fill the bubble with love, light and Reiki, and let that love and light permeate your physical body, imagining every cell within it filling with love and light.

2. Tell your body you love it—all of it—every day, and thank it for the wonderful job it does of being your vehicle for this life. (Even though parts of it may perhaps not be working exactly as you would like them to, there's a lot more of your body that *is* working, and it needs appreciation for the work it is doing, and will respond lovingly to a loving response from you.)

3. Tell yourself every day—many times—that you love and approve of yourself. Louise Hay, the famous metaphysical teacher from America who pioneered affirmations and understanding the causative levels of physical ill health, believes we don't love ourselves enough, so she recommends saying affirmations (positive statements) aloud many times each day (at least 20 times). Her favorite is "I love and approve of myself," preferably said aloud while looking at yourself in a mirror. I would add another affirmation: "I deserve to be healthy, fit and vibrantly well."

4. Visualizing yourself happy, whole and healthy can be an important part of any recovery process, so if you have any illness or disease at the moment, spend 5 minutes or so *every hour* that you're awake actually

imagining yourself happy, whole and healthy. Imagine how it will feel to be like that. Imagine the things you will be able to do—ordinary things like shopping for new clothes, as well as things you dream of doing, like having holidays in beautiful places, or having someone special in your life.

Note that you can't help the world by focusing on the negative things either—if you absorb and focus on world problems, you not only add to them, but also bring more negative things into your own life. I made a decision some years ago not to listen to or watch the news on radio or television, and not to read newspapers, because they were so full of negativity, and I didn't want to be "polluted" or pulled down by that kind of energy, so you might like to try that, too. I find that if anything is impor-tant enough in the news that I need to know about it, someone will tell me about it.

A THREE-STEP PROCESS FOR CREATING ABUNDANCE WITH REIKI

Abundance isn't just about money; it is about being happy, healthy, fulfilled and enjoying good relationships, so it is about living life to the fullest. These three steps can be used to help you to attract any aspect of abundance, such as a loving relationship or improved health, as well as a more enjoyable job or a higher income. However, Reiki will only work for your highest and greatest good, so if what you are asking for doesn't fulfill that, it won't happen—you will get what you need, rather than what you want. By all means suggest winning the lottery, but if that isn't right for you, it won't happen!

1. Use Reiki to break down your resistance to abundance. Write down a phrase such as "I let go of my resistance to abundance" and hold the paper in your hands for 5 or more minutes, and let Reiki flow into it. Think about the statement as you do so, and you may receive insights into some of your resistances, such as "money doesn't grow on trees" or "you have to work hard for a living," which would indicate that you think acquiring money is difficult—and you can let go of those thoughts.

2. Use Reiki to promote an "attitude of gratitude" for all you have and are. Place one hand on your pelvic area (base chakra) and one hand near your navel (sacral chakra), and allow Reiki to flow into you while repeating a phrase such as "I am grateful for everything in my life." This means everything positive and negative—it is important to feel gratitude for all your experiences, because even the negative ones add something good, such as strengthening your character.

3. Use Reiki to attract abundance into your life:
   ◆ Decide what it is you wish to attract into your life, and create a simple, clear affirmation in the present tense as if you were already there. Some examples are: I am healthy, energized and full of vitality; my job is fulfilling and

rewarding; my life is joyful and abundant; my relationships are happy and loving.

◆ Get into a comfortable position, either sitting or lying down, close your eyes and allow your breathing to become slow and steady.

◆ Place one hand on your forehead, over the brow chakra (third eye) and the other hand on the back of your head over the indentation at the base of your skull.

◆ Then intend that Reiki flow into the issue you want to work on, always remembering to add "for my highest and greatest good."

◆ Repeat your affirmation as you hold this position, and feel the Reiki flowing into you and into your wishes and intention, for about 5 minutes.

◆ Remove your hand from your forehead, but keep your other hand in place at the back of your head. (You can now have both hands behind your head if you wish.) Spend about 5 minutes in meditation, visualizing yourself as you would be if you were to achieve what you want.

◆ Gassho, and give thanks for the Reiki.

I hope what I have said in chapters 9 and 10 will help you to create a more enjoyable and fulfilling life, and make it easier to "live with gratitude." In Part 6 we look at kindness as part of "living the Reiki way," and how being kind to yourself and others can really turn your life around.

part six

LIVING WITH KINDNESS

No act of kindness, no matter how small,
is ever wasted.

Aesop

chapter eleven

KINDNESS BEGINS
WITH YOURSELF

Living with kindness is a vital part of living the Reiki way, and "just for today, be kind to others" is another of the Reiki Principles passed on to us by Dr. Usui. For many people this will be something very familiar, and probably something their parents and teachers will have passed on to them. It may also seem a fairly obvious statement, because we find that if we are kind to others they are usually kind to us.

This seems all the more reasonable when you consider that, at an energetic level, we are all connected, and as your consciousness is raised with Reiki you become more aware that every living thing is a part of you, and that you are a part of it, and that everything is a part of the Divine, God, the Source or whatever you choose to call it. The realization will come that there is no place for prejudice, harsh judgment, cruelty or indifference in a world where we are all connected, all a part of the whole, all one. All people and other mammals, birds, reptiles, fish, insects and plants—and even the planet itself—have a vital role to play and should therefore be valued, respected and treated with kindness.

LIFE AS A MIRROR

It isn't always easy to be kind to everyone—at least, not all the time. The way you relate to other people will be influenced by the following three things:

- A projection or a mirror of the qualities you suppress or do not accept within yourself.
- A reflection of the way people related to you when you were young.
- A reflection of the core beliefs that you have about life.

You may have heard theories about how life mirrors our inner selves, so that what annoys us about other people is really reflecting what we are annoyed about within ourselves. Perhaps it's a disturbing thought, but if you look at the people in your life, they are all mirroring some belief you have about yourself.

- If you are always being criticized at work, you are probably critical of others yourself.
- If you resent being judged too quickly, you probably do that, too.
- If you get cross with people who find it difficult to make decisions, perhaps you're a bit indecisive yourself at times.
- If you're a bit intolerant of fat people, maybe you're concerned about your own weight, or don't like your own body.

Everything in our lives is a reflection of who we are, but it takes courage and honesty to take a good hard look at ourselves, take stock of our beliefs and behavior patterns, and make up our minds to change them—for the better.

DISADVANTAGEOUS BEHAVIORS

In other chapters I mentioned that we are all programmed mentally and emotionally by the significant adults in our early lives, and that our core beliefs about life and the ways we relate to others are usually reflections of, or reactions to, our parents' patterns. However, these negative patterns hold us back. Louise L. Hay, in her book *The Power Is Within You*, refers to "The Big Four"—four categories of behavior that, if you let them run your life, will impede your progress, make you unhappy and sabotage your future. They are:

◆ Criticism
◆ Fear
◆ Guilt
◆ Resentment

We all have beliefs and behaviors that were induced by our families, and it's easy for us to blame our parents, our childhood or our environment, but that just keeps us stuck. We remain victims, and we perpetuate the same problems over and over again. If there are negative patterns that have passed down through our families, we do have the chance to break those patterns so that we don't pass them down to our children or grandchildren. Today is a new day. Now is the moment in which we are creating our future. We can be positive about people. We can value people. We can be kind to people.

LOVING YOURSELF

If you have grown up in Western society, even if you are not a Christian you will probably have heard of the parable of the Good Samaritan, and although it is a very old story, I think it is a useful example here, and I hope that those of you who are not Christians will bear with me for a few minutes.

> A teacher of the Law came up and tried to trap Jesus. "Teacher," he asked, "what must I do to receive eternal life?"
>
> Jesus answered him, "What do the Scriptures say? How do you interpret them?"
>
> The man answered, "Love the Lord your God with all your heart, with all your soul, with all your strength, and with all your mind and love your neighbor as you love yourself."
>
> "You are right," Jesus replied; "do this and you will live."

There is a phrase there that I think is crucial: "Love your neighbor as you love yourself." My feeling is that most people, when they hear that, only really hear the first part—love thy neighbor. They completely forget about loving themselves. They rush about helping everyone else, doing things for everyone else, being kind to everyone else. But the very last person they think of helping, or doing things for, or being kind to, is themselves.

Without wishing to be sexist here, I think it's probably true to say that women are particularly likely to behave in this way—the caring for others is sort of built-in, especially in those who are mothers. Indeed, this type of action has become a normal part of what we might describe as a good life, or as some might say, a Christian way of life. Further, I think that many people believe that lacking consideration for themselves, always putting other people first, never finding time to do the things they enjoy and living life as a kind of martyrdom, is the right way to behave. But is it? Is that what Jesus was reported to have said? I don't think so.

What he said was "Love your neighbor *as you love yourself.*" Surely, then, that means it must be okay to love yourself? Naturally that doesn't mean to the exclusion of everyone else, but at least treat yourself as well as you would treat other people. After all, Jesus didn't say to love your neighbor *better* than you love yourself! Moreover, surely a bit of practice at loving yourself would mean you'd be better equipped to love your neighbor?

The trouble here is that many people have real difficulty with the concept of loving themselves. Even liking themselves can seem pretty hard. Most of us have some problems with self-esteem, and we're not likely to suggest that we're perfect. In fact, we can usually come up with a long list of what we think is wrong with us—but when do we ever come up with a long list of what is right about us: our skills, talents, knowledge, experience, or our nice eyes and kind heart?

If you were born and brought up in Britain, for example, you almost certainly have a harder time liking yourself than do many other nationalities. In our culture it is seen as being "good" to be modest, polite and unemotional (all those stiff upper lips!), and to "keep yourself to yourself." No wonder we find it so hard to accept praise, say what we feel, cry when we're sad, hug each other, admit when we're lonely—or, heaven forbid, actually say good things about ourselves.

One of the most inspirational spiritual messages of the twentieth century is a quotation from "A Return to Love" by Marianne Williamson, and I think it is relevant here.

Our deepest fear is not that we are inadequate. Our deepest fear is that we are powerful beyond measure. It is our light, not our darkness, that most frightens us. We ask ourselves: "Who am I to be brilliant, gorgeous, talented, fabulous?" Actually, who are you *not* to be? You are a child of God. Your playing small doesn't serve the world. There's nothing enlightened about shrinking so that other people won't feel insecure around you.

We were all meant to shine, as children do. We were born to make manifest the glory of God that is within us. It is not just in some of us—it's in *everyone*!

And as we let our own light shine, we unconsciously give other people permission to do the same. As we are liberated from our own fear, our presence automatically liberates others!

This extract encompasses much of what I believe in. We *are* all brilliant, gorgeous, talented and fabulous . . . although we have many different ways of expressing these aspects in our lives. We are *all* valuable and special; every life, every person, has a role to play in the whole. We all impact each other in so many ways, and I think it's important to recognize our own value, to acknowledge how important *we* are, as well as acknowledging and respecting others.

Some years ago I started to act on my beliefs, because I realized I was falling into the trap of always trying to help others and forgetting to look after myself, so I began to treat myself much better. I learned how to say no when people asked me to do things I didn't really want to do; I also learned to say yes more often to things that I thought I might enjoy. I started buying myself fresh flowers for the house every week, and taking myself out for a nice lunch—or at least coffee and cake—regularly. I decided to buy myself a little present each week—nothing too extravagant, but just something that took my fancy, like a magazine, a bar of perfumed soap or a scented candle. I discovered that giving yourself presents is fun, and it doesn't have to be for any special reason, but just because *you* are *you*, and you want to celebrate the fact.

One of the things I bought really helps me with my self-esteem—it's a mirror with a cheeky face painted on the wooden frame, just above the words "Hello Gorgeous." I've hung it by my front door, so every time I go out or come in, or just open the door to a visitor, I see myself in that mirror and just have to smile—and yes, I do sometimes say "Hello Gorgeous" aloud to myself as I go past, and it makes me feel good!

I also began to give myself more time. Time to read a book, meditate or chat with a friend on the phone, or simply time to do nothing. I found that as I gave myself

201

these little treats my "happiness factor" got higher, and as I became happier it was much easier to try to pass that happiness on by helping other people. It felt absolutely fine to give some of my time to others, even if it wasn't always convenient, because I knew that I would also allocate some time just for me. I wasn't feeling under any obligation, or forcing myself to be kind to my neighbor—I was doing it because I wanted to.

In my experience, people who deny their own needs and desires and constantly do what other people want either end up feeling angry and resentful, or, possibly even worse, develop a "holier than thou" attitude, looking down their noses at others who don't choose to work themselves to a frazzle in the name of helpfulness.

♦ Think of one person with whom you've had some conflict, or with whom you feel uncomfortable, and write down three things you really don't like about that individual, or three things (or behaviors) you wish he or she would change.

♦ Now close your eyes and go within, and ask yourself if there is any part of you that is a reflection of the things you don't like about that individual. Be honest with yourself, and don't react with guilt or blame—you always do the best you can with the knowledge and experience you have, but when you gain new knowledge, it helps you to change.

♦ Spend a few moments sending Reiki to the situation between you and the individual, for the highest and greatest good. You can either simply *intend* that Reiki flow to the situation, or write both your names on a piece of paper and hold it in your hands, letting Reiki flow, or if you have Reiki Second Degree, you can connect with the other person by drawing the Distant symbol in the air over the paper, then the Harmony symbol and finally the Power symbol, and let Reiki flow to the situation between you.

◆ When you've finished, clap your hands a couple of times to break the connection.

◆ Spend a few moments giving Reiki to yourself, with your hands placed on your heart chakra or solar plexus chakra, while still sending loving thoughts to the other person (even if this is difficult).

◆ End by visualizing yourself and the other person shaking hands, hugging or whatever feels most appropriate.

Practice kindness toward yourself and others as often as possible. I really like what Wayne W. Dyer says in his book *Manifest Your Destiny*: "Make it your own special mission to be kind to others each day at least once, and to extend the same privilege to yourself as much as possible."

So it is good for us, as well as good for other people, to follow Dr. Usui's precept and "just for today, be kind to others"—including yourself. And remember, *what goes around, comes around*, so as you are kind to others, so you will experience more kindness from them.

In the next chapter I take the concept of kindness to

others a step further, and talk about how the way in which we treat others can build up Karma—or in other words, a debt that has to be repaid in some way, either in this life, or, if you're happy to consider the idea, in the next life.

chapter twelve

KINDNESS AND KARMA

We've probably all heard phrases such as "You reap what you sow," and "Treat others as you would like to be treated," and each would seem to indicate that it's a good idea to be kind to others, because then they are likely to be kind to us. This is the basis of the concept known as Karma.

WHAT IS KARMA?

The way in which Karma is explained depends upon individual religious traditions, but basically it is believed that the sum of everything that an individual has done, is currently doing and will do, will affect his or her future fate. Each person is thus responsible for his or her own life, and the pain and joy it brings to others. In religions that incorporate a belief in reincarnation, Karma extends through each person's present life and all past and future lives as well. It is cumulative.

The basic ethical purpose of Karma is to behave responsibly, and the tenet of Karma is essentially "if you do good things, good things will happen to you, and if you do bad things, bad things will happen to you." Millions of people around the world believe in Karma, and it is a part of many cultures, even those without religious backgrounds. According to Karma, whether you are performing positive or negative actions, the results of either can be seen straightaway, producing a pleasant or difficult life, or they may be delayed—even, potentially, until a future life.

The idea of Karma originally came from Hindu and Buddhist teachings, but was popularized in the West mainly through the work of the Theosophical Society and the New Age movement. It became transmuted into a belief in a kind of good luck and bad luck, depending upon whether someone performed good, spiritually valuable acts, or the opposite. There is also the metaphysical idea that Karma is universal, and not dispensed by something or someone judgmental, that it is about positive and negative *energy*, where negative energy can include things not seen as "being bad," like sadness and fear, and positive energy can be caused by being creative and solving problems, as well as by exuding love and doing virtuous acts.

Karma can therefore be a logical and understandable way of making sense of good and evil, the different qualities of different lives and the different moral statuses of different people, without having to involve rules laid down by a higher power. Ill fortune can be best avoided by behaving well at all times so that no bad Karma is attracted. Which brings us back to kindness.

RANDOM ACTS OF KINDNESS

A random act of kindness is defined as a selfless act performed by a person or persons wishing to either assist or cheer up a complete stranger. There will generally be no reason for it, other than to make people smile or be happier. Random acts of kindness can be either spontaneous or planned in advance. They can include all sorts of things, from giving gifts to family or friends for no particular reason, to mowing a neighbor's lawn or taking a meal to an elderly person, to paying for a stranger's bus fare or parking ticket.

Pay It Forward

In the year 2000 the film *Pay It Forward* was released, starring Kevin Spacey, Helen Hunt and Haley Joel Osment, and it had a profound effect on many of the people who watched it because it was based on the idea of random acts of kindness.

It is the story of twelve-year-old Trevor McKinney, who was given an assignment by his new social studies teacher to think of something that will change the world, and put it into action. Trevor comes up with the idea of, rather than paying back a favor, paying it forward. He decides that if he can do good deeds for three people, and they in turn can "pay it forward" to three new people, who in turn pay it forward to another three, and so on and so on, positive changes can happen.

He describes his idea to his mother and teacher, saying that if he does a favor for three people, and they ask how they can pay it back, he suggests that instead, they pay it forward, to three new people. Then he gets out his calculator, and shows them how this would spread out so that 9 people get helped, then 27, then 81, then 243, then 729, then 2,187, and so on.

Trevor's efforts to make his idea work bring a revolution not only to his life and the lives of his mother and teacher, but also to an ever-widening circle of people completely unknown to him, as they spread from city to city. People begin to help others, and to bestow kindnesses in completely unexpected ways. The investigative reporter who eventually finds Trevor and publicizes the idea so that it can spread even more widely is one of the recipients of a random act of kindness, which has sparked his curiosity. He was given the keys to a man's two-year-old car when his own car broke down. The man took the old car in exchange and explained that a great deal of generosity had come into his life lately, so he thought he could pass it on. So an idea from a young boy who believed in the good hearts of people became something that changed the world for the better—just as his school assignment had asked him to do. It was a world where generosity and kindness became commonplace— a happier world.

The film was based on the book of the same name written by Catherine Ryan Hyde, who wrote it because she became the recipient of almost the same kind of random act of kindness as the reporter in the story— a complete stranger helped her with her broken-down car. Although it started as an idea in a novel, since the book and the film were released a real-life social movement has begun, not just in the United States where the story is set, but elsewhere too. If you look up "random acts of kindness" on any Internet search engine, you will find hundreds of websites dedicated to this idea of being kind to others just for the fun of it.

Don't you think that's an inspiring story? Wouldn't it be wonderful if we *all* did that? The great thing is, when you do something kind for someone, you feel good too, so everyone benefits. I had heard the phrase "random acts of kindness" a few years ago, although I didn't know where it had come from, but I have been putting it into practice ever since. Not on a daily basis, I'll admit, but every now and then. Recently I was in the local pharmacy, where I overheard the assistant telling a lady that they didn't have the medication she needed in stock, but the pharmacy in a village five miles away had it. The lady was rather distressed by this news, as she needed the medication fairly urgently, but unfortunately she didn't have a car, and country bus services aren't particularly frequent. I decided to offer my help—I drove to the next village, collected the prescription and delivered it to her, as she actually lived farther down the same road as I do, although I had never met her before. Why did I do it? Well, it was a nice sunny day, I had some time to spare, and I'm lucky enough to have a car and enjoy driving, so why not? And anyway, I do try to "live the Reiki way," so being kind to others has become a natural thing for me.

His Holiness the Dalai Lama says: "When we feel love and kindness toward others, it not only makes others feel loved and cared for, but it helps us also to develop inner happiness and peace."

Giving Gifts

What can you give easily, effortlessly and happily, as random acts of kindness? Here are a few ideas found on an Internet site, which I thought were lovely:

- Gift of service—do something useful for someone, like carrying their groceries, sending their letters or tending their garden; or donate to a good cause.
- Gift of affection—be generous with hugs, kisses and pats on the back.
- Gift of laughter—share funny stories verbally or by e-mail, cut out cartoons from the paper and give them to someone.
- Gift of writing—send a thank-you note, write a letter to an old friend, keep in touch regularly by e-mail.
- Gift of a compliment—a simple "you look great today," a sincere "thank you for a wonderful meal."
- Gift of listening—no interrupting, no daydreaming, no responding, just listening.
- Gift of solitude—spend some time in silence, and respect others' need for silence.

DEVELOPING LOVING-KINDNESS

In a Buddhist tradition, Loving-Kindness is the first of four meditation practices to develop the four qualities of love: Friendliness (*metta*), Compassion (*karuna*), Appreciative Joy (*mudita*) and Equanimity (*upekkha*). The idea is that the warmth of friendliness reaches out and embraces others, spreading loving-kindness, compassion, empathy and appreciation of other people's good fortune and good qualities, so that ultimately you remain kindly disposed and caring toward everybody, with an equal spread of loving feelings and acceptance in all situations and relationships.

That may sound like a tall order, but as with any meditation practice, you start wherever you feel comfortable and progress as you gain confidence in the process. There are recommendations for the people you might try to develop acceptance and loving-kindness toward, in these stages, as part of your spiritual practice:

- First, and perhaps not unexpectedly, yourself.
- Then you might include someone you respect, such as a spiritual teacher.
- Then someone close to you who you care about.
- Then a neutral person, someone you know but have no particular feelings about.
- And finally someone with whom you are currently having problems.

There are a number of methods of developing feelings of loving-kindness, and you can use all of them or just the one that works best for you as your meditation practice:

- Visualization—picture yourself smiling, or the other person smiling at you, and showing that he or she is feeling happy, and hold this picture in your mind for several minutes or longer.
- Reflection—think about the positive qualities of yourself or the other person, and reflect on these for several minutes or as long as you wish.
- Auditory—repeat a mantra or phrase such as "loving-

211

kindness" aloud or silently in your mind for as long as is comfortable for you, while thinking about yourself or the other person.

However, the purpose of this meditation practice is to enable you to develop loving-kindness toward everyone around you, not just to the few people you have chosen in the above exercise. So take the attitude of friendliness, openness and empathy into your daily life, at home, work and into all your relationships.

USING REIKI TO LET KINDNESS FLOW

You can use the flow of Reiki as part of being kind to others, as well as to yourself. Giving yourself a daily Reiki self-treatment is one way of being kind to yourself, and offering Reiki to family and friends is a lovely way of being kind to them—providing you don't make your offer in such a way that they feel obliged to accept! It doesn't always have to be a full treatment.

◆ If someone you know has a headache, you could ask if they would like you to place your hands on their head to help to alleviate the pain.
◆ If they're feeling agitated, you could offer to stand behind them and place your hands on their shoulders and let the Reiki flow until they feel calmer.
◆ If you have done a Reiki Second Degree course, you could offer to send a distant treatment to someone who is ill (you should have their permission before sending it).

◆ You could send Reiki to a world situation by writing it down on a piece of paper and holding the paper in your hands for a while, letting Reiki flow into it for the greatest and highest good. If you have Reiki Second Degree, you can draw the Distant symbol in the air over the paper to connect to the situation, then the Harmony symbol to bring peace and harmony, then the Power symbol to bring the Reiki in powerfully. (If you are sending the Reiki to some kind of disaster such as a great flood or a volcanic eruption, it will flow to everyone involved, from those directly affected by the disaster, to the aid agencies, medical and emergency staff, government departments who can release funds, and so on.)

Using Reiki in this way is a wonderful method of fulfilling your commitment to "be kind to others" every day. There is so much pleasure to be found in the power of kindness, but actually it is one of the most difficult things to give away, because it is almost always returned to us. I saw a phrase on a website that I thought summed this up: "When we bring sunshine into the lives of others, we're warmed by it ourselves; when we spill a little happiness, it splashes on us."

Developing loving-kindness as a way of being makes us feel good inside, because it brings enjoyment and gladness back to us—and if there is such a thing as Karma, then being kind to others is likely to benefit us in that way, too!

I'd like to finish this chapter with another saying, this time from Lao Tse:

Kindness in words creates confidence.
Kindness in thinking creates profundity.
Kindness in giving creates love.

Let kindness flow in your spoken and written words, in your thoughts and in the generosity of your giving. As Dr. Usui suggested: just for today, be kind to others.

In Part 7 we look at the last of Dr. Usui's Principles, "just for today, work hard," both in terms of working hard in our daily lives, perhaps for an employer, and working hard on ourselves, for our personal development and spiritual growth.

part seven

LIVING, WORKING
AND LEARNING

You are a limitless being in a limitless universe, with the
power to create whatever you want.

Reverend Simon John Barlow

chapter thirteen

WORKING HONESTLY AND DILIGENTLY

There are various translations of Dr. Usui's Principle, "Goo hage me" (pronounced *gyo oh hah gay may*):

- Work hard.
- Do your work diligently.
- Do your work honestly.
- Be honest in your work.

But what does it really mean? Each interpretation could be seen in different ways. In terms of "work hard," from one perspective it could sound as though we're being encouraged to become workaholics—although I'm pretty sure that's not what is intended—it certainly wouldn't be "living the Reiki way." Is it about "doing a fair day's work for a fair day's pay"? Possibly, but there's probably more to it than that. Or are we just being reminded that we shouldn't steal anything from our workplace? Well, maybe that is valid too, but I don't suppose that was uppermost in Usui's mind, either. No, it's much more likely that he was keen for us to work hard on ourselves, or in other words, work on our personal and spiritual development, but that isn't necessarily the way this Principle has been interpreted in the West over the years, so I'll come back to spiritual growth later in this and the next chapter.

WORK HARD/DO YOUR WORK DILIGENTLY

In our fast-paced society, when we talk about work we are usually referring to paid employment, although "work" can include all those everyday tasks in the home, too. But "work hard" has become even more a part of our way of life today as many organizations downsize or introduce new technology to reduce their workforces. This leads to a culture of working longer and longer hours to cope with a greater workload for those who are left, alongside an increase in stress and feelings of insecurity. In the UK, for instance, people work the longest hours in Europe, and many work in excess of 60 hours a week, especially those in supervisory or management positions; on top of that, many people commute to their jobs for several hours a day. This inevitably leads to an unhealthy imbalance in a person's life, because there is less time to spend with family and friends, or in leisure pursuits, or simply relaxing and getting enough sleep.

I think one of the mistakes we make is believing that "work hard" means "work faster" or "work longer." There's a really good book by Richard Carlson and Joseph Bailey entitled *Slowing Down to the Speed of Life*, which tackles this problem. They maintain that you actually "need to slow down in order to deal with increased demands, because when people are feeling rushed and frantic, they make more mistakes, deal with others poorly, burn out and lose their ability to think clearly, creatively and intelligently." Does that sound familiar? Or do you recognize those traits in someone close to you? As someone who used to teach time management and stress management, I can certainly agree with what they say, and I know that if I'm rushing around trying to get too many things done at once, I become much less efficient and a bit grumpy.

Carlson and Bailey talk about "working smart" as the ideal in a fast-paced world. That means "listening, reflecting, and then acting, rather than reacting out of habit. It means knowing how to live your life in the moment—doing one thing at a time, with presence and at a pace that lead to balance in your personal and work life."

They use a really good example of what that means, and they call it "living above the line":

Visionary
Dynamic
Self-motivated

Stressed
Survival Oriented
Bureaucratic/Dysfunctional

If you are living below the line, then your working environment is unsatisfactory, fear-based and out of control; your employers have a poor understanding of their employees' needs, and there will probably be a high turnover of staff—if this resonates with you, it might be time for you to go too.

If you're living above the line, however, your working life will be productive and satisfying, and you will feel part of a team if you work for an organization, rather than just a cog in a wheel—or of course, it could describe how you would feel if you worked for yourself, for instance as a writer, Reiki practitioner or Reiki Master. (I'm definitely an "above-the-line" worker!)

Part of this issue relates to the following questions:

♦ Do you do your work willingly and with a good heart?

♦ Or are you reluctant, only doing your work because you have to, or because it is the only way you can see to earn a living?

The attitude you have to your job, or to your work in the home, makes a great deal of difference. If it is done gladly and cheerfully, with a loving heart, any work can become more enjoyable, even boring, difficult or dirty tasks. But if it is done grudgingly, apathetically or under duress, everything will seem so much harder, and it becomes a vicious circle—you hate the work, so it feels more difficult, so you hate it more . . . ad infinitum!

VALUING YOUR WORK

It is therefore important to respect any work that you have chosen for yourself and to honor yourself by doing your best to create a feeling of satisfaction in it. *All* work is valuable to the extent that we choose to value it, so it is possible to take satisfaction from even the simplest tasks, and to be willing to do everything to the best of our ability. There is an old Zen Buddhist saying: "Before enlightenment chop wood, carry water; after enlightenment, chop wood, carry water."

No matter how much of your life you dedicate to spirituality, you will probably still need to work in some manner to feed yourself, clothe yourself, keep yourself warm and live comfortably.

So if working too hard is an issue in your life—or even if it isn't—sometimes feeling unhappy or unsettled or even just bored at work can be an indication that it is time to move on—perhaps you need to ask yourself some more questions:

- What is your role or job?
- What drives you?
- What are your ambitions and dreams?
- How do you feel about what you do to earn a living?
- What do you believe to be your life purpose?

As you may know, one of the effects of Reiki is to help you to grow spiritually, and this usually calls for change. Even if you have previously been happy in your job, or have felt settled in your career or been comfortable with the ethics (or lack of them) in your place of employment, you might feel differently now, so take a little time to consider the questions above. Maybe you've just gone on from day to day in the job you're doing out of habit, and perhaps it's time to reconsider and reassess, look at new options, reevaluate how you feel and consider other types of work that you might find more satisfying and more in tune with the real you, now, rather than the you of however many years ago you chose that type of employment.

Empowering Goals with Reiki

One way of helping yourself is to use Reiki to work on your goals and ambitions, and you can use the following technique for this. Decide what it is you wish to work on, then create simple, clear affirmations or goals in the present tense, as if they were already in existence, such as "I have the perfect job which is fun, fulfilling and financially rewarding," then place one hand on your forehead, the other behind your head, and let Reiki flow, allowing yourself to visualize your life as it will be when you have achieved your goal.

Write Down Your Goals

Another way of working with affirmations and goals—such as getting the perfect job for yourself—is by writing them down, holding the paper in your hands and letting Reiki flow into them for your greatest and highest good, saying the affirmation over and over to yourself while giving them Reiki for a few minutes. If you have Reiki Second Degree you can draw all three symbols in the air over the paper, saying their mantras in the usual order—Distant, Harmony and Power—before beginning to say the affirmation. Do this for at least 10 minutes a day until you achieve what you want—or until you change your mind, because we don't always realize what we really want straightaway, but by working on it in this way, the issue becomes clearer.

Think About Your Goals

Yet another way of creating what you want is to work in harmony with the Law of Attraction (see chapter 10) by focusing on what you want, such as a fun, fulfilling and well-paid job, as mentioned above. Visualize it often, but don't keep thinking about what you dislike about your current job, because you get what you focus on, and you'll just stay in your unsatisfactory employment.

DO YOUR WORK HONESTLY/BE HONEST IN YOUR WORK

Another translation of this Principle is "do your work honestly" or "be honest in your work." Being honest and truthful are obviously good traits in anyone, whether in the workplace or at home, but my feeling is that this Principle is about being honest with yourself, as well as with others. It means accepting yourself for who you are. We often confuse what we *do* with who we *are*, taking our sense of identity from the kind of job we have—or do not have. I'm frequently amused when I attend a gathering of new people, because one of the first questions I get asked is, "And what do you do?" as if my job title is the most important thing about me. As previously noted, what we all need to remember is that we are human *beings*, not human *doings*. We shouldn't be judged as a person simply by what work we do, although of course it is one of the valid aspects of our makeup. As Marianne Williamson said, we are *all* valuable and special. Every life, every person has a role to play in the whole, and we all impact one another in many different ways. Society

223

seems to have a built-in hierarchy of jobs that are seen as important and high status, such as doctors and lawyers, and those that are seen as less valuable and low status, such as manual laborers and garbage collectors. But realistically that's ridiculous.

Okay, doctors can save lives and lawyers can sort out our legal problems, but think what a mess we'd be in if no one collected our garbage, or worked on building or repairing our homes and roads. We are all interdependent in modern society, because humankind has become collectively specialized, rather than self-sufficient, so we should honor and respect everyone for the important part they play in our lives, because without them life as we know it today would be unrecognizable. For most of us it would mean no food in our refrigerator (and no refrigerator!), no transportation to work, no schools for our children, no hospitals for our sick, no clothes to buy, etc. Get the picture? We rely heavily on everyone around us to "do their work honestly"; to do the best they can, for our benefit as well as theirs.

One of the ways of being honest in your work is to follow your life purpose, and sometimes we already have a strong sense of what that is, especially if we are following a spiritual path and learning to "live what we love." However, if you don't currently have a clue about your life purpose, you can use Reiki to help you to discover it.

LIFE-PURPOSE MEDITATION

1. Start by sitting or lying down comfortably, and steady your breathing until it is deep and slow and you feel centered.

2. Begin to fill yourself with Reiki from head to toe, until you can feel the Reiki vibrations in your hands, and sense that it is flowing all around you, within your body and outside your body, in your aura, raising your consciousness.

3. Imagine yourself somewhere beautiful, like on a beach, or in a flower-filled meadow, or a sunlit forest glade, and spend a few moments connecting with that image with all your senses.

4. Then imagine that a little ways in front of you is a ladder, a rainbow or a beam of light coming down from way, way up high, and walk toward it and begin to climb up the ladder, or allow yourself to slide up the rainbow or beam of light. (If you have Reiki Second Degree, you can imagine that the ladder or beam of light is the Distant symbol, connecting you with the higher realms.)

5. As you climb higher, you become aware that your body is becoming lighter, until you realize that while you are still recognizable as you, you no longer have a dense physical body, but a body of beautiful, rainbow-colored light.

6. As you reach this realization, you also reach another higher dimension, and waiting for you are some wise beings of light, and you can feel the

happiness and unconditional love flowing from them as they welcome you.

7. You follow them to a place where you can all sit together, and they invite you to ask whatever you need to ask. On this occasion you have come to ask about your life purpose, and how much progress you have made so far on your life path, and what else you need to do to fulfill your purpose and your potential in this particular life.

8. Give yourself plenty of time to receive the replies, which may be in words or images, symbols or physical objects, or even charts or maps showing where you are now and where you are going. If you are presented with anything you don't understand it's okay to ask for an explanation—these are high spiritual guides, including your own Higher Self, and their intention is purely to help you as lovingly as they can.

9. When you sense that you have been given all the information that is there for you at this time, thank the beings of light for their help, and let them lead you back to the top of the ladder, rainbow or beam of light, but know that you may return here whenever you wish to ask for guidance.

10. With a final wave goodbye, allow yourself to slowly descend until you reach the bottom of the ladder, rainbow or beam of light, and spend a few minutes in that beautiful place you have created, remembering what you have experienced.

11. Allow your awareness to return to your body, feeling the chair or bed beneath you, and hearing the sounds in the room. If you feel a little woozy, clap or shake your hands for a moment to bring you back into full awareness.

12. Finally, write down what you have just experienced, so you can examine it a few times to gain as much insight and inspiration from it as you can. You may find you have been given a full life plan, or just one or two points, or the first time you do this visualization you may just get a feeling of deep peace—but persevere and in time you will get the information you are seeking about your life path and life purpose.

I'd like to finish this chapter with some advice adapted from an old Irish prayer (author unknown):

Take time to work—it is the price of success
Take time to meditate—it is the source of power
Take time to play—it is the secret of perpetual youth
Take time to read—it is the way to knowledge
Take time to be friendly—it is the road to happiness
Take time to laugh—it is the music of the soul
And take time to love and be loved—it is the path to joy and contentment.

In the next chapter we explore ways in which you can work on your spiritual development and personal growth, to fulfill what I believe Dr. Usui wanted us to do—just for today work hard—on yourself.

227

chapter fourteen

SELF-AWARENESS, PERSONAL GROWTH AND SPIRITUAL DEVELOPMENT

As mentioned at the beginning of the last chapter, it is most likely that Dr. Usui's original Principle, "work hard," was intended to mean work hard on yourself, or in other words, work on your personal development and spiritual growth with Reiki and meditation. In this penultimate chapter I suggest a range of other self-help techniques too, such as an NLP technique, and ways to connect to your Higher Self, to help you to develop spiritually and achieve self-awareness and understanding, mindfulness, a sense of purpose, and feelings of joy, bliss and fulfillment. Of course, there are other ways to help your growth and development:

- ◆ Reading inspirational books—there are literally hundreds nowadays in bookstores and libraries, and there is a selection I recommend in Further Reading (see page 255).
- ◆ Learning yoga or t'ai chi—your local library or college should have details of classes in your area. Or check offerings at a fitness or community center.

- Learning various types of meditation practice—again, your library or nearby college might have information about classes, or you may find brochures in a health-food store.
- Spending time in nature—visiting the beach or countryside, or a nearby park or your own garden, can all be uplifting.
- Studying academic subjects such as psychology or theology, if these interest you—and again, your local college might have suitable day or evening courses, or you could try an online university, which has a wide variety of courses at various levels, not just for those wanting to pursue a degree.

The essence here is that this is a personal journey; it should be what you want it to be, and at the pace you set for yourself. However, it is important to remember that *doing* something spiritual isn't necessarily the same as *being* spiritual. Reading many spiritual or self-help books is only useful if you put what you read into practice.

We're all spiritual, all of the time, because that is what we are—*spirits having a human experience, not humans having a spiritual experience!* However, developing your spiritual awareness can help you along your spiritual path in this life, and it doesn't have to be deathly serious—loads of meditation, difficult yoga postures, chanting "om" at every opportunity—all of those things can be great, if you want to do them. However, each person's spiritual journey has to be taken at a pace and in the way that suits him or her, and we are all individuals, so what suits one person may not suit another. In this chapter I introduce

229

you to a variety of "spiritual experiences" and ideas that can become part of your own spiritual toolbox, to be taken out when you're ready to use them.

DEVELOPING YOUR SPIRITUAL AWARENESS

Unfortunately many people don't have much awareness of their spiritual selves, so they spend a lot of time trying to fill an inexplicable void within themselves by seeking power, money and material success. But the answer doesn't lie outside ourselves; it is internal, not external, and it is the essence within us all, the wise, loving, powerful and creative inner core of our being that some call the Higher or Inner Self. Connecting with it is easier than most people think, yet without this connection it is often difficult to find the strength, understanding and inspiration we need to live our lives.

Some people's spiritual "wake-up call" happens during major changes or traumas in their lives such as a near-death experience, the birth of a baby or the serious illness of someone close to them. At these times we become very focused, so the more superficial preoccupations of everyday life get pushed into the background, enabling us to reach a different state. The spiritual awareness of others grows slowly over time, usually through developing a spiritual practice such as meditation or prayer—and practicing Reiki can also act in this way.

SPIRITUAL FITNESS

Some years ago I read an interesting article by Caroline Reynolds in *Here's Health* magazine, on how to be spiritually fit, which was about our need to develop a lifestyle and attitude to help us to rediscover the real meaning and sacredness of our lives. We all want to have clarity, inner strength and a sense of purpose in our lives, but like physical fitness, it can take effort and ongoing commitment. Getting spiritually fit means living authentically, being true to yourself in everything you do in your work, relationships and leisure time, and making life choices from a place of courage, love and trust, instead of from fear— which is really what "living the Reiki way" is all about, too.

Being spiritually fit means living more consciously by being more grounded, clear and compassionate. This helps us to make more sense of our lives, because it allows us to connect with others from a place of deeper understanding. When we're spiritually connected we can experience improved relationships, enhanced creativity, a sense of purpose and direction, a deep inner peace and real enjoyment of our lives. Being spiritually "switched on" gives us greater happiness and fulfillment.

To get spiritually fit we need to use soul-level awareness, which means raising our thinking to a higher level and viewing our lives in the context of the bigger picture. Instead of just reacting to life in the ways we've done in the past, we can start asking ourselves "What is the purpose, the highest truth, the soul gift for me in this situation?" This will change things in ways that, to begin with, we can barely imagine.

As well as trying some of the other techniques in this book, we can start by appreciating our unique gifts and taking better care of ourselves, partly by living consciously and directing our attention to the areas of life that most fulfill us and bring us the most joy.

Make a list of the ten things that bring you the greatest happiness, and start to incorporate at least one of them into your life every day. This could be spending more time out in the fresh air, doing something creative like painting or writing, listening to music, spending time with friends, baking, reading or stargazing—or any number of other things you might enjoy.

Make a commitment to doing something special for yourself every week, like buying fresh flowers for your home, taking yourself out to lunch (even if it's just a bowl of soup or a sandwich, shared with friends or enjoyed on your own) or buying a scented candle to light each evening.

Practice happiness, because as His Holiness the Dalai Lama says: "The purpose of life is to be happy!"

CONNECTING WITH YOUR HIGHER SELF

There are various ways of connecting with your Higher Self, and the simplest involves finding somewhere quiet where you can be alone and undisturbed for a while (somewhere in nature is especially good—a garden, park, riverbank, etc.), then either sitting or lying down, and *intending* to connect with your inner voice. (Energy follows thought, so your intention sets up the connection.) You may have some questions to ask, so feel free to ask whatever you need to know.

When answers pop into your mind it can initially be rather confusing, and you may think the answers are just your own imagination, but one thing that can help you distinguish between guidance and your own thinking process is the speed of the answers. When it is guidance from your Higher Self, the answer often pops into your mind even before you've finished formulating the question. Gradually you will begin to trust this intuitive sense more, and the more you trust it, the more guidance you will receive.

Automatic Writing

Another way of getting guidance from your Higher Self is through a process called automatic writing. The method I describe is one I use regularly myself, and it is really quite simple. It involves activating the creative and intuitive side of your brain—the right side—by initially writing with your left hand. (Left-handed people may be able to do it this way too, or they may initially have to use their right hand—it depends where their creative blocks are.) Having a special notebook for your automatic writing can be a good idea, as you may want to refer back to some guidance you received last week, last month or even after several years, so do date each entry.

1. First of all, with your pen held in the hand you usually write with, write down one or two questions you would like answered. You can try something like: "Who am I?" "Why am I here?" or "What is my purpose?" and "How do I achieve that?" They are pretty profound questions, but you may be amazed at the answers you will get—sometimes people get just a few words, a sentence or two, or images or symbols, but at other times they get page after page of information. Or you can address an issue you are struggling with, such as: "What can I do to help myself to be healthier?"

2. Next, hold your pen in your left hand and write the statement: "Activate right brain." This may feel pretty strange at first, but you may be surprised at how easy it can be. However, if what you have written is barely legible, and you found it really difficult, still with the pen in your left hand write down the statement: "Yes, I can." That is just giving yourself permission to access your creative, intuitive side, and it really works.

3. Begin to concentrate on your breathing, and as you breathe in, silently say to yourself whatever question you want answered; as you breathe out, continue silently saying the question to yourself. Then, in the pause between breaths (i.e., when your lungs are empty), begin to write (with the pen still held in your left hand) whatever pops into your head. At first you may get nothing or very little, or even some words that don't make any sense. Don't worry about this—it is just your ego putting up

resistance and getting in the way. Persevere, and this technique can result in some amazing insights and guidance.

4. When you need to breathe in again, stop writing, and let yourself inhale and exhale, then, during the pause between breaths, continue your automatic writing. Carry on like this until you no longer get any further response to your question. You can then go on to your next question, and the process is the same.

5. Breathe in, breathe out and write during the pause between breaths until you are no longer getting any information.

6. If the answers are flowing easily and quite fast, you have obviously established an easy rapport and good connection with your Higher Self, so you can stop writing with your left hand and transfer the pen to your right hand (if that is your usual writing hand) and carry on. You may even be able to just continue writing without waiting for the pause between breaths, but try the full exercise several times first.

7. You can then either go on to another question, or stop and read and contemplate what you have written.

CONNECTING WITH GUIDES AND ANGELS

If you are comfortable with the idea, you can connect with a spirit guide or angel in a visualization, and there are many ways of doing this. The simplest is to sit quietly, close your eyes, and ask and *intend* at the beginning of a visualization to meet a guide or a guardian angel, then allow your mind to imagine yourself meeting him or her in a forest glade or on top of a spiritual mountain (for example). If you have Reiki Second Degree, you can enhance that connection by using the Reiki Distant Symbol to connect the two of you. Then just ask any questions you like and wait for the answers, which might be in words, images or symbols (for instance, an oak tree might mean strength is needed), or an object as a gift (such as a map to show you the best way forward). When the answers stop coming, remember to thank your guide or angel, then allow your awareness to return so that you can hear, sense and see your actual surroundings again.

Another way of connecting with angelic guidance is by using a variety of Angel Cards. My favorites are the Archangel Oracle Cards and Healing with the Angels Oracle Cards, both by Doreen Virtue, but there are many others on the market. Find a pack that appeals to you— sometimes holding packs in your hands for a few moments while you are in a store can help you to decide which pack feels "right" before you buy it.

When using the pack, hold it in your hands for a few moments to connect it with your energy. Then shuffle the cards and either lay them out in a fan on the floor or a table and select one, or let the pack fall open in your hands, select a card that is revealed and read whatever it says and think about its guidance.

Why does this work? Because everything is energy, and each card has different illustrations and words on it that give it a different energy from those around it. Your guardian angel (or Higher Self) knows what guidance you need, and helps you to select the right card for that moment in time, based on its energetic vibration.

A PIECE OF CAKE

This is a very useful NLP process that can be used in many varied ways, from accessing your natural healing abilities to helping you to learn more easily, but here we use it to help with your spiritual development—to make it easy or, in other words, "a piece of cake."

First you need to create three spaces on the floor. These can be in your imagination, or you can place pieces of paper down on the floor to indicate which is which.

1. A time when it was easy for me to feel peaceful, whole and spiritually aware, or when meditation was easy.

2. A time when I found it difficult to feel peaceful, whole and spiritually aware or when it was hard to meditate.

3. Neutral Space.

1. Stand on the Neutral Space and think about a particular situation, such as your spiritual development or personal growth, and how you would like to become more self-aware and peaceful, for instance, or if you find it difficult to meditate successfully or anticipate that it might be difficult.

2. From the Neutral Space, step forward and to your right and "anchor" how it feels for you to find meditation or spiritual development difficult, i.e., use your inner vision and all your senses to bring that alive. Step back to the Neutral Space.

3. Take one step forward to your left and really remember and anchor a time when you felt peaceful and self-aware, and found meditation easy and fun—when it was "a piece of cake." Step back to the Neutral Space.

4. Step forward and left from the Neutral Space into the Easy to Meditate Space, then right into the Difficult to Meditate Space and back to Neutral.

5. Repeat this process for as long as you wish, finishing in the Neutral Space.

6. From there, step to the space that was the Difficult to Meditate Space, and notice how that feels to you now. If it now feels really hard to imagine that meditation or spiritual development could be difficult, and you feel much happier and more relaxed about it, you have succeeded, but if you want to, you can step back to the Neutral Space and repeat Step 4 to enhance your feelings even more.

7. When you feel you have successfully completed this

exercise, step away from the three spaces you've been using and spend some time assimilating the feeling that now you will find meditation or spiritual development easier—and smile!

DEVELOPING A MORE SPIRITUAL LIFESTYLE

Here are a few ideas for living your daily life in a more spiritual way—but more important, perhaps, for doing things in whatever way makes your life happier and more joyful.

- ◆ Regularly review what you want your life to be like—the summer and winter solstices (around June 21 and December 21), and the spring (March) and autumn (September) equinoxes, are ideal times for this.
- ◆ Make time just to "be"—time for joy and relaxation, taking a bubble bath, walking in the country, quality time with loved ones.
- ◆ Look after your body—give it good, nourishing food, plenty of water, some enjoyable exercise and enough sleep, and some occasional treats, like an aromatherapy massage.
- ◆ Devote some time to spirituality—daily meditation, reading self-help books, or going on an occasional inspirational course, workshop or retreat.
- ◆ Try to simplify your life—clear your clutter, spend your time and money wisely rather than wasting them on things that are not your priorities.

- Release any old emotions, thinking patterns or habits that are clogging up your energy, including any idea that life is a struggle. Commit to a life filled with joy and ease instead.
- Raise your vibrational frequency with regular Reiki self-treatments and some of the Reiki activities described in this book.
- Make some time for fun and laughter, because they raise your vibrations, too.
- Trust your inner guidance and "go with the flow," allowing the Law of Attraction to bring you what you want and need, easily and effortlessly.
- Find your higher purpose through meditation, visualization, NLP, EFT or any other self-help methods that appeal to you, and then *live it*.

And of course, *live the Reiki way*:
Just for today, do not anger
Do not worry, and be filled with gratitude
Devote yourself to your work and be kind to people

I hope Part 7 has brought some insight into your working life, and given you ideas to help with your personal growth and spiritual development. In Part 8 I suggest a couple of daily practices that will also help you to "live the Reiki way."

part eight

LIVING WITH THE REIKI PRINCIPLES TODAY

Every journey starts with a single step;
make today your first step into a better future
and begin living more joyfully.

Penelope Quest

chapter fifteen

LIVING THE REIKI WAY AS A DAILY PRACTICE

In the preceding chapters I gave you a range of Reiki techniques and other self-help methods to help you to deal with each aspect of the Reiki Principles, which I hope will lead you to being able to live in the present, without anger or worry, with gratitude and kindness and with an acceptance of working on yourself as a life-long process. In this final chapter I add to all the techniques I suggested by providing a daily practice to support you in "living the Reiki way." I am proposing this as a practice that you can do every day, but of course, just as Dr. Usui began his Principles with the phrase "just for today," you can decide each day whether it feels right to do it.

1. SELF-TREATMENT

Giving yourself a Reiki treatment each day would be a good way to start. If you place your hands for about 3 minutes in each of the 12 hand positions suggested in chapter 1, your self-treatment will take just over half an hour, and of course you can schedule this for any time of day that is convenient for you. You can make it feel even more special by lighting a candle, and perhaps an incense stick, and playing some soft music, so that the occasion is deeply relaxing.

2. A REIKI MEDITATION AND CLEANSING TECHNIQUE

This is called Hatsurei-ho in Japan, and it can provide a beautiful, peaceful start or end to the day. Its basic functions are three-fold:

1. To cleanse the outer part of your energy body (the aura) with dry bathing or brushing.
2. Then to cleanse the inner part of your energy body by bringing Reiki into yourself with the cleansing breath.
3. When you are cleansed internally and externally, it allows you to bring more Reiki into yourself for your own personal healing, and to send Reiki out for global healing.

This technique may look a bit long, but actually it's fairly simple and can take as little as 10 minutes, or you can stretch out the more meditative parts of it (the Cleansing Breath, and Concentration or Meditation) to half an hour or more—it's up to you.

1. Make yourself comfortable, sitting either on the floor or on a chair, then close your eyes, allow yourself to relax and bring your breathing into a slow, steady rhythm as you center yourself and focus your thoughts.

2. Place your hands in gassho (prayer position) and *intend* to begin the Reiki meditation and cleansing technique.

3. **Dry bathing or brushing off** This combines loud exhalations (make a sound like "haaaaah") with rapid hand movements as you brush quickly from one shoulder to the opposite hip, or down each arm from shoulder to fingertips.

4. Place your right hand near the top of your left shoulder, hand lying flat, fingers and thumb close together, and draw it swiftly diagonally across your chest down to your right hip while exhaling noisily—"haaaah."

5. Do the same thing on the other side, placing your left hand on your right shoulder, and brush down from the right shoulder to the left hip, again exhaling loudly.

6. Return your right hand to your left shoulder and repeat the process again, with your right hand brushing diagonally from your left shoulder to your right hip and exhaling loudly.

7. Place your right hand on your left shoulder again, and this time draw it quickly down the outside of your arm, all the way to the fingertips of your left hand, while exhaling loudly as before.

8. Repeat this process on the other side, with your

left hand on your right shoulder, brushing down quickly and positively to the fingertips of your right hand, and expelling your breath loudly.

9. Complete the process by once more sweeping your right hand down your left arm from shoulder to fingertips, again exhaling loudly.

10. **Connecting to Reiki** Raise both your hands high up in the air above your head, with your palms facing each other about 12–15 inches apart, and *intend* that Reiki begin to flow into you. As you sense a change in your hands— warmth or tingling—lower them and place them on your lap with your palms facing upward.

11. **The Cleansing Breath** Breathe naturally and steadily through your nose, and as you breathe in, visualize Reiki as white light pouring into you through your crown chakra, into your Reiki channel and down the hara line (an energy line that connects all your chakras from the crown down to the perineum), and through your major chakras. *Intend* that the Reiki expand beyond the hara line to fill the whole of your physical body and aura, and as it flows around your energy system, *intend* that it break through any blockages and pick up any negativity, so that as you breathe out, the Reiki takes with it any negative energy to beyond your aura, where it can be healed and transformed by the Reiki.

12. Continue this process for a few minutes, or as long as you wish, breathing in Reiki to cleanse yourself, and breathing out Reiki so that it takes away any negativity.

13. Finally, take a really deep breath, then blow out the rest of the negativity and move your hands into the gassho position in front of your chest at the level of your heart chakra.

14. **Concentration or Meditation** Keeping your hands in the gassho position, imagine that you are breathing in Reiki through your hands directly into your heart chakra, from where the Reiki flows up and down the hara line, and then spreads out to fill all of your physical body and aura.

15. This time *intend* that you are breathing in Reiki for your own healing, on all levels—physical, emotional, psychological and spiritual—wherever it is needed. As you breathe out imagine that you are breathing out Reiki in all directions, radiating out through your hands, around the world and into the Universe, to spread its healing, balancing, harmonizing energy wherever it is needed—for the planet, people, animals, birds, fish, plants and other living organisms.

16. Continue this process for as long as you wish, and let your mind settle into a peaceful, meditative state.

17. Finally, place your hands back on your lap with palms facing downward, and *intend* that the Reiki meditation and cleansing technique be now complete. When you feel ready, open your eyes and shake your hands gently for a few seconds, to bring you back to a greater state of physical awareness.

3. DAILY CONTEMPLATION

This is a way to bring the Reiki Principles into your everyday life with a fairly short visualization that you combine with verbal instructions to yourself.

- Place your hands in gassho (prayer position) in front of your heart chakra.
- Start by saying "Just for today, I won't get angry." Imagine yourself *now* beside a lovely, calm lake, where there is no wind, the sky above is a beautiful blue and there is sunshine reflecting on the smooth surface. Stay with this image in your mind for a few minutes, or until you feel ready to move on.
- Then say to yourself "Just for today, I won't worry." In your imagination, create a sanctuary for yourself where you feel safe. This might be sitting beside a tall, strong tree with your back against its trunk, sheltered by its branches and leaves, feeling the warmth of the sun on your skin; or it might be inside a chapel, temple, mosque or even your own bedroom or some other space that feels right to you, which you can furnish in any way you wish, so in your imagination you can place beautiful pictures on the walls, and a comfortable bed or couch or large cushion to sit or lounge on. Stay with this image in your mind for a few minutes, or until you feel ready to move on.
- Say to yourself "Just for today, I will be kind to others." Think of someone—a friend, a member of your family, a child you know or a favorite pet— for whom you have strong feelings of love and compassion, who brings joy to your life. Imagine

being with them right now, perhaps giving them a hug or kiss, or if it's a pet, stroking its fur lovingly. Stay with this image in your mind for a few minutes, or until you feel ready to move on.

◆ Then say to yourself "Just for today, I will be grateful." Think of your family, friends, home, best-loved possessions, wonderful places you've visited that hold special memories, and feel and know the richness these people, possessions and places bring to your life and to your experiences. Feel love and gratitude and appreciation for them, and remember how fortunate you are to have them in your life. Stay with this image in your mind for a few minutes, or until you feel ready to move on.

◆ Finally, say to yourself "Just for today, I will work hard." Think of a task or hobby you really love, which is fun, brings you joy and makes you feel passionate—perhaps cooking for your loved ones, tending your garden, painting a beautiful landscape, wood carving, creating a tapestry or meditating, or giving someone a Reiki treatment. Let that love and passion and joy fill your being; let it spread out to other tasks, other parts of your job that you may not always like as much, but that you realize can still be valuable and enjoyable and useful experiences. Stay with this image in your mind for a few minutes, or until you feel ready to move on.

◆ When you are ready to finish, take a few deep breaths and allow yourself to become fully aware of your real surroundings again, then perhaps clap your hands a few times to bring yourself fully back to alertness.

At any point in the day, you can bring the images in the exercise back to mind, whenever life is challenging or distressing, or simply not much fun. If you are feeling worried about something, return for a few minutes to your sanctuary; if you feel anger welling up, think of that still, calm lake and allow your breathing to become deeper and slower. If you are faced with a task you don't like, spend a short time remembering the feelings you get when doing something you love, and allow those feelings to help you to change your attitude to whatever you have to do right now. If you're feeling despondent, think of all the people or possessions you are fortunate enough to have in your life and allow those thoughts to lift your spirits. If you are experiencing a difficult time with someone, allow your mind to bring back the joyful, compassionate feelings you have for someone you love, and remember that people are simply the sum of all their experiences, so their reaction to any given situation is bound to be different from yours.

Remember that "living the Reiki way" doesn't mean you have to be solemn and serious—life is meant to be enjoyed, so have fun, live life to the fullest, share happy times with people you love and bless Reiki for the gift it is in your life. If you don't yet have Reiki in your life, maybe now is a good time to think about taking your first Reiki course, so you can have its healing, harmonizing, loving energy literally at your fingertips, for the rest of your life. To all of you, I wish you joy on your personal Reiki journey.

Blessed be.

RESOURCES

USEFUL CONTACT ADDRESSES AND WEBSITES

Penelope Quest
For information about Reiki courses and other
workshops with Reiki Master Penelope Quest,
and for details of all her books and CDs:
Websites: www.reiki-quest.co.uk and
www.penelopequest.com
E-mail: info@reiki-quest.co.uk

REIKI TEACHERS AND PRACTITIONERS IN THE UK

For details of other Reiki Masters and Practitioners,
and useful information about Reiki and other
forms of healing, you might like to try the following
organizations and websites:

The UK Reiki Federation
Website: www.reikifed.co.uk
E-mail: enquiry@reikifed.co.uk

The Reiki Association
Website: www.reikiassociation.org.uk
E-mail: co-ordinator@reikiassociation.org.uk

The Reiki Council
Website: www.reikicouncil.org.uk
E-mail: info@reikicouncil.org.uk

The General Regulatory Council for Complementary Therapies (GRCCT)
Website: www.grcct.org
E-mail: admin@grcct.org

The Reiki Alliance—UK and Ireland
Website: www.reikialliance.org.uk
E-mail: mail@reikialliance.org.uk

Reiki Healers and Teachers Society (RHATS)
Website: www.reikihealersandteachers.net
E-mail: info@reikihealersandteachers.net

National Federation of Spiritual Healers (The Healing Trust)
Website: www.nfsh.org.uk or
www.thehealingtrust.org.uk

British Complementary Medicine Association (BCMA)
Website: www.bcma.co.uk
E-mail: chair@bcma.co.uk

Institute for Complementary Medicine (ICM)
Website: www.i-c-m.org.uk
E-mail: info@i-c-m.org.uk

REIKI TEACHERS AND PRACTITIONERS IN THE U.S.A. AND CANADA

The Reiki Alliance—Worldwide
P.O. Box 41, Cataldo, ID 83810-1041
Website: www.reikialliance.com;
E-mail: info@reikialliance.com

Usui Shiki Ryoho (The Office of the Grand Master—Phyllis Furumoto and Paul Mitchell)
Website: www.usuireiki-ogm.com

The International Center for Reiki Training
(William Lee Rand)
21421 Hilltop St., #28, Southfield, MI 48034-1023
Website: www.reiki.org
E-mail: center@reiki.org

International Association of Reiki Professionals
P.O. Box 481, Winchester, MA 01890
Website: www.iarp.org
E-mail: info@iarp.org

Southwestern Usui Reiki Ryoho Association
P.O. Box 5162, Lake Montezuma, AZ 86342-5162
Website: www.reiho.org
E-mail: adonea@msn.com

**The Radiance Technique International Association, Inc
(TRTIA)**
P.O. Box 40570, St. Petersburg, FL 33743-0570
Website: www.trtia.org
E-mail: TRTIA@aol.com

Canadian Reiki Association
Box 54570, 7155 Kingsway, Burnaby, BC, V5E 4J6
Website: www.reiki.ca
E-mail: reiki@reiki.ca

Usui-Do (Traditional Japanese Reiki)
The Usui-Do Foundation, Toronto, Ontario, Canada
Website: www.usui-do.org;
E-mail: askme@usui-do.org

WORLDWIDE CONTACTS

Reiki Dharma (Frank Arjava Petter)—Translations available in English, Spanish and German
Website: www.reikidharma.com
E-mail: Arjava@ReikiDharma.com

Australian Reiki Connection
Website: www.australianreikiconnection.com.au

Reiki Australia
Website: www.reikiaustralia.com.au

International House of Reiki (Frans and Bronwen Stiene)
Website: www.reiki.net.au
E-mail: info@reiki.net.au

Shibumi International Reiki Association
Website: www.shibumireiki.org

Reiki New Zealand Inc.
Website: www.reiki.org.nz
E-mail: info@reiki.org.nz

The Wellness Directory
Website: www.thewellnessdirectory.co.nz

The Reiki Association of Southern Africa
Website: www.reikiassociation.co.za

Reiki Masters Association of South Africa
Website: www.reikihealing.co.za

World Reiki Association
Website: www.worldreikiassociation.org

International Holistic Therapies Directories
Website: www.internationalholistictherapiesdirectories.com

FURTHER READING

The following books are my recommendations from the many available on each subject. I have placed them under headings to make it easier to find the topics you want to pursue, but many of them cover several categories.

Abundance Theory, Law of Attraction and Cosmic Ordering

Boyes, Carolyn, *Cosmic Ordering in 7 Easy Steps*, HarperCollins, 2006

Byrne, Rhonda, *The Secret*, Simon & Schuster, 2006

Cainer, Jonathan, *Cosmic Ordering*, HarperCollins, 2006

Carlson, Richard, *Don't Sweat the Small Stuff About Money*, Hodder & Stoughton, 1998

Dyer, Wayne W., *Manifest Your Destiny*, Thorsons, 1998

Edwards, Gill, *Life Is a Gift*, Piatkus, 2007

Frank, Debbie, *Cosmic Ordering Guide to Life, Love & Happiness*, Penguin, 2007

Hicks, Esther and Jerry, *Ask and It Is Given*, Hay House, 2005

Hicks, Esther and Jerry, *Money and the Law of Attraction*, Hay House, 2008

Horan, Paula, Abundance *Through Reiki*, Lotus Light Publications, 1995

Losier, Michael, *Law of Attraction*, Hodder & Stoughton, 2007

Mohr, Barbel, *The 21 Golden Rules for Cosmic Ordering*, Hay House, 2011

Roman, Sanaya, and Duane Packer, *Creating Money*, H. J. Kramer, 2008

Emotions, Thinking, Anger and Worry

Blanchard, Ken, *Whale Done!: The Power of Positive Relationships*, Free Press, 2002

Bloom, William, *The Endorphin Effect*, Piatkus, 2001

Carlson, Richard, and Joseph Bailey, *Slowing Down to the Speed of Life: How to Create a More Peaceful, Simpler Life from the Inside Out*, Hodder Mobius, 1998

Carnegie, Dale, *How to Stop Worrying and Start Living*, Pocket Books, 2004

Dyer, Wayne W., *Change Your Thoughts, Change Your Life*, Hay House, 2007

Dyer, Wayne W., *You'll See It When You Believe It*, Arrow, 2005

Edelman, Sarah, *Change Your Thinking*, Vermilion, 2006

Fisher, Mike, *Beating Anger: The Eight-Point Plan for Coping with Rage*, Rider & Co., 2005

Gentry, W. Doyle, *Anger Management For Dummies*, John Wiley & Sons, 2006

Goleman, Daniel, *Emotional Intelligence*, Bloomsbury, 1996

Hamilton, David R., *The Contagious Power of Thinking*, Hay House, 2011

Hamilton, David R., *It's the Thought That Counts*, Hay House, 2006

Hay, Louise L., *The Power Is Within You*, Hay House, 2004

Hicks, Esther and Jerry, *The Astonishing Power of Emotions: Let Your Feelings Be Your Guide*, Hay House, 2007

Holden, Robert, *Living Wonderfully*, Thorsons, 1994

Holden, Robert, *Shift Happens*, Hay House, 2011

Jeffers, Susan, *End the Struggle and Dance with Life*, Hodder Paperbacks, 2005

Jeffers, Susan, *Feel the Fear and Do It Anyway*, Vermilion, 2007

Leahy, Robert L., *The Worry Cure*, Piatkus, 2006

Lindenfield, Gael, *Managing Anger*, Thorsons, 2000

Neill, Michael, *Feel Happy Now!*, Hay House, 2007

Purdie, Jeni, *Life Coaching For Dummies*, John Wiley & Sons, 2010

Ricard, Matthieu, *Happiness: A Guide to Developing Life's Most Important Skill*, Atlantic Books, 2007

Wood, Eve A., *10 Steps to Take Charge of Your Emotional Life*, Hay House, 2006

EFT and NLP

Craig, Gary, and Garry A. Flint, *Emotional Freedom: Techniques for Dealing with Emotional and Physical Distress*, Garry A. Flint, 2001

Dilts, Robert, Tim Hallbom, and Suzi Smith, *Beliefs— Pathways to Health & Well-being*, Metamorphous Press, 1990

Eden, Donna, *Energy Medicine*, Piatkus, 2008

Feinstein, David, Donna Eden, and Gary Craig, *The Healing Power of EFT & Energy Psychology*, Piatkus, 2006

Gallo, Fred P., and Harry Vincenzi, *Energy Tapping: How to Rapidly Eliminate Anxiety, Depression, Cravings and More Using Energy Psychology*, New Harbinger Publications, 2000

Lynch, Paul and Valerie, *Emotional Healing in Minutes*, Thorsons, 2001

Mallows, Michael, and Joseph Sinclair, *Peace of Mind Is a Piece of Cake*, Crown House, 1998

McDermott, Ian, and Joseph O'Connor, *NLP and Health*, Thorsons, 2001

O'Connor, Joseph, and John Seymour, *Introducing NLP*, Thorsons, 2003

Ready, Romilla, and Kate Burton, *Neuro-linguistic Programming For Dummies*, John Wiley & Sons, 2010

Gratitude and Kindness

Ban Breathnach, Sarah, *Simple Abundance: A Daybook of Comfort and Joy*, Bantam, 1997

Clinton, Bill, *Giving: How Each of Us Can Change the World*, Hutchinson, 2007

Dalai Lama XIV Bstan-dzin-rgya-mtsho, *Kindness, Clarity, and Insight*, Snow Lion Publications, 2012

257

Demartini, John, *The Gratitude Effect*, Burman Books, 2007

Hay, Louise L., *Gratitude: A Way of Life*, Hay House, 2004

Hyde, Catherine Ryan, *Pay It Forward*, Black Swan, 2007

Salzberg, Sharon, *The Force of Kindness*, Sounds True, 2005

Salzberg, Sharon, *Lovingkindness: The Revolutionary Art of Happiness*, Shambhala Publications, 2003

Wallace, Danny, *Random Acts of Kindness: 365 Ways to Make the World a Nicer Place*, Ebury Press, 2004

Weissman, Darren R., *The Power of Infinite Love and Gratitude*, Hay House, 2007

Reiki

Ellis, Richard, *Reiki and the Seven Chakras*, Vermilion, 2002

Hall, Mari, *Reiki for the Soul*, Thorsons, 2000

Horan, Paula, *Empowerment Through Reiki*, Lotus Press, 1995

Lubeck, Walter, Frank Arjava Petter, and William Lee Rand, *The Spirit of Reiki*, Lotus Press, 2001

Lubeck, Walter, and Frank Arjava Petter, *Reiki Best Practices*, Lotus Press, 2003

Quest, Penelope, *The Basics of Reiki*, Jeremy P. Tarcher/Penguin, 2012

Quest, Penelope, *Reiki for Life*, Jeremy P. Tarcher/Penguin, 2010

Quest, Penelope, and Kathy Roberts, *The Reiki Manual*, Jeremy P. Tarcher/Penguin, 2011

Quest, Penelope, and Kathy Roberts, *Self-Healing with Reiki*, Jeremy P. Tarcher/Penguin, 2012

Steine, Bronwen and Frans, *The Japanese Art of Reiki*, O Books, 2005

Steine, Bronwen and Frans, *The Reiki Sourcebook*, O Books, 2003

Spiritual Development

Myss, Caroline, *Anatomy of the Spirit*, Bantam Books, 1997

Myss, Caroline, *Entering the Castle, An Inner Path to God and Your Soul*, Simon & Schuster, 2007

Myss, Caroline, *Sacred Contracts*, Bantam Books, 2002

Potter, Richard N., and Jan Potter, *Spiritual Development for Beginners*, Llewellyn, 2006

Roberts, Jane, *The Nature of Personal Reality*, Amber-Allen, 1974

Roman, Sanaya, *Living with Joy*, H. J. Kramer, 2011

Roman, Sanaya, *Personal Power Through Awareness*, H. J. Kramer, 1986

Roman, Sanaya, *Soul Love*, H. J. Kramer, 1997

Roman, Sanaya, *Spiritual Growth*, H. J. Kramer, 1989

Ruiz, Don Miguel, *The Four Agreements*, Amber-Allen, 1997

Tolle, Eckhart, *A New Earth: Awakening to Your Life's Purpose*, Penguin, 2006

Tolle, Eckhart, *The Power of Now: A Guide to Spiritual Enlightenment*, Hodder Mobius, 2001

Walsch, Neale Donald, *Conversations with God*—Books 1, 2 and 3, Hodder & Stoughton, 1996, 1997, 1998

Williamson, Marianne, *A Return to Love*, Thorsons, 1996

Zukav, Gary, *The Seat of the Soul*, Rider, 1991

SUGGESTED MUSIC AND ORACLE CARDS

Chapman, Philip, *Soul Mates*, New World Company, 1988

Cooper, Diana, and Greg Stuart, *Wisdom Cards,* Findhorn Press Ltd, 2007

Hay, Louise I., *Power Thought Cards,* Hay House, 2009

Hicks, Esther and Jerry, *Well-Being Cards,* Hay House, 2004

Llewellyn, *Music for Reiki Heating,* New Beginnings, 2001

Llewellyn, *Reiki Gold,* Paradise Music, 2005

Wiese, Klaus, *Touch of Silence: Tibetan Singing Bowls,* Aquarius International, 2005

Index

ABOUT THE AUTHOR

Penelope Quest has been a Reiki Practitioner since 1991 and a Reiki Master/Teacher since 1994, and did further training in Reiki from the Japanese lineage in 2000 and 2003. She is a former vice chairman and education coordinator of the UK Reiki Federation, and has been a consultant on Reiki for both the Open University and Britain's NHS. She currently teaches all levels of Reiki and runs occasional retreats in the UK in a beautiful area called the Cotswolds.

Quest is a qualified teacher and former college lecturer, and her academic qualifications include a master's degree (MSc) in Health and Healing Science, and a BA in psychology and education. In addition, she has extended her knowledge and experience by studying a wide range of subjects, including meditation, visualization, NLP, EFT, sound healing, Hawaiian Huna healing, shamanism, kinesiology, dowsing, feng shui, abundance theory and cosmic ordering, energy psychology, and other topics that promote understanding, personal growth and a holistic view of the person. She is the author of the bestselling titles *Reiki for Life, The Reiki Manual, Self-Healing with Reiki* and *The Basics of Reiki*.